SHOES

D1332353

SHO

A HISTORY FROM

SHOES

SANDALS TO SNEAKERS

EDITED BY GIORGIO RIELLO AND PETER MCNEIL

⊕BERG

london and new york

English edition
First published in 2006 by Berg
Paperback edition published 2011

Editorial offices:
49–51 Bedford Square, London WC1B 3DP, UK
175 Fifth Avenue, New York, NY 10010, USA

Berg is an imprint of Bloomsbury Publishing plc.

Library of Congress Cataloging-in-Publication Data
A catalogue record for this book is available from the Library of Congress.

British Library Cataloguing-in-Publication Data
A catalogue record for this book is available from the British Library.

ISBN 978 1 84520 443 3 (Cloth)
ISBN 978 0 85785 038 6 (Paper)

Designed by Sunandini Banerjee, Seagull Books
Printed in China

www.bergpublishers.com

PREFACE

The publication of this book comes at the end of a three-year long journey for the editors and for twenty energetic scholars who joined us in this project. It is the result of a collective effort that is global both in scale and scope. Contributors have been drawn from the Old and New World: Europe, North America, Africa, Asia and Australia. This volume has been shaped, organised and edited simultaneously in London and Sydney, a task impossible before the age of modern communication and the Internet. It is the result of 10,000 emails, 2,000 document and image files, late-night calls across time zones, laptops on airlines, and editorial meetings in three continents.

Shoes: A History from Sandals to Sneakers has also been the pretext for an adventure. We have explored many shoe collections in Europe and America and we are very grateful to The Bata Shoe Museum in Toronto, Canada; the Musée de la Chaussure at Romans, France; and the Northampton Boot and Shoe Collection, UK, for their intellectual and practical assistance. We have tried to avoid using the shoe as a pretext for academic debate. This book has been shaped through an in-depth engagement with the materiality of the shoe and some significant exchanges with curatorial staff and librarians. We have thus prompted our writers never to use the shoe as "illustration"; we wished for a volume in which an article of dress was explored from various angles without losing sight of its status as artefact and representation. As the numerous images – many not reproduced before – in this volume show, the shoe itself and its dissemination to new viewers and readers has been our priority.

Our debts extend widely and are heartfelt. We include firstly the contributors to this book. The publication of this book was made possible by the financial support of A.C.Ri.B., the Design History Society 25th Anniversary Scholarship, the University of New South Wales College of Fine Arts, The Australian Research Council – Discovery Projects, the 2006 PRIN on "Made-in-Italy," financed by the Italian Ministry of Education and University, and the especially gracious assistance of the Bata Shoe Museum, the Northampton Boot and Shoe Collection and the Veronika Gervers Fellowship at the Royal Ontario Museum. We would like to thank Katie Andrews, Rebecca Arnold, Franco Ballin, Sonja Bata, Maxine Berg, Manolo Blahnik, Richard Butler, Christopher Breward, Michael Carter, Sue Constable, Giovanni Luigi Fontana, Joe Fountain, Sakis Gekas, Sally Gray, Ian Henderson, Martin Kamer, Vicki Karaminas, Ulrich Lehmann, Roger Leong, Emanuele Lepri, Elizabeth Little, Desley Luscombe, Margaret Maynard, Suzanne McLean, Gianpiero Menegazzo, Lidia Minceva, Alexandra Palmer, Stefania Ricci, Toni Ross, Elizabeth Semmelhack, Rebecca Shawcross, Valerie Steele, John Styles, Gerry Torres, Amanda Vickery, Stuart Weitzman, Elizabeth Wilson, and Lye-Yew Yeo for their intellectual and moral support.

Our thanks extend also to Juliet Ash, Susan Best, John Clarke, Elizabeth Hackspiel-Mikosch, Ulrich Lehmann, Beverly Lemire, Elisabetta Merlo, Ann Matchette, Alison Matthews David, June Swann, Norma Wolff, Andrea Vianello, and Paola Zamperini, who kindly acted as reviewers for the chapters included in this volume. Our thanks extend also to Guy West and Susan Cutts who allowed us to use their art-works. At Berg, we wish to thank Tristan Palmer, Veruschka Selbach, Hannah Shakespeare, Ken Bruce, Fiona Corbridge, Kate Shepherd, Kathryn Earle and the designer for all their hard work.

This book is dedicated to Peter's parents Kevin and Mary McNeil, Giorgio's mother Mirella Riello and to the memory of Giorgio's father Mariano Riello.

Giorgio Riello and Peter McNeil

A LONG WALK

SHOES, PEOPLE AND PLACES

giorgio riello and peter mcneil

> I did not have three thousand pairs of shoes.
> I had one thousand and sixty.
>
> Imelda Marcos

Shoes are ever present, with a long and complex history. *Shoes: A History from Sandals to Sneakers* is the first book to present a global history of shoes from ancient times to the present. In revealing the complex and intricate world of shoes, the chapters here draw on examples from Europe, America, Asia and Africa. Our book will present you with fine examples of Western and non-Western shoe fashions, as well as explaining some of the mysteries of your favorite object. We will also show you some of the types of banal, occupational, military and mass-produced footwear, which used to be much more common before twentieth-century production transformed the range of shoe possibilities. The ordinary shoe can inspire your favorite designer today, or transport you to another sense of yourself.

Within these pages is pretty much everything you ever wanted to know about shoes – the eroticism of ancient shoe lacing, medieval moral panic about long-toed shoes, the role of shoes in religious rituals, the infamous woman's chopine, with its twenty-three-inch platform heel, eighteenth-century male show-offs, from red-heeled courtiers to flashy macaronis, to austere dandies. We will explore the creation of the Wellington for war, the cruel and utilitarian boots of the First World War, the rise of men's shoes as symbols of conservatism, and the shoe in fairy tales, both splendid and ghoulish. Finally, we examine the story of the high heel, the sexualization of the shoe after Freud, the meaning of the "gay shoe," shoes in gallery art, the extraordinary rise of the sneaker, and the cult of shoe designers themselves. Throughout our book, contributors consider the shoe from a variety of perspectives. Without losing sight of the aesthetics – the potential sheer beauty and sculpture of the shoe, from delicate satin to glossy black leather, our writers help you understand how your shoes have reached your closet and your foot. Perhaps for the first time, thoughts about making, designing, distributing, promoting and disseminating fashion ideas for shoes are brought together, for a wide historical period, across cultures. We hope we have done so without diminishing the magic or mystery of shoes, in which we now believe more firmly than when we commenced our long trek.

THE MEANING OF SHOES

Footwear is more than a simple wrapping or protection for the foot. The notion that shoes indicate a great deal about a person's taste (or disdain for such things) and identity – national, regional, professional – class status and gender, is not an invention of modernity. Shoes have, for centuries, given hints about a person's character, social and cultural place, even sexual preference.[1] Shoes are powerful "things," as they take control over the physical and human space in which we live. They allow us to move in and experience the environment. They are the principal intersection between body and physical space. The psychologist Nicola Squicciarino has called this "extensions on the corporeal ego." Shoes, then, are always more than simple garments allowing us to walk, stroll and run on streets, parks and fields. They are tools that amplify our bodies' capacities. Everyday shoes allow us to walk to work, to run for the bus, to look smart at a party. High-tech shoes have permitted the demonstrable improvement of the world record for the 100 meters during the last hundred years (in conjunction with training and nutritional regimes). Shoes thus extend our social and emotional capacities, as well as our physical capacity.[2]

Navigating between the ground and one "edge" of the body, i.e. the foot, footwear acquires different meanings related to sex, attractiveness, group membership and power.[3] Such meanings appear in different ways through time from ancient Greece to premodern Japan and present-day Western societies. A case in point is the theme of identity, be it personal or collective (Figure I.1).

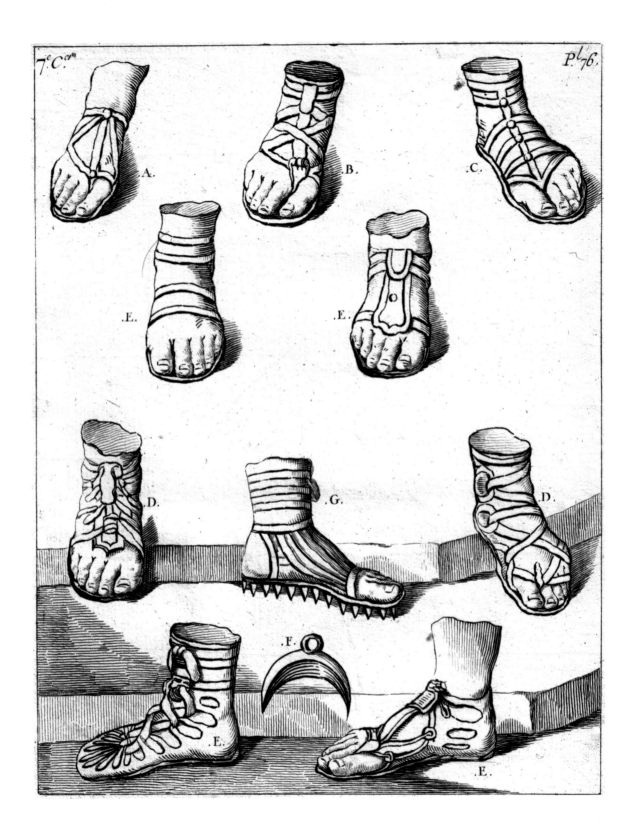

A.

B.

C.

E.

E.

D.

G.

D.

E.

F.

E.

To wear white sneakers in present-day northern Europe is a signifier of membership of a specific type of youth culture: "trainers," kept rigorously white and spotless, are used by working-class youngsters. This means resorting to blacking and painting. An unexpected parallelism can be demonstrated in late eighteenth-century Europe, where the bleaching of boots was part of the ritual of a gentleman's behavior (Figure I.2).

These social rituals related to the wearing of footwear are apparent in different cultures over time, although they take myriad forms. In many instances, social rituals can assume religious connotations, as in the case of premodern Japan, where shoes were, on the one hand, polluting agents but also at the center stage of rituals of purification. In other societies, it is religious and moral values that shape footwear. In medieval Europe, for instance, moral precepts formulated from the Bible were used to limit the height of shoes and the wearing of footwear made of luxurious materials such as silk, embroidery and pearls. A tension is present, through history, between the power of shoes as tools of self-presentation and their persistent sociocultural nature. On the one hand, shoes are very personal garments. A pair of red stiletto shoes is quite different, in every way, from a pair of boots. An attractive young lady can decide that her ankles look better in stilettos than in boots. But her choice is rather more sympathetic for a smart party than a rock concert. The issue of the appropriateness of shoes reminds us that they must always adapt not only to the physical terrain but also to the social one.

Shoes differ not only according to their use, but also according to their wearer. Several chapters in this volume touch on the fact that shoes are used not only to differentiate between the sexes but also as tools in gender relations. The smallness of women's feet, for instance, is a feature emphasized by many cultures over time. If the most classic example is premodern China, where women's feet were bound to limit their growth, the use of small shoes was also common in eighteenth- and nineteenth-century Europe. The smallness of the foot made walking more sinuous, but also more difficult. It clearly inferred that feet were organs of locomotion for men, but part of the sensual appeal of women.[4] A man's boot, however, in creating the sense of the extension of calf and encasing the lower leg in glistening leather, was just as erotic as any slipper worn by a woman. Several chapters in this book thus consider the very act of walking in socially defined space. Mobility within space is in part connected to the nature and quality of shoes. But it would be a mistake to think that this relationship is just about the physical.[5] As previous writers have demonstrated, the role of the shoe in slave and other enslaved communities, such as the prisoners of the Nazis, was central to their ability to survive, escape, and stay alive.[6] If women in society encountered barriers against free movement, such barriers often had little to do with real bodily limits. The limits were social, and shoes played their role in constructing and reinscribing these roles.

FIGURE I.1 (FACING PAGE): ROMAN SHOES FROM AN EIGHTEENTH-CENTURY PRINT. PRIVATE COLLECTION.

FIGURE I.2 (ABOVE): THE SUPREME BON TON NO. 5: LES DÉCROTEURS EN BOUTIQUE. HAND-COLORED ETCHING, LONDON, PUBLISHED BY MARTINET, C. 1802. BRITISH MUSEUM, 1856-7-12-596.

FIGURE I.3 (BELOW): SHOES AND VIOLENCE: A MAN THREATENS TO HIT A WOMAN WITH A STRAP IF SHE DOES NOT PICK UP A LAST. LITHOGRAPH BY A. D. LAJOU, PARIS, C. 1815–25. BATA SHOE MUSEUM, TORONTO, P79.586. REPRODUCED BY KIND PERMISSION OF BATA SHOE MUSEUM.

Figure I.4a (above): The Macarony Shoe Maker. Engraving, c. 1770, published by M. Darly. By kind permission of the British Museum, London.

Figure I.4b (below): A Beautiful Pair. Print, New York, published by Currier & Ives, c. 1872. Library of Congress, PGA – Currier & Ives–Beautiful pair.

FIGURE 1.5: WREN'S: THE MAN'S POLISH. ADVERTISEMENT, 1950S. NORTHAMPTON MUSEUMS AND ART GALLERY, BOOT AND SHOE COLLECTION, BC14329. REPRODUCED BY PERMISSION OF NORTHAMPTON MUSEUMS AND ART GALLERY.

The examples so far have concerned the wearing of shoes. But shoes are also commodities. They are objects that are produced, exchanged and eventually worn. They can be used as tools of self-defense or violence and they appear in endless narratives of marital bliss as well as unhappiness (Figure I.3). This book also engages with shoes "behind the scenes." Several chapters purposely address the relationship between making and consuming. Shoes are not just "packages" of signs, meanings and messages. They are products that acquire certain shapes, colors and forms through a process of creation (creativity), application of technologies, choice of materials and the understanding of consumer markets. Shoes, more than any other realms of sartorial taste, have produced global names and international brands. As shoes are recognizably one of the most powerful but also most complex items of apparel, the relationship between wearer and producer is often portrayed as an intimate one (Figures I.4a and b). Carrie Bradshaw, the heroine of the series *Sex and the City*, is a case in point. Although her relationship with world-famous shoe designer Manolo Blahnik is surely not a personal one, her passion for Blahnik shoes makes the designer an intimate character in the series. Jimmy Choo also appears in her imagination as the type we have coined the "male Cinderella" maker, explored in the concluding chapter of this book.

Shoes have both a personal and private nature, which has been preserved even in a global media society like ours. Shoes, like handbags, do not generally look good in advertisements, unless they are manipulated through artful lighting and digital means (Figure I.5). They are far too small, near to the ground and difficult to set in a stage-like way. By themselves they are, in many ways, too prosaic. It was perhaps for this reason that many shoe advertisements were drawn, such as Roger Vivier shoes for Dior and the famous torn-style motifs of Andy Warhol. Some of the most visually successful campaigns for shoes, such as Serge Lutens' photographs, distort the appearance of shoes to underline their fantastical possibilities.

Shoes are a nightmare for museum curators and provide a challenging experience for window dressers (Figure I.6). As worn shoes soil very easily, and as their materials (such as leather) tend to corrode more swiftly than woven textiles, the "worn" shoe in the museum can tend to have a slightly forlorn appearance. Even when their provenance is famous, such as the shoes in the Marlene Dietrich Archive in Berlin, they will most likely be abject items of clothing. Note here that the current trade in retro and secondhand clothes often does not extend to shoes, as they cannot be dry-cleaned or washed, and customer resistance to the secondhand shoe is palpable. It was a sign of poverty for children in the West to wear hand-me-down shoes.

Their difficult character is not just the result of their size or spatial position. Of all garments, shoes are uniquely independent from the physical body. They have a shape that they keep even when the wearer is absent. Most clothes can only be displayed through the use of props such mannequins, but shoes are "self-standing." This peculiar nature explains why they often stand for something else

FIGURE 1.6 (ABOVE): POCOCK BROS., SHOEMAKER'S SHOP IN BRIGHTON, C. 1909. NORTHAMPTON MUSEUMS AND ART GALLERY, BOOT AND SHOE COLLECTION, BC16228/B. REPRODUCED BY PERMISSION OF NORTHAMPTON MUSEUMS AND ART GALLERY.

FIGURE 1.7 (BELOW): THE FAMILY OF STYLES (JOHN, AMANDA AND THEIR THREE DAUGHTERS). JANUARY 2011. GENDER, AGE AND FAMILIAL RELATIONS ARE EXPRESSED THROUGH SHOES.

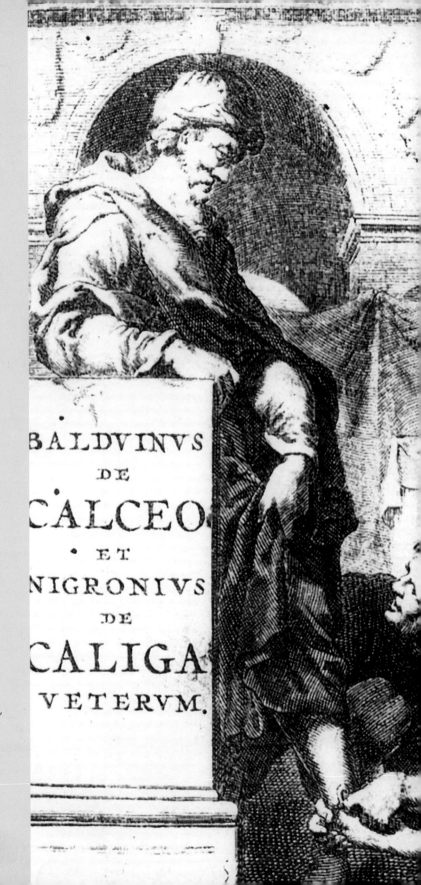

FIGURE 1.8: COVER OF *DE CALCEO ANTIQUO*, 1667.

that is not physically present. Piles of shoes were one tragic reminder of the millions of Jews who perished in concentration camps. But a group of shoes can also symbolize the comfortable presence of a family unit with gender and age divisions, conspicuous consumption, or an interest in a complex range of garment choices and image types (Figure I.7).

The very presence or absence of shoes is one of the most recorded facts in history. The Musée International de la Chaussure in Romans (France) includes a *kurdaitcha* (*kadaitcha*) feather, fur and twine shoe from Australia, giving a lie to the myth that the indigenous Australians were everywhere naked on their feet. Many of the chapters included here rely on the testimony of people through the ages commenting on how shoes appeared and were used. Until recent times, a lack of shoes could be a fact of life even in the relatively prosperous Western world. And to be barefoot meant that all avenues of life were closed. "The boy is barefoot," wrote a certain Thomas Cleare from Braintree (England) to the Parish authorities in 1829, seeking financial support, "if he can get work & find him Shoes it is not in my Power for I Cannot get any for myself."[7] One can say that the association between bare feet and poverty has entered our genetic code in such a way as to inform new notions of acquisitiveness through shoes. The cliché wants women to be "mad for shoes." The Imelda Marcos inside seems to burst out in front of the shoemaker's window. This has often been taken as one of the best examples of the irrational (female) consumer. But is it really so? The inferior social and cultural position imposed on women for centuries is refused by engaging with the acquisition of one of the most important symbols of movement, richness and worth: shoes.

SHOES, HISTORIES AND STORIES

These introductory remarks serve to contextualize shoes within a long history stretching over several centuries. As far back as 1667, *De Calceo Antiquo*, written in Latin, was the first book dedicated entirely to shoes (Figure I.8). It was published jointly by the breechmaker turned scholar Benoît Baudouin and Giulio Negrone, a Jesuit and instructor in rhetoric and theology.[8] This early interest in the lineage or history of shoes was continued in the Enlightenment. In the seventeenth and eighteenth centuries, shoes circulated in popular culture through stories, visual imagery and health advice. As shoemaking was one of the most common occupations in towns and villages, the shoemaker was a principal character in many stories of everyday life in pre-industrial Europe. As late as the 1960s, mechanical tin toys for children included the by-then archaic figure of the cobbler. In children's literature there seems to be something reassuring about the repetition of comforting and rhythmic work effected by the shoemaker. Illustrations of the two patron saints of shoemakers, St Crispin and St Crispianus, were accompanied by entertaining ballads such as *The Gentle Craft's Complaint: Or, The Jolly Shoe-makers Humble Petition to the Queen and*

FIGURE I.9 (ABOVE): A SHOEMAKER'S WORKSHOP. REPRODUCTION FROM MELCHIOR TAVERNIER'S COPPERPLATE ETCHING, 1640–70. BATA SHOE MUSEUM, TORONTO, P97.140. REPRODUCED BY KIND PERMISSION OF BATA SHOE MUSEUM.

FIGURE I.10A (LEFT): RARE FRENCH WOODCUT PRINT OF TWO SHOEMAKERS, PROBABLY THE PATRON SAINTS OF THE TRADE, C. 1500. BATA SHOE MUSEUM, TORONTO, P87.161. REPRODUCED BY KIND PERMISSION OF BATA SHOE MUSEUM.

FIGURE I.10B (RIGHT): A POPULAR IMAGE OF ST CRISPIN AND CRISPIANUS. COLORED LITHOGRAPH, 1875. BATA SHOE MUSEUM, TORONTO, P83.0289. REPRODUCED BY KIND PERMISSION OF BATA SHOE MUSEUM.

Parliament (1710) mocking the frequent petitions sent by the guild of shoemakers (the so-called Cordwainers) to the authorities (Figures I.9 and I.10a and b).

John Gay's *Trivia, or, The Art of Walking*, first published in 1716, became a well-known poem of the very act of moving within the physical and social world of the eighteenth-century metropolis, a genre that inspired the later social commentary of Louis-Sébastien Mercier's *Tableau de Paris* (1783) and *Nouveau de Paris* (1790), and Rétif de la Bretonne's *Nuits de Paris* (1786–8).[9] But perhaps the most enduring of all popular narratives on shoes is *The History of Goody Two-Shoes*, which is thought to have been written by Oliver Goldsmith, first published in 1765. It is the story of a poor young woman who manages to make it through life with only one shoe and is finally rewarded with another.[10] Shoes, as a chapter by Hilary Davidson in this volume argues, appear frequently in fairy tales, from Andersen's famous *The Red Shoes* to Perrault's *Cinderella* and popular stories such as *The Old Woman Who Lived in a Shoe* (Figure I.11).[11]

The popular tradition of storytelling using shoes, shoemakers and walking as the pretext for social commentary, and the comparison between the good old days and the displeasures of the modern world, is accompanied by two other more scientific strands of literary production considering the history of shoemaking. From the second half of the eighteenth century, the "gentle craft" became the subject of "scientific" investigation. Diderot and D'Alembert's *Encyclopédie* (1751–65) dedicated a chapter to the productive methods used in shoemaking and a few years later, an entire volume entitled the *Art du Cordonnier* (1767) was published by François Alexandre de Garsault (Figure I.12).[12] Both books provided visual as well as written information on shoemaking and neatly described the productive processes adopted in the craft.[13]

During the same years, another strand of polemic discussion was concentrating on shoes. A new type of medical literature was analyzing the shape of footwear and its suitability for healthy living. Books like Andry de Bois-Regard's *Orthopaedia* (1743), Camper's *Abhandlung über die beste Form der Schuhe* (1783), Sokosky's *Imperfections de la Chaussure* (1811), and the anonymous *Art of Preserving the Feet* (1818) are just a few of the works examining the relationship between footwear and wearer in present and past times.[14] This strand of research warned against the evil outcomes of debauchery and heavy drinking and eating, such as gout or frequent bunions (Figures I.13a and b).

It was, however, only in the nineteenth century that the significance of shoes came to the fore. *Crispin Anecdotes* (1827) was – as the title said – a collection of "interesting notices of shoemakers who have been distinguished for genius, enterprise, or eccentricity." Shoemakers and wearers, rather than shoes, were the center of stories suitable for entertaining the whole family in

Figure I.11 (facing page): Earthenware tile, painted in blue, gold and white depicting Cinderella and the two ugly sisters. Probably by Edward Borne Jones, c. 1862. By kind permission of the British Museum, London.

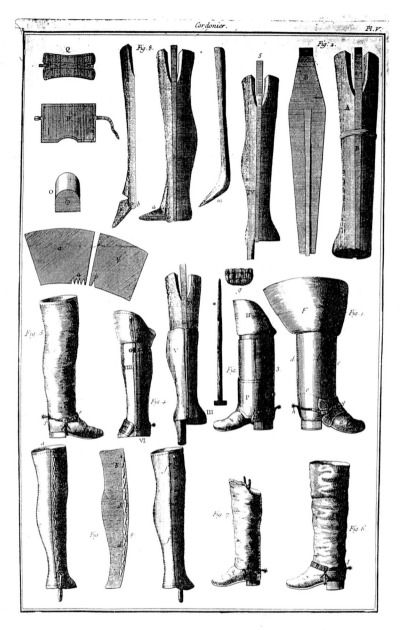

FIGURE I.12: PLATE, ALEXANDRE DE GARSAULT'S *ART DU CORDONNIER*, 1767.

front of a fireplace.[15] In a similar vein, although autobiographical in nature, was John Brown's *Sixty Years' Gleanings from Life's Harvest* (1858), concerning the life of a shoemaker during the first half of the nineteenth century.[16] The hard life of a boot- and shoemaker in the nineteenth century is also the biography of one of the most prolific writers on shoes, the London bootmaker James Dacres Devlin. For many years, he wrote about the meager salaries of shoemakers in London and the deterioration of their professional and personal standards of living in the transition of shoemaking from "gentle craft" to "sweated trade" (Figure I.14).[17] His books, reminiscent of the interviews by Henry Mayhew with the "London poor" are a touching reminder of the author's tragic death in utter poverty in mid-Victorian London.[18]

Devlin's sad end contrasts with the meteoric success of another Victorian bootmaker, Joseph Sparkes Hall. In 1846 he published his *Book of the Feet*, which in just over a hundred pages collected all available information about boots and shoes from ancient Egypt to the mid-nineteenth century.[19] This was neither an academic exercise nor an in-depth analysis of footwear. As in his later *History and Manufacture of Boots and Shoes* (1853), Hall's historical analyses ended with his own triumphal invention of the elastic-side boot.[20] In the same years, monthly journals (the *Innovator*, also called the *Boot-and-Shoemakers Monitor*, and later the *St. Crispin*) discussed technical, commercial and productive issues, but did not deign to amuse their audience with historicized stories. This tradition of the analysis of shoes and shoemaking, mixing history and inventions, productive traditions and new industrial ways of production, was further developed in the second half of the nineteenth century both in England and France by books such as Horlock's *A Few Words to Journeymen Shoemakers* (1851), Sensfelder's *Histoire de la Cordonnerie* (1856), Ratouis's *Théorie et Pratique de la Fabrication et du Commerce des Chaussures* (1866) and his later *Histoire de la Cordonnerie* (1886).[21]

COLLECTING AND STUDYING SHOES

Shoes have not only been the center of attention of academic and literary scholars. In the last two centuries they have been also avidly collected. Most of what we know about shoes today is the result of the painstaking research by museum curators who have discovered precious information about footwear of different periods and cultures and, over the years, have collected an impressive number of examples. One of the most prolific collectors and scholars of shoes was the Scottish photographer T. Watson Greig. He published precise drawings of his collection of shoes in two volumes entitled respectively *Ladies' Old-fashioned Shoes* (1889) and *Ladies' Dress Shoes of the Nineteenth Century* (1900).[22] The importance of his collection lies in the fact that it has survived to the present day and is now available to scholars at the Victoria and Albert Museum in London and the Royal Ontario Museum in Toronto. Each of these two museums owns half of a vast collection

Figure I.13a: The Modern Job! Or John Bull and his Comforts! Hand-colored etching, London, F. Johnston, 1816. Library of Congress, Prints & Photographs Division, PC 1 – 12798.

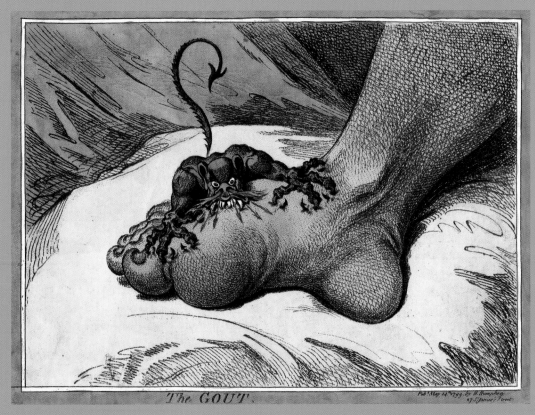

The GOUT.

FIGURE 1.13B: THE GOUT BY JAMES GILLRAY, HAND-COLORED ETCHING, PUBLISHED BY HANNAH HUMPHREY, LONDON, 1799. BY KIND PERMISSION OF THE BRITISH MUSEUM, LONDON.

FIGURE I.14: SHOEMAKER. LATE SEVENTEENTH CENTURY. BUNION. NORTHAMPTON MUSEUMS AND ART GALLERY, BOOT AND SHOE COLLECTION, BC16177. REPRODUCED BY PERMISSION OF NORTHAMPTON MUSEUMS AND ART GALLERY.

that constitutes the core of their shoe collection, now including several extra-European and twentieth-century pairs of shoes, boots, sandals, slippers and clogs (Figures I.15 and I.16).

Specialized museums of shoes and shoemaking now receive the interest of thousands of visitors. The Boot and Shoe Collection at the Northampton Art Gallery in England is the oldest museum of shoes in the world, dating back to 1865.[23] Its collection includes over 30,000 objects and extends into material culture associated with shoes, such as pottery and domestic instruments representing shoes. The more recent Musée International de la Chaussure in Romans in the South of France (opened in the late 1960s)[24] and the Bata Shoe Museum in Toronto (opened in 1995)[25] are the other two most important shoe museums in the world, both of which aim to provide an understanding of shoes from antiquity to the present day (Figure I.17).

Other shoe museums are located in Europe. The Deutsches Ledermuseum in Offenbach (Germany) opened as early as 1917, and owns a remarkable collection of shoes as well as leather goods.[26] In Switzerland, the Bally Shoe Museum in Schönenwerd has been open for several decades, whilst in Spain the Museo del Calzado at Elda near Alicante is active in both the historical and critical understanding of shoes.[27] The Ferragamo Museum in Florence opened in 1995 and is the most important collection with regard to the relationship between the design process and footwear.[28] Other museums that attract visitors from all over the world are the Shoe Museum in Street, Somerset, England owned by the shoe producer C. and J. Clark Ltd., the Museo della Calzatura "Bertolini" in Vigevano (Lombardy) and the Museo della Calzatura of the A.C.Ri.B. at Villa Pisani in Dolo near Venice.[29]

In the twentieth century, and more specifically in the last twenty-five years, there has been a tremendous change in the research carried out on shoes. Footwear is no longer the forgotten Cinderella of dress, but an integral part of the study of fashion. This is the result of wider research on the topic, but also of important changes in the way shoes are understood. Since the 1980s, postmodernism and minimalism have proposed new visions of fashion and the body. They have underlined the fragmentary nature of fashion. The international catwalk has been subjected to new ideas based on the "disintegration" of dress, unusual and clashing combinations, and the conception of the body as composed of single "body parts" or details, rather than as a figure or silhouette. These theoretical changes have a profound impact on the way footwear is represented in the media, and very often on how it is advertised. Emerging designers sometimes eschew shoes altogether, as they are a major expense for fashion shows, sending models down the runway in socks or bare feet. Lifestyle magazines, arch comedies and cable television programs have in recent years created a new awareness of the cultural importance of shoes as elements of consumption and identity in contemporary society.

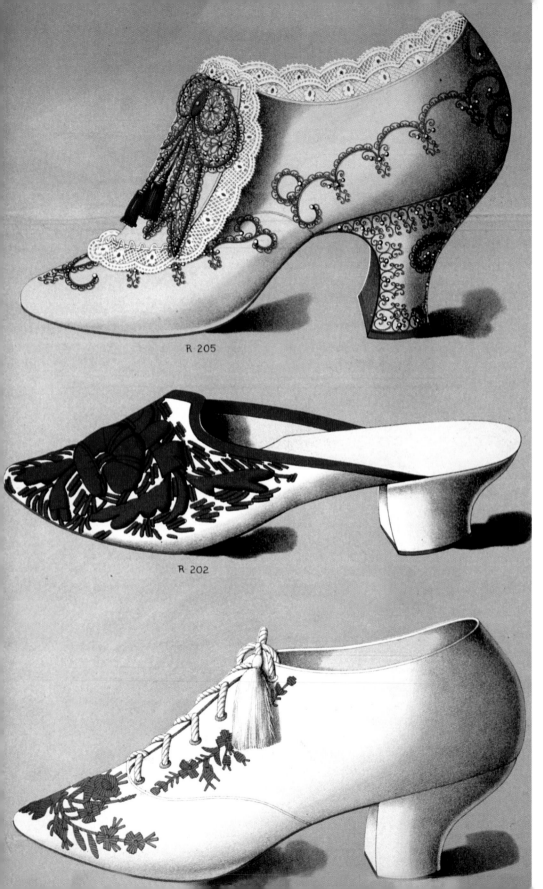

R·205

R·202

FIGURE I.15: PAGE FROM T. WATSON GREIG'S *LADIES' DRESS SHOES OF THE NINETEENTH CENTURY* (EDINBURGH, 1900). COURTESY OF THE VERONIKA GERVERS FELLOWSHIP AND THE ROYAL ONTARIO MUSEUM.

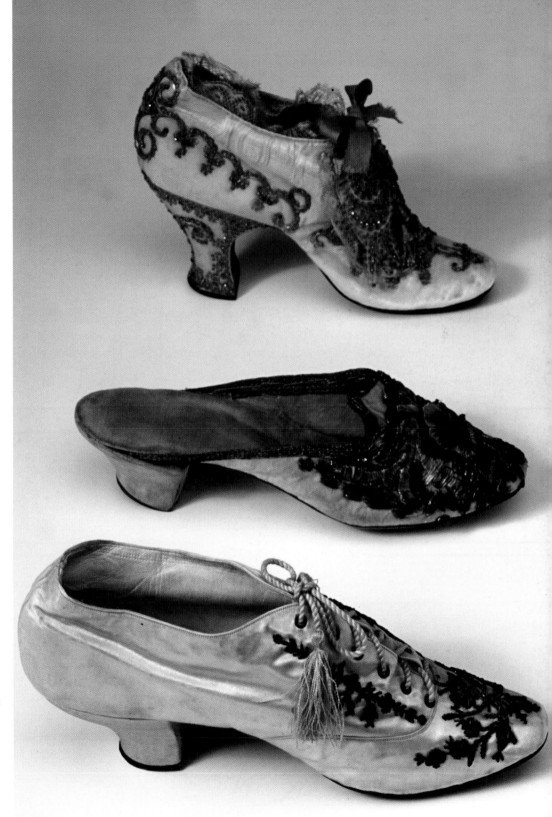

FIGURE 1.16: THREE PAIRS OF
WOMEN'S SHOES FROM THE T.
WATSON GREIG COLLECTION,
ROYAL ONTARIO MUSEUM,
921.2.82.A-B, 923.30.4.A-B
AND 923.30.7. COURTESY OF THE
VERONIKA GERVERS FELLOWSHIP.

From a historical perspective, the theories of social and psychological behavior which have informed the recent attention paid to shoes suffer from a lack of historical specificity and tend to be atemporal. The focus on the twentieth century makes it difficult to fully appreciate the dynamic relationship between footwear, culture and society within much of fashion history. History adds at least one important dimension to our understanding of the role played by clothes in contemporary societies. It not only focuses on the way in which people relate to their clothes and express particular *choices* in a world full of goods, signs and meanings; history also deals with *constraints* imposed culturally or socially, or created economically. The classic fashion theory that sees "fashion leaders" being imitated by "fashion followers" becomes, in the context of the early modern, modern and postmodern societies, a theory limited by social rank, wealth, strategies for saving, composition of households, costs of textiles and the availability of ready-made garments. Several chapters in this book thus refer to groundbreaking research by Eunice Wilson, Iris Brooke, Florence Ledger, Francis Grew, Margrethe de Neergaard and, in particular, June Swann, whose analyses have provided a great deal of crucial information about the history of shoes.[30] This book attempts to integrate in-depth analysis of footwear and recent scholarship on the cultural, social, economic and personal meanings of shoes.[31] It is unfortunate that analyses of the object or artifact, and social theory, have tended to become so specialized and polarized that these communities no longer communicate effectively.

A WALK THROUGH THE BOOK

Shoes, perhaps more than other objects or items of dress, have a history or "life" of their own, which we have tried to capture in the initial part of this book. The book is divided into four "steps," the first of which is dedicated to "A Foot in the Past." Six chapters in this section chart the history of shoes from ancient Greece to the beginning of the twentieth century. Sue Blundell's chapter introduces the reader to the footwear used in the ancient world. It examines the role of women's footwear in ancient Greece through the analysis of sculpture, vase paintings and literature. Giuseppina Muzzarelli also uses a wide variety of sources in her analysis of medieval footwear. She shows how, during the later Middle Ages and the Renaissance, shoes were the center of attention of a public authority keen to curb conspicuous consumption and exaggerated spending (Figure I.18).

Andrea Vianello investigates further the theme of Renaissance shoes by showing how women, in particular, were subjected to close scrutiny. This was not just the scrutiny of the state, but also of religious leaders who frowned upon the high heels used by Venetian women. The fair sex seemed to have enjoyed as little freedom of expression as they had freedom of movement. When the tall *pianelle* used in the sixteenth century were replaced by shoes similar to modern footwear, women still faced severe obstacles limiting their mobility. A chapter by Peter McNeil and Giorgio Riello investigates eighteenth-century shoe fashions, examining the impact of changes in the artifacts themselves and shifts in the ideas surrounding shoes. The rise of the modern city, as chapters by Alison Matthews David and Nancy Rexford show, meant a separation between male and female spheres of action. Men walked freely in town and country by wearing sturdy boots, whose military image contributed to reinforce the notion of male power (Figure I.19). In contrast, as Nancy Rexford shows, women only slowly adopted practical boots. In nineteenth-century America, women continued to wear flimsy shoes in town and country, thus following European fashion, but also reinforcing a perceived inferior role.

The second "step" in the long walk of this book is dedicated to "Encounters and Cultural Interactions." Three chapters by established scholars of extra-European dress illuminate the way in which shoes appear as symbols of cultural understanding, in particular in the relationship between the West and other major civilizations such as Japan, China and West Africa. A chapter by Martha Chaiklin provides a sharp analysis of the role of footwear in premodern Japan. In a society dominated by symbolic associations, shoes were tokens of material culture embodying the spiritual, but also physical principles of cleanliness and dirt. Established categories of thought on the use of footwear are also the subject of a chapter by Tunde M. Akinwumi, examining the way in which Africa's cultural, social and political position was influenced by European nations in the nineteenth and early twentieth centuries. Shoes, the prerogative of the emperor and his court, became widely available and much sought after by the rising Europeanized elite. The "English" shoe was a tool of social competition within African social hierarchies, but also a symbol of cultural oppression in its more global context. A final chapter by Paola Zamperini connects past and present in Chinese footwear by analyzing the links between established moral and social views on shoes and the challenge of the global market for footwear in which China is imposing itself as the major producer of cheaper types of products and imitations.

The English shoe, as the modern man's shoe, is the topic of the first chapter of "step" three of this book, "Shoes, Bodies and Identities." Christopher Breward shows how early twentieth-century men's shoes were taken as examples of "good design" in opposition to women's shoes, whose abundance of decoration was abhorred by modernist architects such as Adolf Loos and Le Corbusier. Elizabeth Semmelhack further develops the topic of female extravagance in a chapter on the history of high heels. She shows how, in the last five centuries, high heels have been integral to the formation of bodily appearance and, in the twentieth century, have created specific social and cultural constructions of femininity, from the pinup to the "girl power" of the 1990s.

Bodily appearance has also been central to the way eroticism has been conceptualized and performed in the twentieth century. A chapter by Valerie Steele details the way in which sexuality,

FIGURE I.17 (TOP LEFT): EIGHTEENTH-CENTURY SNUFFBOXES IN THE SHAPE OF A SHOE AND A BOOT. TWO OF THE MANY EXAMPLES OF THE MATERIAL CULTURE OF FOOTWEAR AT BATA SHOE MUSEUM, P84.97 AND P84.176 (DATED 1740). REPRODUCED BY KIND PERMISSION OF BATA SHOE MUSEUM.

FIGURE I.18 (TOP RIGHT): WOMEN HAVE OFTEN BEEN PORTRAYED AS CONSPICUOUS CONSUMERS. THE DIALOGUE BETWEEN A SHOEMAKER AND A WOMAN. FRENCH ENGRAVING, SEVENTEENTH CENTURY. BATA SHOE MUSEUM, TORONTO, P79.0588. REPRODUCED BY KIND PERMISSION OF BATA SHOE MUSEUM.

FIGURE I.19 (RIGHT): A PAIR OF POLISHED GENTLEMEN BY JAMES GILLRAY. LONDON, H. HUMPHREY, 1801. PRINT, 1849 VERSION.

eroticism and fetishism interact and their representation through shoes in subcultures and also in mainstream cultural settings. Hilary Davidson explores the importance of shoes in the construction of sexual profiles, and also in the "performativity" of sex, in a chapter about the magic of red shoes. From a nineteenth-century literary construction, red shoes have become, in the twentieth century, iconic symbols of female "deviance" and have only been more positively interpreted in recent years (Figure I.20). The concluding chapter, jointly written by Clare Lomas, Peter McNeil and Sally Gray, examines the notion of the "queer" dress of non-normative men and women, as well as gay and lesbian urban subcultures after the Second World War, and the interrelationship between the foot, footwear and sexual identity during the last fifty years.

The final "step" of this book is dedicated to what the shoe can affect and effect: "Representation and Self-Presentation." Stefania Ricci examines the life of Salvatore Ferragamo from his American period to his success in postwar Italy. Ferragamo was the father of the shoe-maker-*célèbre* and constructed a myth of the diva in divine shoes through an interplay between the historical past of Florence and the new world of cinema and fashion. Ferragamo was central in putting Italy back on the map of fashion, with a continuing focus on footwear. Giovanni Luigi Fontana argues that Italy's success in footwear manufacturing in the last fifty years is the result of a notion and practice of good taste, but also good training in design and the recovery of the skills and talents in footwear production that Italy had held in the Renaissance.

Shoes are not just tools of personal or collective self-presentation. Julia Pine shows how shoes are widely present in conceptually sophisticated and avant-garde art from the eighteenth century to the present day. At times they have been used to signify sexual behavior and gender identity, but often they have become widely accepted ciphers for ideas about late-capitalist art and society, as in the case of Andy Warhol. As Benstock and Ferris have demonstrated, the power of shoes to suggest the nature of postmodern society, style and even modes of art practice is suggested in Warhol's gold-dust paintings of that banal object, the shoe. The mass nature of shoes in present-day societies is also the topic of Alison Gill's chapter on sneakers. Global shoe manufacturers sell the ideal of the athletic body through the use of well-known brands. Sneakers, trainers or "runners" are central to the construction of contemporary consumer identity and have become enduring symbols of affluence, youth and social mobility.

A STEP FORWARD

The editors have the privilege of concluding this volume by considering the various threads of the history of footwear. Shoes are peculiar objects. We believe this even more so at the end of the project than upon its commencement. We have been amazed at the large numbers of shoes, from the banal to the luxurious, stored in museum depositories and rarely displayed. We have been astonished at the tenacity of a small group of researchers who for decades have argued for the significance of this essential but everyday object. We have been intrigued by the way discussion of the project raises, in all those who overhear it (from academic to generalist listeners), instant and passionate reactions, more marked than the general idea of "fashion." Few people have any idea of how or where their shoes are made, whereas these understandings are clearer in the labeling and purchasing of fashion. This tension is evident in the titles of numerous texts designed to explicate the "mystery" of shoemaking. Shoes are thus ubiquitous and mysterious.

The chapters gathered in this book show how shoes are far from the pedestrian level of the street that they are designed to navigate. They encapsulate a huge range of meanings, prejudices and tensions in society. Shoes are part of daily life – from the Manolo Blahnik exclusive dream of limousine shoes to the million of sneakers invading alleys, streets and squares all over the world. They are produced in large factories, artisan workshops and South Asian sweatshops. They are consumed by us all from the cradle to the grave. They are a necessity of life and the *necessaire* of social living.

Figure 1.20 (facing page): Madonna's shoes. Red satin platform d'Arcy pumps, size 37½, made by Sergio Rossi, 1992. This pair of shoes was worn by Madonna in Rochester, Michigan during her Girlie Tour of 1993–94. Bata Shoe Museum, Toronto, P95.69.AB. Reproduced by kind permission of Bata Shoe Museum.

1.
BENEATH THEIR SHINING FEET

SHOES AND SANDALS IN CLASSICAL GREECE

sue blundell

For the Greeks of the classical era, shoes could have multiple meanings.[1] The egalitarian flavor of much of their civic ideology meant that footwear did not figure greatly as a marker of status distinctions. The Greeks tended instead to invest shoes with symbolic value, and to deploy them – or their absence – as expressions of their relationship with the natural, social or cultural environment. In exploring the significance of Greek shoes, this case study will hopefully help to remedy the neglect of this crucial item of clothing in contemporary Classical scholarship. Ancient Greek dress has only begun to receive critical attention fairly recently, and only two scholars have studied footwear in detail during the last 100 years.[2]

I start with a brief examination of issues relating to the use, manufacture and form of shoes, and their role as signifiers of gender, class, or ideology. Next, I look at their symbolic associations, investigating the meanings most commonly ascribed to shoes, especially those related to journeys and travel. The concept of "boundary" is explored in connection with the removal or donning of footwear. These actions are often employed to mark the passage between different spheres – public and private, or secular and sacred – or to underscore the transitions associated with wedding or funerary rituals. I also consider the erotic connotations of shoes, and discuss the issue of "monosandalism," a puzzling mythological and artistic motif that appears to take its root meaning from a religious cult.

WITH OR WITHOUT SHOES?

Ancient Greek shoes hardly ever survive,[3] and most of the evidence used in this chapter is derived from literary or visual sources. Such literature is wide ranging, and includes epic poetry, drama, history, philosophy, and law-court speeches. Vase paintings and sculpture also provide valuable visual evidence.[4] Very few of these media are noted for their realism, and although some detailed representations of shoes are to be found in sculpture, both literature and art are problematic when considering the complexity and intricacy of stylistic conventions. Symbolism, however, is another matter. Drama and the visual arts in particular are rich in imagery and can help us to reconstruct some of the meanings that were attached to shoes in real-life cultural practices.

A casual observer might be forgiven for thinking that in classical Greece, people often went around without shoes, or without any clothes on at all in the case of some of the men. Sculpture and vase paintings, the two principal visual media of the fifth and fourth centuries BC, can easily lead us astray in the matter of Greek clothing. In sculpture, the convention of the male nude means that men often appear naked and shoeless in situations where in real life they would have been fully clothed. Shoes are even less common in vase paintings, where people of both sexes are often shown with bare feet. This again seems to be an artistic convention, determined in part by the difficulty of depicting an intricate item such as a sandal in such a small-scale medium.

In reality, it is clear that both sexes generally wore shoes when they went out of doors, and sometimes when they were at home as well. Both females and males (when not conventionally naked) are often shown wearing shoes in sculpted representations. Similarly, there are many references to footwear in Greek literature. In Athens, when people went shoeless in public it seems to have been taken as a mark either of poverty or of philosophical asceticism. It was, for example, seen as a remarkable occurrence when Socrates took the trouble to bathe and put on some shoes before going out to a drinking party.[5] Bare feet would have been rather more common in Sparta, where the constitution stipulated that boys in military camps should go without sandals in order to toughen their feet.[6] But these are clearly the exceptions. For most people, even in Sparta, footwear was the norm.[7]

The prevalence of footwear meant that shoemakers as well as shoes received plenty of attention from Greek writers. Plato lists these craftsmen alongside farmers, weavers and house-builders as essential workers supplying some of life's basic necessities in the prototype for a city.[8] This suggests that one of the reasons why shoes had a loaded symbolic significance for the Greeks was that they were seen as one of the fundamental items of civilized life. Everyday manufacturing processes supplied Plato's mentor, Socrates, with many a philosophical analogy, and his talk was peppered with homely references to "mules and metalworkers, shoemakers and tanners."[9] It is little wonder that he was familiar with the production of footwear, for men in Athens often used to pass the time of day at "the perfume-seller's, the barber's, or the shoemaker's," especially if these establishments were close to the marketplace.[10] One enterprising craftsman named Simon was in the habit of taking notes when Socrates was giving forth in his workshop, so that eventually he was able to publish thirty-three philosophical treatises known as *The Leather Dialogues*.[11]

These shoemakers were responsible for producing many different types of footwear. As explained by Bryant:

> There were shoes for men and shoes for women; there were good shoes and poor shoes; leather shoes and felt shoes, and shoes with wooden soles; there were sandals and slippers, and half-boots, and top-boots; tall shoes for short people, thin shoes for tall people; shoes for winter and shoes for summer.[12]

Shoes came in a large variety of styles with precise names, not all of which are understood today. I shall be using the term "shoe" in its generic sense, although sandals seem to have been the most common item of footwear worn in ancient Greece. Sandals were used by both sexes, and ranged from heavy-duty types with stout straps and thick soles to more refined and ornate artifacts. Men sometimes wore shoes with leather uppers covering the whole or part of the foot, or boots that laced together over the ankle or shin. Women's shoes made from soft white leather were used indoors, as were various kinds of inexpensive light slippers. On occasions, women might also be seen in *kothornoi*: soft boots without lacings that came high up the shin. Since a *kothornos* fitted either foot, the term was used as a nickname for the slippery Athenian politician Theramenes who, during the upheavals of the late fifth century, transferred his allegiance from the democratic to the oligarchic system and then back to democracy again.[13]

GENDER AND STATUS

The precise differences between male and female versions of footwear are not always clear to us, although there are clues that suggest gender identity. Xenophon tells us that there were shoemakers who specialized in the manufacture of either male or female footwear, and some styles were certainly exclusive to one gender.[14] Wearing *kothornoi*, for example, could make a man appear effeminate. For this reason the Persian king, Cyrus, was advised to force some of his male subjects to wear this style of footwear in order to turn them into pseudo-women and neutralize their rebellious tendencies.[15] These gender distinctions mean that shoes feature in some of the cross-dressing fantasies that are a highlight of fifth-century Athenian comedy. When a hapless old man is to be dispatched to a women-only festival disguised as a female worshipper, he is first taken to visit a poet famous for his effeminacy in order to borrow a frock, a girdle, a wrap and some women's shoes.[16] In another play, a revolutionary women's leader steals her husband's shoes so that she can infiltrate a meeting of the Athenian Assembly masquerading as a man. In her absence, her disgruntled spouse is forced to snatch up his wife's slippers when a sudden call of nature sends him dashing out of the house.[17]

Footwear may have been less reliable as an indicator of distinctions in wealth or status. Some shoes were certainly fancier than others. Sandals might have elegant cutout patterns and multi-layered soles, and occasionally they sported gilded straps or decorative discs attached to the central thong.[18] On the other hand, shoes that were roughly made or were worn and patched would no doubt have been worn in the main by the poor or by those of lower social status. However, these distinctions were not particularly clear-cut. In Athens low-quality shoes might, for example, be adopted as a way of declaring one's political sympathies: a man could advertise his opposition to democracy by "playing the Spartan" and wearing crude shoes with thin soles.[19] The majority of Athenian men probably preferred stouter footwear if they could afford it, but this did not mean that they wore showy shoes. By the classical period, luxurious display of any kind was seen as unsuitable for the citizens of democratic Athens, and Athenian males seem to have adopted the Spartan fashion for simplicity in dress, with "the rich leading as much as possible a life like that of the ordinary people."[20] It is therefore not particularly surprising to find that shoes are hardly ever remarked on as a sign of inferior class status. Even slaves, it seems, looked much the same as many other people when it came to footwear. Some of them may have gone barefoot, but many appear to have worn shoes of some kind. When a corner-cutting shoemaker in an Athenian comedy is accused of palming off some poorly made shoes onto a group of citizen farmers, one of the slaves who is present complains that he has been a victim of the same con merchant.[21]

JOURNEYS, BOUNDARIES AND LIMITS

Symbolically, shoes are associated most obviously with movement and journeys. In Greek art, divinities are generally distinguishable from humans only by virtue of their clothing or accessories, and in the case of Hermes, patron deity of travelers, these include a pair of high-laced sandals or boots, often with wings attached. The hero Perseus was presented with similar winged sandals to enable him to fly off to the eastern edge of the earth and dispose of the monstrous gorgon Medusa. Shoes of a less magical kind play a significant part in the life story of another hero, Theseus, who was brought up by his mother Aithra. By the age of sixteen he was strong enough to roll back a large boulder and uncover the sword and sandals left there by his absent father, King Aegeus, shortly after his conception. These tokens prompted him to undertake a perilous expedition to Athens, wearing the sandals and wielding the sword, and there he was eventually reunited with his father. In this myth shoes provide the impetus for a life-changing journey, but the story also furnishes a fairly rare example of footwear as an emblem of identity.

In Greek art, conventional human footwear can serve as a sign of movement on a more mundane level. When sandals make one of their relatively infrequent appearances in a vase painting, they seem even more striking if the wearer is standing next to someone with bare feet. On one painted wine cup, for example, young men with quite elaborate sandals are paying court to barefoot companions – women on one side of the vessel (Figure 1.1), and boys on the other. Here the men's sandals, coupled with their walking sticks, seem to signify their freedom of movement, thus highlighting the privileges that they enjoy as Athenian citizens. Their companions, by contrast, are marked out as people who do not enjoy the same freedom to move around in the world. As women or underage males, they are formally excluded from the public sphere in which they are temporarily appearing. In a different context, the juxtaposition of bare feet and shoes can assume a different meaning. When, on another wine cup, a naked man who is still wearing shoes is seen having sex with a totally nude slave girl, it is the male and not the female who is seen to be out of place.[22] The man's shoes tell us that he belongs in the outside world, not to the brothel. This is just a fleeting visit, and soon he will be gone; unlike the slave girl, he has the freedom to leave.

Figure 1.1: Young men courting women. Red figure wine cup, 525–475 bc. Berlin, Antikensammlung, F2279.

FIGURE 1.2: SANDALS OUTSIDE A HOUSE IN OLD CORINTH, GREECE.

The symbolic association with journeys is extended in situations where people are either putting their shoes on or taking them off. Frequently, these actions mark the crossing of one of the boundaries encountered in travel. The ancient Greeks, with their highly developed sense of community, invested the dividing line between private and public spheres of activity with particular significance. It is not surprising to find shoes among the items that mark the transition from one to the other. In Greece today, as in many other countries, people commonly take off their outdoor shoes before they enter a house (Figure 1.2). There is no surviving evidence to prove that this was a regular practice in ancient Greece; but it is clear from written sources that leaving one's home for the wider world was an event associated with the donning of shoes.

FIGURE 1.3: YOUNG MAN PREPARING TO JOIN THE PROCESSION (THE STRAPS OF THE SANDAL WOULD ONCE HAVE BEEN PAINTED IN). CAST OF THE PARTHENON WEST FRIEZE, XV.29, 440 BC. THE BRITISH MUSEUM.

In Homer's poems, deities regularly "bind beautiful sandals beneath their feet" before flying off from Mount Olympus to intervene in some troubled sector of their earthly domain.[23] Down among the humans, when the Greek commander Agamemnon prepares for another day of action in the campaign at Troy, he throws a cloak over his shoulders, grasps a weapon, and fastens fair sandals "beneath his shining feet."[24] Withdrawal from the public domain can also be linked to shoe-handling. Notoriously, Agamemnon's wife Clytemnestra greets the victorious commander on his return from Troy by spreading a crimson textile over the threshold of their palace. Resistant at first, he eventually orders an attendant to remove his shoes before he consents to set foot on this magnificent floor covering.[25] For Agamemnon, the step is to be a fatal one. When he reenters his home, crossing the boundary that separates public exploits from private interactions, his desperate and implacable wife murders him. Clearly, lacing or unlacing one's sandals could be the prelude to momentous events, and it is little wonder that the actions attracted superstitions: for example, according to the Pythagoreans, when putting your shoes on you should always start with the right foot.[26]

In Greek art, a figure who stoops to adjust a sandal strap may similarly be signaling a movement from one sphere to another. In the Parthenon frieze, created circa 440 BC, we witness a large-scale public spectacle, a religious procession staged by the Athenians every four years in honor of their patron goddess, Athena. In the western section of the frieze – the side that faced visitors when they entered the Acropolis – we see a series of young men preparing to join the procession, getting themselves ready for public display. The second in line has one foot on a mounting block and is bending to lace a sandal (Figure 1.3). Further along, the pose is repeated. The gesture serves as a signal to the viewer that the procession is about to move off. We are present at the start of a journey, observing two young men on the point of crossing the boundary that separates the private individual from the active citizen – someone who is equipped to represent his community in both a religious and a military capacity. More broadly, the gesture identifies the men as part of the wholesale creative process that defines the city of Athens. Like many of their companions elsewhere in the frieze, they are seen in the act of adjusting their clothing, transforming themselves through their dress into worthy and well-ordered Athenian citizens.

Conversely, shoes that have been removed by their owners may be used by an artist to mark a passage from the outside world to the domestic interior. In vase paintings, they are to be seen standing on floors or hanging from invisible walls, and they often help to identify a scene as one that is taking place in an indoor location. At a male drinking party ("*symposium*") shoes left underneath a couch suggest that public concerns have been placed on one side along with the shoes – they signal informality, wine, song and relaxation.[27] At the same time, they remind the viewer that these men are free to move back into the public arena when the party is over. Here discarded shoes are used to underscore the notion of a versatile masculine community, publicly engaged but still capable of enjoying interactions of a more personal character. In mixed company, their meaning is sometimes harder to fathom. Shoes placed beneath a couch shared by a man and a woman leave us in little doubt about the nature of their relationship.[28] But they are also to be seen hanging on walls in rooms where groups of women are entertaining male visitors.[29] Many people are likely to have hung their shoes on hooks as a precaution against invasion by scorpions; but when an artist takes the trouble to include them in a domestic scene, he may be letting us know that this is no ordinary household. If these women are in the habit of stepping out of the house, then it is possible that they are being presented to us as sex workers rather than housewives.

Although sexual segregation was undoubtedly a significant aspect of Greek social life, it would be a mistake to imagine that many women were kept in anything approaching seclusion. Ideologically, females were closely identified with the domestic interior, and in real life they were certainly more restricted in their movements than men. As we have seen, this distinction is occasionally drawn to our attention in vase paintings where sandaled male feet are juxtaposed with naked female ones. But plenty of women seem to have left their homes to visit neighbors or friends, to fetch water from public fountains, to attend weddings or funerals, or to take part in religious celebrations. Their journeys, though generally quite short, could be invested with considerable symbolic significance. This situation seems to be reflected in Greek art, where women are no less closely associated with shoes than men. Female mobility was important to Greek men, above all because the reproduction of the family unit depended on it: marriage involved the formal transfer of a woman from one household to another. When she made

FIGURE 1.4 (LEFT): EROS FASTENS A BRIDE'S SHOE. RED FIGURE OIL JAR, 450–400 BC. BOSTON, MUSEUM OF FINE ARTS, 95.1402. DRAWING BY LLOYD LLEWELLYN-JONES.

FIGURE 1.5 (FACING PAGE): LIA TSEKI'S WEDDING, FERES, GREECE, AUGUST 2004.

FIGURE 1.6: NIKE (THE
GODDESS OF VICTORY)
ADJUSTING HER SANDAL
STRAP. SCULPTURE FROM
THE PARAPET OF THE
TEMPLE OF ATHENE NIKE,
THE ACROPOLIS, ATHENS,
C. 410 BC. ATHENS,
THE ACROPOLIS MUSEUM,
973.

this crucial journey from her father's home to that of her new husband, a bride was generally equipped with new sandals known as *nymphides* ("bride's sandals"). This stage in her adornment is quite often featured in vase paintings showing the preparations for a wedding. The sandals may be laced by the bride herself, by an attendant, or even by the young god Eros,[30] present on a metaphorical level as a deity responsible for sex, love and desire (Figure 1.4). Present-day Greek weddings include a similar ritual, in which the "best man," before escorting the bride to church, has first to find a shoe hidden by one of the bridesmaids, and then to fit it onto the bride's foot (Figure 1.5). For the bride in ancient Greece, shoe-tying underscores the notion of marriage as a vital transitional stage in a woman's life, incorporating both social and sexual meanings. Like other examples of the action, it also presages a movement from the private to the public sphere. In the wedding procession that is to follow, the bride will be displayed to the outside world as a visible token of the formation of a new union.

Matrimonial shoe-lacing is rarely represented in sculpture, but it does receive some spectacular treatment in the sculptural group from the east pediment of the Temple of Zeus at Olympia, created in the 460s BC. Here a chariot race that will decide whether the hero Pelops will win the hand of Hippodameia, daughter of a local king, is about to take place. As the contestants and their companions come together in a tense and fidgety lineup, the potential bride offers the viewer a few hints as to the likely outcome of the contest. She herself holds back a corner of her veil in a gesture that anticipates a wedding day ritual, while a servant who kneels at her feet is almost certainly, in a part of the work now lost, engaged in tying her sandals.[31] Greek viewers, well acquainted with all the ramifications of this story, were being reminded that one of the most notable marriages in the whole of their mythology was about to take place. The union was destined to produce several generations of outstanding and tormented personalities. These included Atreus (who tricked his brother Thyestes into eating his own children in a stew), Atreus' son Agamemnon (who was assassinated by his wife), and Agamemnon's son Orestes (who murdered his mother to avenge the death of his father).

The handling of shoes can also signify a transition from secular to sacred space. Every sanctuary and every religious festival had its own distinctive regulations, of which only a fraction are known to us. But it is not surprising to find that in some of them the removal of shoes was stipulated: worshippers had to be barefoot when carrying out a sacrifice, but also when entering a temple, approaching the statue of a deity, or undergoing initiation.[32] A hymn to the agrarian goddess Demeter praises the young women who walk in her procession "unsandaled and with hair unbound," so that "their feet and heads may remain unharmed for ever."[33] So when Nike, goddess of victory, is depicted in a sculpture from the Athenian Acropolis stooping to untie her sandal in a beautiful sweeping gesture, the fact that she is about to perform a sacrifice in honor of her patron Athena is the most likely explanation for her action (Figure 1.6). However, the gesture may also signify the end of a journey, reassuring the viewer that this is no fleeting visit, and that Victory is here to stay. This sculpture was produced in the late fifth century BC, in the course of

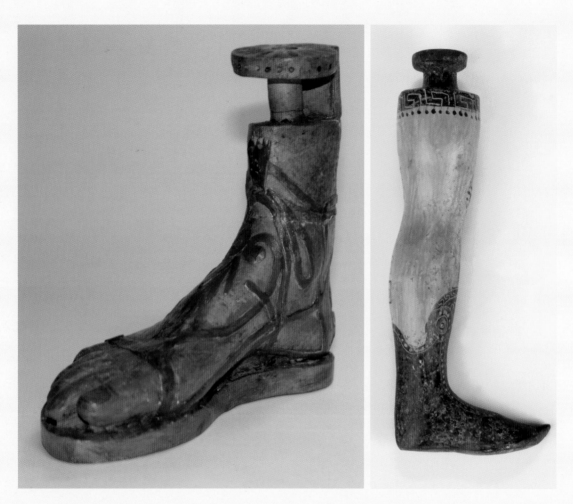

Figure 1.7 (left): Pottery vessel from Attica in the form of a foot and sandal, 550–525 bc. Bata Shoe Museum, Toronto, P84.76. Reproduced by kind permission of Bata Shoe Museum.

Figure 1.8 (right): Pottery vessel in the form of a leg and laced boot, originally from Rhodes, c. 570 bc. Height 8 in. Bata Shoe Museum, Toronto, P83.3. Reproduced by kind permission of Bata Shoe Museum.

FIGURE 1.9: A SLAVE GIRL FITS A SHOE ONTO
A DECEASED WOMAN'S FOOT. A RELIEF ON
AN ATHENIAN TOMBSTONE OF THE LATE FIFTH
CENTURY BC. ATHENS, NATIONAL
ARCHAEOLOGICAL MUSEUM, 718.

a major war between Athens and Sparta, and the idea that Victory might be preparing to settle down in their city would have had tremendous appeal for the hard-pressed Athenians.

The Greeks conceptualized death as a journey to the Underworld, and clearly it involved the crossing of the most crucial boundary of all. Shoes were naturally included among the articles needed to accomplish it. In the sixth century BC, terracotta vases in the shape of sandaled feet (Figure 1.7), or occasionally sandaled or booted legs (Figure 1.8), were placed in tombs in several parts of the Greek world.[34] Since most of them are quite small (2–4 in. high in the case of the feet), their meaning seems to lie in their symbolism rather than their functional value as containers. These shoes will presumably help to make the long journey from this life to the next less arduous. The same idea probably lies behind the occasional inclusion of real shoes among the objects deposited in graves: iron frames for wooden soles, and sometimes the wooden soles themselves, have been found in tombs of the sixth and fifth centuries BC.[35] This theme of departure may be subtly alluded to in sculpted gravestones showing the deceased in a domestic setting, among relatives or household slaves. Most of them are wearing shoes, as though ready for their journey, and in one rare example a sandal is being fitted onto a deceased woman's foot by a kneeling slave girl (Figure 1.9).

EROTICISM AND MONOSANDALISM

For the Greeks – as for most civilizations up to the present day – shoes could be sexually alluring, particularly when worn by women. In the early Christian era, shiny black shoes with pointed toes were included in the list of immodest items of female dress denounced by John Chrysostom, Bishop of Constantinople.[36] However, Greeks in an earlier age may have been less bothered by seductive displays of footwear. The lovely young women of the late sixth century BC, whose statues were dedicated to the goddess Athena on the Acropolis at Athens, were in many cases raising their skirts to reveal a pair of shapely feet and some delicate sandals.[37] Shoes with built-up platform soles might be worn by women who wanted to make themselves look taller, although in Xenophon's famous *Treatise on Household Management*, one young bride is reprimanded by her stuffy husband for sporting these items around the house.[38] More assertive wives might not hesitate to exploit the erotic potential of footwear, at least when they were characters in a comedy. In Aristophanes' *Lysistrata*, the heroine (who is campaigning for an end to war) urges her fellow activists to put on "little saffron dresses, perfumes, flimsy slippers, blusher, and see-through chitons" if they want to inflame their men's passions and bring their sex strike to a successful conclusion.[39] Later in the same play, a male official makes use of the sexual imagery implicit in footwear when illustrating the many opportunities for misbehavior that careless husbands have been presenting to their wives:

> Another chap goes to the shoemaker, a young lad with a very grown-up prick, and says,
> "Oh shoemaker, the strap of my wife's sandal is pinching her little toe, it's so very tender.

FIGURE 1.10 (FACING PAGE): A NAKED WOMAN FASTENS HER SANDAL. RED FIGURE AMPHORA, 525–475 BC. PARIS, MUSÉE DU LOUVRE, G2. PHOTOGRAPH: RMN/© HERVÉ LEWANDOWSKI.

Go round at midday and loosen it up a bit, will you? Give her something with a bit more breadth to it."[40]

Footwear might also feature in the equipment used by a brothel-keeper to improve the appearance of some of her apprentices. A thin woman would be supplied with padding, a pale one with blusher, while a short woman would have cork soles stitched into her shoes, and a tall one would be made to wear thin slippers.[41] Sometimes shoes could have a more direct erotic impact. In the Christian era, streetwalkers might advertise their trade by incorporating invitations to clients into the nails on the soles of their shoes, "thus stamping the lustfulness of their own feelings onto the earth."[42] Much earlier, if we trust the evidence of Athenian vase painting of the fifth century BC, male customers in brothels used to engage in a form of sadistic practice that involved beating prostitutes with slippers or the soles of shoes.[43] There was even a Greek word, *blautöo*, meaning "to beat with a slipper," which suggests that the activity was not uncommon.

When represented in vase paintings, shoes or shoe-handling can help to intensify the erotic atmosphere of a scene. Discarded boots or shoes imply release from normal constraints. They can be seen standing by washbasins where naked women are bathing, or placed beneath couches that are the site of sexual activities ranging from fondling to full-scale intercourse.[44] In other pieces, naked women may be raising one of their legs to pull on a boot or fasten a sandal. When attended by Eros, they are clearly dressing for love and if a male spectator is included in the scene, the action may appear seductive even if the sandal-lacer is fully clothed.[45] Often the status of these females is left unclear. The woman on the neck of the wine jar in Figure 1.10, who is lacing her sandal, could be a wife, a mistress or a streetwalker. But whoever she is, we can easily imagine that she is extending a sexual invitation to the viewer, an impression reinforced by her position above an image of erotic pursuits among the followers of Dionysus. Salaciousness of a more overt kind is achieved by a woman in the center of a wine cup, who is tying her sandal while squatting over a footbath (a household article that seems to have doubled as a bidet). Meanwhile a large shadowy dildo looms up to one side of her.[46]

Of the transitions with which shoe-tying was associated in real life, one at least was partly sexual in character. As we have seen, a Greek bride put on new sandals when she took the step that would transform her from unmarried virgin to sexually active wife. This is an aspect of her journey that is underlined in vase paintings where Eros is playing the part of her attendant. But any action that involves raising one's leg might be seen as potentially titillating, so that other transitions could easily be invested with erotic overtones by artists who chose to focus on the shoe-handling aspect. Removing one's shoes when attending a sacrifice would not generally be seen as a sexually charged event. However, the act appears quite suggestive when it is performed by the sensuous Nike, whose pose has allowed the sculptor to insert a shadowy hollow between the goddess's thighs. It is hardly surprising that this Nike became the model for numerous nude or nearly nude Aphrodites who, in the post-classical period, unlaced their sandals with a more obviously

FIGURE 1.11 (FACING PAGE): APHRODITE, EROS AND PAN, C. 100 BC. ATHENS, NATIONAL ARCHAEOLOGICAL MUSEUM, 3335.

erotic intent. The trend culminates in a superbly flamboyant piece in which a smiling goddess of love playfully uses her sandal to fend off the attentions of a marauding Pan (Figure 1.11).

This last image furnishes a somewhat unorthodox example of the motif of "monosandalism," common enough in myth, literature and art to have provoked discussion by a number of scholars.[47] The hero Jason provides the best-known mythological example. Smuggled away into the countryside as a baby after his wicked uncle has usurped his father's throne, he returns at the age of twenty to reclaim his birthright, wearing a single sandal on his right foot. The uncle's doom is sealed, for he has long since been told to "beware a man wearing one sandal when he comes from his mountain retreat to the sunlit plain."[48] A real-life event described by the historian Thucydides[49] seems even more puzzling. In 427 BC, the members of a garrison in the town of Plataea, under siege from the Spartans, made a daring escape through enemy lines with each man wearing one sandal on his left foot, "so that they would be less liable to slip in the mud." Monosandalism of a more sensuous kind is to be seen in a set of Greek-inspired paintings from the Villa of the Mysteries in Pompeii. Here the god Dionysus reclines in the lap of a seated woman, his left foot encased in a sandal, but his right foot naked.[50]

The general consensus among scholars is that the single sandal motif derives from religious ritual, and more specifically from the worship of chthonic deities – deities associated with the earth rather than the sky. One writer links it with the chthonic rites performed by ephebes, young men in a transitional phase of their lives who were undergoing military training.[51] Jason, seen at the point where he is passing out of the wild and into the city, strikingly illustrates this kind of coming-of-age. The arch-rationalist Thucydides may, in his account, be misinterpreting a ritual of adolescence that the real-life Plataeans resorted to in a desperate situation. In general, the motif may signify a liminal state where the wearer has one foot in contact with the natural powers of the earth, while the other, sandaled foot gives him a toehold in the realm of human culture. It is a particularly appropriate image for Dionysus, god of wine and drama, whose offices were important to the civilized life of the city, but who also had close ties with the untamed natural world. We should probably not make too much of the motif in the Aphrodite and Pan piece, where it is used primarily to comic effect. Even here, however, we might say that the goddess is poised between the sphere of socially approved relationships, and the chaotic instinctive impulses represented by Pan.

CONCLUSION: SHOES AND MEANING

On or off the foot, a shoe was an object that was rich in meaning for the Greeks. In a culture where performances of all kinds were colored by the dynamic of ritual, it is not surprising that the most potent symbolism was attached, not so much to footwear itself, but to the human actions in which shoes appeared. Binary systems of thought, firmly established in Greek ways of looking at the world, led to an emphasis being placed on the opposition between shod and unshod feet. This was linked to other contrasts – between culture and nature, outdoors and indoors, public and private, secular and sacred, male and female – though meanings were fluid and always governed by context. So actions with shoes – covering or exposing the feet – were highly significant, and were associated in particular with movement between different sectors of the human environment. Change, transition and the crossing of boundaries were vital components of the meaning of shoes, and the rites of passage with which they were associated included coming-of-age, marriage and death. But actions with shoes can also be erotic, and in the hands of some Greek artists they became heavily charged with sensuality. Here, more than anywhere else, gender became a notable factor. Although shoes were worn by both sexes, most of the sandal-lacing poses depicted in Greek art are assigned to female figures. The tendency, in Greek culture, to confer on women the status of erotic object, is certainly present in representations of their relationship to footwear.

2.
SUMPTUOUS SHOES

MAKING AND WEARING IN MEDIEVAL ITALY
maria giuseppina muzzarelli

When we talk about "shoes" we mean a wide variety of different footwear: sandals, boots, clogs, pumps and so on. During the Middle Ages and the early modern period, shoes were not only different for men and women, but came in a diverse range of materials and shapes. There were sturdy types for labor, practical urban footwear, and delicate, elegant shoes for special occasions. Of course, shoe types changed over time, although the basic typology remained roughly unaltered throughout this period, preserving crucial differences between men's and women's shoes, between low- and high-heeled shoes, and between three materials: textiles, leather and wood. Perhaps more puzzling is the fact that there were at least as many names as types of footwear in medieval Italy: some footwear had several names; others had different names in different cities. The famous *pianelle*, for example, were called *sibroni* or *solee* in Lombardy, *pantofole* (literally "slippers") in Ferrara and *calcagnini* both in Venice and in Tuscany (Figures 2.1a and b).

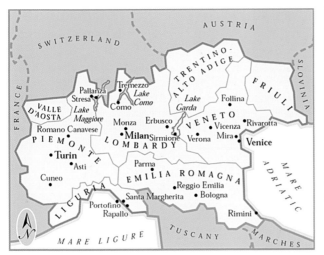

Figure 2.1: Maps of northern and central Italy.

Among such a variety of names and types of footwear, this chapter aims to chart the worlds of making and consuming from the thirteenth to the sixteenth century. How were shoes produced? Who wore what? And why were certain shoes preferred to others? These questions can be answered only if we consider the specific social and economic environment of medieval Europe. By concentrating on the cities of central and northern Italy, I would like to show how the wearing of certain shoes was not entirely left to personal preference. Moral and legislative constraints regarding shapes, materials and uses came to influence the choice of footwear made both by men and women.

PRETTY SHOES AND OLD SHOES

We know a great deal about medieval shoes from paintings and frescoes. However, not all shoe types are found there. Women's shoes were often invisible as they were hidden under long skirts that reached the ground; men's shoes, however, were emphasized by the tight hose that men wore. Imagery is thus not only biased as it belongs to a specific genre of representation, but also because it provides few clues about women's shoes. Visual representations also show how, similarly to adults, children wore both practical shoes for walking and footwear for "appearance."[1] The former were made of leather, while the latter were made of fabric: delicate shoes of red cloth with contrasting borders, such as the ones worn by the young Jesus in Carpaccio's painting (Figure 2.2).

More is known about men's shoes. In the early Middle Ages they had low heels and came mainly in dark colors; some had substantial tongues, or rose to cover part of the calf. They were made of leather or fabrics, sometimes with some minor variations – for instance to highlight the use of colorful hose by young men. They often covered the ankle and were secured with strings on the side.[2] It is not uncommon to find men shown wearing soft, boot-type footwear reaching their knees or *calze solate* (literally "soled hose," soft footwear with leather soles). The tailor

VICTORIS CARPATIO
VENETI OPVS

represented in one of the frescoes of the Castle of Issogne in Valle d'Aosta in northern Italy is intent on producing this type of footwear or garment (Figure 2.3).

These paintings and frescoes provide a partial understanding of medieval footwear as they concentrate on the representation of good-quality products, either in the act of being produced, or as new and unworn. Most men, women and children in the Middle Ages belonged to the vast social class of the poor. For them footwear was possible, although not probable, and could be worn only in times of prosperity or on special occasions. Shoes were worn until they disintegrated, and were passed down from men to women and children. Visual representations of the poor (normally embodied by old women, sick men and cripples, and iconographically associated with beggary) show them wearing clogs, humble slippers and, for the most destitute, simple rags folded around their feet. A recurrent image is that of a man with no feet who walks with the use of wooden crutches, a kind of footwear for the hands, as represented in the Cupola of the Baptistery in Parma (Figure 2.4).

During the later Middle Ages, the men and women of the populace usually wore clogs made of wood or cork. These were particularly common among peasants, but were also used by wealthier citizens to protect their *calze solate* from mud or from the damage caused by the bad state of public roads. During the summer, bare feet were preferred to hard clogs. Paintings show how men and women could choose from a wide range of clogs, from the low-heeled and thin-soled to more substantial types, normally attached through a simple string of leather. A similar type of footwear was adopted by the Minor Observant Friars, whose common appellation of *Zoccolanti* derives from the clog (*zoccolo*) they adopted (Figures 2.5a and b).

Clogs were made of different types of close-grained wood such as walnut, plane or elm and were worn for a variety of occasions. For some classes, however, clogs were compulsory: the peasant from the Florentine countryside, for instance, was not allowed to use *calze solate* or *pianelle* but, according to the 1464 sumptuary legislation that regulated the dress of the citizens of Florence, had to wear simple clogs fastened with black *ghuigie* (leather straps) fixed at both ends of the wood.[4] In Sicily, prostitutes were forbidden to wear shoes and were forced instead to wear clogs called *tappini*, from which the Italian colloquial verb *tappinare* was derived, meaning a sexual act performed by a prostitute.[5] Not all clogs, of course, were reserved for such functional or identifying purposes. Double-heeled clogs (not dissimilar from traditional Japanese clogs) characterized by one additional support halfway through the sole were worn for social occasions and even at court (Figure 2.6). Women's double-heeled clogs were richly decorated and skillfully carved (Figure 2.7). At the end of the seventeenth century, one-piece heels began to be used, first in small sizes and later as very tall elevations for shoes.[6]

In the Italian courts, the most common type of footwear was a velvet or silk shoe, normally in a light color or bright red. These were similar in shape to the more common and far more durable leather shoes worn by the populace. Other types of footwear included *cosciali*, the subject of

FIGURE 2.2 (FACING PAGE): VITTORE CARPACCIO, VIRGIN MARY WITH BABY JESUS AND SAINT JOHN, 1493–5. STÄDELSCHES KUNSTINSTITUT, FRANKFURT AM MAIN, INV. NR 1075.

much medieval legislation on footwear. These were a sort of light boot or heavy stocking that covered the calf and fell back softly toward the ground. In order to prevent it dropping, the *cosciale* was secured to the leg with laces. Underneath the *cosciale*, tight hose were fastened to the doublet with strings. The foot, covered by stockings – sometimes with soles – was further protected by a shoe or clog. Iconography shows how women wore silk stockings and girdles that functioned as garters in conjunction with high-rise *pianelle*. This was an elegant ensemble, which was at the same time practical.

Shoes had purposes other than to facilitate walking. For the elite, there were elegant shoes to distinguish oneself from the crowd. These were worn with the intent of making one's physical presence felt and were normally far from durable or comfortable. The Catalan Franciscan preacher Frances Eiximenis (1330–1409) condemned the use of shoes worn to attract the interest and glances of passers-by. Their erotic value was highlighted by the cleric as he commented upon the fact that women "graze the ground only with the toe when they wear long, pointed shoes."[7] Those women who wore golden gloves, painted their eyelashes with fourteen different colors and smeared their bodies with perfume from Tunis embodied the *vanitas* that Eiximenis was fighting against. According to the Franciscan, they also wore shoes with cut toes and used narrow – sometimes spiky – sandals and shoes, or little shoes with ermine, which often made walking difficult for them.[8] Of course, he was exaggerating. We know, for instance, that both men and women wore sandals, but they were mainly worn in the home. Women's covered feet were a symbol of chastity and this explains why sandals are common in representations of Christ but are very rare in depictions of women.[9]

LEGAL AND ILLEGAL SHOES

The sources used by historians to reconstruct the history of shoes and shoemaking are as numerous as the types of shoes available to medieval men or women. If paintings, frescoes and miniatures provide an exceptionally important "visual memory" of past fashions, garments and shapes, historians also rely widely on documents reporting the activities of shoemakers or the laws regulating dress. These laws were called sumptuary laws, and from the middle of the thirteenth century to the end of the eighteenth century they were passed for the purpose of regulating dress – in particular women's dress – including footwear.[10] Some of the laws forbade the use of certain footwear, although they more frequently limited the height of shoes or the materials used in their production according to precise social criteria. This is particularly striking if we consider the richness of information they provide for medieval and early modern Europe – Italy included – where a war of "appearances" was fought between consumers keen to express taste and choice and legislators keen to preserve strict conventions.

Sumptuary laws were important in influencing production and structuring the market for clothing and fashion in medieval Europe. But they had a more profound significance in the way

FIGURE 2.3 (FACING PAGE): CLOTHIER (DETAIL OF A TAILOR SEWING A "SOLED STOCKING"). SECOND HALF OF THE FIFTEENTH CENTURY. CASTELLO DI ISSOGNE, VALLE D'AOSTA. KINDLY REPRODUCED BY PERMISSION OF THE REGIONE AUTONOMA VALLE D'AOSTA, ARCHIVI DELL'ASSESSORATO ISTRUZIONE E CULTURA, FONDO SERVIZIO CATALOGO E BENI ARCHITETTONICI.

FIGURE 2.4 (ABOVE): UNKNOWN ARTIST, THE MIRACLES OF CHRIST (DETAIL). THIRTEENTH CENTURY. DOME OF THE BAPTISTRY, PARMA.

FIGURE 2.5A (FACING PAGE): BERNARDINO DA SIENA WITH HIGH HEELS. POLYCHROME GOLDEN STUCCOED WOOD. MUSEO CIVICO MEDIEVALE, BOLOGNA. FIFTEENTH CENTURY.

they shaped collective notions of consumption, which were not simply expressed according to specific economic possibilities. These were the outcome of cultural and social variables such as one's social condition, gender, moral attributes, age and so on. Taste – the very essence of preference – was just one element within a large set of factors influencing choice. A clear example of this are the *pianelle*: they were adored by women of every rank in the latter part of the Middle Ages, but were also one of the most castigated items of apparel by legislators throughout Europe. Sumptuary laws are thus fundamental to understanding what men and women wore on their feet. During the five centuries preceding the French Revolution, the state controlled dress and banquets, processions and coaches, paying constant attention to dress. It did so in relation to women's dress in particular, by examining, granting and prohibiting the use of cloaks and trains, hats and jewelry, belts and hosiery.[11] By focusing on central and northern Italy in the period between the thirteenth and the sixteenth century, it is possible to use sumptuary laws to compare which types of shoes were actually worn and what, theoretically, was available on the market. The testimony of visual representations is thus contextualized within its social milieu.

Sumptuary laws also highlight the absence of the modern distinction between hose (or stockings) and shoes (Figure 2.8). This apparently banal confusion was generated by the process of production and the overlap between makers of stockings and producers of footwear. Were *calze solate* (soled hose) produced by a tailor or by a shoemaker? What type of garment were *cosciali*? Both were essential components of a gentleman's apparel. The *calze solate* had strong leather soles and could be worn without *pianelle* or clogs, especially within the home. The *cosciali* were used outdoors, and as such attracted (especially in the sixteenth century) the attention of legislators whose aim was to curb public display.[12] In Bologna in 1568, men were allowed to wear *cosciali* lined with taffeta d'ormesino (a very light silk that was named after the Persian city of Ormuz) or satin, although it was specified that a maximum of 4 "arms" (90 in.) of material could be used.[13] A few years earlier, the city of Modena had forbidden men to wear *cosciali* made of more than 2½ "arms" (67 in.) of velvet or other cloth, or *cosciali listati*, that is to say made with more than one material for a total length of 1⅔ "arms" (37 in.) – hose included. It was also stated that this footwear could not be lined with more than one layer of a permitted textile but without any embroidery (*lavori d'ago*) or whatever type of string.[14] In 1564, the city specified that only *cosciali* lined with taffeta or taffeta d'ormesino were allowed, but not those finished in gold or silver or produced by using more than 2 "arms" (45 in.) of velvet.

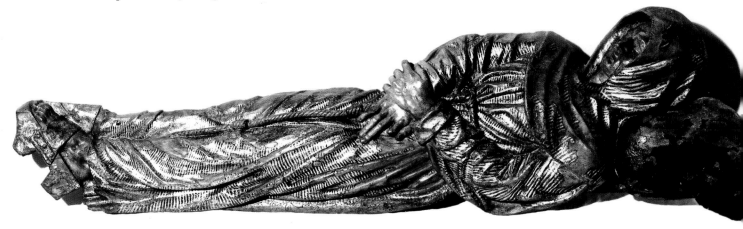

FIGURE 2.5B: "BRIDGE" PATTEN CLOG SIMILAR TO THE ONES USED BY BERNARDINO DA SIENA, C. 1400. BATA SHOE MUSEUM, TORONTO, P.85.65. COURTESY OF BATA SHOE MUSEUM.

To forbid or allow the use of a particular fabric, or to stipulate the maximum quantity of it to be used in the production of shoes, stabilized the prices of each material and commodity. The case of the *pianelle*, however, shows how the legislative intentions went well beyond economic intents. If on the one hand sumptuary laws curbed urban spending, on the other they functioned as a public demonstration of the civic respect for social hierarchy. This was shown through specific rules for apparel and footwear. In Emilia Romagna, and also in Florence and Umbria, sumptuary laws were enacted to limit the consumption of footwear, allowing and forbidding specific materials and also regulating shapes, lengths and heights. These laws, infrequent in the later Middle Ages, became common in fifteenth-century Italy. An example is the 1401 sumptuary legislation of Bologna, which forbade the use of *pianelle* with toes longer than half an *oncia* (¾ in.) or those painted, carved, embroidered or made of any type of leather apart from black or white. The law also established a five-lira fine for not following the rule. This had to be paid both by the wearer and by the producer of such unlawful footwear.[15] The city of Perugia decided, in the sixteenth century, to forbid *pianelle* "*de alcuna sorte de drappo*" (of any type of textile) even if this was used just as decoration. The same rule extended to golden, silver and silk embroidery on leather. The only *pianelle* allowed had to be made of leather and lower than five fingers in height.[16] The prohibition of golden or silver embroideries was very common in many Italian cities in the sixteenth century. Silk, another expensive material for sumptuous decoration, was allowed in only a few cities – as in Assisi and Perugia in the sixteenth century, where it could be used for trimmings and the decoration of shoes and *pianelle*.[17]

It is important to examine sumptuary laws over time. What was allowed in one statute could be forbidden in the following one. In Perugia, for example, the 1559 law allowed golden, silver and silk embroidery on gloves, sleeves, shoes and *pianelle*, but a subsequent law of 1575 made them all illegal. In other cities, the law did not forbid or allow specific footwear, but simply set maximum values for garments. In 1511 – and later reiterated in 1549 – the town of Foligno, not far from Assisi, decreed that all elite women – normally the wives and sisters of men belonging to the civic administration (the so-called *Consiglio Cittadino*) – could use silk shoes and *pianelle*,

FIGURE 2.6: THE EMPEROR WITH CLOGS. MS I, 147. BIBLIOTECA ARIOSTEA, FERRARA.

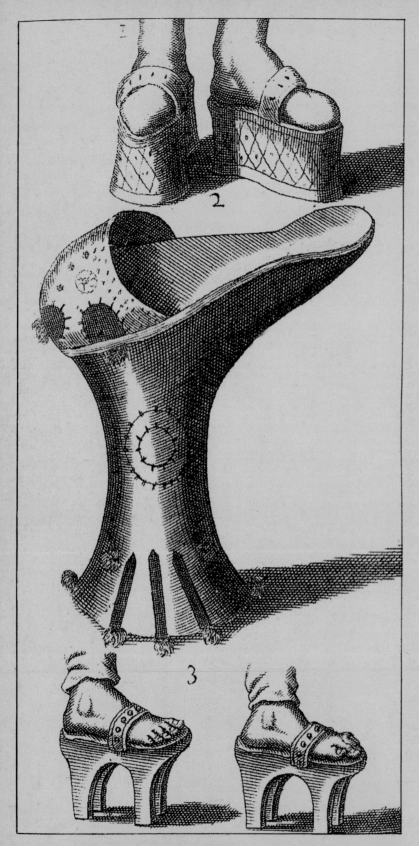

FIGURE 2.7: *PIANELLE*, PLATE FROM BENOÎT BAUDOUIN AND GIULIO NEGRONE, *BALDUINUS DE CALCEO ANTIQUO, ET JUL. NIGRONUS DE CALIGA VETERUM* (1667).

but they were not allowed silver or gold decorations. Lower down the social scale, the wives and daughters of men belonging to the inferior *Ordine del Priorato* were not allowed to wear shoes with silk uppers, but only (as clearly established in a later law) those of wool fabrics. These examples suggest that there were three different types of *pianelle*, identifying three separate categories of women: first, at the top of the social hierarchy the wives of cavaliers and doctors could wear *pianelle* of every color and material, including golden and silver textiles; second, women belonging to the civic structure of the town could wear *pianelle* that ranged from silk to other inferior textiles, according to their social status. Finally, women from the countryside, as made clear in the 1581 law of the city of Todi, could not wear *pianelle* made of any textile, but had to use leather footwear.

The public authority of the city of Forlì in Emilia Romagna was far less restrictive. In 1556 it was established that female citizens were allowed to wear *pianelle* of every type of fabric. It was also established that only the servants of citizens of the city could wear stockings, jackets, berets and shoes passed down from their masters. The law, however, was more restrictive with artisans (*artesani*) and other inhabitants (*popolani*) of the city who could wear only stockings – but no other garments – lined with taffeta and taffeta d'ormesino. They were also expressly forbidden to wear berets, hats and shoes made of velvet.[18] Again in Forlì, in 1559 women were allowed to own two pairs of silk *pianelle* (of whatever color, even made of crimson velvet, but with no silver or gold decoration and worth less than twenty soldi) or leather *pianelle* (with no ornaments of any type). Men, too, were included in this law. They were allowed to own a maximum of three pairs of velvet shoes, with no restrictions on color apart from intense crimson, *paonazzo* and *morello di grana* (all intense reds with purple shades), and no ornaments.[19] When, as in the case of the city of Spoleto, women were allowed to wear *pianelle* made of velvet "or any other sort of cloth," gold, silver, pearl and stone decorations were prohibited. This probably means that the use of heavily embroidered *pianelle* was widespread. Prohibition could extend to other types of decoration such as lace, gold and silver cloth, and precious stones.

Legislators were keen to regulate not only the value of materials and decorations, but also the shape, size and design of footwear. In fourteenth-century Florence, for instance, the maximum height of *pianelle* was fixed at 3⅛ in.[20] In the city of Todi, it was established in 1444 that *pianelle* could not be taller than 4 in., as visible from the measure carved on the wall of the Chapel of Saint Anastasia in the Church of Saint Mary.[21] A fine for contravening this law was set at half a golden ducat.[22] The height of *pianelle* was a subject of particular interest for women, probably much more so than their embroideries and decorations. This can be fully grasped by considering the peculiar dialog on the topic between the inhabitants of Orvieto and the city's legislators in 1537. Early that year it was established that only *pianelle* lower than four inches could be used. We can imagine that the reaction was strong, in particular from women, as a few months later another law followed. This established that *pianelle* of all heights could be used.[23]

Regulations and acts forbidding the wearing of specific garments help us to understand the taste of men and women who had continuously to negotiate choices within rules imposed by both their gender and their class. Men liked to wear velvet shoes with decorations and *cosciali* lined with fine fabrics. Women loved *pianelle* of every type, in particular those embroidered or enriched with golden threads and precious stones (Figure 2.9). Such *pianelle* were normally no taller than four inches, but could go up to twenty inches, causing extreme problems when trying to walk. Sumptuary laws tell us also about the hierarchy of value of footwear. The most precious shoes were made of crimson silk and deep red velvet, and were often decorated. The most common shoes, made of leather and wood, were systematically ignored by the legislator.

BELOVED *PIANELLE*

Pianelle seem to be at the center of our attempt to reconstruct the "shoe world" of medieval Europe. They are not only at the core of sumptuary laws, but also frequently represented in paintings, frescoes and prints, suggesting that they were very sought after. Although their name reminds us the concept of flatness (from *piano*, meaning "flat level"), they were surely far from being flat shoes.[24] Originally, people used them to keep out of the dirt and mud so common in the streets of many medieval towns. They were therefore shoes to be worn outside. Their soles were made of cork rather than wood, making them light. They were not just worn by women: men too wore *pianelle*, of a type that often covered the foot entirely, unlike *calcagnini*, the popular women's *pianelle* that were open at the back. Another difference between men's and women's *pianelle* was the fact that men had soles just a few inches high, while women indulged in more extravagant types with elevations as high as twenty inches.

The shape of *pianelle* changed from place to place. In Venice, the cylindrical form was the most used.[25] It is less easy to categorize *pianelle* in Florence. In the fifteenth century, *pianelle* had uppers covering the entire foot, sometimes exposing the toes, and were higher at the back. However, in the sixteenth century, *pianelle* were open at the back and closed at the front; their uppers had round shapes and were often carved with geometrical designs through which colorful internal linings could be seen. The elevation was usually covered with white leather. Some *pianelle* were sustained by two supports – the so-called "bridge" type – probably derived from similar models used in the Near East and known in Venice as Turkish and Syrian *kub-kab* or *kab-kab* (Figure 2.10). In the Middle East, *takunya* are traditional clogs used in a hammam in order to keep one's feet dry, and analogous bridge-type sandals are still used in India in ceremonies involving water. Similar types of footwear have also been found in Japan at archaeological sites in Karako and Toro, suggesting their widespread use by workers in rice cultivation during the period between 300 BC and AD 300. These types of high clogs remained in use in Japan throughout the centuries and served to protect the hem of the kimono.[26]

The use of rich *pianelle* in Renaissance Europe is substantiated not only by paintings and other visual representations, but also by historic records. The wardrobe accounts of Eleanor of

FIGURE 2.8: OPERE DI MISERICORDIA. VISITARE GLI INFERMI BY DOMENICO GHIRLANDAIO (DETAIL), LATE FIFTEENTH CENTURY. ORATORIO DEI BUONOMINI DI S. MARTINO, FLORENCE.

Toledo record few shoes but plenty of *pianelle*, most of which were made of velvet. They were red (thirty-two pairs), violet (ten pairs), green (ten pairs), chestnut brown (five pairs), gray (three pairs), as well as white (two pairs) and black (one pair). A note suggests that it was common to match the color of the dress and that of *pianelle*. Not all *pianelle* were covered with fabric. The *pianelle* produced in Florence had supports made of wood, which were covered with the same fabric used for the uppers. Shoemakers needed from ½ "arm" (11 in.) of fabric for the low types to 2 "arms" (45 in.) for tall *pianelle*. Eleanor owned one pair covered with silver-colored leather, which were probably a very rare type as the maker, a certain Master Michele, is expressly mentioned. Other leather *pianelle* were worn by Eleanor when traveling or during the winter months. She also owned half-boots lined with fur similar to the ones worn by her husband, the duke.[27] Other noble ladies, such as Drusiana Sforza, owned twelve pairs of half-boots, eight of which were made of velvet and four of golden fabric. Bianca Maria Sforza owned twenty-four pairs of similar footwear in several colors, some decorated with silver.[28]

The use of *pianelle* was associated with several meanings. They were expensive types of footwear that clearly prevented women – and sometimes men – from engaging in practical or manual activities.[29] They "confined" women and restricted their mobility in a way similar to foot-binding in China. However, unlike in China, the lack of mobility was not considered a negative attribute or a reason to reject the *pianelle*. The lack of functionality of *pianelle* was also often paired with clear erotic meanings. The high types worn by women gave them a sensual gait. Both the height and the lack of balance caused by the front rise in the shoe provided, according to

FIGURE 2.9: *PIANELLE* WITH OPEN TOE, 3⅛ IN. AT THE TOE AND 5½ IN. AT THE HEEL, 1580–1620. BATA SHOE MUSEUM, TORONTO, P91.80.AB. COURTESY OF BATA SHOE MUSEUM.

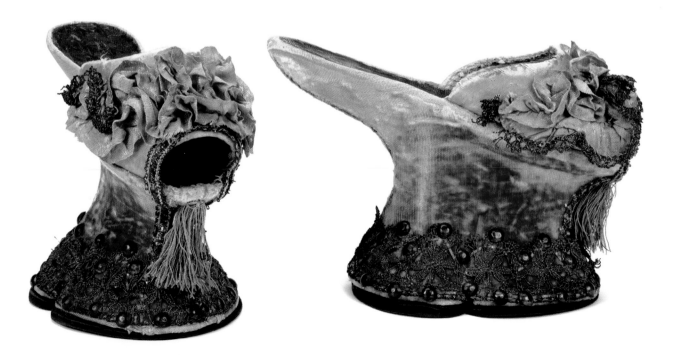

Castiglione, "*grandissima gratia*" (very high grace) to the posture and walk, as the leg and foot itself were hidden behind long skirts.[30]

This relationship between restrained mobility and erotic meaning was important in the choice of *pianelle* by courtesans. These high-class prostitutes wore *cioppine* or French *eschapins* as part of their work attire. Courtesans and prostitutes used high *pianelle* as a tool to identify their sexual availability and social position (Figure 2.11). As examined by Andrea Vianello later in this book, iconography suggests that *pianelle* could also characterize virtuous women. It is more likely that the exaggerated height of certain *pianelle* allowed courtesans to be clearly identified as women living outside "the ordinary." And it was not just a matter of what was worn; it was also the way that *pianelle* were worn. Courtesans paired their insolence with the exhibition of conspicuous footwear.

In Florence, as in Venice, Perugia, Terni and Orvieto, the height of *pianelle* was considered to be a public problem. Again we find how women's willingness to indulge in high-heeled shoes was curbed both by legislators and clerics. Preachers went so far to forbid them on the grounds of the gospel by Matthew 6:27, according to which no person should increase his or her physical stature. Tertullian, in his *De Cultu Feminarum* (*The Ornaments of Women*) dated to the third century AD, further explained that to increase one's stature was both a contravention of God's creation and a deception, as one's physical shape, size and proportions were hidden from the judgment of suitors.[31] In the fifteenth century, the problem of high *pianelle* was discussed by the Franciscan Bernardino da Feltre, who in his *Confessionale* – a textbook for confessors written at the end of

FIGURE 2.10: TURKISH WOODEN CLOGS (*KAB-BABS* OR *NALINS*). BATA SHOE MUSEUM, TORONTO, P84.22.AB. COURTESY OF BATA SHOE MUSEUM.

FIGURE 2.11: Courtesan showing her legs, from Roger de Gaignières, *Raccolta di Costumi Strenieri*.

the century – reminded readers that sinners were often guilty of looking for "the glory of clothing, *pianelle* … and other vanities."[32] Another *Confessionale*, known as *Interrogatorio Volgare Compendioso et Copioso* (*A Complete Digest for Questioning*) recognized as a conceit also the production of "women's ornaments that are vain, such as the trains, red shoes and embroidered and adorned clothes."[33] According to the anonymous author of this *Confessionale*, it was not just the height of shoes that made them indecent. Embroideries and warm colors were morally unacceptable, even if they were the "latest fashion" of the Middle Ages.[34]

Legislators, too, were worried about the wearing of high *pianelle*. Their motivations were far from moral as they accused *pianelle* of being the source of personal endangerment and a waste of the costly fabrics used to produce very long skirts. Tailors and dressmakers were allowed to take a lady's measurement only "without her shoes at her feet."[35] The same laws also imposed limits on the height of shoes. In Venice, for instance, shoes higher than *mezza quarta* (about eight to ten inches) were categorically forbidden. The law was probably ignored, as we know that the use of *trampoli* (trampolines) – as very tall *pianelle* were dismissively defined by contemporaries – was widespread.

BRIGHT RED WITH LONG TOES

Imagery shows how, notwithstanding the moral advice of preachers and the prohibitions of legislators, medieval and Renaissance men and women favored elevated shoes. These were often of bright colors, such as red, and had long toes. The use of long toes became widespread all over Europe at the beginning of the fourteenth century, and coincided with the adoption of the doublet.[36] This fashion lasted until the beginning of the sixteenth century, when both men's and women's shoes went back to a rounded shape called the "bull's head" (*a muso di bue*). Between 1300 and 1500, however, the most famous shoes were the *poulaine*, as shoes with enormous toes were called in France. The origin of such a name is not clear. It could be that they were originally adopted in Poland, although some historians prefer to think that it was the elongated shape of a ship's figurehead (*polena*) that inspired *poulaine* shoes.

Historians agree about the sexual symbolism of long, pointed shoes worn by both men and women.[37] Preachers fought against this fashion, especially bright red shoes, but their main moral criteria were social rather than material (Figure 2.12). Like legislators, they believed that shoes had to be appropriate to one's station in life, although their arguments were often colored by moral overtones. According to the famous preacher Giovanni da Capestrano (1386–1456), it was sinful for women to wear "soldier's" shoes, especially if long, as "these are the principal and exclusive prerogative of men. And even if such shoes are not too long, this is not a good reason to allow women to wear military shoes for the ornament of their tibia, as women must show more humility than men."[38] He thus inferred that it was also sinful to wear *pianelle* taller than a span (or a "palm") and that the only morally acceptable shoes were those that were just high enough to protect the wearer from the dust and mud of the streets.

This insensate footwear – defined by Giovanni da Capestrano as "sandals with nibs, perforated or sharpened" ("*sandali rostrati, perforati ed appuntiti*") was so uncomfortable as to be instrumental in the martyrdom of the feet. But human stupidity did not limit itself to self-punishment. The shape of these shoes showed a lack of respect for Jesus Christ, who for the love of mankind, had had his feet nailed to the Cross. Giovanni da Capestrano also added that long dresses and trains were conceived to hide the feet and thus to show honesty and modesty. It was therefore even more detestable that feet were at the center of such a show. Similarly, he commented unfavorably on the use of precious shoes with ornaments. These were not only morally unacceptable. Certain shapes suggested an association between the human foot and the claws of animals. It was even worse if these shoes were red, as all cloth of such color was worn "especially outside the house, to demonstrate hauteur and pride."[39]

Preachers considered honesty to be the guiding principle when garments and footwear were chosen. And honesty was not just a moral value, but also the correspondence between a person and his or her dignity and position in life. This was particularly true for those men who participated in public life and, by extension, for their wives, daughters and sisters. In turn, these moral views informed the legal action of legislators who specified the precise length of the trains of women of different social ranks. The sumptuary laws adopted in the town of Foligno in the mid-sixteenth century allowed different lengths of silk, or quantity of decoration for *pianelle*, according to social rank. Nothing was said about the length of the toes of shoes. This is a significant absence, as the matter was carefully regulated not only in Italian cities, but also throughout Europe – particularly in Burgundy, where since the fifteenth century snug and slender forms for clothes, hats and shoes had been in fashion.[40] Here, both shoes and hats could be more than twenty inches long. The aforementioned *poulaine* shoes had toes up to three times as long as the foot. They were so difficult to wear that devices were invented to fix the padded toes to the leg by means of a string or a metal wire.[41] The length of shoe toes was a way to distinguish the rich from the poor. Sumptuary laws confirmed such practice by allowing the use of long toes only by the upper classes. Folklore tales about the battle of Sempach reverse such class associations. The legend tells that the defeat inflicted by the poor Swiss peasants against the mighty Hapsburg cavaliers was partially due to wearing long, pointed shoes (Figure 2.13). The peasants, although ill-equipped and few in number, were able to defeat the emperor's army by removing them from their horses. The cavaliers' enormous shoes made it impossible for them to walk, thus giving the peasants, who wore very practical footwear, the advantage.[42]

MAKING AND BUYING SHOES

Pianelle, poulaines, embroidered shoes and cheap, ragged shoes were among the enormous variety of footwear available to medieval and Renaissance consumers. If consumers enjoyed choice, so producers organized production in an array of ways. Medieval shoemakers belonged to different productive categories. In Venice, for instance, the producers of shoes and sandals (*caligari*) were distinguished from the so-called *zavateri*, who dealt exclusively in low-quality and secondhand

CAPVT TRICESIMVMQ VINTVM.

 Nde quidam feruus nomine Theophilus, & pre
sbyter in li.prophetiarũ, quẽ fcripfit Anthonius
Theodorus tempe quo erat dux Ianuæ, in quo li
bro fpecialiter cõtinenẽ oĩia quæ futura funt de
regimie eccliæ, & qualiter debeat renouari, ficut

M ij

Figure 2.12: The cutting of long toes, fifteenth century. Bata Shoe Museum, Toronto, not cataloged.
Courtesy of Bata Shoe Museum.

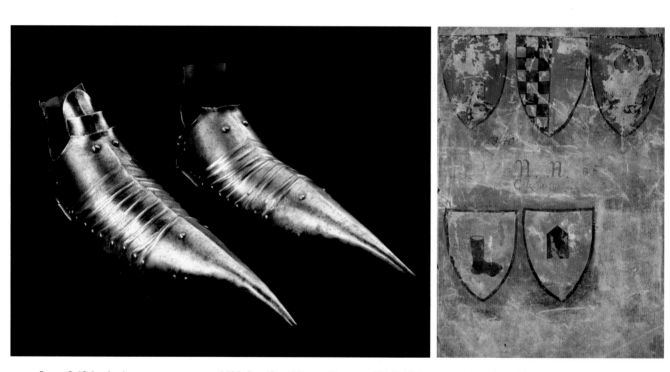

Figure 2.13 (left): Armor with long toes, 1490. Bata Shoe Museum, Toronto, P92.1.AB Courtesy of Bata Shoe Museum.

Figure 2.14 (right): Illuminated statute with the image of a boot (1340). Archivio di Stato di Bologna, "Callegari e calzolari," b.IV.

shoes. The latter were peddlers or humble artisans who repaired shoes; the former were producers of new shoes and were often suspicious of the activities of the *zavateri*, who were invariably accused of improving their meager income by illegally producing new shoes. Both categories of producer were in turn closely connected to the tanners and curriers who supplied them with the necessary raw materials to produce and refurbish shoes.[43]

The shoemakers, the proper producers of footwear, were organized – as most productive activities were in the Middle Ages – into a guild. L'Arte dei Calegheri, as it was called in Venice, was one of the most ancient guilds in the city. Its foundation, in 1268, was not the first in the Italian peninsula. In Bologna, the first *schola* (school) for the training of artisans was that of the shoemakers, which was founded in 1144. All shoemakers worked in the same place, as was usually the case before 1200. By the middle of the thirteenth century, the economic complexity of urban centers in Italy meant an overall change in the basic structures regulating specific branches of the manufacturing economy. The major occupations were granted statutes by which they were conferred rights and privileges. In some cases, these statutes distinguished between the shoemaker proper and the "shoemaker of cow" (*calzolaro de vacca*) who produced shoes from cowhides. One of these statutes, from the 1340s, is a parchment with colorful coats of arms and an image of a boot (Figure 2.14).[44]

Inventories, that is to say lists of goods recorded after a person's death, provide us with a snapshot of what a shoemaker's shop contained in the later Middle Ages. The inventory of the shop of the shoemaker Filippo di Matteo, working in Rimini in the fifteenth century, records several shoe uppers for men's and women's shoes, some of which were embroidered.[45] There were also hides of several sizes, white and black sheepskins, cordovan leather, as well as the less prized leather backs and sides. The stock in the shop was impressive: sixteen pairs of men's shoes with low heels (three of which were vermilion in color), nine pairs of men's shoes with high heels, eleven pairs of women's shoes, and two pairs of *mamolitti* (children's shoes). The inventory also records thirty lasts for children's shoes, a hundred lasts for adults' shoes and five lasts for *pianelle*.

The large number of shoes in stock and the abundance of lasts suggest that medieval shoemakers produced bespoke as well as ready-made shoes in different sizes. Archaeology also helps the historian. The shoes found in medieval buildings present very different sizes, from present-day European size 16 (a small shoe for a child) to size 42 (for adults).[46] In Filippo di Matteo's shop there were also four pairs of boots. There were also more than fifty buckles and a variety of tools. Alas, only a few of these tools are included in the surviving parts of the inventory: a saw, a plane and a knife. The inventory of another shoemaker's shop in Rimini tells us that the space was furnished with two small desks, a chair, two buckets, a pail, two containers filled with vinegar and a straw basket.[47]

Representations of shoemakers' shops in the Middle Ages tell us that shoemakers used to show ready-made shoes on the shop counter or on their workbench, as can be seen in Jaume Serra's famous fourteenth-century painting, *The Saint Healing a Shoemaker* (Figure 2.15). Saws and knives are usually included among the objects represented in workshops, as are punches, scissors, needles and thread. The simplicity of a shoemaker's tools allowed him to peddle his wares. In was not uncommon, as a 1437 statute of the city of Bolzano (in present-day Trentino Alto Adige) tells us, for shoemakers to go to their customers' houses. All a shoemaker needed to take with him was a small table, a carver, some wooden lasts, awls and alum. The statute specified how much a shoemaker and his assistants could charge a client when working in his/her house. Prices varied according to shoe type, such as new shoes with low heels, new shoes with high heels, or boots (called "shoes to the knee"); repairs and remodeling of old shoes were also carried out. The products and their relative costs were fixed by law. Boots, for instance, cost six times the price of a pair of new shoes.[48] The way in which shoes were made implied substantial differences in their final price. The records of the Compagnia dei Bianchi of the city of Gubbio in central Italy, for the period 1419–25, show how out of a total price of fourteen soldi for a pair of calfskin shoes, the manufacture accounted for about two-thirds of the total cost.[49]

Pricing was another matter frequently considered by legislators in various Italian towns and cities. In 1323, the authorities of the city of Piacenza intervened to stop prices for clothing and shoes from increasing any further. These rules extended not only to producers of shoes and clogs, but also to "all others who produce and sell shoes and other footwear."[50] It was established, for instance, that shoemakers could not charge more than two soldi and three denari[51] for a pair of men's shoes that were either "light, closed or carved" (*subtiles, integre vel intagiate*). Women's shoes could not cost more than twenty denari, men's *pianelle* were three soldi, and women's *pianelle* were three soldi and six denari. The same regulation that fixed prices also established precise rules about quality and materials. Men's and women's *pianelle*, but also shoes and clogs, could only be produced with cordovan leather uppers (*corollos de cordoano vel manzollo*). Clogmakers could charge a maximum of twenty-two denari for a pair of clogs and eight denari for repairing them. But prices were not just measured in terms of the commodity sold. The price of a pair of clogs had to be less than twenty-two denari if the client was sixteen to twenty years old, and even less if he or she was a child younger than twelve.[52]

As previously shown, shoemakers produced a wide range of different footwear. The most elegant shoes were made of cloth, velvet and satin; those commonly used in the streets were made of leather. Leather was also used to make *pianelle*. The skins of the bullock, calf, goat and kid were the types of leather used most frequently. Ordinary shoes were made of cheap buffalo hide and cowhide, whilst expensive types were made of horsehide and the renowned cordovan leather, a soft, curried leather originally produced in Cordoba. The 1271 Venetian statute of the shoemakers distinguished different types of shoes. The *calçarios* were probably leather leggings that could cover the foot and might also be made of fabric. These differed from *stivalli* (boots) – shoes covering the calf, which were worn by both men and women. Paintings show us half-boots, tied at the side with metallic hooks. These were used for hard walking, like the long trips made by medieval pilgrims (Figure 2.16). Down the social scale, the clogs used by most people were *patitos*, which were made by the shoemakers (*caligari*); while the *solarii* could only produce shoes.

FIGURE 2.15: JAUNE SERRA, SAINT HEALING A SHOEMAKER (DETAIL OF THE TAILOR'S DESK). SECOND HALF OF THE FOURTEENTH CENTURY. MUSEU NACIONAL D'ART DE CATALUNYA, BARCELONA. PHOTOGRAPHERS: CALVARES/MÉRIDA/SAGRISTÀ.

FIGURE 2.16: Marco Marziale, La cena di Emaus (detail of half-boots with side lacing), 1506. Gallerie dell'Accademia, Venice. Courtesy of the Ministero per i Beni e le Attività Culturali.

The production of shoes in medieval and premodern Europe had five different phases: the sawing of the upper, lasting (giving shape to the upper), the sewing of the upper and the internal linings, the insertion of the insole, and the sewing of the sole. The thread used for sewing shoes was almost certainly made of strong hemp.[53] The coloring of leather was another important part of the production process. Hides were dyed red and violet by vegetable tanning with woad and sumach, or alum was used to produce white leather. Valonia oak and sumach were used to produce black leather.[54] In the *Piazza Universale di Tutte le Professioni del Mondo*, the description of all occupations published in the mid-sixteenth century, Tomaso Garzoni portrays shoemakers as a deceitful class of people. It was common, and a well-known fact, that shoemakers sold bullock instead of calf or "a mended slipper instead of a shoe" ("*una scarpa nuova una ciabata rinovata*"). According to Garzoni, shoemakers embodied the worst of shopkeeping: "Smears and lies are common for them, as they are for all those people who serve others, as today the city trades are so full of fraud that it is hardly possible to find someone who would wish to speak the truth."[55] This harsh judgment came as no surprise, as shoemakers had enjoyed a poor reputation for most of the Middle Ages. However, by the late fifteenth century, their social profile began to change. Shoemaking was, for the first time, considered to be a necessary – even valuable – employment. Garzoni himself admitted that the occupation was of "ornament for all the general world, as everyone appears swift and courteous when wearing a nice pair of shoes at their feet, be they in Spanish, Neapolitan or Savoyard style, or when wearing a pair of *pianelle* or good clogs, as it is common in our times."[56] Thus the medieval shoe, shoemaker and shoe-wearer are far from peripheral. Despite covering a tiny part of the human body, their significance in terms of social positioning, mobility and attraction are out of all proportion to their relative size.

3.
COURTLY LADY OR COURTESAN?

THE VENETIAN CHOPINE IN THE RENAISSANCE

andrea vianello

TWO MYSTERIOUS LADIES

Costume historians use the word "chopines" as a generic expression to identify the platform shoes that were worn in Europe between the fourteenth and seventeenth centuries. These were characterized by thick soles, made of cork or wood, which could be up to twenty inches tall, as in the case of the stilt-like clogs now at the Correr Museum in Venice (Figure 3.1). These very peculiar shoes – perhaps the most extreme ever produced for European women – were worn in the streets of early modern European cities both by noblewomen and commoners. However, the wearing of chopines did not indicate a single common meaning or shared fashion message understood by women belonging to different social groupings or living in different historical periods. What appeared to be essentially the same kind of shoe was in reality a diverse form of footwear conveying precise information about the wearer's status and identity. A few inches' difference in the thickness of the soles seems to have originally revealed the distinction between the famous and the infamous, and between appropriate and inappropriate behavior in the sixteenth century.

Contemporaries frequently recognized these subtle differences – they were able to "read" clothing and to form judgments about a person's social and moral standing within a particular community. Historians have the difficult task of reconstructing the meaning of clothing from scattered evidence in order to clearly identify the conventions that were frequently implicit in early modern culture. This is the background of one of the more famous *causes célèbres* in the history of art, that of the "mistaken identity" of Carpaccio's *Two Ladies* (Figure 3.2). This painting dates from the last decade of the fifteenth century and is now also a prime exhibit of the Museo Correr in Venice. Carpaccio's *Two Ladies* has been interpreted in the English-speaking world mainly through John Ruskin's *St Mark's Rest* (1877–84), in which the painting is ranked as "the best picture in the world."[1] Ruskin identified the two women depicted as "two Venetian ladies with their pets," hence going against the established interpretations of the painting's subjects. One of the major Italian historical guides to Venice, published in 1852, had instead named the painting the *Due Giovani Maliarde* (*Two Young Vamps*), alluding to their presumably dubious moral reputation. The famous Venetian historian Pompeo Molmenti also endorsed this idea a few years later by giving to the picture the more elegant, but still disparaging, title of *The Courtesans*.[2] This title is still used today, even though most art historians believe that the two were in fact noblewomen and thus prefer the title of *The Two Ladies*.[3]

This confusion about the social and moral identity of the two women originates from the abundance of objects and animals with potential symbolic meanings present in the picture. The two white doves, for instance, have been alternatively interpreted by art historians as symbols of sensual love (as they were traditionally depicted following Venus' chariot) or of marital fidelity (an idea already present in Ovid's *Amores*). Among all these symbolic elements, modern art historians are particularly doubtful about the meaning of a pair of red shoes – the high-heeled chopines that feature so prominently in the picture.[4] On the one hand, the iconographical strand of art historical study exemplified by Erwin Panofsky encourages and demands a "decoding" of each element as relevant and interrelated – as Panofsky did in his analysis of another iconic Renaissance painting in which shoes carry meaning, Jan Van Eyck's *The Arnolfini Double Portrait* (1434).[5] On the other hand, the difficulty of such a system of interpretation is that subsequent writers have presented different interpretations of the symbolic value of these shoes, which have then entered circuits of "knowledge" regarding dress history.[6]

What might have been a clear message for the people of the time thus requires understanding of codes of representation, which can be obtained only though detailed research into an object's meaning in its historical context. The high-heeled chopines in Carpaccio's painting were clearly extravagant shoes for those nineteenth-century male viewers who first interpreted this painting and who probably believed that this footwear was inappropriate for a lady. Indeed, the

FIGURE 3.1: HIGH CHOPINES. MUSEO CORRER, VENICE. COURTESY OF THE MINISTERO PER I BENI E LE ATTIVITÀ CULTURALI.

term *zoccola* (a feminine form of the word *zoccolo*, meaning "clog") is still used in modern Italian slang for "prostitute."[7] Even Ruskin, who seems to have recognized the correct social value of these shoes, had only unkind words for them. He believed that Carpaccio was commissioned to paint a portrait of the two women but, disliking the arrogant ostentation of their wealth, had dropped satirical elements into his painting such as the chopines.[8] He wrote that "to mark the satirical purpose of the whole, a pair of ladies' shoes are put in the corner, (the high-stilted shoe, being, in fact, a slipper on the top of a column) which were the grossest and absurdest means of expressing female pride in the fifteenth and the following centuries."[9] This misinterpretation of the cultural meaning and significance of these and similar kinds of shoes, determined by nineteenth-century preconceptions of excess and vanity, may have been thus at least partly responsible for nearly two centuries of misunderstanding and the "defamation" of these two women depicted by Carpaccio. Apart from the shoes' clear extremism, Ruskin's fame and importance on topics ranging from painting to architecture rendered this case, in the public imagination, as one of the best-known episodes regarding fine art, women and the shoe as an emblem.

FROM CLOGS TO CHOPINES

Chopines appear to be the result of the evolution of the humble clog. Leather shoes that cover the entire foot, like those we wear today, were not available to the vast majority of the European population in the early modern period. Even in sophisticated Paris, most people started to wear "proper" shoes only in the eighteenth century, as a consequence of what French historian Daniel Roche has called the victory over the "fragile life" which characterized that of the masses in the *ancien régime*.[10] Those who could not afford to buy a pair of shoes, but were not in the predicament of having to go barefoot, could opt for wooden clogs, which were much more economical and long-lasting than leather footwear. In the Middle Ages, however, clogs were also used by wealthy people – not so much to protect the foot, but rather to protect delicate soled stockings from the mud and dust of the street. Even a European monarch such as Bernardo, Charlemagne's grandson and Frankish king of Italy, was buried in 818 wearing a pair of clogs.[11]

By the fourteenth century, clogs had evolved into a new kind of shoe, with uppers made of leather or fabric and the sole of wood or, more often, of lighter cork. These shoes, called *chapins* in Spanish and French (from which comes the English "chopines"), were generally known as *pianelle* or *pantofole* (slippers) in Italy. There were, however, different regional denominations: in Milan they were also known as *zibre* or *solee*, while in Venice they could be called *zoccoli* (clogs), *calcagnini* (also *calcagnetti*, a word related to the Venetian *calcagno*, or heel), or *mule* (from which comes the English word). A Venetian family account book of 1460 talks about "very tall *zoccoli*, i.e. very tall *pianelle*," while a 1522 law refers to "*zoccoli* otherwise known as *pantofole*," which seems to indicate that these terms were used more or less interchangeably.[12] Some historians believe that these tall chopines originated in Venice, a theory that seems to be confirmed also by a Milanese manuscript of the year 1461, where they are described as "Venetian-style *zibre*."[13]

FIGURE 3.2: VITTORE CARPACCIO, TWO LADIES, C. 1490. MUSEO CORRER, VENICE. COURTESY OF THE MINISTERO PER I BENI E LE ATTIVITÀ CULTURALI.

Indeed, from at least 1308, the Venetian shoemakers' guild was the only one in Italy to have a separate subguild for the *zoccoleri*, who specialized in the fabrication of this kind of shoe.[14]

Large sums of money were spent on these delicate shoes, which then became a focus of sumptuary legislation in many Italian cities. Grazietta Butazzi has found eleven laws in northern Italy between 1512 and 1595, which forbade the use of gold, silver and embroidery for shoes and especially chopines.[15] Golden chopines, however, were neither new nor just an Italian prerogative: Lorenzo Strozzi, member of one of Florence's richest families, apparently saw a pair of splendid golden chopines in Valencia in 1450, but did not have enough money to buy them.[16] Furthermore, while chopines were worn by both sexes, their use by men would be eventually forbidden in cities such as Florence, where in the late fourteenth century men were fined for wearing them, as they were considered to be too effeminate.[17] Chopines thus became heavily gendered objects by the early sixteenth century, when Baldassare Castiglione, the Italian master of style and author of *The Courtier* (1528), even advised ladies to "show with some womanly disposition a little bit of leg, covered by a graceful and tight stocking and velvet *chiapinetti*."[18]

That the chopines covered but only partially hid women's feet, the public exhibition of which had always been regarded as negative, increasingly worried scholars and churchmen alike during the Renaissance. Physician and writer Michelangelo Biondo ironically claimed in the 1540s: "Maybe it would have been better if women had been born without feet, or even without legs, because then they would not entice us [men] to lustful amusements, [to] our dissipation and their satisfaction."[19] But Biondo was merely following an established tradition of the moral condemnation of women's dress. As early as 1333, the bishops of Siena and Lucca had forbidden shoemakers to fit shoes on women, thereby highlighting their sensuality and their danger to morals.[20]

Indeed, as the chopines' soles grew taller, they increasingly provoked the criticism of both Church and State. In the late thirteenth century, for example, Friar Jacopone da Todi criticized what he called the "*suvarate*," a kind of shoe with soles of thick cork (in Italian *sughero*, hence their name) used to "make the small woman pass for a giant."[21] By the late 1370s, some Florentine women were apparently wearing *pianelle* taller than one-sixth of an "arm" (1 arm = 22 in.). Francesco Sacchetti, prior of the city in 1384, commented sarcastically in his poem "Against the Bearing of Florentine Women," that if they wore such tall *pianelle* as a penitence for the love of God instead of for themselves, "they would be all saints."[22]

These concerns reached a crescendo by the third decade of the fifteenth century. In 1427, the Franciscan and future Saint Bernardino da Siena lamented in a sermon that handbreadth-tall *pianelle* were not only foolish and dangerous, but needed longer dresses to cover them, requiring more cloth and making women's dresses more expensive. Bernardino's words were echoed about ten years later by another Franciscan, Giovanni da Capestrano, who condemned tall chopines in his *Treatise on Embellishments, Particularly Those of Women* (written between 1434 and 1438), in which he railed that *pianelle* both threatened the natural order created by God and distorted the

proportions of the human body. In addition, they encouraged large expenditure in order to ornament the body's most inferior parts, the feet, which Nature had deliberately made lowest and thus
most vile. The respect of order, be it natural or social, was of paramount importance and, as far
as Fra Giovanni was concerned, the tall *pianelle* violated both.[23]

CHOPINES, COURTESANS AND PROSTITUTES

Giovanni da Capestrano's *Treatise on Embellishments* recalled some of the ideas that he originally
developed for a sermon on the perils of luxury, which he preached in Venice in 1434. He is likely to have had a receptive audience, since four years earlier the Venetian Major Council (the
largest legislative body of the Republic, which expressed the will of its male ruling aristocracy)
had passed legislation regulating the height of these controversial shoes.[24] The law lamented that
Venetian women, both married and unmarried, were following a new and "despicable" fashion.
They wore *zoccoli* that were incredibly tall and "deformed," which not only generated great
expense and "infamy" for the wearer, but had also apparently caused pregnant women to fall and
abort, with great harm to "both their bodies and their souls." To avoid similar events in the future
and "to alleviate the expenses about which everybody knows," the Council thus forbade shoemakers to sell clogs more than 3–3½ in. tall, on pain of a fine of 25 lire and three months' imprisonment. To avoid possible misunderstandings, the Council's secretary even drew a picture of the forbidden shoe, which looks like a kind of platform sandal (Figure 3.3). Probably realizing that
merely threatening the shoemakers would not in itself have been sufficient, on the same day the
Council also decided on an even larger fine of 100 lire, which was instead aimed both at the
women who wore forbidden *zoccoli* and at their husbands or fathers who were legally responsible
for them.

Within a half century, however, the height of the highest of these platform shoes was again
on the rise. In the 1470s, Father Hernando de Talavera, confessor to Queen Isabella of Castile,
claimed to have seen chopines "an elbow tall" and complained that hardly enough cork existed
in Spain to satisfy the demand there.[25] By that time the same height had also been reached in
Venice, where in 1494 Canon Pietro Casola from Lombardy described *pianelle* ½ "arm" (11 in.)
tall, which he said made women look like giants, but forced them to lean on slaves to keep their
balance.[26] Two years later, pilgrim Arnold von Harff, passing through Venice, wrote: "Women
walk on great high soles covered with cloth, three of my fists high, which cause them to walk with
such difficulty that one pities them."[27] Chopines seem to have reached similar heights in
Florence, but not in Milan or Genoa, where in 1480 the Florentine Giovanni Ridolfi was surprised to see women either "without *pianelle* or with really low ones."[28]

Even in Florence, *very* tall shoes were not considered appropriate for respectable women, and
in 1465 the indomitable noblewoman Alessandra Macinghi Strozzi, for example, approved of her
future daughter-in-law particularly because she had seen her wearing "low *pianelle*" (Figure
3.4).[29] The daughters of Queen Isabella of Castile likewise kept the height of their platforms to

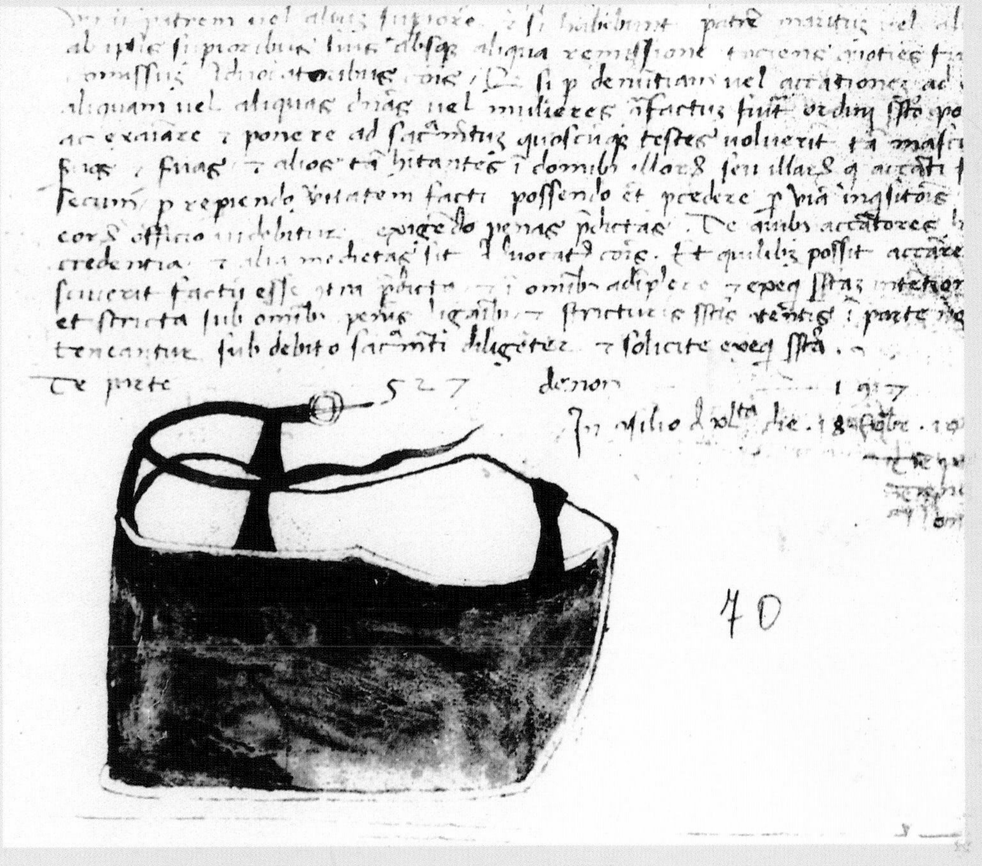

FIGURE 3.3: PICTURE OF A FORBIDDEN PLATFORM SHOE DRAWN BY THE VENETIAN COUNCIL'S SECRETARY. ARCHIVIO DI STATO DI VENEZIA, AVOGARIA DI COMUN, REG. 25, "SPIRITUS," C. 58. KIND CONCESSION N. 41/2005.

Figure 3.4: Two low chopines. Left: Wine red velvet chopine trimmed with gold-colored metallic braid, 1580–1600 (P88.60). Right: Gold-colored velvet chopine, 1600 (P83.338). Bata Shoe Museum, Toronto. Courtesy of Bata Shoe Museum.

Figure 3.5 (facing page): Cesare Vecellio, "Prostitutes of the Public Places." Habiti Antichi et Moderni di Tutto il Mondo, Venice, engraving, 1598.

a relatively modest single handbreadth in 1497.[30] Such testimonies indicate that in the 1490s, the comparatively low handbreadth-tall chopines painted by Carpaccio may well have been perceived as a sign of good taste and moderation, rather than as a symbol of licentious behavior. The "female pride" that Ruskin read in the wearing of the chopines seems in fact to have been very much the opposite: a compliment by Carpaccio to his sitters' virtues and fashionable moderation.

Such a cultural connection between the height of shoes and moral character continued throughout the sixteenth century, as indicated in Cesare Vecellio's famous book, *Ancient and Modern Clothes from Various Places of the World*, published in Venice in 1590. A major source for early modern costume, Vecellio's work has primarily been consulted for its numerous and frequently reprinted engravings. Each of these engravings is, however, accompanied by a short description designed to illuminate and prevent misconceptions arising from the consultation of the images alone. In one of his most famous prints, entitled *Prostitutes of the Public Places*, a woman raises her gown to show a pair of peculiar, column-like chopines, characterized by wide soles (which probably helped the wearer to keep her balance) and by hexagonally shaped central platforms (Figure 3.5). In addition, Vecellio writes that such "streetwalkers" used *pianelle* more than a quarter of an "arm" tall, worn together with "breeches, as if they were men, and for these and other marks . . . are easily recognizable."[31]

Similar chopines, characterized by the same wide soles and thinner rhomboid platforms, but which seem at least twice as tall, were depicted in 1589 on the feet of a so-called "Venetian Courtesan" (together with the aforementioned breeches) by printer Pietro Bertelli in his *Diversarum Nationum Habitus* (Figure 3.6).[32] An analogous combination of stilt-like chopines

MERETRICI PVBLI-
CHE.

Figure 3.6 (this and facing page): Pietro Bertelli, Venetian Courtesan. Engraving, 1589. Bayerisches Nationalmuseum, Munich.

Gentilledona Venet.ª come uano l'inuerno nele
loro Case

and breeches appear also in a late sixteenth-century print titled *Venetian Woman with Movable Skirt*, which shows the woman about to be hit by Cupid's arrow.[33] This image has been frequently reused in contemporary cultural studies for all types of purposes, notably in Marjorie Garber's book on cross-dressing, where she discusses the contemporary fascination with intercourse with female prostitutes and sodomy with pageboys.[34] Similarly shaped chopines are also depicted in a Venetian painting of the second half of the sixteenth century in the Walters Art Museum (Figure 3.7).[35]

In all of these representations, the subjects were either professional prostitutes or otherwise famously sensual women, and the depiction of these peculiar, column-like chopines, similar to those preserved in the Correr Museum, seems as a result to have been emblematic of their carnal habits and sexual availability. On the other hand, noblewomen in the 1530s, according to Vecellio, had worn "low *pianelle*, which in Venice are called *zoccoli,* in red or turquoise," and which remained relatively low throughout the 1550s. These were, he asserted, a "most honest costume" for ladies of the time,[36] particularly when compared to the somewhat taller *pianelle* that had apparently become fashionable among rich and noble women in the late sixteenth century.[37] It is thus possible to imagine that the city's courtesans and prostitutes, whose number and beauty Venice was particularly famous for, used the distinctively taller kind of chopine as an effective means of personal display in public squares.[38]

Vecellio's descriptions, together with his engravings, are particularly important for understanding the cultural value of chopines in late sixteenth-century Venice. As Traci Elizabeth Timmons has written, Vecellio's work was not just a costume book, but also a representation of what has been called the "Myth of Venice." The Serenissima (Most Serene Republic), as Venice was commonly known, was portrayed as a divinely ordained and perfectly balanced government devoid of divisive influences. Indeed, the Republic relied heavily on appearances to demonstrate the ideal of a society governed by male nobility, which was supposed to be dedicated solely to the welfare of the state without indulging in personal competition or conspicuous consumption. The noblemen's wives and daughters were thus "embodiments of display for Venice," and ideally had to be modestly dressed, except in exceptional circumstances such as a king's visit, when their "well-guarded visibility" could be relaxed in the name of glorifying the splendor of the Republic.[39] In this context, it is improbable that Vecellio's display of extremely tall chopines for prostitutes and not for noblewomen was without meaning or significance. Rather, it is likely that their use was largely associated, at least in this period, with women involved in the sex trade.

As for courtesans, who were involved in the same kind of activities but who could assume the appearance either of ladies or of women paid for their company, Vecellio wrote that they were usually dressed by their go-betweens even more elegantly than noblewomen before being taken to foreigners who, often "not realizing the deception, boast[ed] about what is very far from reality," that is to say, having encountered real Venetian ladies.[40] It is thus revealing that in the engraving of *Venetian Women at Home*, which Vecellio carefully clarified in the accompanying

Figure 3.7 (facing page): Portrait of a Woman as Cleopatra, c. 1550. The Walters Art Museum, Baltimore.

VENETIANE CASA.
PER

description as being an image of a courtesan in her apartment, the subject is depicted wearing much lower, steeply inclined chopines (Figure 3.8). This was a deliberate explanatory gesture on the part of the artist, I would argue — so as not to give the impression that the tall, stilt-like chopines were a fixed element in courtesans' more ambiguous system of dress. While Vecellio's work, as a guidebook, could attempt to nuance the discussion of courtesans' amorphous clothing system, isolated images such as paintings and prints would have had instead to rely upon elements emblematic of prostitutes in order to differentiate them more clearly from noblewomen, and vice versa. In this context, it is even clearer that the relatively low *pianelle* worn by the women depicted by Carpaccio were not emblematic of immoral behavior.

INTERPRETATIONS AND MISUNDERSTANDINGS

Once we have solved the problem of the identity of the women in Carpaccio's painting, another still remains: explaining the numerous accounts by foreigners in the late sixteenth or seventeenth century, like that of Tomaso Garzoni in 1586, which describe "Venetian ladies ... transformed into giants". Although brimming with useful narratives and details, travel writing is a notoriously fraught genre. Considering also what Vecellio wrote about the practice of dissimulation followed by Venetian courtesans, it is likely that foreign observers could have easily misinterpreted the nuances of status, the conventions of respectability, and/or the complex social system of Venice. Garzoni, for example, could not even claim direct observation of the cultural practices he described, as he had relied on the writings of the Bolognese Leonardo Fioravanti rather than on firsthand experience in his comment on the wearing of chopines by Venetian women.[41] Others could have simply been prone to exaggeration, such as the English diarist Fynes Moryson, who in 1617 encountered "women of Venice wear[ing] choppines or shoes three or foure handbredths high,"[42] or John Evelyn, who recounted in 1645 "the Noblemen stalking with their Ladys on Choppines about 10 foote high from the ground," and who stood so tall that they had to "set their hands on the heads of two matron-like servants or old women to support them, who are mumbling their beades."[43]

Lastly, travel narratives are inextricably tied to the cultural framework of the author, and still other foreign visitors may have misidentified these "ladies" entirely. Like the gondolas studied by Dennis Romano, chopines were highly visible artifacts used differently by persons of different social classes "to define themselves and their social relations and to give expression to their vision of Venetian society."[44] Chopines, as we have already seen, were not a uniform category of footwear. It is possible that foreign observers (and subsequent generations of their readers) missed the distinction between what were essentially two different kinds of shoes: the modest, lower *pianelle*, a form of platform sandal that permitted an appropriate amount of aristocratic display; and the tall, stilted wooden clogs, which were emblematic of moral excess. Such a distinction

FIGURE 3.8 (FACING PAGE): CESARE VECELLIO, "VENETIAN AT HOME." ENGRAVING FROM HABITI ANTICHI ET MODERNI DI TUTTO IL MONDO, VENICE, 1598.

would be analogous to today's perception of the "suitability" of heels two inches high, versus the perceived overt sensuality of five-inch heels. Indeed, the old women described by Evelyn may have appeared as chaperones only to a foreign eye; iconographically, prostitutes and courtesans were traditionally associated with the presence of older women (themselves frequently former prostitutes) who acted as their go-betweens or *ruffiane*, and the stilt-like clogs may have therefore provided an excellent excuse for them to keep a close eye on their charges.

The confusion between these variations of the *chopine* must have been heightened even more when Venetian noblewomen themselves seem to have started wearing taller *pianelle* in the seventeenth century. Perhaps to avoid such dangerous misunderstandings, in the 1650s the Venetian nobleman Nicolò Bon proposed the placing of another limit on the height of all women's shoes, which was nevertheless twice as tall as that imposed in 1430. Interestingly enough, this measure was soundly defeated, not only because the ruling nobility did not want to supersede the original limit, but also because they did not want new legislation that associated noblewomen with their plebeian counterparts.[45] The story of the Venetian chopines demonstrates that fashion history has to be very careful not to attribute one generic truth to sources and stereotypes within travel writing and the "cultural tourism" that they fostered.

WOMEN OF "ELEVATED" STATUS

By the late seventeenth century, the fashion for chopines eventually faded away even in Venice, perhaps because of a new style of delicate and small shoes popular in Paris, which was becoming the new fashion capital of Europe. This change forced the artisans who made the chopines, the *zoccoleri* – still in business in the 1660s – to recycle themselves as cobblers in the following century.[46] The *zoccoleri* were not the only ones unhappy with this change. Ironically, in the centuries following their introduction, these shoes were finally recognized as offering certain advantages from the male point of view. After all, they were an efficient way to control women's movements. When, in 1655, the Venetian senate belatedly discussed reducing the height of women's shoes in order to limit also the length of their dresses and thus their cost, an old senator argued instead that eight-inch heels (which were by then already in decline) should be *increased* by law, in order to keep wives and daughters from leaving home easily and going freely about the city. Otherwise, he was supposed to have said, they "would go to all the parties and scorn their houses and such bad government (*mal governo*) would ruin the family."[47] Alexandre Saint Disdier confirmed this changed male attitude toward chopines, writing in 1680 that husbands had found them "very handy" ("*se trouvent fort bien*"), while Richard Lassels, the Englishman who coined the term "Grand Tour" in the mid-seventeenth century, believed that they were just "a pretty ingenious way, either to clog women at home by such heavy shoes ... or at least to make them not able to go either far alone or invisibly."[48]

It is unlikely that men simply forced women to wear chopines. As the senate had observed, *pianelle* allowed them to wear dresses that were longer and, as a result, to display more silk, brocade and embroidery, which were clear indicators of their wealth and social status. Walking to and from church in these platform shoes was a way to create a spectacle with multiple messages: it demonstrated the power of the aristocracy to the other classes of the city, while at the same time it showed the wealth of the woman's family to her peers, in a society where a noblewoman's contact with the rest of the world was otherwise limited to her serving maids.[49] Wearing chopines, as Robert Davis writes, was also a way of "feminizing the public space," highlighting women's presence in a city which was dominated, physically and culturally, by their male counterparts. Men reasserted their control by ensuring that women would never feel secure moving around by themselves. Nevertheless, when one of these "giant" women in a sumptuous gown, surrounded by her maids, walked slowly to church, she took physical control of the space surrounding her, the kind of control that the psychologist Nicola Squicciarino describes as the "extension of the corporeal ego."[50]

Considering the chopines as a method of self-assertion for women helps also to explain the long persistence of this footwear in Venice. By the beginning of the seventeenth century, chopines had largely disappeared in other Italian cities; this was precisely when Venetian ladies began wearing taller ones. It is true that Venetian noblewomen could not avail themselves of sumptuous carriages or sedan chairs, which would have permitted them to move without soiling their dresses in dirty city streets. However, it is also possible that chopines continued to be used in Venice because of the relatively strong economic role played by noblewomen in Venetian society when compared with other Italian cities. Women's control over their dowries, as explained by Stanley Chojnacki, gave them a degree of economic independence from their husbands and sons, although it did not open "productive, economic or political outlets" for self-assertion. Heavy spending on lavish dresses could thus have been a way of "calling visual attention to individual identity and demonstrating the autonomous possession of wealth."[51] In this context, Venetian women may have considered the chopines perfect instruments to assert publicly their own wealth and autonomy.

The various kinds of chopines thus helped to make all classes of Venetian women figures of social importance, at the very least within their appearance in public. As Davis has observed, these platforms provided them with a type of public stage on which to "show off and compete for honor,"[52] demonstrating not only wealth and status, but also their perceived modesty or sexuality. Venetian nun and author Angela Tarabotti even defended women's use of these peculiar shoes, when she declared in 1660, "You never find wonderful and great things on the ground, but instead placed on high, to fill others with wonder and reverence."[53] In the process, she was not only ingeniously responding to the satires of those men who for centuries had ridiculed women for wearing tall shoes, but was also expressing her own vision of women's elevated role in Venetian society. Exalted by the chopines, enveloped in their finery, wealthy Venetian women took their place in this most physically precarious and polychromatic of European cities.

4.

WALKING THE STREETS OF LONDON AND PARIS

SHOES IN THE ENLIGHTENMENT

peter mcneil and giorgio riello

Shoes convey a wide range of meanings associated with fashion, style, personality, sexuality, class and gender. New studies have given us awareness of the personal, social and sexual connotations attributed to footwear and created by footwear. Although discussions of gender were present in design and fashion history in the 1980s, the research on footwear proposed by cultural studies has focused mainly on the psychological, affective and emotional values of footwear.[1] Theorists of gender – notably Kaja Silverman – gave prominence to dress in new analyses of the social construction of masculine and feminine self-identity.[2] These models, sweeping across several centuries, had by necessity to generalize across categories of clothing. They tended to repeat the assertion of earlier writers that until the Industrial Revolution and the dominance of the bourgeois sphere, men and women of the elite classes existed in a type of sartorial symmetry.

The relationship between gendered differences in eighteenth-century discourse and the evidence of surviving artifacts have by no means been exhausted by historians. On a fundamental level, the weight and pattern repeats of the dress silks of the male and female elite were essentially different due to the cut and relative surface area of masculine and feminine clothes. But how did shoes differ? Today the public thinks, incorrectly, that men and women wore equally high and beautiful shoes throughout this period. Important questions regarding gender and class, around the topic of footwear, are revisited in this chapter. Today the different shapes and colors of men's and women's shoes revolve primarily around the construction of gender difference. It will be argued that many of these gendered distinctions developed in the so-called "long eighteenth century."

This chapter will focus on English dress, but by necessity will include French examples, as English identity in dress was defined in a constantly shifting relationship to continental types of fashionability.[3] The notion that the English character was being compromised by the spread of fashion was part of the process by which nationhood and gendered identity were defined.[4] By focusing on France and Britain, this chapter shows how, in the eighteenth century, attitudes toward shoes and their merchandising were bound up with intertwined notions of nationhood, health and science. Starting with the physicality of the subject and their "body" in the past, the chapter shows how the changing nature of the built environment in the towns and cities of Enlightenment Britain and France led to new relationships between footwear, wearers and walking. Important differences regarding materials and forms marked the way in which men and women "navigated" public space and were able to walk for pleasure in eighteenth-century cities. The limitations in enjoying the physical space of the town and city translated themselves into psychological, cultural and social restraints. Shoes, and wearing them to walk in, connected national debates over practicality, fashionability, health and the gendered body.

WALKING, FOOTWEAR AND PLEASURE

It was difficult – physically and culturally – to move in the material world of an eighteenth-century city.[5] During the first half of the eighteenth century, the physical mobility of the upper orders in urban or rural environments had been considerably restricted.[6] In town, the poor condition of the streets did not allow "walking for pleasure" outside private parks or pleasure gardens. Streets were dirty, there were few pavements, rubbish was everywhere and the British climate did not help. Walking could be a risky business. The terrible state of roads, always flooded and muddy, created a metropolitan underworld of shoe-cleaners and street sweepers (Figure 4.1).[7] It is probably for this reason that the shoeblack and the "crossing sweeper" feature so often in descriptions of the "types" of London and Paris, as well as in caricature prints.[8] The shoeblack was nearly always paired, in visual imagery, with either a fashionable woman or a fop shod in delicate, slipper-like shoes. Much of the point of the visual joke is carried by the degradation of an occupation on the ground, near filth all the time, cleaning those devices designed to keep others above it.

146 You *are clean* Fair Lady *but our* Ways *and* Means *are* Dirty.

London Printed for ROBERT SAYER, *Map & Printseller, Nº 53 Fleet Street, as the Act directs 16 August, 1791.*

FIGURE 4.1: YOU ARE CLEAN FAIR LADY BUT OUR WAYS AND MEANS ARE DIRTY. MEZZOTINT. LONDON, PRINTED FOR ROBERT SAYER, 1791. GUILDHALL LIBRARY, PRINT ROOM, Q8035021. REPRODUCED BY COURTESY OF GUILDHALL LIBRARY, CORPORATION OF LONDON.

FIGURE 4.2: MARCHANDE DE SOULIERS DE FEMME (WOMAN SELLING SHOES) FROM VERNET'S SERIES CRIS DE PARIS. COLORED LITHOGRAPH, 1820, BATA SHOE MUSEUM, TORONTO, P81.405. REPRODUCED COURTESY OF BATA SHOE MUSEUM.

References to walking are not abundant in early eighteenth-century texts. Surprisingly, this is truer for urban spaces – the very focus of this chapter – than for rural spots where, both in France and in England, country life had always been dominated by a lifestyle of outdoor activities, including hunting and rambling. For instance, in eighteenth-century London, foreign visitors' experience was restricted to touristic places and involved a series of movements through boats, stagecoaches and Hackney coaches. Walking was considered to be an activity for the lower sorts or those who could not afford a coach (Figure 4.2). Most of the eighteenth-century "walks" around London – such as *Gay's Trivia, or The Art of Walking Around London* (1716) – referred to an intellectual geography, far from suggesting any concrete action.[9]

This situation underwent a sudden change in the mid-eighteenth century, with the provision of public spaces in which to walk as part of improvement measures implemented in many British cities.[10] The first act for paving London was passed in 1762 and during the following decades similar acts were enacted in many country towns. By the end of the century, town centers were provided with walking facilities. Sophie von la Roche marveled, in the diary of her visit to London of 1786, about metropolitan street life:

> What number of people, too! How happy the pedestrian on these roads, which alongside the houses are paved with large, clean paving-stones some feet wide, where many thousands of neatly clad people, eminent men, dressy women, pursue their way safe from the carriages, horses and dirt.[11]

By the early nineteenth century, Paris, Berlin and Vienna also had spaces where pedestrians could walk (Figure 4.3).[12] Walking was made a pleasure only in specific spaces designed for the purpose, such as pleasure gardens, but the number of these spaces increased. Navigation became smoother and less dangerous. Even better were the interiors such as the Rotunda at Ranelagh, the Pantheon or the *Colisée*, which deflected both rain and mud.[13] However, as noted by Jane Rendell with reference to early nineteenth-century London, public space had different impacts and possibilities for men and women.[14]

A STEP FORWARD: CLASS, GENDER AND FOOTWEAR

The obstacles to the "appropriation of space" were not merely physical. There was a second set of limits that were very much created by social and cultural barriers. Mental space and physical space interplayed in the definition of gender and class divisions.[15] Inequality in the use of space was legitimized by a clear sense of social hierarchy. In the eighteenth century this was true of what we would now call public space. At the Palais Royale in Paris, for example, in the late eighteenth century, guards denied access to people who were not respectable (Figure 4.4).[16] The émigrés in London were insulted for the difference of their sartorial appearance when they adventured in places where they were unprotected from the scrutiny of laborers and working people.[17] Many of the puns of fashion caricatures revolve around such class-based encounters in public space, notably the street. While the elite carefully avoided social mixing, caricatures insisted on the misplacement of elite dress within the vulgar public space, and the wearing of formerly elite dress by

Le Friseur, et le Savetier à Vienne.

Der Friseur, und der Schuhflicker in Wien.

Wien bey Joseph Eder.

FIGURE 4.3: LE FRISEUR ET LE SAVETIER À VIENNE. ETCHING, 1797. BATA SHOE MUSEUM, TORONTO, P89.289. REPRODUCED COURTESY OF BATA SHOE MUSEUM.

FIGURE 4.4: PALAIS ROYALE, PARIS.
PHOTO: P. MCNEIL.

Figure 4.5a: Early eighteenth-century woman's shoe with cream silk brocade and motif of large roses, c.1725–50. Royal Ontario Museum, Toronto, 921.2.30b. Photo: Brian Boyle. Courtesy of the Veronika Gervers Research Fellowship.

the lower orders. The set of the feet and the contrast of shoe types marked a distinction in the "use" of space according to gender and class differentiation. Many images of the elite show them gathered in salons, ballrooms, galleries and assembly rooms, where there was a boundary between themselves and the common folk.

These attitudes toward walking through public spaces and their changes over time were manifested in the material artifact of fashionable footwear (Figures 4.5a, b, c and d). Pattens, clogs and other devices designed to keep feet above the dirty and wet ground level soon disappeared, and ease of mobility increased still further. At the beginning of the eighteenth century, men's and women's shoes began to look very different. In the eighteenth century, as in the present day, a gender-related distinction in footwear was filtering into production. Contemporary descriptions of the boot and shoe trade underlined the differences between "ladies' shoemakers" and "men's shoemakers."[18] The production of men's and women's shoes implied different skills, as the products were essentially different. Men wore more "sober" footwear, not very dissimilar to modern shoes.[19] Their shoes were entirely made of leather and this provided resistance to rain, mud and bad weather. Women's shoes had uppers made of textiles – silk, satin, cloth or brocade – and their resistance to bad weather and dirty streets was very limited. Only the lower ranks of women wore leather shoes of a form similar to men's. An eighteenth-century French commentator wrote that leather shoes were only worn by women "*destiné à la fatigue, chez les femmes de la campagne*," not even by domestics from urban centers.[20] The high-quality leather shoes for women were often embroidered and were normally worn with clogs or pattens, as they too were prone to spoiling (Figures 4.6 and 4.7).

The history of footwear (and especially women's footwear) is dominated by such devices to keep the feet above the ground. This differentiation is important because it reveals contrasting patterns of consumption and production related to gender. Most scholars of dress agree that the dress style of the male elite was as colorful, flamboyant and sumptuous as that of females from the mid-fourteenth century (the beginning of the development of the Western fashion system) until the "great renunciation" of such flamboyance at some point in the second half of the eighteenth century.[21] The theory is often advanced that, for much of this time, men were in fact more gorgeously apparelled than women. Silverman, for example, writes that the history of Western fashion poses a serious challenge to the "naturalized" equation of spectacular display with female self-identity, and the assumption that

Figure 4.5b: Mid-eighteenth-century woman's shoes with pale blue satin and blue silk ribbon, embroidered in a fashionable design, c.1765–80. Royal Ontario Museum, Toronto, 921.2.42.A-B. Photo: Brian Boyle. Courtesy of the Veronika Gervers Research Fellowship.

exhibitionism is synonymous with woman's subjugation to a controlling male "gaze." She notes that ornate dress was a class rather than a gender prerogative from the fifteenth to the seventeenth century, a prerogative protected by law.[22] That the form and nature of men's and women's shoes became such divergent features of gendered modern dress is not something that has featured in histories to date.

The shoes of men and women related to broad dress systems and aesthetic models in different ways. Female footwear of the wealthy harmonized with dresses, a harmony that could be effected through matching textiles, general color, embroidered detail, or buckles. Elsewhere in this book, we have learned how the velvet shoes of a Renaissance female courtier might match her dresses. In the eighteenth century, men's shoes harmonized in different ways, through a correlation of glossy black, red or pink heels. The male shoe also acted as a type of emphatic punctuation stop at the end of silk-stockinged legs and marked out a man's gender distinction from young boys and women, and his class distinction from working men wearing leather or cloth protective leggings, ragged shoes and clogs. The symbolic marking of the entry of a wealthy young man into manhood through his shoes as well as his breeches and other dress, may have been more pronounced than is acknowledged in costume history.

FOPPISHNESS, FRENCHNESS AND THE FREEBORN ENGLISHMAN

Different types and qualities of footwear were not the only signifiers of social distinction. In *ancien-régime* societies, the use of high heels was considered a physical sign of wealth and power. High heels provided not only higher stature, but also the embodiment of "constrained mobility." Only the upper classes, and especially women, could wear shoes that clearly defined an inability to walk very far.[23] If, on the one hand, shoes for the lower classes normally had low heels, rounded toes and were made of goatskin, leather or cloth (especially for women), on the other hand Louis XIV could impose a rigid protocol allowing only himself and his court to wear red heels in France.[24] By the mid-eighteenth century, red heels had become increasingly common in Britain also (Figure 4.8). Charles James Fox popularized the use of red heels accompanied by a blue powdered wig when he returned from his Grand Tour in the 1770s, worn as a gesture to irritate more conservative elites.[25]

The relationship between French and English fashion during the so-called long eighteenth century is particularly important in order to contextualize the different social and cultural role of footwear in the two countries and the diverging symbolic role they assumed. The work of Aileen Ribeiro and Valerie Steele has underlined the existence of an eighteenth-century European "fashion system" in which France – or more precisely Paris – was the engine of innovation, change and taste.[26] Court dress and the role played by a restricted but influential number of international travelers allowed the spread of transnational fashion. Already by the mid-eighteenth century, tailoring was dominated by French taste, with the so-called *habit à la française*.[27] Magnificent dress was compulsory, as its absence would be insulting to the king. Concentric rings of courtiers, attendants, servants and the more affluent members of what Daniel Roche calls the "appearance industries" (wigmakers, tailors, mercers, *marchand merciers* and dealers, etc.) spread from the center of the court. The sartorial grammar of French taste "corrupting" the English nobility was a part of the meaning of fashionable foppishness that undermined social hierarchy and an English pragmatic sense of style.[28] Charles James Fox and the Earl of Carlisle thus paraded in the Mall "in a suit of Paris-cut velvet, most fancifully embroidered, and bedecked with a large bouquet; a head-dress cemented into every variety of shape; a little silk hat, curiously ornamented; and a pair of French shoes, with red-heels."[29]

The French shoe, the Louis XIV heel or the notoriously undemocratic red heel were all elements reinterpreted and used around Europe to signify sophistication, international travel and refinement. The slipper-like shoe and ostentatious buckles of the male courtier, visiting fop or English macaroni, and the poised and balletic performance of such types negotiating the streets, featured in parodic descriptions and caricatures of fashionable men such as *What Is This My Son Tom* (1774), in which the father's rustic boots contrast with the son's flimsy shoes (Figure 4.9).[30] Indeed, apart from the mannerism of the wig, it is the shoe and the gait of the walk which bring together the very disparate ways of satirizing fashionable men. Some are skinny, some are plump, some wear a French-cut suit, others a frock coat; but nearly all sport slipper-like shoes or shoes trimmed with archaic bows or giant buckles.[31]

The references to footwear, posture and gait are not incidental in the critical and satirical writing dominating late eighteenth-century fashion. The image of a fashionable Frenchman as a monkey was widely used. Smollett, for example, claimed the common French people resembled "large baboons walking upright."[32] There was a long tradition that furnished this iconography. A

FIGURE 4.5D: EARLY NINETEENTH-CENTURY WOMAN'S SATIN SHOES WITH FLAT HEELS, SQUARE TOES AND SQUARE VAMP, C.1840. ROYAL ONTARIO MUSEUM, TORONTO, 976. 199.59.A-B. PHOTO: BRIAN BOYLE. COURTESY OF THE VERONIKA GERVERS RESEARCH FELLOWSHIP.

late seventeenth-century poem entitled *The French Dancing-Master* (1666) described the French as "like puppets in a play," adding that "To act the Mimick, fidle, prate and dance, And cringe like Apes, is a le mode France" (Figure 4.10).[33] An early eighteenth-century text, the anonymous poem *The Baboon A-la-Mode* (c. 1704–5), satirized Frenchmen by saying that "Their modes so strangely alter human shape; What nature made a man they make an ape."[34] In this poem, the French take civilization to an extreme and reduce man to a state of bestial nature. Also in this vein is Garrick's *The Sick Monkey* (1765), a parable in verse about a monkey who is a player in a court of other animals.[35]

The "public" value of posture, the manner of walking and the distinction of the shoe help us explain the insistence on representing the fop in the street. The social ideas about fashion were contextualized in the streets of the town and city where visibility, accessibility and contact made fashion evident and indubitable. In this sense, the act of walking was much more than a functional one; it provided life and context to the deployment of fashion. The shoe was therefore central in conveying the overt messages of *la mode*, by setting alive physical demeanor and personal attitude. The brutality and physical strength of the mob can therefore be contrasted with the delicate nature of the impractical shoes worn by foppish men: "Their legs are at times covered with all the colours of the rainbow; even flesh-coloured and green silk stockings are not excluded. Their shoes are scarce slippers, and their buckles are within an inch of the toe."[36]

The suggestion may well be that the shoes of the macaroni or fop are not simply impractical but so flimsy as to be close to disposable. Here they transgress the emergent masculine model of longevity and hard-wearing qualities of dress so dear to English fashion. Foppish dressing may have caused so much cultural consternation and comment precisely because it upset this understanding about the "natural" states of the genders, the more so for its appearance at a time when these were being consolidated in terms of gendered paradigms of dress and demeanor.[37]

"THE GLITTERING BUCKLE UPON THE GOUTY FOOT"

Buckles too, a new product, gained social, cultural and symbolic meanings. In the early eighteenth century, as a result of the success of the product, buckles became a part of the concept of "gentility". Buckles combined the searches for continuously changing shapes to ornament and value. Fashion was not continuously changing entire products, but was quite often confined to changing marginal apparel such as ribbons and laces, scarves, artificial flowers and so on.[38] In opposition to modern buckles, eighteenth-century buckles were removable. In *Pamela* (1741), the father does not have suitable shoes for his daughter's wedding, but the bridegroom "was then pleased to give him the silver buckles out of his own Shoes."[39]

Buckles could be suited to different dresses or different occasions, changing the appearance of a pair of shoes quite substantially. They also reflected the person and were recognized to be an integral part of his or her identity. In 1782, Carl Philip Moritz had been irritated by a young fop

FIGURE 4.6 (FACING PAGE): PAIR OF SILK SHOES AND PATTENS, C.1735–50. BATA SHOE MUSEUM, TORONTO, P85.73. REPRODUCED COURTESY OF BATA SHOE MUSEUM.

sitting behind him at the Haymarket theater, who "continually put his foot on my bench in order to show off the flashy stone buckles on his shoes; if I didn't make way for his precious buckles he put his foot on my coat tails."[40] Even social presumption was expressed through the use of buckles. There was an order in the nature of goods, mediated by social structures and values. The use of large shoe buckles was criticized as inappropriate only for certain classes. The figure of the Parisian *petit-maître* is one case. His social pretentiousness is expressed through his dress and extremely large buckles (Figure 4.11). Exhortations to common sense and suitability were very prevalent in eighteenth-century England.[41] A conduct manual entitled *The Man of Manners: or, Plebeian Polished* (n.d.) included this direction about apparel:

> We must proportion them to our Shape, our Condition, and our Age: The glittering Buckle upon the gouty Foot must be avoided; the white Stocking tightly garter'd upon the lame Leg… Gaudy Grandmothers and gay Grandfathers, are equally contemptible in the Eyes of all People.

Buckles could range from Sheffield plate to pinchbeck, silver or gold. During the 1740s they could be set with stones, paste gems and marcasite (Figure 4.12). Mourning dress buckles, for instance, were japanned black or set with jet.[42] The importance of buckles in men's shoes and also in women's shoes derives from the low degree of design variation a shoe could have in the eighteenth century. Shoes had to have high heels in order for the wearer to stay out of the dirt, and they had to be fairly resistant to the damp climate. With these limitations, the shape of a pair of shoes could not change much. Buckles not only transformed the physical appearance of footwear but also often acted as signifiers of distinction. Such a search for gentility could be the subject of much satirical literature. The new macaroni fashion, from 1776, was for huge metal buttons and Artois silver buckles, satirized in the print *Darly's modern Shields or the virtue of steel buttons* (1777), in which a man shields himself from his opponent's sword with huge buttons the size of dinner plates. A notice from the *Morning Post* is pasted on the British Library copy of this print, claiming that the buckles weighed three to eleven ounces. It points to the difficulty of the less wealthy in following this fashion without resorting to cheap copies: "The macaronies of a certain class are under peculiar circumstances of distress, occasioned by the fashion now so prevalent of wearing enormous shoe buckles, and we are well assured, that the manufactory of plated ware was never known to be in so flourishing a condition."

Prior to the buckle, laces and ribbons on shoes had characterized foppish male dress. Seventeenth-century stage types, such as the "French dancing [master]" engraved in Francis Kirkman's *The Wits* (1673), were distinguished by a feathered headdress and large bows on their shoes. During the eighteenth century, laces became so unfashionable that they assumed new meanings. According to the investigations of Commissioner Foucault and Inspecteur Noël of the Parisian police, only pederasts wore laces, instead of buckles, and this was a code for recognizing each other

FIGURE 4.7 (FACING PAGE): LADY'S METALLIC PATTENS, C.1815. BATA SHOE MUSEUM, TORONTO, P79.808. COURTESY OF BATA SHOE MUSEUM, TORONTO.

Figure 4.8a (this page) and 4.8b (facing page): Buckles were removable and could change the appearance of shoes. Green silk ladies' shoes with pointed toes and 4 in. wood heel covered with red-maroon kid, 1700–20. Bata Shoe Museum, Toronto, P90.186. Reproduced courtesy of Bata Shoe Museum.

in public places.[43] This prejudice against laces remained even when they returned to fashion, as they were deemed to be "effeminate in appearance."[44] (In the chapter on queer shoes later in this volume we learn how, in the twentieth century, slip-on soft shoes carried new meanings.)

LA MALADIE À LA MODE: NOTIONS OF HEALTH AND THE HEALTHY FOOT

The last decade of the eighteenth century saw important changes affecting women's as well as men's footwear. While men's footwear tended toward functionality, women's shoes became expressive of a female environment increasingly considered to be a domestic, protected and private space. Men's boots and stout shoes contrasted with light and flimsy neoclassical women's shoes (Figures 4.13a, b and c).[45] The neoclassical revival provided an aesthetic sense of unity, which was new in eighteenth-century fashion. Natural lines and freedom of movement were embodied in very light footwear, distinctive not only for its difference to old court-society shoes, but also for the reference to classicism. Women were portrayed wearing Grecian *cothurnes*, sandals similar to flat pumps and light shoes.[46]

Shoe fashion of the early nineteenth century, which had no buckles, no red heels and very controlled forms, can be considered a turn toward a world that was perhaps even more widely fashion-addicted than the atmosphere of a court. French shoes, and especially women's shoes, were characterized by a very particular shape. They were narrow, their exterior was of black or white satin or silk, their interior was light leather, and they had square toes and eventually a rosette on the vamp.[47] This new fashion was very different from the pre-revolutionary high heels, pointed toes and leather or brocade uppers. The creation of light shoes (not dissimilar to pumps or today's ballerina shoes) changed the average life of a pair of shoes. It was not uncommon to buy from six to twelve pairs of shoes a time, and their use could be for just a few weeks. In this "multiplication of consumption," fashion changes were magnified and France had a prime role in setting *la mode*.[48]

Such changes had deeper roots. The Enlightenment proposed a new vision of the body very much dominated by ideas of hygiene. The notion of the enervating effects of luxury, so beloved of both puritanical commentators in England and the philosophes in France, was extended from the 1760s when it was married to scientific discourses of health and the body. The anti-court-dress critique of the late eighteenth-century medical establishment should be advanced as another reason for the demise of such modes in Western Europe. The new discourse of masculine health, elaborated by French doctors and scientists, and promoted also in England, was influential in encouraging a shift away from textiles such as silk and velvet, which were characterized as unwashable and impervious – hence unhealthy, to the greater use of woolen broadcloth and cottons. The notion of moderation was introduced as the essence of male attire.

In 1792, the English writer Walter Vaughan merged anxiety about the male role with science in *An Essay, Philosophical and Medical Concerning Modern Clothing*:

> Alas! If our venerable ancestors were but raised from the dead to see their posterity disguised so hideously with paint, powder, and several other articles of dress, they might be led to ask "Where is a Man?"[49]

FIGURE 4.9 (LEFT): WHAT IS THIS MY SON TOM. MEZZOTINT. LONDON, PUBLISHED BY R. SAYER & J. BENNETT, 1774. LIBRARY OF CONGRESS, PRINTS & PHOTOGRAPHS DIVISION, PC3–1774.

FIGURE 4.10 (RIGHT): LE MAITRE A DANCER. PRINT, LATE SEVENTEENTH CENTURY. BATA SHOE MUSEUM, TORONTO, P97.13. REPRODUCED COURTESY OF BATA SHOE MUSEUM.

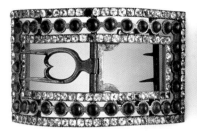

FIGURE 4.11 (LEFT): PAIR OF MEN'S LARGE METAL SHOE BUCKLES SET WITH TWO ROWS OF SQUARE-CUT PASTE BRILLIANTS AND A ROW OF COPPER NAILHEADS, C. 1770–90. ROYAL ONTARIO MUSEUM, TORONTO, 958.134.23.A-B. PHOTO: BRIAN BOYLE. COURTESY OF THE VERONIKA GERVERS RESEARCH FELLOWSHIP.

FIGURE 4.12 (RIGHT): CERAMIC SHOE BUCKLES, C. 1780. NORTHAMPTON MUSEUMS AND ART GALLERY, BOOT AND SHOE COLLECTION, 1997/117. REPRODUCED BY COURTESY OF NORTHAMPTON MUSEUMS AND ART GALLERY. BUCKLES CAME IN A WIDE VARIETY OF MATERIALS AND PRICES. THESE RARE CERAMIC BUCKLES ADDED A HIGHLY DECORATIVE ELEMENT TO SHOES.

Like others, he invoked classical ideals to advocate the use of woolen textiles over silk, "the most natural, the most wholesome," and which were recognized as the clothing of the ancients.[50] Even an endorsement for an elaborate man's wig in the *Cabinet des Modes* of 1785 had to add that these wigs "do not produce any nuisance to health."[51] The ramifications of health discourses have been considered within French cultural history but have had little impact on the revision of costume history.[52] As the fop was so frequently pilloried as enfeebled, impotent and unhealthy, the discourse has particular relevance for reading the fashionable man as a cultural type, a "typing" more convincing for the strength of subsequent discourses rendering the "effeminate" man psychologically sick.

The complexity of such historical discourse regarding the relationship between the body and fashion does not limit itself to how it was shaped by contemporary consumers, intellectuals, physicians and scientists. As in the case of "space," the "body" is a new focus of scholarly investigation, which has recently received enormous attention, especially from psychologists and sociologists, and has affected fields ranging from art history to the history of science. In this schema, the body functions as the primary site of personal values and attitudes and as the elementary expression of personal, collective and social order.[53] The body is central also in shaping the present-day study of fashion – both in its historical and theoretical facets – as it gives life to clothing and enables the metaphorical and material notion of a "fashioned body."[54] It is within this theoretical context that we should adopt a historical perspective as to how and why the debate over fashion in the late eighteenth century assumed dramatic "medical" overtones.

The medical literature of the late eighteenth and early nineteenth century spread more complex ideas related to the physiognomy of the body. The "scientific" credential of such literature

Figure 4.13a (left): Men's leather shoe with silver buckle, English, c. 1800. Bata Shoe Museum, Toronto, P85.30. Reproduced courtesy of Bata Shoe Museum.

Figure 4.13b (centre): Black and brown leather boot with rounded toe, England?, c. 1820. Bata Shoe Museum, Toronto, P85.188. Reproduced courtesy of Bata Shoe Museum.

Figure 4.13c (right): Pair of Melnotte's ladies' pink silk shoes with square toes, fashionable in the 1820s and 1830s. England or France, 1827–40. Bata Shoe Museum, Toronto, P83.27. Reproduced courtesy of Bata Shoe Museum.

made it appear neutral to older moral and fiscal debates on fashion and design, deceivingly concentrating on issues of health and physical well-being. Footwear was at the center of such debate. High heels were considered unhealthy because they allowed only "bad, unsteady walk, something between a trip and a totter, that French women of rank used to acquire from their high heels."[55] Similarly, boots that were deemed to have been made "too small" were disparaged as being "so pernicious to health, and so disagreeable in walking, that I wonder any sensible being should confine himself in them, for the silly purpose of showing the exact shape of his legs."[56] Thus shoes had to be reconsidered not so much in terms of quality or fashion, but according to the new criteria of health and comfort. The most important point – of debatable scientific value – but strong in capturing public attention, was the wide range of deformities caused by the inappropriate use of shoes. Texts warned about the inheritance of such deformities and of the "hereditary shape to the foot" that "ought to have convinced our sharp-pointed grandsirs, and high-heeled grandmamas, that they were not only putting themselves to much personal inconvenience, but also entailing diseases and deformities upon their descendants"[57] The medical literature did not limit itself to reforming fashion, but directed its didactic purpose also toward manufacturers. *Crispin Anecdotes*, a vade mecum for shoemakers and their customers, warned against the production of fashionable shoes and cautioned that shoemaking was not the slave of fashion, but an "art" for "discovering the most perfect mode of answering the purposes required," that is to say the health of the individual.[58]

SIR JOHN DINELY BAR.ᵗ

A Celebrated Writer of Epistles to the Ladies.

Pub.ᵈ as the Act Directs for R.S. Kirby 11 Paternoster Row & J. Scott S.ᵗ Martins Court March 25, 1803

FIGURE 4.14: SIR JOHN DINELY, A CELEBRATED WRITER OF EPISTLES TO THE LADIES. PRINT, 1803.

COMING OUT: BODY, SPACE AND GENDER

The physical experiences of the body, the action of walking, the nature of the built environment and the very notion of fashion are all interrelated concepts that must be simultaneously considered when analyzing the study of dress and shoe-fashion.[59] This chapter asks how much their interplay is conditioned by the construction of gender identities in the public arena. From the 1760s, Rousseau and the philosophes' circle attacked the urbanity of mode and manners characteristic of court society with a focus on that masculine transgressor, the *petit-maître*, the macaroni's French counterpart. In literature and art the *petit-maître* occupied the "feminized" space of the *toilette* and the boudoir, female zones and practices which corrupted men's reason. The *petit-maître*, it was claimed, deferred to women not only in matters of dress and deportment, but in literature and statecraft. His effeminate behavior, the philosophes argued, led to a corruption of the corporeal body and the body politic, and a set of moral and health discourses were mobilized against him. In Rousseau's *Emile*, the dancing master is discussed as particularly pernicious:

> I wish there were fewer of these dressed-up old ballet masters promenading our streets. I fear our young people will get more harm from intercourse with such people than profit from their instruction, and that their jargon, their tone, their airs and graces, will instill a precocious taste for the frivolities which the teacher thinks so important, and to which the scholars are only too likely to devote themselves.[60]

Rousseau would have been pleased by the dramatic reform of late eighteenth-century public spaces. The street was the new social background in which the elite of the old regime metamorphosed into a modern liberal class, displaying more virtue and respectability within their fashionable clothing. Daniel Roche has argued convincingly that the period witnessed a transfer of the "motors of distinction" from the sphere of the court to public space and the arena of production. Such a transition had different outcomes for men and women: "Men gained in real power what they lost in the realm of appearances."[61] So much so, that masculine dress became removed from those traits now aligned with feminine behavior. This point is clearly expressed in the caricature of Sir John Dinely, whose masculinity is diminished by the wearing of "effeminate" metal pattens (Figure 4.14).

As the public street and outdoor space became sites of masculine prerogative, the changing notions of women's shoes, fashion and politeness saw the creation of a distinct association between small feet and gentility. The skills of a shoemaker were measured in relation to his ability to produce shoes that made the female foot appear particularly small: "With these shoes, large feet look normal, and normal feet become remarkable for the grace of their smallness."[62] We thus return to an intersection of gender, the body and the material artifact. From this point on, the fashion plate reiterates the myth of impossibly small female feet and shoes in a manner unimagined in previous fashion imagery. Thus, material changes in the urban world had very different effects according to gender, and this manifested itself in the shifting appearance and understanding of footwear. If many physical barriers against free movement had been removed in eighteenth-century life, the same cannot be said about psychological, social and cultural ones.

5.
WAR AND WELLINGTONS

MILITARY FOOTWEAR IN THE AGE OF EMPIRE

alison matthews david

> Wellington, when asked the most important part of a soldier's equipment, replied
> "Firstly, a pair of good shoes; secondly, a second pair of good shoes, and thirdly, a pair
> of half-soles."
>
> Captain Cecil Webb-Johnson, *The Soldiers' Feet and Footgear*, 1915

The nineteenth century was an era of European military imperialism. Armies marched forth on numerous campaigns at home and abroad. Yet the success of these campaigns hinged on the state of an army's feet: as Wellington knew, a soldier needed solid and comfortable footwear to be an effective fighter. No activity put more stress on feet than the long marches over rugged terrain undertaken by infantry or "foot" soldiers while on campaign; the heavy pack each man carried added to the strain on his shoes. A poorly shod man risked injury, lameness, frost-bite and disease, and footsore stragglers were easily picked off during a retreat. Yet despite military leaders' understanding of the crucial importance of sturdy footwear, the nineteenth century was a period in which provision for shoeing the common soldier was lamentable: chains of supply were often hopelessly inadequate and the design of military boots was ill-adapted to the physical demands placed on troops and the climes of battlefields. Many sets of knowledge were mobilized to solve the persistent problem of providing enough good boots for European armies – new shoemaking technologies, military medicine, chiropody and ergonomics. Dressing and shoeing large numbers of men proved a catalyst for larger innovations, in fields from statistical analysis to social hygiene. While the design of boots had improved by the early twentieth century, the muddy trenches of the First World War proved a bloody testing ground for innovations such as the rubber Wellington boot. Focusing on the Blücher ankle boot worn by nineteenth-century foot soldiers and the Wellington boot worn by their officers, this chapter explores the politics of class embodied in the design, construction and provision of military footwear from 1800 to 1918 (Figure 5.1).

MARCHING AND THE MILITARIZED FOOT

When Jules-Etienne Marey photographically recorded human locomotion in the early 1880s, a soldier served as his model. Yet nineteenth-century soldiers did not stand or move like civilians. In his *Théorie de la Démarche* (*Theory of Walking*), Honoré de Balzac wrote unflatteringly that soldiers' natural gaits were permanently tainted: "Military men have an instantly recognizable gait. Almost all of them are firmly planted on their lower backs like a bust on a pedestal; their legs bustle about under their abdomen…"[1] John Rolt's 1836 manual for officers confirmed Balzac's observation: "The grand principle of marching is, that from the hips upwards the body be held perfectly steady, without jerking or balancing from side to side…"[2] Martial movement was highly specialized and ritualized. Generals and superior officers had to know the exact pace of their men for tactical reasons. By knowing how many miles or kilometers a troop could cover in an hour or a day, they could calculate how much time it would take to deploy battalions or bring in reinforcements.

In order to achieve this end, recruits were drilled until they could move with mechanical precision. Soldiers never "walked" in formation: they marched. Both pace and cadence were crucial. According to an early nineteenth-century drill manual, "pace" was the exact length of the soldier's step, which was thirty inches in the British army.[3] Both the length and speed of these steps varied: drums beat out the rhythm or cadence, which ranged from 75 steps per minute for ordinary time to 120 steps for "quicker time," which enabled the army to cover 300 feet per minute.[4] Each soldier moved left and right foot in synchrony and advanced the same distance regardless of his individual height. Rudyard Kipling's poem *Boots* (*Infantry Columns*) captures this rhythmic tread and the repetitive drudgery of military marching more eloquently than any prosaic description:

> Seven—six—eleven—five—nine-an'-twenty mile to-day—
> Four—eleven—seventeen—thirty-two the day before—
> (Boots—boots—boots—boots—movin' up an' down again);
> There's no discharge in the war![5]

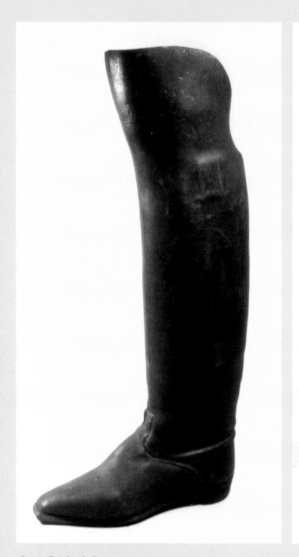

FIGURE 5.1 (LEFT): TALL MILITARY BOOT EXTENDING ABOVE THE KNEE WITH SQUARE TOE AND 1¼ IN. LEATHER HEEL, 1820–45. BATA SHOE MUSEUM, TORONTO, P86.6. REPRODUCED BY KIND PERMISSION OF BATA SHOE MUSEUM.

FIGURE 5.2 (RIGHT): BLACK LEATHER HESSIAN BOOT WITH SQUARE TOE ROUNDED OFF AND 1⅜ IN. LEATHER HEEL. HESSIAN BOOTS WERE WIDELY USED BY MOST MEN IN THE EARLY NINETEENTH-CENTURY. AMERICAN, 1845–60. BATA SHOE MUSEUM, TORONTO, P83-181. REPRODUCED BY KIND PERMISSION OF BATA SHOE MUSEUM.

The staccato repetition evokes the uniform and relentless progress of soldiers during the heyday of British Imperialism.

On the parade ground, exactitude was necessary but even on campaign soldiers were forced to march in formation regardless of the terrain. When puddles or muddy ground barred their way, men marched through rather than around them. Discipline and rigid formations took precedence over clean uniforms and dry feet. Yet forcing soldiers to maintain a "spit and polished" appearance was also used as a way of maintaining order among the troops. Soldiers expended a great deal of time and effort cleaning and blacking boots, which were immediately soiled on marching drill. This endless toil was considered an effective way of occupying unruly soldiers, an integral part of the army's culture of inspection and surveillance. These elements of discipline and punishment could be read as fetishistic rituals. However, I am more interested in the class and gender implications of military footwear than its psychosexual dimension. Army boots were a clear marker of masculinity. While the army boot can encapsulate ideas of masculine dominance and power, these meanings are mitigated by the social class of the wearer. Polished to a mirror-like surface, the officer's Wellington embodied male authority while the infantryman's Blücher ankle boot was a sturdy and unfashionable badge of servitude.

THIS MISERY OF BOOTS

Footwear is always an indicator of class status and social aspirations. The solid, well-kept soles of a man's boots gave him the right to be called "well-heeled" or affluent. While many of the poorest men, who would simply have gone unshod, were delighted to be issued boots when they enlisted in the army, their footwear could not be called elegant or stylish. The army, with its rigid hierarchical structures, echoed civilian class divisions in dress. As a general rule, the cut, tight fit and fine fabric of an officer's uniform was based on the fashionable gentleman's wardrobe, while the looser-fitting, coarser cloth of his soldiers' clothing followed the more practical design of working-class garments.[6] Footwear was no exception to this rule: the soldier's ankle boot resembled the laborer's low-cut, wooden-soled clog or thick hobnailed boot, while the officer's knee-length Hessian or Wellington, impractical for walking, advertised its equestrian origins (Figure 5.2).

In his 1905 Marxist tract *This Misery of Boots*, H. G. Wells stated that most working-class men were ashamed of their shabby footwear but could not afford to invest in solid, reliable boots. Forced to purchase cheap and shoddy goods, they walked the streets distinctly "down at the heel." In the section using Marx's concept of base and superstructure, playfully entitled "The World as Boots and Superstructure," boots symbolize the working-class base of social hierarchy as well as its physical base, a literal pedestal for proletariat bodies.[7] Despite the fact that regulation boots were issued to soldiers for free, there is substantial evidence to suggest that military footwear caused a great deal of misery to men drawn from the ranks of the working classes. In fact, they proved so useless that in many colonial theaters of war, native soldiers setting out on a march took off their boots and tied them to the muzzles of their muskets.[8] This section looks at three conflicts

FIGURE 5.3A (LEFT): A LATE NINETEENTH-CENTURY AGRICULTURAL LABORER'S CLOG AND A 1840S SOLDIER'S BOOT FOUND BENEATH FLOORBOARDS AT THE WEEDON BARRACKS. NORTHAMPTON MUSEUMS AND ART GALLERY, BOOT AND SHOE COLLECTION, 1955.56.1. REPRODUCED BY PERMISSION OF NORTHAMPTON MUSEUMS AND ART GALLERY.

FIGURE 5.3B (RIGHT): FRONT VIEW. THE WELL-WORN BLÜCHER BOOT SHOWS THE BOWLEGGED GAIT OF THE SOLDIER WHO WORE IT AS WELL AS A LACK OF ANKLE SUPPORT IN THE COMMON SOLDIER'S BOOT.

where footwear caused grave problems and became a subject of public debate: the retreat to Corunna during the Peninsular Wars (1808–9), the Crimean War (1854–56) and the First World War (1914–18). These historical examples will be elaborated by two case studies of actual boots held in the Northampton Boot and Shoe Collection: an infantry soldier's boot of the 1840s and a First World War boot found on the battlefield of the Somme.

SHOES AND WAR

The Napoleonic Wars increased the demand for military footwear across Europe. The boots, shoes and uniforms of the troops were largely supplied by military contractors, who vied with each other to obtain lucrative government contracts. In order to offer the lowest prices and bid successfully for contracts, many of these suppliers cut corners on quality. Despite the British army's high annual spend on footwear, which reached £150,000 in the early nineteenth century, some of the soldiers' shoes fell apart after one day's march: unscrupulous contractors had inserted heavy clay between the soles of their boots to make them seem sturdier.[9] In warm weather, the clay was excruciatingly hot and when it rained, it mixed with water and dissolved away, causing the boots to disintegrate.[10]

In the case of Sir John Moore's disastrous retreat to Corunna in Portugal during the winter of 1808–9, slipshod manufacture and supply problems left soldiers fighting each other for proper footwear. One private recalled that he was unable to obtain shoes for his bleeding feet because the stores were mobbed by desperate soldiers. An officer cleared the stores and called the men to fall in for the march before they were fully equipped. The private offered all his money to a man from his own company who had managed to obtain three pairs but the "rascal" would not sell his spoils, knowing he could make a greater profit from them before they had reached Corunna.[11]

When they landed at Portsmouth, many of Moore's troops were unshod and "dragged themselves along the quay on lacerated, festering, rag-bandaged feet."[12] This pitiful sight supposedly moved the inventor Marc Isambard Brunel to put his engineering talents to work in developing a new procedure for manufacturing boots and shoes for the army. Brunel, father of the more famous Isambard Kingdom Brunel, obtained patent number 3369 on August 2, 1810, only a year after the Battle of Corunna, and set up a manufactory at Battersea on the Thames near London.[13] In 1812, the Foreign Secretary, Lord Castlereagh, persuaded Brunel to expand production to fulfill all army requirements and output soon reached 400 pairs a day. His machinery was manned by approximately twenty-five crippled veterans of the Peninsular Wars, who were employed to provide other soldiers with shoes for feet that were still capable of marching. In Brunel's system, each man performed only one operation and machines hammered metal rivets into thick boot soles to keep them in place. While this produced unprecedented numbers of boots, the technology was not perfect and rivets could work their way through the soles, piercing soldiers' feet. Brunel's machines and procedures foreshadow the mechanization that occurred in the shoemaking trade during the final decades of the nineteenth century, and the Taylorist approach to assembly-line production that began to prevail during the First World War.[14] Unfortunately, Brunel's invention did not have a permanent effect on the design and supply of British military footwear. As the construction and wear of the following pair of mid-nineteenth-century boots suggests, the common soldier was not properly shod for the demands of campaigning abroad, a problem that was to cause great suffering during the Crimean War.

SHOES, SIZING AND SUFFERING

A pair of Blücher ankle boots from the 1840s was discovered under the floor of the Weedon barracks near Northampton.[15] Named after the general of the Prussian army who had helped Wellington win the Battle of Waterloo, this humble, unassuming footwear is simply constructed, unlined and cut low to the ankle so as to save on leather. It is rare to find surviving examples of boots worn by ordinary foot soldiers, since most of them were used until they fell apart. Unsurprisingly, the right boot shows signs of heavy wear: the sole has been repaired with a half-sole, the leather sock lining the inner sole has been pushed to one side, and the heel, despite its metal reinforcement, has been worn down on the outside edge. The leather itself bears the literal footprint of the soldier who wore it. Though there is some attempt at stylishness in the squared toe, the shape is not nearly long and narrow enough to make this a fashionable item. Its shape recalls a wooden-soled clog worn by the agricultural laborers from whom his ranks were drawn (Figures 5.3a and b).

Unlike sturdy clogs, however, these thin boots bear the trace of their wearer's bowlegged gait as he rolled over on the outside or "supinated" his foot while carrying a heavy pack. From the marks of his big and little toes, which hung over the edge of the sole, it seems that this boot was the right length but too narrow for the man's wide foot. Though gaiters protected his lower legs, the unlined leather of the boot would not have supported his ankle and as the army did not always provide its soldiers with socks at this period, any protruding seam would have chafed his feet as he marched.

Like much military equipment, produced in large lots and seven standard-issue sizes, this boot did not fit the soldier who wore it. As James Dowie wrote in 1861, "Feet are very different as to shape, irrespective of size; but there is no difference in the shape of the regulation boots of the army, generally speaking, the only difference being in the size; so that in a whole regiment a proper fit will rather be the exception than the rule."[16] Feet, like marching soldiers, were forced to adapt to the physical mold the army imposed upon them.

The problems encountered with footwear were typical of more general complaints over mass-produced clothing during the same time period. Though large quantities of "slops" had been produced for sailors as early as the mid-seventeenth century, the nineteenth century saw the widespread rise of men's garments made in standardized sizes.[17] The army's demand for thousands of uniforms was the catalyst for innovations in clothing production. The system of small, medium and large sizes was well established in the French army by 1800 and Thimonnier, a military tailor, was responsible for inventing the first sewing machine in 1831. However, despite the abstract logic of this system, actual male bodies did not correspond to mathematical models.[18] Problems of fit and quality persisted and troops were often badly clothed. In spite of problems of quality, techniques gleaned from military models were applied to the civilian arena, where ready-made garments were gaining in popularity with working-class and middle-class men. While *confection* or ready-made garments accounted for only a third of the total sales of men's clothing in France in 1848, it had already captured half the market by 1860 and its progress continued apace during the rest of the century.[19] In the field of tailoring, the psychological and economic consequences of this impersonal, metrical approach to the human body were wide-ranging. A disgruntled commentator, writing on the products of the clothing industry at the 1867 World's Fair in Paris, complained that the heyday of artisanal custom-tailoring was long gone. Consumers were now forced to wear the three sizes invented by the military:

> There are no more measurements, there are sizes. Just like the old National Guard, chasseurs, voltigeurs and grenadiers. Meters and centimeters. One is no longer a *client*, one is a *size eighty*! A hundred vestimentary factories are leading us toward the absolute and indifferent uniform.[20]

He was not pleased with what he perceived as the increasing "uniformity" of civilian men's dress, men who were dressed in small (*voltigeurs* or light infantry), medium (*chasseurs* or light cavalry) and large (*grenadier* guards, the tallest men in the army). However, continued innovation in this lucrative sector did produce an improved standard of comfort and fit for the vast majority of military and civilian men by the early twentieth century.

FIGURE 5.4 (FACING PAGE): AU PALAIS DU TROCADÉRO. GRANDE MATINÉE DE BIENFAISANCE EN L'HONNEUR DES POILUS DES RÉGIONS ENHAVIES. LITHOGRAPH POSTER, 159 CM X 119 CM, 1917. LIBRARY OF CONGRESS, PRINTS & PHOTOGRAPHS DIVISION, POS – FR. B377.

A. Barrère
Somme 1917

ŒUVRE DES PARRAINS DE REUILLY
= CASERNE DE REUILLY - PARIS =

Le Dimanche 3 JUIN 1917
à 2 heures précises
AU PALAIS DU TROCADÉRO
GRANDE MATINÉE DE BIENFAISANCE
EN L'HONNEUR DES
POILUS DES RÉGIONS ENVAHIES

EN PRÉSENCE DE Mʳ LE PRÉSIDENT DE LA RÉPUBLIQUE
ET SOUS LA PRÉSIDENCE DE Mʳ LE MINISTRE DE LA GUERRE
ASSISTÉ DE Mʳ LE PRÉSIDENT DU CONSEIL MUNICIPAL DE PARIS
ET DE Mʳ LE PRÉSIDENT DU CONSEIL GÉNÉRAL DE LA SEINE

AVEC LE CONCOURS DES ARTISTES DE L'OPÉRA,
DE L'OPÉRA-COMIQUE, DE LA COMÉDIE-FRANÇAISE, DE L'ODÉON
ET DES PRINCIPAUX THÉÂTRES ET CONCERTS DE PARIS
= MUSIQUE DE LA GARDE RÉPUBLICAINE =

Pour la Location des places s'adresser :
à l'ŒUVRE DES PARRAINS DE REUILLY, 20, Rue de Reuilly, ou au PALAIS DU TROCADÉRO

IMP. ROBERT & Cⁱᵉ, PARIS

However, during the first half of the nineteenth century, ready-made garments and footwear still presented problems for their wearers. Not least amongst these was the low prestige accorded to men who had to rely on ready-made rather than made-to-measure items before they became common among middle-class civilians. The sole of this boot reveals the low class status of the man who wore it. It is crisscrossed with metallic studs and hob or grip nails to reinforce the strength of the sole and to give the soldier traction over uneven or muddy terrain. No gentleman's boot would have had these utilitarian but essential features. Another telling design feature is the heel of the boot, which has a small, inverted metal horseshoe-shaped reinforcement hammered into the leather itself. Unlike officers, soldiers were beasts of burden who carried packs weighing up to sixty pounds. Like the horses that served in times of war, they were literally "shod" to protect their feet from lameness. The thin, smooth sole with a few small, invisible nails was the hallmark of a man who sat on a horse, rode in a carriage, or wore his boots on newly paved urban streets. James Dowie, a Scottish shoemaker who invented a rubberized leather sole for shoes and boots, wrote extensively about the problems of regulation army footwear. In fitting Dr. Charles Bell, professor of surgery at the University of Edinburgh, with a pair of shoes in the 1830s, Dowie wondered aloud why a veterinary surgeon had to undergo training before he could shoe a horse while any untrained cobbler could make boots for the army. The surgeon's sarcastic response was that you could not get a good horse under £200, but you could buy a man at any time for £4, referring to the bounty the crown paid for a soldier.[21] Dr. Bell asserted that the lack of scientific attention paid to the human foot reflected the low monetary value many members of the upper classes attached to the lives of working-class men.

A final important design feature of the sole of the boot is the high "toe-spring" it exhibits. This measurement is central to understanding the gait of the soldier and the class status of his footwear. The toe of thick-soled working-class boots and clogs rises up to a curved point rather than lying flat on the ground like a thinly soled and malleable gentleman's boot, which yielded to the foot in walking. Dowie complained of the pivoting gait these boots forced soldiers to adopt: "It is this bump-bumping that gives to the tread of soldiers in marching its peculiarly rocking and undignified trampling character, so destructive to pontoons, bridges, and everything under their feet… ."[22] Using what later writers would call ergonomic principles, Dowie argued that this plodding gait injured and flattened the soldiers' feet and caused them to waste muscular energy while marching. Based on material evidence and the texts of writer-shoemakers like James Dowie, ready-made footwear, like much of a common soldier's uniform and equipment in the mid-nineteenth century, was designed with cost-effectiveness, rather than comfort or practicality, in mind.[23]

THE WANT OF BOOTS

Footwear like the Weedon boots proved woefully inadequate for soldiers on campaign. In the Crimea, disease and exposure claimed more lives than battle and ill-adapted footwear contributed to many injuries and deaths. Catastrophic problems with the supply chain, general administrative incompetence and the suffering of the soldiers became public knowledge through the despatches of war correspondents such as *The Times'* William Russell. The resultant scandal eventually caused the downfall of the Aberdeen government.[24] A Captain Dallas used boots as a symbol of the army's lack of organization:

> What kills us out here is the utter want of system and arrangement in every department. I must give you an instance while I think of it, of the clever way in which everything connected with the Army is done, at home as well as here. We got up at last about 20 pair of boots per company, a great want as the men were all in a wretched state. Would you believe that they are all too small! & except for a very few men useless! How curiously the vein of Incapacity seems to wind about thro' everything, not omitting even the humble boot.[25]

French and British troops were unable to maneuver on the muddy, unpaved Crimean soil and when the troops found themselves still stationed there in the winter of 1854–5 their wet boots froze, shrank and became impossible to wear. Sockless, exposed feet were quickly frostbitten. Modern systems of communication and the rise of mass-circulation newspapers ensured that grisly firsthand accounts of the conflict reached comfortable Victorian parlors. One letter from Sebastopol to the *Daily Mail* described local conditions in early January 1855:

> The ammunition boots are villainous affairs; the leather is bad, the workmanship is bad… When the plain was covered with adhesive viscid mud it separated the seams, and made openings between the layers of the sole; as the snow melts the leather soaks up the water, and in the morning the boot is frozen, and so hard that the soldier cannot get his swollen and tender foot into it.[26]

By contrast, Russian troops were familiar with the terrain and had been issued with sturdy, well-fitting half-boots. The footwear of dead Russians was "one of the most coveted prizes to the poor, footsore rank-and-file-man, as he went *booty*-hunting among the slain after the terrible conflicts…"[27] The health inspector of the French army recalled how the Russians would taunt French sharpshooters and "showing the point of their feet they would call out in good French, 'Venez les prendre' or 'Come and get them.'"[28]

It would appear that the army had learned little in the half-century since the retreat to Corunna: once again unscrupulous military contractors had supplied shoddy goods to the French and British armies. The shoemaker James Devlin railed against these abuses of power and equated the plight of the underpaid shoemaker with that of the soldier: both were forced to suffer physical and economic misery on account of military footwear. Writing after the deadly winter of 1855, Devlin singled out firms such as Messrs Almond of St Martin's Lane in London, experts in leather equipment, who had been awarded a contract for footwear they had no experience in making, or corrupt army inspectors, who overlooked manufacturing defects in order to send

FIGURE 5.5: FIRST WORLD WAR OFFICER'S BOOT FOUND AT THE SITE OF THE SOMME BATTLE OF MAMETZ WOOD (1916), FRANCE. NORTHAMPTON MUSEUMS AND ART GALLERY, BOOT AND SHOE COLLECTION, 1987.214. REPRODUCED BY PERMISSION OF NORTHAMPTON MUSEUMS AND ART GALLERY.

some boots to the Crimea rather than none. Even when footwear was sent, chains of supply were unreliable and shipments regularly were destroyed or went missing. One of the worst losses of the war occurred when the steamship Prince was sunk in Balaclava harbor, along with the 40,000 boots it was carrying. It became clear that reforms in design and supply were needed in the wake of campaigns like the Crimean War.

MILITARY HYGIENE AND THE FIRST WORLD WAR

During the seventy years between the production of the Weedon barracks boots and the beginning of the First World War, the design of infantry boots improved out of all recognition. Unlike its precursors, the modern army boot was designed with solidity, hygiene and ergonomics in mind. The late nineteenth century saw physiologists and doctors begin to treat the body as a machine and armies devised scientific tests to maximize efficiency and minimize fatigue. The First World War proved a testing ground for "scientific" theories aimed at improving soldiers' performance, many of which were based on American Taylorist models designed to improve industrial productivity.[29] For example, in 1900 the American army formed a shoe board headed by Edward Munson, which measured military feet to calculate average conformation. Using new X-ray technology developed in 1895, Munson X-rayed soldiers' feet in boots and gave suggestions for improvements in design and sizing. Though Munson's recommendations seem impractical, his research led him to call for boots made in fifteen half-sizes and six widths, giving ninety varieties of boots to choose from.[30] The advent of methods of statistical analysis in the nineteenth century contributed to this rationalization and quantification of military bodies based on statistical data. Because the army recorded the heights and weights of its conscripts, it proved a seedbed for this type of systematic reform.[31]

At the same time, medical experts began to pay more attention to the health and treatment of feet. Army manuals of chiropody were published and men with experience as barbers or masseurs were trained and assigned to battalions to look after soldiers' feet. This stress on specialized medical care stands in stark contrast to the early nineteenth-century surgeon's claim that horses had more value than foot soldiers. In an age when cavalry had less importance in military operations, one manual makes the claim that: "In a sense, the chiropodist is to an infantry regiment what a veterinary surgeon is to a cavalry regiment."[32]

In addition to advances in medical science, shoemaking technology had progressed during the second half of the nineteenth century and many more of the processes involved in heavy boot-making had been mechanized. Machines able to stitch uppers and sew and stitch soles had become commonplace, and shoemaking work increasingly took place in factory settings.[33] Because of these technological developments, supplying adequate numbers of well-made boots for soldiers entering battle had become a viable proposition by the early twentieth century. Northampton was one of many cities that turned its wartime production to military boots. As a traditional center for the production of welted men's footwear, it found itself in a particularly strong position to direct its output toward the army. Family firms such as A. Lee in Northampton, which advertised itself as a producer of "reliable gents' footwear," produced sealed patterns for government inspection, such as a pristine 1915 British infantry boot.[34] At this stage, the British term "Derby" had replaced the "Germanic" term "Blücher" to designate a lace-up ankle boot of this type.[35]

The boot is fashioned from black chrome-tanned leather, with metal eyelets for reinforcing the laces and a welted sole with metal studs and the familiar horseshoe-clad heel. Chrome-tanned leather was introduced early in the war because it reinforced leather and accelerated the tanning process.[36] Like the Weedon boots, it is unlined for economy but it is much more solidly constructed and weighs at least twice as much as its predecessor. The thick and unyielding leather of First World War footwear explains the almost obsessive interest military hygiene publications paid to clean feet, good socks and proper fit. Unlike the Weedon boots, the 1915 model would not have molded to its wearer's sockless foot and blisters would have appeared almost instantly. Many manuals advised troops to break in their boots gradually and by one writer's estimation, European armies sending unseasoned troops on marches could expect to lose an average of 10 percent of their force, while several days' marching would cause foot injury to 25–30 percent of infantrymen (Figure 5.4).[37]

Prototype boots provide a sharp contrast with boots worn in combat. A lone Australian boot, also in the Northampton Boot and Shoe Collection, was found on a battlefield in the Somme, France in 1986. Its current state demonstrates that regardless of soldiers' training and the quality of their equipment, war put men and military footwear through grueling tests (Figure 5.5). Preserved in the mud of the battlefield, this boot is a testimonial to the destructive force of war: its heel and half of the sole have been ripped off, bare metal screws jut from the toes like jagged teeth and sharp objects have cut scars in the leather. The acid soil has eaten away the linen thread used to stitch it together but it still speaks eloquently of its trials. It was found at Mametz

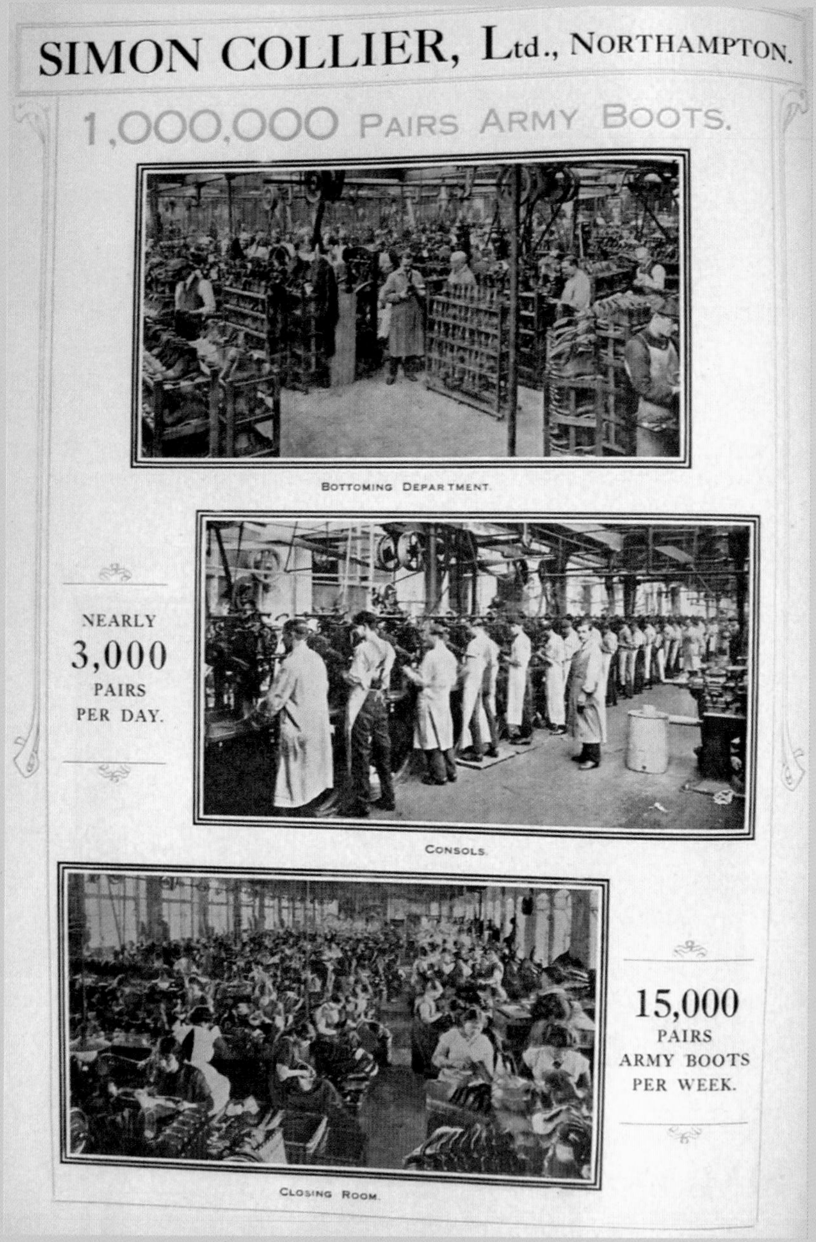

SIMON COLLIER, Ltd., NORTHAMPTON.

1,000,000 PAIRS ARMY BOOTS.

BOTTOMING DEPARTMENT.

NEARLY 3,000 PAIRS PER DAY.

CONSOLS.

15,000 PAIRS ARMY BOOTS PER WEEK.

CLOSING ROOM.

FIGURE 5.6: WARTIME PRODUCTION OF ARMY BOOTS IN NORTHAMPTON AT THE FIRM OF SIMON COLLIER. FROM *THE ILLUSTRATED BIOGRAPHIC DIRECTORY OF THE BRITISH SHOE AND LEATHER TRADES, SHOE AND LEATHER NEWS,* LONDON, 1919. NORTHAMPTON MUSEUMS AND ART GALLERY, BOOT AND SHOE COLLECTION. REPRODUCED BY PERMISSION OF NORTHAMPTON MUSEUMS AND ART GALLERY.

Wood, the scene of one of the bloodiest conflicts of the First World War. On one day – July 1, 1916 – 19,240 British troops were killed and 35,493 wounded.

This lone boot, unearthed seventy years later, is a marker and memento mori of the grisly confusion that reigned at this infamous battle. While the well-shod First World War soldier, whose body was likened to a machine by medical and industrial science, was still haunted by potential death and dismemberment, the actual machinery that produced army boots assumed a technical perfection.

On the home front in mainland Britain, the broadsheet press celebrated wartime technologies with patriotic fervor. Northampton firms proudly announced their impressive output. In 1915, *The Times* printed an article on Northampton that claimed: "Its output of Army Boots is prodigious, and one cannot meet a manufacturer who is not profoundly convinced that no battalions have ever been so well shod as ours."[38] For example, the firm of Simon Collier photographed its orderly factory floors, including the bottoming department, consols and closing room peopled by women (Figure 5.6). The tidy, soldierly rows of operatives at power machinery in the consols and serried ranks of boots on shelves in the bottoming department were accompanied by the claim that Collier had produced one million pairs of boots, or close to 3,000 pairs of boots per day. This output represents a significant improvement on Brunel's 400 pairs a day, 100 years earlier. Mass-production techniques and mass warfare went hand in hand, yet while soldiers might be better equipped to go on campaign, the conditions of trench warfare still wreaked havoc on soldiers' fragile feet.

Despite technological improvements and better chains of supply, improved footwear design proved no match for the waterlogged trenches of the Western Front. While many soldiers were issued with rubber Wellington or thigh boots, these did not allow the foot to breathe and often caused "trench foot."[39] Other soldiers complained that rubber boots gave them no traction on the wooden planks set up in the trenches and caused many slips, falls and broken bones. At its worst, rubber footwear got caught in the sucking mud, forcing soldiers to abandon their boots. In a letter home dated January 18, 1917, Private Richard Stevens described his first tour of duty in the trenches. When being relieved from trench duty, he got stuck in the mud only 300 yards from his post. His friends freed him but he was forced to abandon one rubber boot in the process. He walked ten miles back to camp in his stocking foot, painfully cutting it on barbed wire. On doctor's orders, Stevens was merely relieved from parade but three others, who lost both boots that night, were sent back to England with bad feet.[40] Despite the lessons learned in over a century of disastrous conflicts such as Corunna and the Crimea, no amount of technological or administrative progress could fully surmount the challenges of dressing men for the conditions of battle.

THE OFFICER'S FOOT: WELLINGTONS AND STYLE

Officers' boots present a very different picture to soldiers' footwear. Their history is much more closely tied to the vagaries of high fashion. Much of the male (and also sometimes female) wardrobe has been inspired by military styles. Cravats, lapels, pocket flaps, khaki pants, camouflage gear, even the simple T-shirt, worn as an undershirt by American troops in the Second World War, have all crossed over from military to civilian dress.[41] Even the Crimean War inspired fashion trends, including raglan sleeves and cardigans, named after British officers, and gowns dyed in hues christened Alma brown and Solferino purple after battles there. Nineteenth-century officers were renowned for their dash and elegance, and unlike common soldiers given standard-issue dress, they always had their own made-to-measure uniforms and boots. This practice made them less prone to the pitfalls of ill-fitting regulation sizes and boots that fell apart due to cheap construction and materials. Fashion, however, placed its own constraints on the practicality of boot types worn by stylish officers. The Hessian, and later Wellington, boots were exorbitantly expensive to acquire and a servant was required to keep their black, mirrorlike surface polished.

At the beginning of the nineteenth century, gentlemen's boots rose up almost to the knee. This design feature reveals their origin as an equestrian fashion, intended to protect the wearer's legs from the chafing of the saddle. This connection with equestrianism is the key to understanding the authority these boots commanded, since they signaled the rider's membership of the horse-owning set. In a military context, cavalry regiments were far more prestigious than infantry regiments and cavalry officers wore the most elaborate and expensive uniforms in the army.[42]

The increasing importance of the Wellington and other styles of knee-length boot in military and civilian attire is linked to more general shifts in early nineteenth-century men's dress. This period saw radical changes in men's fashions: developments that required a new form of footwear. As tightly fitting, ankle-length pantaloons began to replace knee breeches in the gentleman's wardrobe, Hessian boots conveniently covered the wearer's lower leg and replaced buckled shoes and silk hose. However, the accordion-pleated and tasseled Hessian could only be worn outside leg coverings. As more loosely fitting pants came into competition with pantaloons, boot design changed accordingly. The plainer Wellington boot was a more versatile style and could be worn inside pants or outside pantaloons at a time when men wore both almost interchangeably (Figure 5.7). It became popular from about 1817 and by 1830 an advice manual on gentlemanly attire claimed that Wellingtons were "the only ones [boots] in general wear."[43] In an age before elasticized panels and zippers, Wellingtons had to be made to measure because the shape of the wearer's legs was central to their construction. Owners required bootjacks to put them on and swollen or gouty feet made them even more difficult to take off. In the museum of the Royal Hussars in Winchester, several boots show slits up the front where the owners have cut the leather to achieve greater ease and comfort.

In stark contrast to the wide, flattened feet of the soldier who wore the Weedon Blücher boots, the fashionable male foot was relatively small and above all narrow, with a high arch or instep. One doctor wrote that bending the bones of the instep upward produced "that peculiar

FIGURE 5.7 (FACING PAGE): PATENT LEATHER WELLINGTON BOOTS WITH RED TRIM. ENGLAND, 1870, BATA SHOE MUSEUM, TORONTO, S86.181. REPRODUCED BY KIND PERMISSION OF BATA SHOE MUSEUM.

FIGURE 5.8: PAUL PRY (WILLIAM HEATH), A WELLINGTON BOOT OR THE HEAD OF THE ARMY, CARICATURE ETCHING, 1827. BRITISH MUSEUM, PRINTS AND DRAWINGS COLLECTION, CARICATURES 15430. © THE TRUSTEES OF THE BRITISH MUSEUM.

prominence that some have called *aristocratic* and beautiful."[44] Those who had them were proud to show off their "neat" small feet, and suffered accordingly from corns, hammer toes, bunions, ingrown toenails and other painful conditions. Toes were crammed into the tips of boots that alternated between exaggeratedly square and round-toed models. The heels of men's boots were called either "high" or "military" at the time. Medical men compared fashionable male footwear with the barbarous practices of tight-laced corsets for women and Chinese footbinding. In the 1840s, a surgeon and chiropodist-general to the United States army made the excessive claim that tight new boots caused:

> … sickness at the stomach, nausea, headache, palpitation of the heart, nervousness, inability to mental labor, pain in the feet or limbs, and the thousand-and-one forms of suffering which causes a new pair of boots to be dreaded as instruments of torture.[45]

They were certainly unfit for marching on foot: they looked good on parade but confined the instep and "annoyed soldiers on a long march."[46] As a solution to this problem, some recommended half-boots or ankle boots of the same design as cheaper and more comfortable, and by the 1840s and 1850s, the ankle boot had largely replaced the full-length Wellington in civilian circles. Many examples of "dress" Wellingtons survive in museum collections, with decorative tops and tooling in red or purple morocco leather. Unlike the heavily worn and resoled boots found at the Weedon barracks, most show little sign of wear on the soles, which are tooled with designs. According to the shoemaker James Devlin, patterns were made on boot soles displayed in shop windows. One pair at Northampton still exhibits decorative tooling and an instep covered with black ink squiggles imitating wood grain.[47] Because the style of these boots was more subject to the vagaries of fashion than that of practical footwear, gentlemen's boots are much more commonly found in museum collections than those of the common infantryman.

The exact origins of the "Wellington" boot are obscure, but the boot does not seem to pre-date September 1809, when Arthur Wellesley was awarded the title of Viscount Wellington of Talavera. Some trace the design to the Duke of Wellington himself. Indeed, he had many pairs of Wellington boots in his own wardrobe, which is kept at Stratfield Saye. While he may have been the first wearer of these simple, elegant boots, it seems more likely that patriotic bootmakers adopted it as a clever marketing tool designed to capitalize on the nationalistic fervor spurred by the British victory at the Battle of Waterloo in 1815.[48] The Duke as military hero became a commodity in his own right and his famous profile adorned "snuff-boxes, tea services, fans, bells, door-stops, brooches, note-books, clocks, watches, barometers, and razors" and even a black basalt Wedgwood service.[49] Like Lords Cardigan and Raglan, who fought in the Crimean War, other dress items were named after him, including Wellington hats, collars and pantaloons.[50] Despite this proliferation of Wellingtoniana, only the boot has retained his name. While the original version was made from leather, rubber versions have existed since the 1850s and the domesticated "Welly" or rubber boot is now a familiar part of our wardrobes for wet or muddy activities.[51]

Another reason for the longstanding association between the Duke of Wellington and his eponymous boot is the famous caricature penned in October 1827 by Paul Pry (Figure 5.8). The Duke's body is replaced by a Wellington boot. He "stands" in front of the Horse Guards, who are parading before St James's Palace, not far from the premises of Hoby, Wellington's bootmaker. Hoby had premises on St James's Street, which was located at the heart of London's center for elite masculine consumption, not far from Savile Row (Figure 5.9).[52] The spurs are engraved with the initials of his many orders. The caption reads: "A Wellington Boot: Or the *Head* of the *Army*" and refers to his role as commander-in-chief of the British army, which he assumed from January to April 1827 and again in early August 1827, until he was elected as prime minister in January 1828.[53] One the one hand, the image plays on the boot's association with class privilege and command; on the other, the title puns on the contrast between the connotations of head and foot. It invites us to see the Duke of Wellington as the "foot" of the army, contrasting the head as the seat of intellectual powers with the feet, which are literally "low" and represent all that is earthly and grounded. Perhaps Pry alludes to the Duke's well-known practicality and attention to detail, and as the quote at the beginning of this essay suggests, he was frequently quoted as stating that "a pair of good shoes" was the most important part of a soldier's equipment.

While the shape of officers' boots changed in line with general fashion trends during the course of the late nineteenth and early twentieth centuries, the Wellington and Hessian remained an important part of full and mess uniform dress. Boots worn in the field were more practical in design but maintained features that marked their wearer's class status. During the First World War, officers wore both ankle boots and knee-length boots, often fashioned from elegant, smooth-grained tan or black leather. Like the Wellingtons from a century earlier, the knee-length boots have a perfectly flat sole with tooled decoration around the edges. Both low and high boots have a narrow and stylish toe shape and a flat, as opposed to a "sprung," toe. Even at a time when horses were beginning to be replaced by tanks in "cavalry" regiments, the quality of leather, style of sole and elegance of the narrow toe recalled the officer's equestrian associations and reinforced his elite class status. These same equestrian associations could prove lethal in battle conditions; German snipers aimed at officers because they could distinguish the cut of the riding breeches and knee-high boots they wore – "the legs of the officers [are] thinner than the legs of the men."[54]

SOLDIERS AND GENTLEMEN

The Wellington gradually became domesticated as an ankle-length boot worn under pants by the middle of the century. It was later replaced by more practical boot styles with buttons or elastic sides to help men get them off and on. By the First World War, men's footwear for both civilians and the military had become broader, more comfortable and more affordable. The technologies developed during the second half of the nineteenth century allowed a broader public access to stylish and practical shoes and boots. Yet differences in class were still clearly visible on the battlefield. While the British "Tommy" was said to have a "special affection for his boots" because

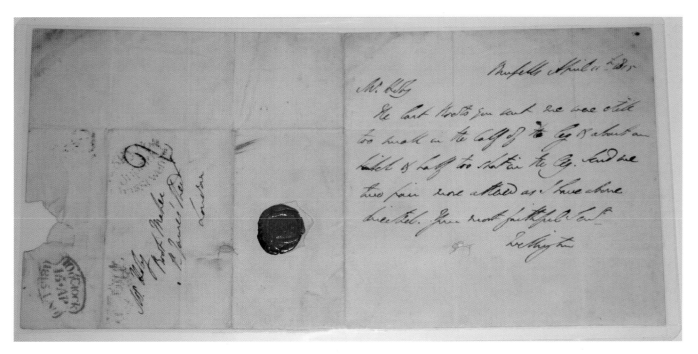

Figure 5.9: A letter from Wellington to his bootmaker, George Hoby, Bootmaker of St James's Place, London, April 11, 1815. The letter orders from Hoby two pairs of new boots as "the boots you sent me were still too small in the calf of the leg & about an inch & a half short on the leg." Bata Shoe Museum, Toronto, P98.13. Reproduced by kind permission of Bata Shoe Museum.

they were his "best friends" in wartime, his boots still marked him as a working-class man.[55] They had thick, metal-studded soles and laced up to the ankles. Most importantly, they had an unfashionably broad toe. A small, narrow "smart" foot still held cachet. By the early twentieth century, infantry soldiers complained not that their boots were shoddy, but that they were too large and wide. While vanity about small shoe size has been perceived as a female trait, Webb-Johnson paternalistically advises officers to supervise the distribution and fitting of boots because:

> If the soldiers are allowed to choose their own boots without official supervision, they are apt to let "vanity override wisdom," and choose too narrow or too small a boot. This is known in the army as "fitting the eye instead of the foot," and even after the proper sizes of boots have been issued, the soldier will often have them altered in shape at his own expense to make them look smarter.[56]

Soldiers who had access to more elegant, narrower shoes in civilian life had their own ideas about what constituted suitably fashionable footwear, even on the battlefield. They were willing to go to great trouble and expense to alter and personalize their boots, bringing a standardized item into line with their own concepts of sartorial elegance (Figure 5.10). There was undeniable progress in the design, ergonomics and supply of military footwear from a century which saw unshod soldiers returning from Corunna and disintegrating boots during the Crimean War, to the battlefields of the First World War. A century of reforms had minimized differences in design between the ranks: like his officers, the well-equipped First World War infantryman was concerned with both function and fashion in footwear.

Figure 5.10 (facing page): First World War soldier's boots vs. officer's boots: two models of boots showing the wide toe of the black soldier's boot and fine leather and narrow toe of the officer's boot. Northampton Museums and Art Gallery, Boot and Shoe Collection, 1973.89.21 (black soldier's boot) and 1920.1.32 (tan officer's boot). Reproduced by permission of Northampton Museums and Art Gallery.

6.

THE PERILS OF CHOICE

WOMEN'S FOOTWEAR IN NINETEENTH-CENTURY AMERICA

nancy rexford

The most important development in American women's fashion footwear in the nineteenth century was the dramatic increase in variety – variety in the sense of real functional diversity as well as in color and ornament. In 1800 most women had only lightweight, thin-soled, low-cut, slip-on shoes to wear, whatever the occasion. By 1900 they could choose from over a dozen different types of footwear, each one designed for a particular social or occupational setting. This expansion resulted in large part from mechanizing the shoe industry, which made footwear cheaper and more plentiful and drove manufacturers to develop new styles to increase their sales. By the early twentieth century, competition within the industry was fueling an uncontrolled explosion of new variations, to the point that the pressure to produce them menaced the survival of the manufacturers. While the impetus for variety came from the manufacturing side, the whole culture of fashion changed as a result of it. Footwear had always reflected gender and class, but now choice itself opened new avenues for expressing personal identity. Indeed, the wide availability of choice in all types of ready-made clothing eventually destroyed the tyranny of Paris fashion, but footwear paved the way because it was the first fashion trade in the United States to reach industrial maturity.

Imagine the nineteenth century as divided into two acts, with the first-act curtain coming down about 1860. In Act One, shoemaking is already a well-established cottage industry, and our middle-class heroine routinely buys her shoes off the shelf rather than made to order.[1] She aspires to buying French shoes (and is deceived by fake French labels). Styles do not change quickly, nor is there much variety at any one time. Not counting protective overshoes,[2] she has only three kinds of footwear to choose from and none of them is likely to have heels. She can buy what she calls "slippers" – thin-soled, low-cut shoes of silk, wool or kid, with ribbons that tie around the ankle. Or she can buy higher-cut "tie shoes" with more substantial soles and leather uppers. The tie shoes, however, she disdains, because she associates them with working folk in the country. The only other alternative is ankle-high boots. If she is shopping before 1830, what few she can find are front-lacing English "half-boots" with substantial soles. After 1830, they are side-lacing French "gaiter-boots" that imitate the look of a cloth gaiter over a leather shoe. Within any one category, most examples are very similar, and variety actually decreases after skirts lengthen to veil the shoes in 1834. The stylish woman chooses either slippers or boots and, as we shall see, in the United States this means that she has hardly any choice at all.

In Act Two, manufacturers can make huge quantities of shoes because the work is now concentrated in factories where the processes are mechanized and powered by water or steam. Having put so many shoes on the market, they must compete for our protagonist's business, and she discovers that shoes are getting cheaper and that they come in many more styles than they used to. She doesn't buy French shoes – real or fake – anymore. American manufacturers are beginning to drive fashion change rather than merely reacting to what they see in Paris, and they export their shoes around the world. She can find elegant slippers, shoes and boots made of leather, silk and wool, having high and low heels and fastened with ribbons, ties, buttons, straps and elastics. Many of them are ornamented with pretty rosettes or beading. Now the problem is which to choose? What to wear on which occasion? The stakes are high, because she knows that, to her neighbors' discerning eyes, every detail of her costume, including her shoes, reveals all too much about her personal taste, lifestyle and level of income.

ACT ONE: FRENCH SLIPPERS OR ENGLISH BOOTS?

In 1828, the English writer Frances Trollope traveled to the United States to gather material for what would become one of the most famous books about early nineteenth-century America: *Domestic Manners of the Americans* (1832). She spent three years in the United States, much of it in Cincinnati, a thriving western town on the Ohio River. Her depictions of the new republic are not always flattering, but they make lively reading even today. Her accounts of American dress – and footwear in particular – are important evidence:

FIGURE 6.1: WALKING IN THE
SNOW. ONE OF TWENTY-FOUR
ORIGINAL ILLUSTRATIONS DRAWN
BY AUGUSTE HERVIEU FOR
FRANCES TROLLOPE'S DOMESTIC
MANNERS OF THE AMERICANS
(1832). MRS. TROLLOPE WAS
BOTH AMUSED AND EXASPERATED
BY AMERICAN GIRLS WHO CON-
SIDERED FLAMBOYANT HATS AND
TINY SHOES APPROPRIATE GEAR
FOR WINTER WEATHER.

XX WALKING IN THE SNOW

Though the expense of the ladies' dress greatly exceeds, in proportion to their general style of living, that of the ladies of Europe, it is very far (excepting in Philadelphia) from being in good taste. They do not consult the seasons in the colors or in the style of their costume … They never wear muffs or boots, and appear extremely shocked at the sight of comfortable walking shoes and cotton stockings, even when they have to step to their sleighs over ice and snow. They walk in the middle of winter with their poor little toes pinched into a miniature slipper, incapable of excluding as much moisture as might bedew a primrose.[3]

While Mrs Trollope was poking fun at the Americans (Figure 6.1), the Americans were also passing judgment on Mrs Trollope. According to Timothy Flint, who befriended the writer in Cincinnati:

[She was] of appearance singularly unladylike, a misfortune heightened by her want of taste and female intelligence in regard to dress or her holding herself utterly above such considerations, though at times she was as much finer and more expensively dressed than other ladies, as she was ordinarily inferior to them in her costume. Robust and masculine in her habits, she had no fear of the elements, recklessly exposing herself in long walks to the fierce meridian sun or the pouring shower.[4]

Another Cincinnati acquaintance remembered seeing Mrs Trollope "in a green calash, and long plaid cloak draggling at her heels … walking with those colossean strides unattainable by any but English women."[5] The two nations may have shared the same language, but apparently they were not speaking the same dialect when it came to dress.

How did Mrs Trollope and her American friends come to see things so differently? To answer this, it is helpful to look back for a moment to the years just after the American and French revolutions. The period between 1785 and 1805 was one of great change in footwear. For most of the eighteenth century, both men and women had worn buckled shoes for almost all occasions. While men's shoes were normally made of leather and women's of wool or silk, the general form was still similar, though women had the option of higher heels. But by the early nineteenth century, the basic forms of men and women's footwear had diverged. Men tended to wear high boots while women generally wore shoes cut so low that they could slip on and off without any fastening. In that respect, nineteenth-century women's shoes descended from the backless slippers or "mules" that had been worn in the boudoir and other indoor private spaces in the eighteenth century. Men's boots, which had previously been worn only by the military and for active outdoor pursuits such as riding, now became an ordinary part of everyday dress. Thus the nineteenth century began with a new gender disparity in footwear, one that associated women with indoor life and men with the outdoors.[6]

Women in Great Britain, France and the United States all wore these feminine slippers indoors in the period 1790–1815. But once they walked outdoors, national differences began to appear. England and France always had a complex relationship with regard to fashion, and they did imitate each other whenever a new style proved fascinating enough to overcome their mutual distrust. But for about twenty years after the French Revolution, when the two countries were at war and trade relations broke down, they each developed distinctly national styles. In England, women began to wear ankle-high, front-lacing boots with sturdy soles for walking. This was, after all, the era when Dorothy Wordsworth tramped around the Lake District with her poet brother and when Elizabeth Bennett got her petticoat muddy walking to Netherfield to win the heart of Mr Darcy. Ladies in French fashion plates, by contrast, were more likely to be wearing slippers – even for horseback riding. What look like boots in French fashion plates in these early years are often separate gaiters worn over low leather shoes.

In the United States, the evidence suggests that women with any pretence to fashion wore slippers almost exclusively, as Mrs Trollope claims (Figure 6.2). Even though leather half-boots would have been practical in an expanding frontier country, very few boots dating from before 1840 survive in American collections and only one known to this writer has a specific history associated with an American wearer.[7] The fact that boots were an English style did not recommend them. During the colonial period, Americans had been forced to consume English goods. But after the revolution, when Americans were free to choose, they turned toward France, which had supported them in the war, was the acknowledged fountainhead of fashion, and had all the more allure for being until recently forbidden. If Paris wore slippers, then slippers were the rule in every American village from Georgia to Maine.

Another impediment to the adoption of boots was President Jefferson's 1807 embargo, which halted international trade just as boots were coming into wider use in England. After 1815, when normal trade was reestablished and boots also began to appear in French fashion plates, tariffs seem to have discouraged boots (but impressive numbers of slippers survive bearing the labels of the French company Viault/Esté/Thierry).[8] At any rate, long after the French had added several new styles of boots to their fashion arsenal, American women continued to suffer in their "excruciating French slippers."[9]

"Excruciating" may not be too strong a word. Because of their thin soles and lack of any heel (at least in most examples dating 1815–1860), slippers were distinctly uncomfortable for walking on anything but smooth pavements. Even when made out of kid, they provided very little protection against the weather, and many were made only of silk or wool serge lined with linen. Because small feet were valued as a sign of female delicacy, women preferred their footwear to be as minimal as possible. Surviving examples are commonly only two inches across at the widest part of the sole (Figure 6.3). But being impractical can be an advantage in the world of fashion. For a woman to brave the outdoors in elegant but unsuitable footwear implied that she was an indoor creature, only momentarily outside her natural environment, that she normally rode in a carriage and had servants to run her errands – in short, that she was rich. The inclination toward wearing slippers was only encouraged by the fact that the United States was a democracy without inherited rank. The Jacksonian rhetoric of equality claimed that even the poorest American

Figure 6.2 (above): Pink kid slipper, pale green silk slipper and tan kid tie trimmed with blue silk, all dated c.1815–25. Wool serge slipper with rosette, c.1825–30, the period when Mrs Trollope visited America. National Society of the Colonial Dames in the Commonwealth of Massachusetts, Boston.

Figure 6.3 (below). While the incised 1806 date and overlapping hearts suggest this was a wedding slipper, the traces of mud and straw and the abrasion where the foot overspread the sole show that it was worn outdoors for serious walking. Lynn Museum and Historical Society, Lynn, MA.

was every bit as good as anyone else. Therefore, every girl in the country had the God-given right to dress just as fine as she could. The most commonly cited reason for American girls going out to work in the 1830s and 1840s was that they wanted to earn enough to buy a silk dress, and it went without saying that the dress required slippers to go with it. Fashion and appearance became all the more powerful because class was not fixed and the population was mobile. In the American democracy, dressing well was the first and easiest step up the social ladder.[10]

Men and women experienced the world very differently simply because of their footwear. One person who understood the sartorial gender divide during this period was the French novelist George Sand. In her autobiography, *L'Histoire de ma vie*, she describes going to live in Paris in 1831 on an income too small to support a carriage:

> On the Paris pavement I was like a boat on ice. My delicate shoes cracked open in two days, my pattens sent me spilling, and I always forgot to lift my dress. I was muddy, tired and runny-nosed, and I watched my shoes and my clothes … go to rack and ruin with alarming rapidity … [To save money, she began to dress as a young man.] I can't convey how much my boots delighted me: I'd have gladly slept in them, as my brother did when he was a lad and had just got his first pair. With those steel-tipped heels I was solid on the sidewalk at last. I dashed back and forth across Paris and felt I was going around the world.[11]

When Sand mentions her brother, she is referring to the nineteenth-century practice of dressing all children, boys and girls, in dresses until they were about five. When little boys graduated from dresses and donned pants and boots for the first time, they abandoned the indoor world of women and entered the company of men – an event so significant that it is rare to find an American costume collection without the equivalent of "Willie's first boots." In 1856, an anonymous writer for *Harper's New Monthly Magazine* offered the following panegyric on the subject:

> Do you remember, reader, the first pair of *boots* that ever encased your boyish legs? Is there any acquisition of after-life that *quite* comes up to it?
>
> "How many boots," asked a little boy of his father (who had a friend with him at the time …), "do three folks wear?"
>
> "Why, *six*, my son."
>
> "Then," said the little fellow, with conscious pride, "there are six boots in this room!"
>
> Simple arithmetic, surely; but it was the only way in which he could adroitly call the stranger's attention to the fact – with him a *great* fact – that for the first time in his life he had on a pair of little boots.
>
> After all, men are not of much account without boots. Boots are self-reliant – they stand alone. What a wretched creature, slip-shod and discordant, is a human being without boots! In that forlorn condition he can undertake nothing. All enterprise is impossible. He is without motion – a thing fit only to have his toes trodden on. But if the thought

flashes through his brain that he must be up and doing what are the first words that rush to his lips?

"My boots!" …

You have only to say that an effort is "*bootless,*" and the folly of attempting any thing without boots becomes at once apparent.[12]

Thus in the popular imagination, boots became the quintessential symbol of masculine action while slippers both symbolized and even enforced the cultural assumption that women belonged indoors. In the early nineteenth century, women were not equipped either by nature (in theory) or by footwear (in fact) to cope with the world outside (Figure 6.4).

BACKSTAGE BETWEEN THE ACTS: SARAH JOSEPHA HALE AND *GODEY'S LADY'S BOOK*

During the early nineteenth century, Americans depended on model garments and fashion plates imported from Europe for information about changing styles. There were no American fashion plates until 1828, and until the 1840s they were few in number, often rather badly drawn, and presented with minimal commentary. They rarely mentioned footwear, and there were no individual illustrations of shoes until the mid-1850s. Therefore American women seem to have imitated European fashion plates and models without quite understanding the concepts of etiquette that governed their wear in the European context. For all but the most sophisticated American woman, being in fashion simply meant being "fine."

This changed in the 1840s when the editor of *Godey's Lady's Book* began to take a greater interest in its fashion offerings. *Godey's Lady's Book*, the first important and long-lasting American magazine for women, was founded in 1830 by Louis Antoine Godey and edited by Sarah Josepha Hale, who joined the staff in 1837. Mrs Hale, whose lifelong aim was to encourage education for women, tried at first to minimize or even omit fashion coverage. But fashion sold magazines, so in 1843 Mrs Hale announced a new policy:

> Some readers will be surprised to learn that we expect materially to aid the cause of moral improvement by our Fashion Plates. But why should Christian ladies leave the regulation of the fashion of dress entirely to the votaries of the world? Why should this subject be considered altogether vain and frivolous? … Purity of heart, and correctness of mind, as well as elegance of taste, may be shown in the external appearance … We are intending, during the year now commenced, to pay particular attention to this subject, and explain by what means the fashions of dress may be made auxiliary to that moral and mental progress which the Lady's Book has so steadily advocated.[13]

The justification for fashion adopted by Mrs Hale grew out of the nineteenth-century assumption that women were more religious than men and therefore qualified to be the moral guardians of the home. In order to keep easily tempted men from straying out to clubs or bars, women were told to create a domestic environment that was serene, orderly, and attractive – starting, of course,

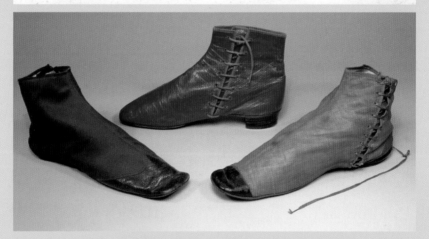

FIGURE 6.4 (ABOVE): THE INTEMPERATE. THIS IMAGE ILLUSTRATES A SCENE FROM A SHORT MORALITY TALE CALLED "THE INTEMPERATE" WRITTEN BY MRS L. H. SIGOURNEY AND PUBLISHED IN *THE YOUNG LADY'S OFFERING; OR, GEMS OF PROSE AND POETRY* (1851). THE FAMILY IN THE PICTURE HAS LEFT NEW ENGLAND TO SETTLE IN OHIO, WHERE THE WIFE HOPES THAT HER ABUSIVE HUSBAND WILL BE ABLE TO OVERCOME HIS DRINKING PROBLEM. THEIR HORSE HAS DIED AND THEY ARE COMPLETING THEIR JOURNEY ON FOOT. EVEN AS LATE AS 1850 AND IN THIS FRONTIER SETTING, THE WIFE WEARS NOTHING MORE SUBSTANTIAL ON HER FEET THAN KID LEATHER SLIPPERS TIED ON WITH RIBBONS.

FIGURE 6.5 (BELOW). SIDE-LACING BOOTS, 1845–60. LEFT: GAITER-BOOT, BROWN SERGE FOXED WITH BROWN MOROCCO LEATHER, C. 1840–47. CENTER: LEATHER BOOT, RED KID WITH SLIGHTLY THICKER SOLE AND LOW STACKED HEEL, C. 1860–65. RIGHT: GAITER-BOOT, LIGHT BROWN WOOL, FOXED WITH BLACK PATENT, C. 1850–55. HISTORIC NORTHAMPTON, NORTHAMPTON, MASSACHUSETTS. THE RED BOOT REPRESENTS A REVOLUTION IN AMERICAN WOMEN'S FOOTWEAR. FOR THE FIRST TIME, OUTDOOR FOOTWEAR COULD BE BOTH STYLISH AND PRACTICAL. BOOTS COULD HAVE THICK SOLES AND BE RED!

with their own appearance. In one fashion writer's pithy wisdom, "Many a man's heart has been kept from wandering by the bow on his wife's slipper."[14] In the modern phrase, beauty was duty.

In her new campaign in 1843, Mrs Hale aimed to replace fashion as "finery" with fashion as "propriety." Being a lady was no longer to be defined as looking like a French fashion plate. From now on, it meant wearing clothing appropriate to your condition in life and also to the needs of the occasion. Her opening salvo in this campaign addressed the question of footwear:

> I wish our young ladies would dress *their feet* in as good taste as the Parisian ladies. You never see ladies in Paris walking in thin slippers, (though it is true they seldom walk;) they wear abroad *gaiter boots*, either thick or thin, according to the season. I think a handsome foot and ankle never appear better than in such boots. And surely there is a propriety when walking out, and exposed to dust or mud, that the feet should be well protected; and propriety is the fundamental law of good taste.[15]

This sounds suspiciously like Mrs Trollope, whose work Mrs Hale would certainly have known. In fact much of the advice offered in *Godey's* repeats themes sounded by Mrs Trollope and other English sources. Even though it is the French who are held up as the paragons to be imitated, the consideration given to practicality as one element in propriety has a very English quality to it. Not that gaiter-boots were all that practical: their great advantage was that they modestly covered the ankle and made the foot look smaller (Figure 6.5).

Since propriety – appropriateness – was "the fundamental law of good taste," *Godey's* felt free, in an 1849 article called "Dress in Rural Districts," to reverse its recommendation of gaiters insofar as it applied to rural women:

> Gaiters and slippers are of no use at all on unpaved roads. The dust penetrates the prunella [wool serge fabric used for shoe uppers] and defaces the patent leather in one instance, and *sifts* through the stocking. … Morocco walking-shoes, high in the instep, no matter what is worn on Chestnut Street or Broadway, are the things for country wear. … What we ask of our fair readers is this: Never to copy a fashion that is not suited to their means, figure, and the climate in which their residence is fixed. We tell them what is worn in cities, that they may modify and arrange the styles to suit their own comfort and pleasure.[16]

Magazines such as *Godey's* assured their middle-class and rural readers that they could be truly ladylike, even with limited resources, if they consulted "neatness and propriety" in their dress. This meant giving up the more flamboyant joys of fashion, such as silk dresses and flimsy footwear, and instead buying sensible dark prints and serviceable leather shoes. The effect of such advice (had it ever been followed) would have been to create two classes of women, the urban rich and the rural poor, each perfectly ladylike but also perfectly distinguishable in their "appropriate" dress. Etiquette thus came very close to advocating class distinctions in a society in which they were not supposed to exist, an idea that made Americans very uncomfortable. "Dress in Rural Districts" tried to ward off resistance by honoring the nobility of labor and taste over the aristocracy of wealth and fashion but the argument seems unconvincing at best:

Do not … ruin your health by wearing thin slippers and low-necked dresses in winter, because [city ladies] are so foolish as to do so. It is but meet that they who have no nobler employment for their time, should set certain styles of dress and furniture; but if you copy them too closely, you are their slaves, instead of their being your workmen.[17]

Americans were much more comfortable with advice that encouraged them to dress up rather than down, so it is no surprise that the "beauty is duty" ideology was heavily promulgated from Mrs Hale's day right into the twentieth century. In *Godey's* story "The Cheap Dress" (1845) for example, poor Mrs Allanby learns to her chagrin that no practical exigency can justify an unattractive appearance. One day, planning to work in her garden, Mrs Allanby decides it is time to get some use out of "the ugliest, clumsiest, stoutest pair of boots ever intended for a lady's feet – boots that had been expressly imported for me from some provincial place in Great Britain by an English friend, on the hypothesis that the slight, pretty articles manufactured for our use on this side of the ocean, were the cause of a national tendency to consumption." Wearing the story-title's cheap dress, which has shrunk so much that it leaves her clumsy boots in full view, Mrs Allanby sets to work, only to be interrupted by an elderly neighbor bringing a handsome young gentleman to call. Mortified at being seen in her ridiculous English boots, she later apologizes to her neighbor, who scolds her sternly, not for wearing that graceless outfit before visitors but for wearing it in front of her husband. "No woman should present herself before her husband in a dishabille which would cause her to blush if seen in it by any other man. The continuance of affection depends upon a strict attention to what may be trifles in themselves." Since the story is a comedy, the husband does not abandon his wife because of her English boots, but her cheap dress brings her nothing but trouble from beginning to end.[18]

Whether to wear thin slippers, English walking boots or French gaiters was only the first of many footwear choices American women had to negotiate in the nineteenth century as new kinds of footwear entered the field of fashion. The next arrival was the boudoir slipper, which returned to fashionable floors in emphatic style around 1850. Boudoir slippers were the ancestors of our bedroom slippers, but less bulky and more ornamental (Figure 6.6). They were distinguished from other slippers by having broader, more comfortable soles, by being more brightly trimmed, and by having no ribbon ties, so they could truly slip on and off. It was appropriate to wear boudoir slippers at home in the bedroom or at breakfast within the privacy of the family. But what if you lived in a boarding house or were staying in a hotel and took breakfast in a common dining room? What if you were traveling overnight on a train or steamship? These situations were problematic because they raised the question of where private space left off and public space began, and boudoir or "dressing" slippers, fashion writers were clear, belonged only in private spaces.

Dressing slippers are well in their way, and often daintily becoming. It is never well to be without a pair, in your bag or basket, for your state-room or the hotel; but a slippered foot, descending from a rail car, or promenading a deck, however pretty and attractive, would be very likely to subject the owner to impertinent, if not unkind remark and criticism.[19]

FIGURE 6.6: BOUDOIR SLIPPERS, 1840–70. LEFT: CROCHETED WOOL SLIPPERS IN SHADES OF SCARLET WITH OILCLOTH SOLES LINED WITH LAMBSWOOL, C.1855–70. CENTER: DEERSKIN MOCCASIN WITH EMBROIDERED VAMP, C. 1840–50. THE LINED ANKLE BAND AND BUCKLED STRAP ARE NOT TRADITIONAL AMERICAN INDIAN FEATURES. THIS SHOE MAY HAVE BEEN MADE FOR THE TOURIST TRADE OR AT HOME. MOCCASINS WERE WORN BY BOTH MEN AND WOMEN AS HOUSE SLIPPERS AND AS CARRIAGE OVERSHOES. RIGHT ABOVE: PINK AND YELLOW SLIPPER OF KNITTED SILK WITH PLEATED SILK RIBBON, C. 1855–70. RIGHT BELOW: BRONZE KID BOUDOIR SLIPPER WITH VAMP CUTOUTS LINED WITH RED SILK, C. 1865–70. LABELED "JOLLY 125," PROBABLY FRENCH. SLIPPERS LIKE THESE SURVIVE IN MANY AMERICAN COLLECTIONS. IN SPITE OF THEIR SHOWINESS, THEY WERE NOT EVENING DRESS SHOES. WELL-TO-DO WOMEN WOULD HAVE WORN THEM IN THE MORNING WITH A STYLISH WRAPPER (A LOOSE DRESS DESIGNED TO WEAR WITHOUT A CORSET). HISTORIC NORTHAMPTON, NORTHAMPTON, MASSACHUSETTS.

FIGURE 6.7: NEW, THICK-SOLED WALKING BOOTS OF THE 1860S. LEFT: ELASTIC-SIDED "CONGRESS" BOOT WITH BLACK WOOL SERGE UPPER AND PATENT FOXING, C. 1865–70, MADE WITH THE MCKAY SOLE SEWING MACHINE (PATENT STAMP SURVIVES ON THE SOLE). RIGHT: FRONT-LACING BLACK WOOL SERGE BOOT WITH BLACK PATENT TOECAP, LACE STAY AND TOP BINDING. SAMPLE SHOE WITH PATENT LABELS DATED 1864 ("WARRANTED. THE C. O. D. MAN") AND 1865 ("BANCROFT & PURINTON. WARRANTED. LYNN, MASS"). LYNN MUSEUM AND HISTORICAL SOCIETY, LYNN, MA. THESE RARE SURVIVORS ARE FAR MORE TYPICAL OF EVERYDAY FOOTWEAR IN THE LATER 1860S THAN THE WHITE WEDDING BOOTS AND SLIPPERS THAT POPULATE MOST MUSEUM COLLECTIONS. THEY WERE MASS-PRODUCED IN NEW ENGLAND AND SHIPPED ALL OVER THE UNITED STATES, EVEN TO THE MOST REMOTE REGIONS.

By the time this was written in 1857, gaiters had largely replaced slippers for outdoor wear, with the result that private indoor and public outdoor footwear were more clearly differentiated than previously. While a plain black slipper might still have escaped notice beneath the long dress, boudoir slippers called attention to themselves with their colorful needlework patterns and elaborate trimmings. Even worse, while ordinary slippers at least fitted tightly and fastened with ribbons, loose-fitting boudoir slippers were easy to slip off. By a sequence of associations from loose shoes to loose morals (prostitutes wore loose "private" clothing in public), a pair of pretty slippers in the wrong place might well make the wearer blush.

ACT TWO: INDUSTRIAL COMPETITION AND THE EXPANSION OF CHOICE

The era of thin soles for indoors and out finally came to an end in 1860, with the following announcement in *Godey's*:

> From Mr. Bowden of the shoe department [of Genin's Bazaar, an early New York department store], we learn that thick walking boots for ladies are universal this winter, and no one will be required by elegance or fashion to shiver along in thin soles. We have examined three or four styles of buttoned boots, and congress [elastic-sided] boots with heels and soles a half-inch thick, lined with cloth, Canton flannel, or flannel, and costing $4.50 to $6.50.[20]

Fashion periodicals and etiquette books deserve some of the credit for this victory, having insisted for twenty years that no garment, however elegant, could be in good taste unless it was suited to the occasion. But more importantly, the conception of woman as a private, indoor being had come under strong attack. Women had begun to speak in public in the abolition and temperance movements. The women's rights convention at Seneca Falls in 1851 demanded property rights and the franchise. Mount Holyoke Seminary and Oberlin College began to provide higher education for women in the 1830s, and the 1840s and 1850s saw the beginnings of the campaign to encourage exercise for women, an effort that would bloom into a series of sports fads starting in the 1860s.

Although thick-soled, practical boots do echo contemporary social advances for women, it is likely that manufacturers hungry for sales were pushing this new development quite as hard as women were calling for it. In the late 1850s, the widespread cottage industry that already produced hundreds of thousands of shoes every year began to centralize in factories where machines could peg a woman's boot in as little as seven seconds.[21] Abundant production required new customers, which the industry found in the soldiers who needed boots during the Civil War (1861–65) and in the Americans who needed practical footwear as they settled the new territories to the west. But until the McKay sole-sewing machine (patented 1860) came into general use, shoes with any pretension to fashion could not be mass-produced. Those lightning-fast pegged soles were thick and inflexible, while fashion required soles that were thin and supple. The McKay machine mechanized the production of shoes with a flexible sole of moderate thickness, suitable for walking, and thus created a revolution in the industry (see Figure 6.7). Over the next forty years,

American shoe manufacturers mechanized every step in the shoemaking process, leading the world in technical innovation.[22] By controlling production, design and marketing, they created an integrated industry analogous to the fashion trades of Paris, and by the American Centennial in 1876 they were in a position not only to design for but to shape the American market.

As manufacturers looked for more buyers, it was in their interest to encourage American women to buy and wear the kinds of shoes they were able to mass-produce – not just thin slippers, which required hand processes, but the more utilitarian footwear they could produce by machine. Manufacturers naturally cultivated connections with the retailers they supplied, men like "Mr. Bowden of the shoe department" and eventually with the fashion magazine editors as well. As early as 1848, *Godey's* published what was essentially a puff piece extolling the virtues of the new elastic-sided "Congress boots," even including an engraving showing women trying them on in a well-appointed shoe store (Figure 6.8).[23]

The enormous expansion of production capacity brought down the average price of shoes. Boots roughly equivalent to those mentioned by *Godey's* as selling for $4.50–$6.50 in 1860 could be had for under $2.00 in 1900. Lower prices meant consumers could consider owning more pairs of shoes, but why bother if they were all alike? Therefore, to encourage consumption, manufacturers developed a variety of styles designed for a variety of occasions. After all, once boots finally displaced slippers on the street, women had to own both.

The number of new footwear types with plausibly "functional" differences expanded quickly. From the 1860s, both boots and shoes might have front lacing, side lacing, buttons, elastic sides, or straps. Heels were available in both stacked leather and covered wood. To the staple black and white kid leathers, manufacturers added tan, suede, reptile skins and new colors and finishes. To address the new interest in sports, manufacturers produced riding boots, rubber-soled canvas sports shoes (Figure 6.9) and bicycle boots with convenient lace hooks and grooved soles to keep them on the pedals. The advent of vulcanized rubber in the 1840s led to overshoes that were both waterproof and reasonably stylish.

The important thing about this development was that one type of shoe or boot did not simply succeed and replace the previous one. Instead, they all coexisted as options for the buyer to choose from. Once front-lacing boots came into use, they didn't completely disappear just because buttoned boots had become more fashionable. They merely slipped down the social ladder where they were worn by working people, only to move back up again a few years later when the style-setters wanted something new. Manufacturers even began to offer a variety of lasts. For example, in the later 1890s "commonsense" lasts with rounded foreparts provided relief from the "needle toe" styles then in fashion (Figure 6.10).

The existence of all these alternatives gave rise to rules of etiquette and standards of usage that both governed and gave meaning to women's choices. While these rules could be subtle in the details (Figures 6.11a and b), the basic categories remained fairly stable throughout the last decades of the nineteenth century. Broadly speaking, shoes were worn indoors and boots were

FIGURE 6.8: SHOE SHOPPING. WHEN THIS ILLUSTRATION APPEARED IN *GODEY'S LADY'S BOOK* IN AUGUST 1848, THE MAGAZINE WAS STILL BEING FINANCED BY SUBSCRIPTION RATHER THAN ADVERTISING. YET THE TONE OF THE ARTICLE IS SO TRANSPARENTLY PROMOTIONAL THAT ONE MUST WONDER WHETHER MONEY CHANGED HANDS. IN ANY CASE, IT IS A VERY EARLY EXAMPLE OF THE AMERICAN SHOE INDUSTRY TRYING TO SHAPE THE MARKET. BY RECOMMENDING THE ELASTIC-SIDED BOOT FOR MEN, WOMEN AND CHILDREN, THE WRITER HOPED TO CREATE SO MUCH DEMAND THAT MANUFACTURERS WOULD FEEL COMPELLED TO PRODUCE IT — AND TO PAY THE SIX-CENT-PER-PAIR LICENSE FEE (PRESUMABLY TO THE INVENTOR CHARLES GOODYEAR, WHO DIED DEEPLY IN DEBT AFTER ATTEMPTING TO DEFEND HIS PATENT AGAINST THE UNSCRUPULOUS MANU-FACTURERS WHO STOLE THE TECHNOLOGY). ELASTIC-SIDED BOOTS WERE WIDELY WORN IN THE 1850S BUT NEVER PROVED CONVINCING AS ELE-GANT FOOTWEAR, AND THEY EVENTUALLY SLID DOWN TO A HUMBLE ROLE AS A "COMFORT SHOE."

FIGURE 6.9: FOOTWEAR FOR SPORTS. LEFT: RED SATIN BATHING BOOT WITH RUBBER SOLE, C. 1920–25. THE PINKISH STAINS SPREADING FROM THE SATIN ONTO THE RUBBER SUGGEST THAT THE WEARER OF THESE CHEERFUL BATHING BOOTS MIGHT HAVE DONE BETTER TO STAY OUT OF THE WATER. AN ALMOST IDENTICAL PAIR MADE OF PEA GREEN SATIN SURVIVES, STILL GRIT-TY WITH BEACH SAND, AT THE DANVERS (MA) HISTORICAL SOCIETY. CENTER: WHITE CANVAS BOOT WITH RUBBER SOLE, LABELED "REGENT KEDS," C.1917–19. THE KEDS BRAND NAME WAS INTRODUCED IN 1917 AND APPLIED TO SEVERAL STYLES OF CANVAS SHOES WITH RUBBER SOLES INTENDED FOR GENERAL SUMMER WEAR. THIS ONE IS CUT LIKE A CONTEMPORARY WALK-ING BOOT, BUT OTHERS WERE SIMPLE SLIPPERS NOT VERY DIFFERENT FROM THOSE BEING SOLD TODAY. RIGHT: BROWN CANVAS BOOT WITH RUBBER SOLE, WORN TO WALK THROUGH THE FIELDS IN RURAL VERMONT IN THE 1920S. RUBBER-SOLED CANVAS SHOES WERE ORIGINALLY MARKETED FOR TENNIS AND BOATING, BUT SOON BECAME EVERYDAY WEAR. HISTORIC NORTHAMPTON, NORTHAMPTON, MASSACHUSETTS.

Common Sense Broadway London Opera

Louis XIV

Opera

Military

Half Military

Common Sense

Women's Patent Leather and Patent Kid Boots, $4.00 and $5.00

No. 286. Women's patent leather whole foxed button boots, dull kid tops, London toes, tipped, military heels, welted and stitched soles, 5.00

No. 287. Same as No. 286, only laced

No. 292. Women's patent kid button boots, whole foxed, dull kid tops, opera toes, Cuban heels, welted and stitched soles, 5.00

No. 293. Women's patent kid laced boots, full foxed, dull kid tops, Broadway toes, straight tips, military heels, welted and stitched soles, 5.00

No. 320. Women's patent kid button boots, dull kid tops, opera toes, tipped, Cuban heels, welted and stitched soles, 4.00

No. 321. Women's patent leather laced boots, Broadway toes, straight tips, military heels, welted and stitched soles, 4.00

Women's Kidskin and Box-Calf Shoes, $4.00

No. 300. Women's kidskin button boots, three-quarter foxed, opera toes, straight kid tips, Cuban heels, welted and stitched soles, 4.00

No. 301. Same as No. 300, only laced

No. 302. For stout women, kidskin button boots, London toes, straight kid tips, extra large ankles, common sense heels, welted and stitched soles, 4.00

No. 303. Our women's bunion shoes, made over a last specially made for this purpose, kidskin laced boots, Broadway toes, straight kid tips, welted and stitched soles, very full and roomy across the ball, common sense heels, 4.00

No. 306. Women's dull kidskin boots, plain common sense toes, heavy single soles, welted and stitched, common sense heels, 4.00

No. 334. Women's kidskin button boots, turned soles, opera toes, straight patent leather tips, high military heels, 4.00

No. 335. Same as No. 334, only lace

No. 312. Women's kidskin button boots, opera toes, straight patent leather tips, military heels, welted and stitched soles, 4.00

No. 313. Same as No. 312, only laced

No. 314. Women's kidskin button boots, dull kid tops, Broadway toes, straight kid tips, half-military heels, welted and stitched soles, 4.00

No. 328. Women's kidskin button boots, plain common sense toes, welted and stitched soles, common sense heels, 4.00

No. 337. Women's kidskin laced boots, opera toes, straight kid tips, Louis XIV. heels, 4.00

Women's Kidskin Shoes, $5.00

Welted and Stitched Shoes, $5.00

No. 252. (For stout women.) Kidskin button boots, plain common sense heels, welted and stitched soles, wide ankles, 5.00

No. 256. Women's kidskin button boots, Waukenphast last, straight patent leather tips, common sense heels, flexible welted and stitched soles, 5.00

No. 260. Women's kidskin button boots, Broadway toes, straight kid tips, welted and stitched soles, half military heels, 5.00

No. 261. Same style as No. 260, only laced

No. 265. Women's kidskin laced boots, straight patent leather tips, high military heels, opera toes, 5.00

No. 266. Women's kidskin button boots, cloth tops, London toes, straight patent leather tips, half military heels, welted and stitched soles, 5.00

No. 276. Women's kidskin button boots, plain common sense toes, common sense heels, welted and stitched soles, 5.00

No. 277. Women's dull kid laced boots, Broadway toes, tips of same, heavy soles, medium extension, welted and stitched, half military heels, 5.00

Women's Turn Shoes $5.00

No. 230. Women's kidskin button boots, common sense toes, common sense heels, light turn soles, 5.00

No. 232. Women's kidskin button boots, full opera toes, diamond shaped patent leather tips, opera heels, turn soles, 5.00

No. 234. Women's kidskin button boots, opera toes, straight kid tips, Cuban heels, turn soles 5.00

No. 235. Same style as No. 234, only laced

No. 236. Women's kidskin button boots, opera toes, straight patent leather tips, military heels, turn soles, 5.00

No. 237. Same style as No. 236, only laced

Women's Comfort Shoes

No. 379. Women's kidskin laced shoes, plain, common sense toes, right and left last, common sense heels, heavy soles, turn, 3.00

No. 380. Women's kidskin button shoes, seam up front, plain common sense toes, common sense heels, heavy soles, turn, 3.00

No. 381. Women's kidskin side-seam laced shoes, plain common sense toes, common sense heels, heavy, turn. 3.00

No. 382. Women's kidskin congress, plain toes, common sense heels, heavy sole turns, 3.00

No. 383. Women's kidskin button shoes, seam up front, plain common sense toes and heels, turn soles. 2.00

No. 384. Women's kidskin laced shoes, plain common sense toes and heels, turn soles, 1.75

No. 385. Women's dull dongola button, seam up front, plain toes, common sense heels, turn soles, 2.00

No. 386. Women's dull dongola laced, common sense heels, turn soles, 2.00

No. 387. Women's dull dongola Congress, plain toes, common sense heels, turn soles, 2.00

No. 388. Women's serge Congress, plain toes, common sense heels, turn soles, 2.00

No. 391. Women's dull dongola, laced buskin, plain broad toes, common sense heels, turn soles, 1.50

FIGURE 6.10: SELECTION OF TOE AND HEEL TYPES. THIS PAGE FROM WANAMAKER'S SPRING/SUMMER CATALOG OF 1901 ILLUSTRATES THE VARIOUS TOE AND HEEL STYLES OFFERED TO THE PUBLIC BY THE END OF THE CENTURY. NATIONAL SOCIETY OF THE COLONIAL DAMES IN THE COMMONWEALTH OF MASSACHUSETTS, BOSTON.

FIGURE 6.11A: RED CROSS SHOES, ADVERTISEMENT IN THE *LADIES' HOME JOURNAL*, APRIL 1908. THEY ARE PRESENTED HERE IN ORDER OF FOR-
MALITY, FROM THE DRESSY BLACK PUMP AT UPPER LEFT TO THE SPORTY TAN BROGUED WALKING SHOE AT LOWER RIGHT.

FIGURE 6.11B: HIGH-CUT BLACK LEATHER DERBY SHOES. CANADIAN. STAMPED ON SOLE "QUEEN ALEXANDRA SHOES," C. 1910. BATA SHOE MUSEUM, TORONTO, S81.0362.AB. REPRODUCED BY KIND PERMISSION OF BATA SHOE MUSEUM.

worn outdoors. Indoor shoes began in the morning with boudoir slippers, graduated to low shoes with fastenings for the afternoon, and ended in the evening with kid or satin slippers with covered wooden heels and rosettes. Outdoor boots were designed either for walking (plainer, with stacked heels and thicker soles) or for visiting and carriage wear (more elaborate, with covered wooden heels). To these standard categories, a woman would add riding boots, tennis shoes, overshoes and so on, as her lifestyle called for them.

There were variations in this practice over the decades. For example, in the 1860s, women quite frequently wore black or white silk side-lacing boots even with evening dresses. For much of the period, middle-class women wore walking boots for everyday wear, inside and out. Later in the century, some women began to wear low, tied shoes outdoors during the summer. In the first quarter of the twentieth century, boots were gradually replaced even in winter by tied or strapped shoes, and even, horror of horrors, by slippers (now called "pumps"), a development that appalled the writers of the 1916 *Shoe and Leather Lexicon*: "Women have shown a tendency in late years to wear on the street shoes suitable only for indoor use; that came about partly because women are much accustomed to follow fashions set by those who desire to drag boudoir suggestiveness through the streets, not only in shoes but in all their attire."[24]

Manufacturers encouraged women to conform to the expectations of etiquette in regard to their shoes. If different occasions required different kinds of shoes, then women would have to buy them ... or would they? In a 1923 article titled "Over-Styling and Over-Capacity", the *Shoe Retailer* reported that the average per capita shoe consumption had remained stable at three pairs per year for the last thirty years but that American shoe factories were over-producing by 50 percent to 250 percent.[25] The journal blamed the shoe stores for not selling enough footwear to correct this imbalance. "Satin slippers ... have been sold for street wear, when they were originally and properly intended only for dress footwear, thus cheating the merchant out of the second pair of shoes he ought to have sold ... Much of the trouble arising out of our multiplicity of styles arises from the fact that we have not taught our customers to buy shoes for the occasion."[26]

This "multiplicity of styles" was a huge problem for both manufacturers and retailers. When the century opened, there had been only two fashion seasons annually. By 1923 shoe manufacturers identified six, each requiring the publication of new styles. Each new shoe style required an investment in design, fabric, last and pattern, but few would ever recoup those costs. Manufacturers felt obliged to present as wide a selection of samples as their competitors did, even though no retailer could afford to stock more than a small fraction of them in a full range of sizes.

It was apparently the tooth and claw struggle for survival within the industry that really drove fashion change, rather than the new roles women were playing in the world at large. It is true that footwear with masculine characteristics was welcomed with growing approval in the decades after 1860. By 1899 women were buying shoes that looked very much like those worn by men (Figure 6.12). "Shoes made on a man's last, laced in front, with broad, projecting sole, and round, boxed toes, with low, flat heels, are worn exclusively for the street, both in tan and black."[27] One could argue that this reflects women's growing role in a masculine world. But if it did, should we also assume that their role diminished when such shoes went out of style again, as they did a few years later? Or was the whole cycle just one more expression of competition within the industry? The *Shoe Retailer* reports that the popularity of mannish shoes threatened the very livelihood of women's shoe manufacturers because they were being produced by manufacturers who had heretofore specialized in men's footwear. To save their business, the women's shoe manufacturers fought back, "introducing new styles, consisting principally of narrower toes than have been in vogue, higher arched insteps and higher heels, also lighter shoes: in short, everything that is diametrically opposite to the characteristics of the mannish shoe."[28] It seems to have worked. What had looked like a little women's liberation movement in 1900 faded before an onslaught of elaborate shoes with fancy straps and beading. Is it cause or effect that the women portrayed in popular women's magazines after 1910 seem far more frivolous and inconsequential than they had in the 1890s?

AFTER THE CURTAIN: LOOKING TOWARDS THE TWENTIETH CENTURY

Competition among manufacturers created plenty of alternatives for women to choose from, but that did not mean women could afford to buy them all. Well-to-do women might own exactly the right shoe to go with every dress, but most women made do with as few as two or three pairs. The woman who could afford only one pair for everyday and one for "best" – and who didn't have the strength of character to resist a fetching shoe – was very likely to be seen at some point on the street in satin shoes, shocking the fashion experts and reminding the historian of Mrs Trollope. Whether it was a matter of economics or of personal preference, it was inevitable that with so many styles to choose from, some people would defy the strictures of etiquette and wear what they liked. Thus fashion was eventually forced to become less monolithic in the twentieth century, as one group or another latched onto a style and wore it with the "wrong" clothes or on the "wrong" occasion.

The extent of choice available even to ordinary Americans by the end of the nineteenth century prepared the ground for a whole new way of generating fashion and expressing identity in the twentieth. Overabundant choice eventually dealt the deathblow to the idea that there was just one correct fashion to which everyone aspired. Even as early as 1900, the *Shoe Retailer* noted that the rubber-soled canvas shoes worn by fashionable folk for tennis or boating had become a uniform for young people: "Thousands of young people virtually 'live in them' all summer … A great many of the sales are to boys, who do all varieties of 'stunts' in them, from riding a wheel to playing ball."[29] These ball-playing boys, and their sisters who wore satin shoes on the street, together lay the foundation for a new attitude toward fashion and identity in the twentieth century, when each cultural tribe would adopt its own idiosyncratic style.[30] From satin slippers to Elvis's blue suede shoes, choice itself became the engine of change.

Two Extremes

The Womanish and the Mannish

The first of these is a patent calf and black velvet tie by B. COHEN & SONS, of New York. The high Louis heel and the finely stitched welt are of the very best workmanship.

The striking mannish Oxford shown opposite—the other extreme—is by E. W. BURT & Co., of Lynn.

FIGURE 6.12: "TWO EXTREMES: THE WOMANISH AND THE MANNISH," FROM *THE SHOE RETAILER*, MAY 22, 1901, P. 22. LYNN MUSEUM AND HISTORICAL SOCIETY, LYNN, MA. AT THE TURN OF THE CENTURY, THE VOGUE FOR MASCULINE FOOTWEAR CHALLENGED THE MANUFACTURERS SPECIALIZING IN WOMEN'S FOOTWEAR.

7.
PURITY, POLLUTION AND PLACE IN TRADITIONAL JAPANESE FOOTWEAR

martha chaiklin

"Statues of Buddha are made from the same wood as *geta*." This Japanese aphorism asserts that all things are fundamentally and intrinsically similar, as their philosophical meaning is based on a shared material form. The strength of the statement is further reinforced by the juxtaposition of a sacred artifact (the statue of Buddha) and a profane and mundane object (footwear). These are not random examples used in constructing a witty argument. The reference to the double meaning of "footwear" versus "Buddha" has deep worth in Japanese culture and its indigenous religion, as it contrasts, in an unexpected way, two fundamental Shinto concepts – purity (*seijō*) and pollution (*kegare*). The insertion of the everyday reference to footwear reminds us that "purity" and "pollution" are concepts that extend well beyond the ceremonial practices of religious life. They also enter as guiding concepts in the material culture of everyday life.

This chapter analyzes the relationship between moral and physical cleanliness and daily life in early modern Japan. It will consider the role of footwear through the lens of commerce, production, family, social structures and the built environment, from their early origins to the end of the Tokugawa period (1600–1868).

ORIGINS OF FOOTWEAR IN JAPAN

While scholarly opinion is divided as to the date of the first Japanese shoes, it appears that footwear only spread in Japan when contacts with the Asian continent increased, sometime in the fourth century. The oldest physical evidence of footwear is the high platform clog (*ta-geta*) used to walk in muddy rice fields, dating from the late Yayoi period (200 BC to AD 250), although these might be considered "equipment" rather than "apparel."[1] The catalyst for the spread of footwear appears to have been the arrival of Chinese and Korean peoples who wore slip-on shoes (*kutsu*) made of woven straw, cloth, fur or leather. These were adopted by the Japanese aristocracy but did not spread beyond this social group.

Funerary relics found in tombs from the Kofun (Tumulus period) (AD 250–552) include gilded bronze replicas of leather shoes with iron spikes of continental origin, which would seem to indicate that footwear was an important possession. In central Honshu, the site of imperial capitals, footwear was reserved for higher classes such as priests. At times, this sartorial distinction was enforced through sumptuary legislation. For example, an imperial edict from AD 718 established that only the aristocracy could wear *kutsu* while all other social classes were forced to wear straw sandals. In the colder climes of some remote provinces, peasants wore rough straw shoes (also called *kutsu*), especially after advances in harvesting technology, such as the use of scythes, made straw more easily obtainable. Leather, cloth and finely woven straw *kutsu* (the word still used to denote "shoe" today) generally remained restricted to the aristocracy, although there were some exceptions to this rule (Figure 7.1). For example, the military classes who were the political rulers from 1185 until 1868 sometimes wore leather boots (Figures 7.2 and 7.3).[2] Shinto priests wore lacquered wooden mules called *asa-gutsu*, which were derived from the shoes of the nobility. Some Buddhist monks wore a type of shoe known as *sōkai*, which could either be of finely woven plant material or composed of wooden soles and brocade uppers.

In addition to *kutsu*, two broad categories of footwear developed in premodern Japan: *geta* and *zōri*. Both are thonged, but *geta* are always made of wood, while *zōri* are woven from straw, bamboo bark, or other materials. *Geta*, although originally used in the field, are believed to have developed as apparel from religious ceremonies performed by the emperor, who as a descendant of the gods, upheld many ritual functions. The word "*zōri*" is thought to originate from Chinese, but the origin of the sandals themselves is less clear. These shoe types began to spread from the aristocracy to other social groups around the tenth century. Diffusion was a gradual process and it was not until the seventeenth century that footwear became common amongst most social strata.

FIGURE 7.1: HEIAN GENTLEMEN WITH CART. UKIYO-E PRINT, C.1750–1900. LIBRARY OF CONGRESS, PRINTS & PHOTOGRAPHS DIVISION, FP 2 – JPD, NO. 798.

In seventeenth-century Japan, the end of a long period of warfare, higher personal incomes and increasing urbanization facilitated the spread of footwear. In burgeoning and prosperous cities, it was considered shameful not to wear shoes, as only the meanest ranks of society had no footwear. However, it was not illegal to be barefoot in the city of Tokyo until 1901; grooms, day laborers and the like were often unshod.[3] Moreover, it was not really until the introduction of public education in the late nineteenth century that footwear was widely worn by children. Many variations on basic *zōri* and *geta* forms developed, including somewhat outrageous extravagances such as *geta* with foot-warming charcoal pans in the sole (Figure 7.4).[4] Footgear differed according to region, class or merely fashion, of which only a few variations can be discussed here, but the preference for a basic, thonged form remained consistent and intact for centuries.

NEVER IN THE HOUSE

Although many factors shape material culture, the nature of Japanese domestic architecture can be cited as one of the main forces as to why thonged footwear remained popular in early modern Japan. A traditional Japanese house "without … uncommon neatness … would not be tolerable to live in."[5] In prehistoric times, people probably went barefoot and lived in pit dwellings. Later, most Japanese lived in elevated wooden houses, an architectural structure that was probably borrowed from Southeast Asia.[6] The spread of raised construction was also facilitated by the concept of purity, as the idea of being lifted from the ground, which was both home to the gods and the source of uncleanliness, was a necessary condition for civilized living.

The concepts of purity and pollution provided two major dichotomies in the abstract wider spaces in which personal, collective and social life took place. Historical examples of how "pollution" was seen to affect the built environment are common in premodern Japan. The belief that death caused pollution meant that, until the construction of more ostentatious Chinese-influenced cities in the eighth century AD, the capital city had to be vacated every time an emperor died. Similarly, especially in rural areas, detached huts were built to accommodate women giving birth, an act that was considered to be highly "polluting." Although such extreme manifestations are no longer part of Japanese religious and secular life today, purification rites are generally performed by Shinto clerics at building sites of all kinds before construction begins. Shrine buildings are only constructed by carpenters who have been ritually purified and whose tools have been blessed.[7]

These examples provide assistance in understanding the relationship between the domestic space and footwear in early modern Japan. Although woven straw or reed flooring mats (*tatami*) did not really come into use until the mid-fourteenth century, outdoor footwear was never worn indoors, even when the floor was made of earth. Nearly all types of footwear were designed to be easily removed upon entering the house (Figure 7.5). The process of removing shoes is in part explained by Günter Nitschke's suggestion that "since Japanese 'places' tend to be very close to each other, they are made to feel larger by reducing the pace and speed by which one can pass between them."[8]

FIGURE 7.2: MAN WEARING BOOTS. UKIYO-E PAINTING, C.1750–1900. LIBRARY OF CONGRESS, PRINTS & PHOTOGRAPHS DIVISION, FP 2 – JPD, NO. 882.

FIGURE 7.3: DIPTYCH (UTAGAWA TOYOKUNI); WARRIORS WITH FURRY TSURANUKI. LIBRARY OF CONGRESS, PRINTS & PHOTOGRAPHS DIVISION, FP 2 – JPD, NO. 638 A, B.

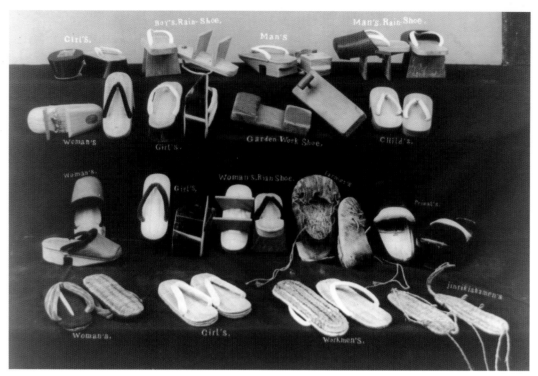

As footwear became increasingly common in the early modern period, many houses were provided with a little vestibule (*genkan*) outside, where shoes were removed, or where deliverymen, peddlers and messengers could stand without removing their shoes. Those inside remained elevated and shoeless. This area had originally appeared in Zen temples as a transition between the outside and the contemplative interior. When it became a part of domestic architecture in the fifteenth century, the deployment of this space was only permitted to people of high rank. While sumptuary laws theoretically prohibited it to commoners, for those who did not flout them, a hard floor space separated from the matted areas was widely incorporated into domestic architecture.

With footwear becoming more widespread, houses were adapted to accommodate it, in order to keep the entranceway clear. Shoes were not simply left in the vestibule, but had to be stored in cupboards (*geta-bako*) especially designed for accommodating footwear. The commonplaceness of these cabinets is demonstrated by a comic poem written in 1798: "Anyone could guess *koma-geta* [shoes] coming from a chest."[9] The humor stems from the parody of a common expression, "A horse [*koma*] from a gourd," meaning something unexpected.[10] The original saying was based on the story of Daoist Immortal Chokaro (Chang-kuo-lao), who could produce out of a gourd a magic horse that would travel great distances in a single day. *Koma-geta,* the most widely worn style of footwear, are formed from a single piece of wood, which supposedly resembled a horse's hoof. Originally designed for muddy streets, they gained wider use, and as a result, a large variety of shapes (Figures 7.6 and 7.7).[11]

FIGURE 7.5: SUZUKOI HARUNOBU. MAN AND WOMAN. UKIYO-E PRINT, C.1750–1900. LIBRARY OF CONGRESS, PRINTS & PHOTOGRAPHS DIVISION, FP 2 – JPD, NO. 1616 (B SIZE).

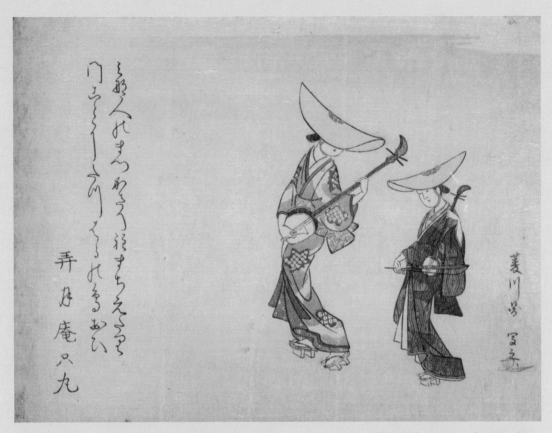

FIGURE 7.6: HISKAWA SHOOL, ITINERANT MUSICIANS, WEARING KOMA-GETA. UKIYO-E PRINT, C.1750–1900. LIBRARY OF CONGRESS, PRINTS & PHOTOGRAPHS DIVISION, FP 2 – JPD, NO. 1338 (AA SIZE).

Footwear was also removed in most public places and it was not allowed in certain interior portions of Shinto shrines and Buddhist temples. Theaters had a shoe check, for which a wooden tag was given in receipt. In brothels, where shoes were also removed, a bundle of these wooden tags would be struck against the floor in front of the house shrine to attract customers.[12] The fact that footwear was removed in many public situations provided only limited opportunities to show it off and this might be one reason why footwear in Japan remained relatively simple.

Geta were usually worn over the bare foot, but the more formal *zōri* were often worn with a split-toed sock called *tabi*. When they appeared in the tenth century, *tabi* were made from tanned leather, often dyed purple or yellow, or sometimes left untanned with the fur still on for additional protection from the cold. Originally worn by the aristocracy under *kutsu* (a shoe that encases the foot), the split-toed sock did not appear until around the thirteenth century, when the warrior class started using them with straw sandals (*waraji*).[13] As footwear became more widely used in early modern Japan, so *tabi* gained in popularity, a process that was surely facilitated by the introduction of *tatami* flooring. *Tabi* kept the bare foot off the floor, keeping the mats clean and in good order.

Cotton, which had only been introduced early in the fifteenth century, made *tabi* not only cheaper but also more hygienic than leather. When members of the warrior class visited the shogun's castle, they would sometimes wear leather *tabi* over cotton *tabi*, removing the leather ones when inside. Although cotton *tabi* could be washed, the uppermost social strata wore a new pair daily. The used ones were handed down to social inferiors.[14] For those who had to wash them, one nineteenth-century source suggests that those with exceptionally "oily" feet put dried loofah, obtainable from "drugstores or sword guard and bamboo craftsmen," in the sole.[15] The concept of purity made white *tabi* usual for formal wear, although there were fashions for specific colors or materials. For example, silk *tabi* were stylish in the mid-1680s; yellowish-brown was the rage in the 1770s.

Simple hygiene was not the only way in which purity, pollution and footwear related to architecture. Habitation requires access to fresh water. In early modern Japan, water was not merely seen as a source of sustenance or as a cleanser: it carried powers of ritual purification. This is the reason why there is always a place for visitors to wash their hands and rinse their mouths at the entrance of Shinto shrines. Evidence of such a relationship can also be found in domestic water supplies. In folk Shinto traditions, it was believed that the god of the well was related to the toilet god and the god of the kitchen through the need for water. Excavations of wells in sites dating from the eighth through to the nineteenth century, along the length of Honshu, the main island in Japan, to the island of Kyushu in the south, have uncovered *geta*. These *geta* were buried at the time of construction because they were believed to have talismanic protective properties.[16]

The symbolism assumed by *geta* had important consequences for the way they changed over time. Although originally developed for wearing in muddy fields, *geta* came to be worn ceremonially, first by the emperor, and later by priests and other dignitaries, in order to prevent

FIGURE 7.7: BLACK LACQUERED POKKURI GETA DECORATED WITH CRANES. BATA SHOE MUSEUM, TORONTO, P87.2. COURTESY OF BATA SHOE MUSEUM.

FIGURE 7.8: KASTUSHIKA HOKUSAI. HOKUSAI
MANGA, VOL.12 (1814), 17.

pollution of holy places by allowing the foot contact with sacred ground.[17] Similar practices were extended to the toilet, which was believed to connect to the gods of the underworld. By the fourteenth century, a separate pair of *geta* was supplied in residential outhouses, a practice continued even today with a special pair of slippers in the toilet. Superstitious beliefs were attached to these geta. For example, it was believed that a toilet *geta*, rubbed gently against the chest of a sleeping person, would cause him to talk in his sleep, revealing all his secrets.[18]

PURITY, POLLUTION AND SOCIAL STATUS

Early modern Japan had a social structure based on modified Confucian ideas, in which the warrior class was at the top, followed by the farmer, the artisan, and the merchant at the base. These class distinctions were enforced through regulations about dress, perhaps the most widely known being the privilege of the warrior class to wear two swords. Footwear was as much an indicator of social class as clothing, and challenges to that order were frowned upon. For example, in the late tenth century, a court noblewoman, Sei Shōnagon (c. 965–1017), in an early Japanese prose piece called *The Pillow Book*, complained in a paragraph entitled "Things that are Unpleasant to See" about "boys who wear high clogs with their *hakama*."[19] She wrote: "This is the modern fashion, but I still don't like it."[20] Her disdain stemmed from the combination of the formal *hakama* with the rough and rustic character of the youths' footwear, which called to mind the tall *ta-geta* used to walk in marshy rice fields. Expectations evolved around footwear in social situations, as João Rodrigues, a Jesuit priest who lived in Japan from 1577 to 1610 noted:

> The Japanese observe certain courtesies regarding their footwear, that is, their sandals and clogs. A man wearing clogs may not greet or pass in front of another man wearing sandals, if he is an honorable person or an equal, if a man wearing clogs is of lowly stock, he takes them off and stands with his feet on the ground while the other person passes, or else he passes with his bare feet. When an honorable person passes on the road a man who is seated, he will greet him by making the gesture of removing his sandals; the seated person, however will dismount and then, after walking past a little way, will remount. If the person passing is of lowly rank, he takes off his sandals and silently passes barefoot, bowing a little as he passes in front as a sign of respect. Thus some have mistakenly written that the Japanese take off their sandals among themselves as a sign of respect just as we take off our hats. But there is no such custom among the gentry. Also when a lowly person or servant is speaking with a noble who is standing, he takes off his sandals, or he pushes them halfway off his feet, while he is speaking or delivering a message.[21]

Another Westerner, the Dutch East India Company's director, François Caron, noted the peculiar practices necessary to adopt when visiting the shogun:

> But no Man whatsoever is suffered to enter the third ring of the Castle, where the Emperor's Palace is, but on foot, and only accompanied with two Servants, and a Boy to carry his Shoes; they of the second rank are allowed but one Servant and a Shoe-carrier; and those of the last rank only a Shoe-carrier.[22]

The "shoe-carrier" was allowed because it would have been beneath the dignity of anyone of this rank to handle footwear, which had to be taken on and off (Figure 7.8). Rodrigues further explains this point:

> It is the general custom throughout the kingdom for any person of quality, from the highest ranking to the lowest, to be accompanied by a lad who takes his sandals at the entrance of the rooms in houses. The boy also carries clogs in case of mud and an umbrella against the sun or rain. He gives his master the sandals on his coming out of the house or room when he has to tread on the ground. If the owner of the house or room comes out to meet his guest in one of the courtyards or sometimes in the street, he too is accompanied by a lad with the same duty of seeing the sandals. This is a very base office, and the pages who are honorable and have the rank of squire will on no account ever take or present the sandals to the lord with their own hands, even if he is waiting for the lad to come. For each of the pages has his own shoe-boy to serve him when he enters the room in the company of his lord or with a message.[23]

The job was base because footwear was strongly associated with impurity. Another of the Dutch East India Company's employees, Hendrik Doeff (1777–1835), even claimed that the Dutch covered their feet with cloaks while waiting to be led into the throne room, because "it was extremely rude to show them."[24]

Efforts were made to enforce class differences through sumptuary laws. In 1750, for example, lacquered *geta* were prohibited for both men and women of the merchant class, as were "three-layer" (*sanmai gasane*) *zōri*, which had soles made from separate layers of bamboo bark, straw and leather.[25] This was just as true in rural environments, where in 1725, tenant farmers were prohibited from wearing *zōri* because they were seen as a luxury.[26] While Japanese footwear was relatively simple in form, excess could be expressed by using imported leathers and textiles, for which blanket restrictions against any use by townsmen and peasants were sometimes issued. These laws were not just aimed at the consumer. In 1721, a series of sumptuary laws were enacted as part of general fiscal reform prohibiting craftsmen from producing a long list of luxury items including several types of footwear. In addition, leatherworkers, *geta*-makers, *setta*-makers (*setta* were a type of *zōri*), and leather *tabi*-makers were ordered to form guilds in order to ensure that the shogunate's orders were followed.[27]

POLLUTION, PRODUCTION AND FOOTWEAR

Those who existed outside the Confucian social order were also subject to footwear restrictions. Craftsmen who produced footwear were part of an outcaste class (Figure 7.9). Their low status was the result of the combination between ideals about pollution caused by illness and death and the Buddhist ideas of the sanctity of life, adopted in Japan from the sixth century. Leather, the very material of footwear, was the result of the death of animals such as cows, wild boar, deer and even monkeys.[28] G. F. Meijlan, a Dutch merchant resident in Nagasaki in the late 1820s, commented that in the Japanese social hierarchy "the absolute lowest of all the craftsman was the leather tanner." He added, "These unfortunate men who practice this profession, in the fullest sense of the words, are cast out of society. They always live in an isolated and remote street, and everyone who is not of their profession despises them, avoiding as much familiarity as possible."[29] By the early nineteenth century, the decline in demand for leather goods caused by the unfashionableness of Edo-period armor (1600–1868) led to economic hardship for the previously prosperous leather-workers, exacerbating their lowly status even more.[30]

The base reputation of shoes and shoemaking did not prevent the flowering of extensive commerce in footwear in early modern Japan. Most leather footwear was produced in urban areas, because of the presence of armor craftsmen in what had originally been feudal castles, and because of the density of the consumer market.[31] In Osaka, the commercial capital of early modern Japan, the southern boundary of the city, the place where outcastes lived, was also the locus of trade in hides for the entire country. The city manufactured large quantities of footwear, which were exported all over the country. In 1714, for example, nearly 60,000 pairs of leather *tabi* were shipped from the port of Osaka to other provinces of Japan.[32]

Not all footwear was made from leather, but the idea of uncleanliness was extended to encompass the entire category. Monopolies with strict, guild-like practices resulted in the designation of all shoemakers as an outcaste class.[33] Even within this outsider world, however, there was space for differences and gradations, mainly related to the specialization of individual shoemakers. A sixteenth-century scroll of poems about craftsmen, for instance, contains an illustration of a producer of *geta* accompanied by an untranslatable pun about how the set of his eyes showed his discomfort. This craftsman is depicted with all the indicators of what the Japanese consider coarse and crude: his eyebrows are thick, as is his beard. He is barefoot, and his kimono is stripped down to his waist. In contrast, the maker of *kutsu*, who served a higher-class clientele, although still stripped to the waist, is depicted as a more refined character.[34] At the very bottom of this "polluted" underworld was the maker of thongs (*hana-o*), the most despised of all shoemakers, even though his products were not necessarily made of leather.[35] Thongs were originally a simple piece of cord, but by the early modern period they were more often sewn in leather or other textiles such as cotton, silk or velvet. The status of these craftsmen was as low as the cobbler who resoled *zori,* inserted new teeth into *geta* or replaced broken thongs, which may have been one reason why by the 1680s many women manufactured *hana-o.*

As social hierarchy could be demonstrated through footwear, so the people living at its lowest boundaries were the subject of precise regulations. Although the specifics of these regulations varied from place to place, in some areas outcastes were only allowed to wear straw sandals, while elsewhere *setta* (a type of *zōri* made of bamboo bark with leather soles, which developed around the end of the sixteenth century) came to be closely associated with, but not exclusive to, outcastes. According to one source, *setta* were originally worn by prisoners, with iron instead of leather soles.[36] *Setta* were regarded as coarse and vulgar, a casual shoe at best.[37] Even as late as the 1960s, in the Kyoto area the wearing of *setta* was seen as an easily identifiable practice of members of this outcaste class.[38] The symbolism of *setta* allowed the word to take on a new meaning in thieves' slang, as "a payoff," while "*setta* leather" is slang for "beef."

Figure 7.9 (left): Making clogs. Kindly reproduced from John L. Stoddard's Lectures v. 3 Chicago & Boston: Geo. L. Shuman & Co., 207.

Figure 7.10 (right): The ubiquitous shoe store. Kindly reproduced from Alfred M. Hitchcock, *Over Japan Way*, New York (1917), 244–5.

Low status or not, footwear was a necessary item and those who were savvy merchants made a good living at it, such as one who held a shogunal warrant to supply boots to the castle. In early nineteenth-century Osaka, a group of twenty-two *tabi* merchants banded together to set prices throughout a distribution network that reached as far as Edo. They called themselves the Kobai (red plum blossom) Group.[39] A survey of 1813 showed thirty members of this group as well as ten *zōri* wholesalers in Edo alone.[40] A guidebook to Edo of the same period also lists fourteen thong wholesalers, forty-eight tabi wholesalers not from Osaka, nine *zōri* wholesalers and twenty-seven *setta* wholesalers.[41] With so much money at stake, even the warrior class became involved in footwear sales, if only indirectly. For example, in the early nineteenth century the regional clan government of Hiroshima was deeply involved in regulating the supply of wood for *geta* production and sales. To ensure that the product was not sent elsewhere and to lock in revenue, in 1813 forty-eight *geta* craftsman from surrounding villages were formed into a cooperative that was compelled to supply the castle town of Hiroshima.[42]

Footwear was sold in shops and on roadside stands (Figure 7.10).[43] While the consumer was not polluted by unclean craftsmen or materials, there were nonetheless customs that linked consumption of footwear and purification, such as those associated with the coming of the New Year. Bills were paid off, the house was cleaned and business brought to a conclusion. The seventeenth-century realist novelist, Ihara Saikaku, writes about how footwear was central to these customs:

> As for *tabi* and *geta*, the artisans of Edo habitually wait to purchase them all just before the New Year begins to dawn. But one year it happened that not even a single sock or a solitary shoe was to be found for sale in all of Edo. As might have been anticipated, in the greatest city of Japan the demand was for thousands of pairs. Whereas in the early evening the price of a pair of *geta* was only seven or eight *bu*, after midnight it rose to one *momme* and two or three *bu*, and by dawn it had soared to two and a half *momme*. Even at this price, although there would have been buyers, there were no sellers.[44]

PURITY, POLLUTION AND THE BODY

In early modern Japan the creation of physical, but also sexual and familial identity, was negotiated through footwear. Many shoe parts are described with terms that derive from the body: the thong, for example, is the "nose cord" (*hana-o*); the wooden piers upon which *geta* stand are "teeth" (*ha*); the portion of the base that sticks out beyond the teeth, the "chin" (*ago*); the loops through which straw sandals are laced are called "eyes" (*me*) or "nipples" (*chi*). Accordingly, footwear was seen as an extension of the wearer. The saying "to have someone's *geta* taken care of" was thus used to mean "to leave matters up to someone else"; charms over *geta* were used to call lovers, while an unwanted guest was chased away by burning moxa in his shoes.

Footwear was unclean both from its contact with the ground, and with the feet. Therefore, leaving the feet exposed was an expression of intimacy. Feet, symbolic of the genitals, had a definite erotic focus.[45] In art, curled toes indicated arousal, and the feet of women who were not prostitutes or of low social status were rarely shown. Imagery for men was quite different: barefoot men were often meant to represent marital estrangement, and piles of shoes meant the probable infidelity of one's husband.[46]

The practice of sex was believed to be the cause of temporary uncleanliness, thus generating a wide and colorful tradition governing the behavior of sexual encounters. For example, in some regions a special hut was constructed in order to consummate marriage, dismantled after the "impure" act took place.[47] Common prostitutes either wore no *tabi* at all, or characterized themselves by wearing footwear in very peculiar colors or materials. In Edo (now Tokyo), they were forbidden to wear *tabi* once they had graduated from serving as attendants to being independent prostitutes. The bare foot was a symbol of sexual readiness and this was clearly the intention in forcing courtesans to expose their feet. In pornographic woodblock prints (*shunga*), the participants are shown – only with rare exceptions and regardless of class – without shoes or *tabi*, even though they are often swathed in layers of clothing. For licensed prostitutes, additional measures were taken to enhance the effect, including whitening the foot with rice powder and rouging the toenails.[48] Indoors, unable to wear *tabi* even in the cold winter months, the courtesans used cloth slippers for walking along unheated passageways.[49]

Courtesans wore *geta* (Figure 7.11), a practice that may have descended from *miko*, female shrine attendants with oracular powers who in ancient times offered more than predictions of the future. As prostitution became more regulated and footwear became increasingly common, the shoes of the courtesans were likewise regulated according to rank, from the simple attendant to the owner of the brothel. From the eighteenth century, courtesans in licensed bordellos were required to wear lacquered *geta*, a style that quickly spread to other classes (Figure 7.12). What really made their *geta* distinctive, however, was their height, which could range from six to nine-and-a-half inches, and were composed of as many as twenty-five layers, rather like the chopines popularized in fifteenth-century Venice.[50] For stability, these tall *geta* sometimes had three "teeth"[51] instead of the usual two and were initially only worn by the highest-ranking courtesans as a status symbol. It required a great deal of practice to walk gracefully in them, and as added enticement, custom demanded that a courtesan who tripped in front of a tea house would have to enter and entertain at her own expense. No one of any position who worked in a brothel was allowed to wear *zōri*.[52]

RICE, STRAW, BINDING AND TRAVEL

Until the twentieth century, Japan was primarily an agrarian nation. Rice was the staple food from the time it was introduced in the Yayoi period (300 BC to AD 300) and during the Edo period was the basis of the economy. Rice, and rice by-products such as sake and straw, therefore took on spiritual significance. Ropes woven from dried rice stalks, strengthened by the weaving together of multiple strands, were used to contain or pacify evil spirits. Straw sandals (*waraji*), the product of both rice straw and binding, came to have religious significance. They were associated with walking on sacred mountains and other holy ground and therefore associated with pilgrimage.

Each shrine in Japan has its own festival and *waraji* were essential for anyone involved in festival rituals. In some instances, *waraji* became the focus of the festival itself. In Mie-Prefecture, for example, the legend of the *waraji* festival is that it began when a giant was disturbing the sea. The villagers showed the giant a huge mat, telling him it was the sandal of the village headman, which frightened him off. Two days before the *waraji* festival, thirty men gather and weave a sandal, which

FIGURE 7.11: ISODA KORYUSAI. THE COURTESAN TAGASODE OF THE DAIMONJIYA. FROM THE SERIES *HINAGATA WAKANA NO HATSU MOYŌ* C.1776–84. ORIGINALLY COMMISSIONED TO SHOW OFF KIMONO PATTERNS, THE HIGH-RANKING COURTESAN IS WEARING GETA WITH THREE TEETH, WHILE THE ATTENDANTS WEAR KOMA-GETA. LIBRARY OF CONGRESS, PRINTS & PHOTOGRAPHS DIVISION, FP 2 – JPD, NO. 130 OIRAN PROCESSION.

Figure 7.12: Black lacquered wooden geta with painted toe covers, early twentieth century. Bata Shoe Museum, Toronto, P84.159. Courtesy of Bata Shoe Museum.

is then dragged to the beach and floated to a nearby island with offerings of rice on it. The ceremonies of the *waraji* festival in Daio-cho machi are conducted to bring good harvests, good catches and safety at sea. In Fukushima, giant straw sandals are carried through the streets to a shrine, purportedly to pray for strong legs.

Straw sandals are so strongly associated with walking and travel that the expression "to put on or remove one's *waraji*" meant "the beginning or end of a trip". It is probably for this reason that straw sandals are part of the dress of the mystical ascetics known as *yamabushi*. The eight points (instead of the usual four) at which the ties meet the sandal sole are said to represent the eight-petaled lotus upon which Buddha is seated. Peace and prosperity under the Tokugawa shogunate brought increased travel for both business and leisure, and often the two were combined in religious pilgrimages. Although the very rich were carried in palanquins or on horseback, most people walked when they traveled, wearing the flexible straw sandals that were easier to walk in over unpaved roads (Figure 7.13).

Straw sandals were, nonetheless, very hard on the feet. In *Hagakure*, a classic of samurai literature, the author tells of how his father was toughened up by being forced to wear the sandals of a warrior from the age of seven.[53] The very first page in *Shank's Mare*, an early nineteenth-century comic novel about travel along the Tokaidō, one of the main highways, describes two travelers leaving home "with their light footgear and their many shells of ointment, which will keep their feet from getting sore for thousands of miles."[54] Similarly, a travel guide from 1810 warns travelers to take the first day slowly so they can break in their *waraji*. The same source also warns that blisters will result if *waraji* of poor quality are purchased, or if they are not softened up before the trip.[55] Travel journals contain numerous references to foot pain, and cures for it. Indigo-dyed *tabi*, often made from worn-out formal *tabi*, were usually worn underneath to help prevent blisters.[56] Pilgrims sometimes wore white *tabi* despite the difficulty of keeping them clean, because this color was associated with purity.

Shrines situated along the roads served the needs of both travelers and nearby villages, which received protection against bad spirits who might enter. Offerings of iron *waraji* were often made at these shrines, because the combination of binding and rice straw was believed to have protective properties. Spirits were also believed to travel, so large *waraji* were often hung at the borders of villages to deflect evil spirits and prevent infectious diseases from entering. *Waraji* were generally a secondary industry for farming families, especially, but not exclusively, in outcaste communities along heavily traveled roads. Because they did not require exotic materials or special skills, they could be made by anyone. In *Shank's Mare*, the wag Yaji teases a samurai who has worn one pair of sandals throughout a journey. The samurai explains that he has made them carefully himself, which is why they have lasted so long.[57]

Travelers often rested at roadside shrines, so naturally rest houses appeared around the more significant of them, which sold replacement sandals and parts in addition to refreshments.[58] *Waraji* wore out regularly, and "one continually sees a great number of worn-out shoes lying on the roads, especially near the brooks, where travellers have changed their shoes after washing their feet."[59] Supplemented by the straw sandals used in place of shoes on packhorses and draft oxen, these piles would eventually break down and decompose, to be carted away as fertilizer. As such a fundamental expression of both daily and spiritual life, it was perhaps inevitable that superstition would develop around *waraji*: for example, if the string broke at the front, misfortune would fall on enemies; if at the back, the wearer would undergo some calamity.[60] There were even beliefs about their manufacture: it was thought that if it thundered while you were making *waraji*, you should throw them away and start again.

TRADITIONAL FOOTWEAR AND THE MODERN WORLD

Cultural preferences for footwear in traditional Japan stemmed from deeply held views about the world, rather than being based merely on protection or changes in fashion. Indeed, open shoes were far from ideal winter garb in most of Japan. Footwear was an expression of self, and many traditions and ideas surrounded it. For example, if you wore a *geta* on one foot and a *zōri* on the other, your parents would die. Or if you spat in your *zōri* and called the spirits of the dead, they would come. Those who wore out their footwear at the front would be wealthier than their parents, and those who wore them out at the back would be poorer (but also unfilial). It was very bad luck to break a thong. Every child knew that one could predict the weather by kicking off a *geta*. If it landed the right way up, it would be sunny; if face down, it would rain. All of these customs show the link between footwear and the spiritual world.

In 1868, the quasi-feudal reign of the shogun ended and a new oligarchy took power with the emperor at its head. Increased contact with the West resulted in government-led initiatives of Westernization, which included the requirement for government officials and teachers to wear Western clothes. While many aspects of the Western world, such as railways, the telegraph, and architecture were adopted wholesale, this was not true for footwear. Rising standards of living actually increased the demand for traditional footwear rather than reducing it. Although *geta*, *zōri* and other traditional footwear are rarely worn today outside ceremonial occasions, Shinto concepts of purity and pollution are to be found in cultural practices such as the use of toilet slippers and *waraji* festivals, and in a plethora of colloquial expressions. They show that traditional ideas about footwear and modern practices do not conflict (or, in Japanese, "*geta* and spirits") but are emblematic of cultural stability, and the belief that the very nature of things cannot be changed. This very concept of permanence is itself explained by the Japanese through the language of footwear: "Even if the shoes are new, they aren't a crown." The study of Japanese footwear underlines a superficial reading of shoes as inferring and conferring protection, ornament and occasionally talismanic charm, to be very partial indeed.

FIGURE 7.13 (FACING PAGE): ANDO HIROSHIGE, YOTSUYA, THE NEW STATION AT NAITO, 1857. LIBRARY OF CONGRESS, PRINTS & PHOTOGRAPHS DIVISION, DONALD D. WALKER COLLECTION, FP 2 – JPD, NO. 1517 (C SIZE).

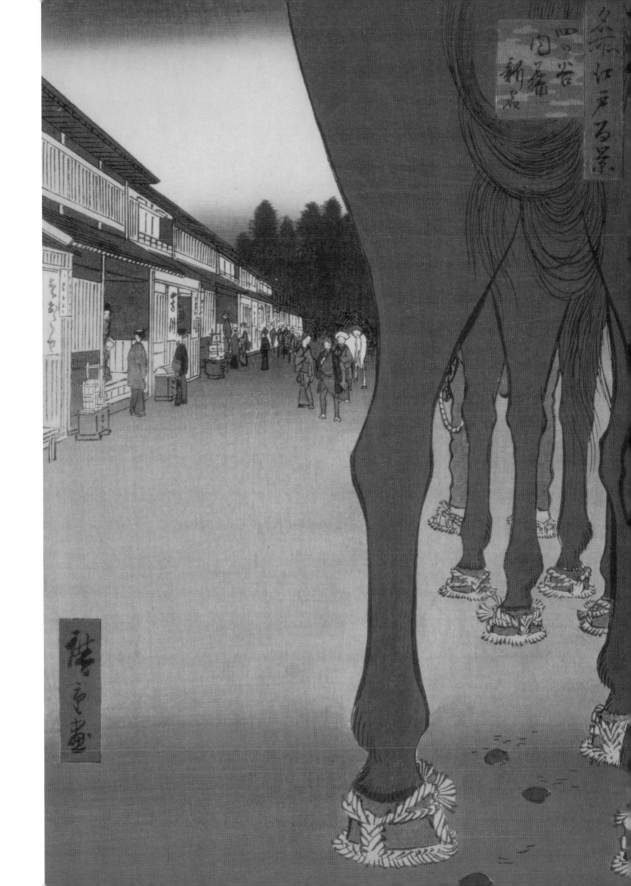

8.

INTERROGATING AFRICA'S PAST

FOOTWEAR AMONG THE YORUBA

tunde m. akinwumi

African history is notoriously difficult to investigate. The scarce premodern indigenous sources are not sufficient to recover the continent's complex past. Historians of Africa have to rely on external views as much as on archeological and written sources. In order to interrogate the role of footwear in the Yoruba country – the southwest area of present-day Nigeria (Figures 8.1a and b) – it is necessary to draw upon Arab accounts dating from the eighth century onward, the works of Europeans since the fifteenth century, and the later narratives by nineteenth-century educated African elites. Nineteenth-century European and American travelogues provide one of the most revealing sources for Yoruba clothing, including footwear. William Clarke, an American Baptist missionary, Alvan Millson, a British colonial official, and other travelers such as Richard Burton, Richard Lander and Daniel May engaged in descriptions of the customs and peculiarities seen while traveling in Africa, keenly capturing the dressing style of the local populations, including the footwear worn by the Yoruba.[1] Contrary to what we might expect, visitors were generally surprised by the high standard of dress of the locals. Similarly, Osifakorede, a Yoruba slave serving in Paris, painted a pleasant dress scenario including the widespread use of footwear in the late eighteenth and early nineteenth centuries.[2]

These accounts provide just a small sample of a type of "testimony" that is useful, but not totally satisfactory, for the historian. They convey an immediacy of observation but do not explain social and cultural phenomena. While providing precious information about use and consumption, they do not reveal insights into production, selection and cultural meaning. This chapter will examine the footwear tradition among the Yoruba from the earliest times to the beginning of the twentieth century by foregrounding the sociopolitical and economic factors that impinged on it. These include the influence of trans-Saharan and trans-Atlantic trade, the importance of ecosystems, the limitations imposed by sumptuary laws, and the subsequent intervention of warlords and the nineteenth-century Yoruba educated elite as they moved toward the establishment of a free society. Particular attention is given to the factors that affected the use of footwear among the various social strata of the Yoruba society over time. Such an ambitious study cannot rest on scattered written sources, but relies on archeological, oral and eyewitness evidence. Hitherto, studies of Yoruba dress history covering the period before the twentieth century have neglected the importance of footwear.[3] This chapter aims to contextualize ideas about footwear and place it within the social and cultural literature concerning African dress.

THE MATERIAL CULTURE OF ABSENCE

European fashion history has shown how the continuous change in dress – its constant and fluctuating redefinition over time and negotiation among classes – thrives in societies characterized by increasing urbanization. Towns and cities are the focal points of change in dress and the catalyst of social and cultural transformation. The Yoruba formed not only one of the largest "civilizations" of tropical Africa, but – in contrast to most of the Continent – presented a high degree of urbanization.[4] European travelers recorded the presence of substantial urban centers in the area of present-day Nigeria as early as the sixteenth century.[5] Such urban centers acted as motors of cultural development and formed the structure of states and empires ruled by local kings and emperors. Notwithstanding such a political fragmentation, Yorubaland was a cohesive entity, well known not only for its riches, but also for its artistic production, ranging from exquisite royal beaded crowns to gowns and footwear.

The social structure of the Yoruba people was related to land, as the economy depended on agriculture. Every member of a household depended on men, slaves and other members for the cultivation of food crops. Agriculture was producing crops beyond subsistence levels and this allowed the flowering of several crafts. Occupations such as carving, weaving, smithing, pottery-making and drumming were performed by an artisan class solely occupied in such trades and in which sons succeeded fathers. Their wares were paid in kind (foodstuff) or by means of cowrie

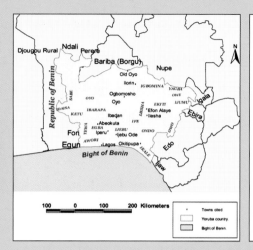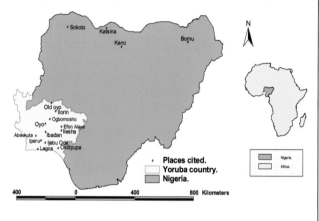

FIGURE 8.1A (LEFT): MAP OF NIGERIA AND THE YORUBA COUNTRY.

FIGURE 8.1B (RIGHT): MAP OF THE YORUBA COUNTRY.

shells. The manufacturing economy was not limited to the production of basic artifacts, but included the making of luxury goods for local rulers and for the monarch (*oba*). This was also a market economy in which, next to copious numbers of petty traders, large merchants sold conspicuous goods such as cloth and engaged in the profitable trade in slaves and palm oil. Trade was encouraged by the *oba,* as it was the source of fiscal returns for the Crown.

The economic prosperity of Yorubaland was as important as its social structure in informing notions of "appropriateness" of dress. The Yoruba articulated the social structure of their kingdom according to a pyramidal notion of power, at the pinnacle of which was the *oba*. He was followed by the court and palace "mandarins" who ranked themselves over the wealthy professional urban elites. At the bottom of the social scale were the urban populace and poor peasants who shared their lowly status with "strangers" – the non-Yoruba. Dress was not only determined by class. All ranks of society were supposed to follow familiar rules of decorum, thus showing choice in dress even for the lowest strata of society. Dress was also established by the prescriptive rules of age, gender, clan, religious affiliation and occupation (hunters, warrior, diviners, etc.), each of which was characterized by specific dress codes.[6] In the midst of rigid dress codes, individual expression was possible to a certain degree, in particular within specific social groups.

One of the earliest representations of *obas'* dress is the Ife classical bronze-work showing an *ooni* (*oba*) of Ile-Ife and his queen, dating from between the twelfth and fifteenth centuries (Figure 8.2). The royal couple are represented in full regalia consisting of beads of various sizes, namely a beaded crown, necklaces, wristlets and anklets. The queen wears a cloth draping from above the bosom to the ankle, while the king wears a waist dress. They are also represented as wearing narrow sashes that cross over the shoulder and end either at the side or at the lap. Most notice-ably, their feet are unshod.[7] Nevertheless, the dress of the *oba* was surely the most lavish and ostentatious, as no other subject was allowed equal the standing of the king. The *oba*'s dress, in this sense, was the personification of his town's prosperity.

The absence of footwear represented the condition of the entire population of Yorubaland before the fifteenth century. It was only with the beginning of the trans-Saharan and trans-Atlantic trade that footwear first appeared in the region. A tradition of "shoelessness" persisted among the Yoruba well after the encounter with Westerners and the spreading of footwear. Tradition defied cultural invasion, as the concept of the "dressing of the foot" remained linked to a wider mental category than its immediate protection through a material artifact. In Yorubaland, one way of "dressing" the foot was to stain the sole of the foot with cam-wood lotion (*osun*). It was compulsory for each groom to paint his feet red with cam-wood lotion, a product that Burton observed on many market stalls in 1861.[8] Foot-painting was meant to distinguish the groom from the crowd on his wedding day.[9] The women painted their feet for fashion, a practice that was particularly widespread during social events. Adéoyè suggests that before the twentieth century, the painting of feet was widely used by the Yoruba as a way to create social bonding, as in the collective worship of deities.[10] As for royalty, Lander observed Alaafin of Oyo being gorgeously dressed in 1830 and noted that: "His legs as far as the knees, were stained with hennah [*osun*]."[11] All these observations reveal that a very large number of Yoruba painted their feet for social inter-actions, before the twentieth century.

THE TRANS-SAHARAN AND TRANS-ATLANTIC TRADE

The introduction of camels as a means of transportation for Trans-Saharan trade enhanced regular contact, linking the central Sudan area with North Africa. From the fifteenth century, trade con-tacts became widespread within Nigeria and could stretch as far as Tripoli and Tunis.[12] According to Yusufu Usman, the commodities that the Fezzani Arabs took to the Hausa consisted of cowries, horses, red woolen caps, linen and silk, carpets, blades, coral beads, looking glasses and brass.[13] In exchange, Fezzani traders took back gold dust, slaves, cotton cloth, hides and skins from Hausaland.[14] The latter became the raw materials from which a strong leatherwork industry devel-oped in North Africa. The unique decorative designs on the Arabian leather products diffused southward with the spread of Islamic culture. The Hausa developed their own leatherwork, some of which was exported to the North African coast as moroccan leather.[15] From the fifteenth century, Hausa traders also featured very prominently in West African trade, marketing various products including leatherwork. This included cheap and simple slippers, expensive embroidered sandals made for the chiefs and wealthy people (*bundin shirwa*), small bags and cushions.[16]

The land trade via the Sahara to North Africa was not the only commercial link between the Hausa and other parts of the world. European traders were supplying increasing quantities of manufactured goods via the Atlantic. The variety and quantity of such goods changed substan-tially over time. In the sixteenth century, Portuguese traders sold brass and copper bracelets,

beads, cloth and caps, some of which were made as presents for the personal ornamentation of chiefs. In the seventeenth century, Portuguese (also Dutch and English) merchants brought in beads, brass, rings, cowries, iron bars, rum, brandy and walking sticks – a wide range of commodities, which in the eighteenth century was supplemented by the import of Indian textiles, guns, gunpowder, tobacco and copper.[17]

The Atlantic trade provided a unique stimulus for the reconfiguration of consumer patterns in Yorubaland. The flow of new and exotic commodities from Europe, and also from North Africa and Asia, reshaped the material culture of the local populations, introducing new habits, garments and social practices. It was in this period that the Yoruba started wearing footwear. Historical evidence is scant, but we know, for instance, that various types of chopines and other platform shoes came into use in Yorubaland after the commercial encounter with Portuguese traders. Chopines were popular in early modern Europe and their use spread to Arabia and North Africa in the Renaissance.[18] In all probability, the wooden types were introduced to Yorubaland by European traders between the sixteenth and eighteenth centuries, as one of the luxury items for barter trade.

We should be careful to avoid the easy conclusion that European and other "foreign" consumer habits became widespread among the Yoruba before the twentieth century. One the one hand, external influences had a paramount effect on the way in which indigenous people conceived the materiality of their possessions and personal apparel. On the other hand, however, only a small proportion of the population could afford to buy such products.[19] In the 1860s, when footwear produced in England began to be sold in Yorubaland, only the aristocratic elite and the small community of African missionaries could afford to buy it.[20] However, sartorial expectations were affected by commodities and behaviors that did not comply with traditional categories of class and dress. In the 1870s, for instance, we find that the Yoruba aristocratic elite had successfully appropriated for itself the practice, previously reserved for the *oba*, of wearing silk velvet slippers of various colors.[21]

INDIGENOUS AND INDIGENIZED FOOTWEAR

The use of footwear was thus the result of a commercial encounter with European and North African traders. The environmental context of Yorubaland provided another strong motive for the Yoruba to "indigenize" clogs and other "foreign" footwear. A process of cultural authentication was accompanied by concerns over the functionality of footwear within the local climate. Much of Yorubaland is covered by rain forest that produces various types of hardwoods such as mahogany, cedar or obeche, suitable for wooden footwear. The variety of raw materials allowed the production of a wide repertoire of products, including clogs made from beautiful hard barks, known as *bata epogi*.[22] The bark was removed and bent to provide a covering for the foot. It was a flip-flop type of footwear, fastened to the foot with rope climbers. Its durability was limited and the wooden "sole" had to be changed frequently (Figure 8.3).[23] A durable flat pod (*panseke*), about three to four inches wide, could also be converted into flip-flop footwear. This was known as *bata panseke* (Figure 8.4).[24] The blacksmith bored a hole in the front and in both sides at the back, for securing rope climbers to the feet. These bark and pod sandals were independent inventions of the Yoruba. However, it is not known when the sandals evolved. It appears the sandals are of great antiquity because they are still part of contemporary rural farming life in many Yoruba communities.

Other footwear used by the Yoruba people included clog sandals, *patako* (also known as *sakoto* or *saka*), about six inches high, artistically carved for the *oba's* use (Figure 8.5).[25] The carvers created beautiful bas-relief patterns on a platform of mahogany, cedar or ebony.[26] The blacksmith assisted in boring three holes in the platform, one in the front and one on both sides at the back. Cane ropes were attached to the holes for fastening the feet to the platform.[27] *Bata onigi*, on the other hand, were not only more conspicuous footwear for their shape but expressed their high quality through an acoustic effect and by the sophisticated imprint patterns left on soft ground and sand. Other more "indigenous" footwear was also developed. *Bata onide*, a type of brass clog, were developed between the sixteenth and eighteenth centuries. The production of such footwear was possible thanks to the Yoruba mastery in producing challenging bronze artworks such as the one shown earlier in Figure 8.2.

Osifakorede, an Ijebu-Yoruba slave born around 1798, who lived in Paris most of his life, recalled the use of golden slippers (*bata golu*) by some Ijebu kings before the second decade of the nineteenth century, when he set sail abroad:

> There is a kind of sandal or slippers called *lagolago* and a more distinguished shoe called *saka* which seems like our galoshes; the latter is worn by the king at ceremonies and, since it is of solid gold of great weight, he is obliged to walk the slow pace which the solemnity of the occasion demands.[28]

Eve de Negri adds that the Ijebu-Ode king (*awujale*) was reputed to have had a pair of slippers of pure gold in 1845.[29] In all probability, these golden shoes were especially made in the Asante country (present-day Gold Coast) for the Kings of Yorubaland. The pair observed by Osifakorede may have been a gift of Nana Osei Kwame Asibe Bonsu (1799–1824), the seventh king of the

Asante nation, or produced by the Asante guild of goldsmiths.[30]

Beaded objects constitute a further type of material culture reserved for a restricted elite. Tradition held that Yoruba gods chose beaded strands as their emblems. This explains why beaded objects were restricted to those who represented the gods: rulers, priests, diviners and ancestor masqueraders.[31] These objects included bead-embroidered crowns and beaded slippers. Simple bead-embroidered crowns, devoid of a conical shape and including bird symbols, have been linked to the pre-sixteenth century, when the *oba* were predominant priest-kings.[32] Ogunba has suggested that thereafter, the prevalent secular kings chose elaborate and gorgeous conical crowns with bird symbols that told various stories.[33] It is credible that this period extended the lavish treatment of crowns to other beaded objects for kings and priests, including their slippers.

The earliest bead-embroidered slippers, the famous *bata ileke,* were most likely developed from the colorful Hausa leather slippers such as *budede takalumi* and *bundin shirwa* (an embroidered type) available in West Africa from the sixteenth century. Drewal and Mason have suggested a much later date, locating *bata ileke*'s introduction to the eighteenth or even early nineteenth century, when European fashions increasingly became the model for prestige wear.[34] The earliest models of *bata ileke* were probably designed using Yoruba cornelian, which was associated with old Yoruba crowns[35] and obtained mostly from Ile-Ife, the center of glass bead manufacture in Yorubaland.[36] They were created by skilled workers who specialized in bead embroidery in a number of centers, especially at Efon-Alaye, Ile-Ife, Oyo, Ilesa, Abeokuta and Iperu-Remo (Figures 8.6 and 8.7).

The example of *bata ileke* makes it clear that the diffusion of footwear among the Yoruba people was possible only thanks to the commercial and cultural contacts developed with the Hausa. The Hausa had a commercial base at Ilorin, the seat of government of the Fulani caliphate in Yorubaland. The Fulani caliphate attempted to annex Yorubaland after the fall of Oyo empire in the third decade of nineteenth century, and to Islamize the people. Although the annexation mission eventually failed, some elements of Hausa/Fulani material culture, including their leathercraft, were introduced to the Yoruba. Thus Rohlfs, the German, commented on the array of available footwear at Ilorin in the mid-nineteenth century as being composed of "very good if rather inelegant shoes with one half red and the other yellow, but most people just wear sandals anyway."[37] Ilorin quickly became a center of footwear production, thanks to the presence of local cattle and a prosperous leather-tanning trade. The town served as a bridge for the introduction, into Yorubaland, of models and practices from the Hausa.

The Oyo kingdom was another center of footwear production in Yorubaland. This southern kingdom expanded considerably during the sixteenth century to form what is commonly known as the old Oyo empire (seventeenth century). Such territorial expansion was possible thanks to an unprecedented military effort based on large squadrons of cavalry.[38] Horseriding was a stimulus for the use of boots, a practice probably borrowed by the Fulani Jihadists. Such boots, together with shoes and sandals, became the specialization of Olulotan, a hunter, during the reign

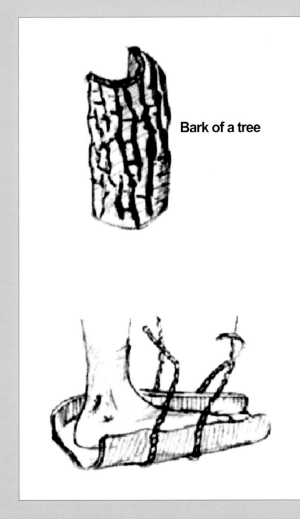

Bark of a tree

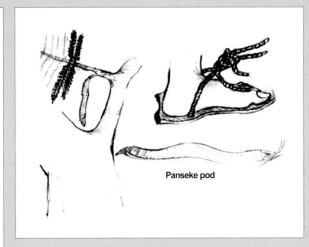

Panseke pod

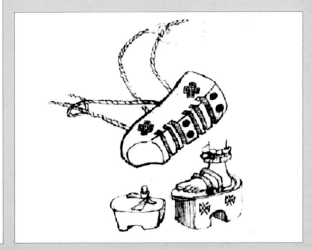

FIGURE 8.3 (LEFT): BATA EPOGI AND STRAPS. AN INDIGENOUS FOOTWEAR MADE FROM HARD TREE BARK AND ROPE FASTENERS, WORN ONLY IN THE COUNTRYSIDE FOR FARM AND HUNTING ACTIVITIES. FROM T. A. A. LADELE, O. MUSTAPHA, I. A. AWORINDE, O. OYERINDE AND O. OLADAPO, *AKOJOPO IWADII IJINLE ASA YORUBA* (COLLECTION OF RESEARCH FINDINGS ON YORUBA CUSTOMS), IBADAN, 1986, 202 AND C. L. ADÉOYÈ, *ASA ATI ISE YORUBA – THE CUSTOM AND PRACTICE OF THE YORUBA*, OXFORD, OXFORD UNIVERSITY PRESS, 1979, 218.

FIGURE 8.4 (TOP RIGHT): BATA PANSEKE. AN INDIGENOUS FOOTWEAR MADE FROM STRONG, FLAT PODS WITH ROPES MADE FROM CLIMBERS FUNCTIONING AS FASTENERS; WORN ONLY IN THE COUNTRYSIDE FOR FARM AND HUNTING ACTIVITIES. FROM T. A. A. LADELE, O. MUSTAPHA, I. A. AWORINDE, O. OYERINDE AND O. OLADAPO, *AKOJOPO IWADII IJINLE ASA YORUBA* (COLLECTION OF RESEARCH FINDINGS ON YORUBA CUSTOMS), IBADAN, 1986, 202 AND C. L. ADÉOYÈ, *ASA ATI ISE YORUBA – THE CUSTOM AND PRACTICE OF THE YORUBA*, OXFORD, OXFORD UNIVERSITY PRESS, 1979, 218.

FIGURE 8.5 (BOTTOM RIGHT): A VARIETY OF PATAKO, A CLOG SANDAL ABOUT SIX INCHES HIGH COPIED FROM THE EUROPEAN MODEL BUT CARVED USING HARDWOOD OBTAINABLE FROM YORUBA FORESTS. THE SANDAL WAS WORN BY THE MONARCHS AND CHIEFS FROM PERHAPS AS EARLY AS THE SIXTEENTH CENTURY. FROM T. A. A. LADELE, O. MUSTAPHA, I. A. AWORINDE, O. OYERINDE AND O. OLADAPO, *AKOJOPO IWADII IJINLE ASA YORUBA* (COLLECTION OF RESEARCH FINDINGS ON YORUBA CUSTOMS), IBADAN, 1986, 202 AND C. L. ADÉOYÈ, *ASA ATI ISE YORUBA – THE CUSTOM AND PRACTICE OF THE YORUBA*, OXFORD, OXFORD UNIVERSITY PRESS, 1979, 212.

Figure 8.6: Oba's beaded regalia, including bata ileke. This kind of bead-embroidered slipper was made indigenously exclusively for Yoruba rulers. By kind permission of Drewal and Mason's Collections.

of Aganju, the fourth Alaafin for Oyo in the sixteenth century.[39]

FROM SUMPTUARY LAWS TO FREEDOM?

Osifakorede, the early nineteenth-century slave, noticed how, in Yorubaland, "footwear, not worn by common people, is reserved for important men." The previous section has examined the way in which the Yoruba "adopted" and "authenticated" the use of footwear either through their contacts with North Africa and Europe, or by commercial exchange with the Norsa. However, the process of adoption was not a straightforward replication of "foreign" shapes, colors and practices. It implied complex cultural and social negotiations that unsettled, but at the same time confirmed, the boundaries and structure of Yoruba society. The lower strata of society were excluded from wearing any kind of footwear until the early decades of the twentieth century, as custom and tradition forbade such a practice.

Osifakorede's observation that "footwear, not worn by common people, is reserved for important men"[40] is not a surprising finding if we consider that footwear belonged, together with umbrellas, fans, flywhisks, beaded scepters and crowns, to a group of artifacts that were strictly associated with royal paraphernalia. Such association between footwear and regal status meant that even nobles could be refused permission to use footwear. When an *oba* wore clogs, his people perceived him as symbolically walking on a dais. The clog, which was about six inches or more high, exaggerated the *oba*'s height, and metaphorically elevated him to the highest position and status in society.

There were exceptions to such sumptuary regulations. Citizens could use footwear outside the town especially for economic purposes. As we have seen, *bata epogi* and *bata panseke* were made for farmers and hunters so that their feet could be protected while working in the bush. Big-time hunters, such as Olulotan of Oyo, even produced special boots and bags for game-hunting.[41] Clarke observed how, as late as the mid-nineteenth century, sandals were hardly worn among the Yoruba unless for long-distance travel or by traders.[42]

The increasing availability of footwear allowed sumptuary restrictions to be challenged by many among the local nobility. The refusal of the "royal appropriation" of footwear came not only from the traditional Yoruba elite, increasingly subject to Western influences. Another class claiming power over the king in the nineteenth century was that of the warlords. Footwear was at the center of the politics of power. For centuries, the *oba* had been "the one in whom supreme authority resides, second only to the gods" (*Alase ekeji orisa*).[43] His power was unrivaled and absolute. The state machine was run by a council of chiefs, who administered civil duties. Paramilitary formation existed in many Yoruba states, whereby recruits were enlisted in times of war and disbanded quickly thereafter. By the nineteenth century, however, the military was becoming not only a permanent feature of Yoruba society, but also an increasingly powerful class. The wars between states caused a shift of power from the monarchy to the military. Military leaders (warlords) started to pose a serious threat to the monarchy in the mid-nineteenth century.

The rise of such military aristocracy coincided with the challenge and ultimate end of many of the sumptuary privileges still retained by the monarch.[44] The arrogance of the warlords was used as a public display of their power. The most famous example of the uneasy relationship between the monarchy and the military aristocracy can be glimpsed from the story of Atiba, who was not only an Oyo prince, but also a seasoned and successful warlord. In 1830, Atiba made the point of appearing before *oba* Alaafin, Oluewu of Oyo, and King Eleduwe, with his feet shod. When asked to remove his shoes, he categorically refused to do so.[45] Johnson provides us with a vivid description of this scene:

> The two kings were one day sitting at a public meeting, and Prince Atiba arrived late with an august pageantry to the disgust of the kings and chiefs present, who could not afford as much. He was preceded by his junior war-chiefs mounted on strong ponies, with their attendant footmen; then those mounted on larger horses came after, then himself followed on a specially powerful animal richly caparisoned, with a large retinue … Olurinde the chief of Sepeteri in the eastern province, could not bear to see this act of disrespect pass unreproved, so he went near and pulled off the sandals from Atiba's feet, and thus reprimanded him: "Know you not before whom you are? How dare you be shod in the presence of our king?" Atiba could not brook a reproof from a commoner and from wounded pride fiercely retorted: "And who are you? And what is that to you? The king is my father and, as a prince, I have privileges which the likes of you can never aspire to. I can even pass by him into the harem which none of you can dare do; but who are you?" The contention was so sharp that Kitoyi the okere of Saki had to interpose, begging Prince Atiba to have respect for the two kings, to take off the sandals, and not to persist merely for the purpose of spiting the Sepeteri chief.[46]

The two kings and those standing by forced Atiba to remove his footwear so as to show respect to the monarchs. This incident was the source of resentment from Atiba, who felt he had been humiliated. According to the story, Atiba looked for revenge by joining the enemy Fulani army in a war against the Oyo *oba*. The war ended in disaster for the Yoruba king and his people.[47] At the battle of Eleduwa, the king was killed, Oyo was sacked by the Fulani and the entire empire collapsed. The Yoruba paid with their lives for the maintenance of regal sumptuary prerogatives. In other cases, however, their behavior was more pragmatic, especially in the light of warlords' insistence on wearing shoes in their communities. It was decided that warlords could appear shod in public but not before the *oba*, a practice that became widespread toward the end of the nineteenth century.[48]

There was a second group of people who also challenged traditional sumptuary rules. This class was formed by the Western-educated Yoruba elite who had moved back from countries such as Brazil, Cuba and Sierra Leone, where their fathers had been sold as slaves. Their influx into Yorubaland, from the 1850s, was greeted with suspicion by local communities as the newcomers comprised mostly Christian missionaries, teachers, clerks, traders — and in smaller numbers,

FIGURE 8.7 (FACING PAGE): YORUBA BEADED BOOT, BATA SHOE MUSEUM, TORONTO, P87.96. COURTESY OF BATA SHOE MUSEUM.

FIGURE 8.8: A WELL-DRESSED ELDERLY COUPLE, MARIA AND SOLOMON ALAWODE, OF BALOGUN NEAR LAGOS, APPEARING BAREFOOT, 1895. MOST PEOPLE WERE STILL RESTRICTED FROM WEARING FOOTWEAR. COURTESY MADAM RHODA MOSUNMOLA JOHNSON, IKEJA, LAGOS.

skilled artisans and craftsmen – in search of their roots. Being literate, fairly wealthy and based in major urban centers, they had access to the press and privileged contact with officials of the British administration. This *émigré* community quickly acquired a prominent position in society. The kings and chiefs of the interior employed them in the business of government as advisers.

The emergence of a prominent Western-educated elite, although strengthening the bureaucratic apparatus of the state, contributed to the progressive erosion of royalty.[49] This was a process that had a profound impact on the use of footwear. Both the educated elite and the visiting European missionaries called for an end to the practice of appearing barefoot in front of the *oba* of Ijebu.[50] Similar calls were made at Abeokuta as early as 1845, when Alake (*oba*) Sokenu was on the throne.[51] Many *oba* eventually allowed the wearing of shoes in the palace. This was seen as the ultimate sign of defeat, as one of the strongest sartorial prerogatives of kingship had come to an end.[52]

The social dynamics created by the warlords and the successful Westernized cultural elite that infiltrated the state echelons after 1850 did not pervade the entire social structure of Yorubaland. Restrictions on the use of footwear were still in place, as sumptuary laws had never been abolished. The majority of the population was still walking around barefoot, while a tiny minority had been able to overcome the ban on the wearing of shoes through exception (Figure 8.8). It was only with another phase of "contact" with Europe that things started changing. In 1893, the British successfully occupied Yorubaland and by annexing other smaller states, constituted what is now known as Nigeria. Colonial rule meant the implementation of commercial policies favoring the consumption of British products in the colonial territories. This was particularly true for the import of large amounts of clothing into Nigeria. Toward the end of the 1900s, a large number of clothing items, including cheap footwear, were provided by the Lagos Stores Ltd., a firm with wholesale and retail shops in several Yoruba towns.[53]

The colonial regime had an economic interest in fostering the wearing of footwear. By importing and constructing a distribution system reaching the far corners of the country, footwear became widely available to society at large. However, the law still forbade the wearing of shoes: *obas'* agents guarded local communities in the attempt to enforce age-long sumptuary laws on footwear use. For example, at Oyo, a plebeian led a protest march of several people, wearing footwear, to the *oba*'s palace in 1908, demanding the abrogation of the sumptuary law regarding footwear use. The protesters were arrested by the palace guards and held for three days.[54] In the long term, this protest seems to have been successful, because soon afterward, the king repealed the sumptuary law. The response elsewhere was different. At Abeokuta, for instance, there was no attempt to enforce the law. Christian missions encouraged converts to wear sandals to church services, and for the purpose of protecting their feet.[55] In the Okitipupa area, the use of stockings without shoes was initially approved by the traditional aristocracy, opening the way for the later use of sandals and shoes.[56] By the second decade of the twentieth century, the use of footwear was widespread in most Yoruba towns. Only the last vestige of the laws requiring visitors to the *oba*'s palace to remove their shoes before entry has been retained as part of court etiquette and protocol.

CONCLUSION: POWER AND FOOTWEAR; THE POWER OF FOOTWEAR

Whilst most sumptuary legislation is aimed at curbing the conspicuous consumption of the few, some has a much wider remit. Hurlock, in her study of sumptuary laws, provides some illuminating examples, such as the eighteenth-century attempt in Spain to abolish the use of the sombrero (causing a revolt), and the rebellions of Turks against their governments when asked to replace the traditional red fez and brimless cap with large turbans as a token of their loyalty to the sultan.[57] In cases such as these, regulations on dress are imposed for entire populations and are normally used as symbolic tokens of submission, despotism or simple political blindness.

This chapter has tried to engage with this second category of cultural meaning of regulation in dress. It has shown how the Yoruba monarchical power claimed for itself the use of footwear for a period of several hundred years. This was first challenged by the dynamic elite classes, appropriating signs of distinction in order to legitimize and consolidate their political power. Much of the population, however, had to wait until the late nineteenth century in order to be able to show any effective choice over their dress, and footwear in particular. However, the price of such freedom was the subjugation to a foreign colonial power. This chapter has added a further element in the analysis of the fall of the old Oyo empire, following Atiba's vengeful action, which resulted in the death of Alaafin (*oba*) Oluewu. It will be recalled that this episode was the consequence of Oluewu's rejection of Atiba because of his wearing sandals at Ogbomoso in 1830. Hitherto the causes of the fall of old Oyo empire have been long debated, although little importance has been given to the specific episode mentioned here.[58] This chapter therefore asserts that footwear was at the very center – perhaps the most important symbolic act – in the fall of the old Oyo empire. A footwear decision can bring down an empire.

9.

A DREAM OF BUTTERFLIES?

SHOES IN CHINESE CULTURE

paola zamperini

Footwear has a very long and complex history in China. As a result of the mesmerizing power of female footbinding for viewers and tourists, most Western scholars have paid very little attention to the diverse customs and styles of other Chinese footwear throughout the centuries. Nor have they properly considered the complex clusters of meanings attached to shoes by the Chinese people. This chapter is an attempt to redress that gender-biased approach. My main goal is to expose and underline the wealth of the Chinese sources at our disposal, by briefly addressing a part of the long history of shoemaking in China. Using a variety of sources, from archaeological evidence in tomb burials to literary narratives, from etiquette manuals to fashion magazines and websites, we will marginally touch upon the well-known lotus feet and "splendid slippers" and will begin to concentrate instead on the wider semantic intricacies of shoes in Chinese culture, present and past. My study of Chinese footwear, which focuses on men, will here attempt to suggest some of this untapped depth. After all, the "butterfly dreams" – possibly one of the most extravagant pairs of shoes to appear in the history of Chinese literature – were worn by a man, not a woman, and thus force us to revise the gendered charge attached to elaborate footwear.

DREAMS, BUTTERFLIES, TEXTS

Throughout the ages, countless Chinese writers and artists have not thought it beneath them to pay attention to feet, shoes, slippers, and socks – their own, as well those of others. Not to be outdone, Confucian scholars, from very early on, went a long way to regulate the proper etiquette and attire for Chinese people of all ranks and social classes. In more recent times, numerous Chinese scholars have studied the significance of shoes and their historical development through careful perusal of classical and vernacular texts. Indeed, shoes appear everywhere within the context of Chinese literary sources. From the Song poet Lu You (1125–1210), for example, we learn how a pair of wooden clogs can buy him happiness and freedom in the context of the rural world he loved so well, as they grant him mobility on muddy roads and relief from the tedium of rainy days in the countryside:

> For one day of rain, three days of mud
> And once the mud dries, the rain starts again
> Going out, obstacles at every step
> Making me utterly miserable
> So I got wooden shoes for one hundred coins
> And now I roam about my village every day[1]

Shoes inspire poetry in female authors as well, albeit of a different type from Lu You's. One of the most romantic poems ever written by a Chinese woman is the one composed in the Tang dynasty (AD 618–906) by the young Yao Yuehua, who imagines that the shoes that she is making for her cherished Yangda will, once on his feet, magically transform themselves into a pair of immortal geese that will literally fly her beloved into her boudoir.[2] Footwear leaves its mark also in the world of fiction and drama in premodern times. One of the most amusing detective stories of late imperial Chinese literature is a Ming (1368–1644) narrative of seduction and detection built around the mysterious manifestations of a handsome god and the leather boot he leaves behind after seducing an imperial concubine.[3]

Of course, the masterpiece of Chinese vernacular fiction, the fabulous eighteenth-century *Hong lou meng* (*The Dream of the Red Chamber*) devotes a great amount of attention to almost each item of dress its many protagonists wear. One of the most charming of such depictions is to be found in chapter forty-five and deals with an article of men's footwear, the very famous "butterfly and falling flowers" shoes (*hutie luohua xie*), otherwise known as "butterfly dreams" (*hutie meng*), which could best be described as low-heeled satin booties with embroidered flowers and appliquéd butterflies whose satin wings would flutter with each step taken by the wearer. Not surprisingly it is Jia Baoyu, the novel's hero (a true Qing dandy if there ever was one) who wears such splendid raiment on a rainy day to visit his beloved cousin Lin Daiyu:

> He had on a somewhat worn-looking tunic of red silk damask tied with a green sash at
> the waist, and trousers of sprigged green silk. The ends of his trousers were stuffed into

socks extravagantly patterned with a design of flowers picked out in gold, and he wore "butterflies and falling flowers" shoes.[4]

PERSPECTIVES ON CHINESE SHOES

A sign that this attention to "foot matters" has not disappeared with the arrival of the modern age is a beautiful illustrated dictionary of Chinese footwear, recently published in mainland China under the auspices of both scholars and shoemakers.[5] This text brings together the literary as well as the cultural and the archaeological sources that form the complex body of Chinese "shoe lore." It is a product of the fascinating interactions between the exploding market economy and the blooming cultural industries that have become so prominent in contemporary Chinese cultural discourses and practices.[6] As the Chinese population "rediscovers" aspects of their shoe culture, new meanings are generated as museums, artists and cultural brokers display the shoe to new audiences and in new media (Figure 9.1).

However, in the West, attention has been devoted almost exclusively to the study and research of women's shoes, because of the widespread knowledge and complex obsession (often racially constructed) with the phenomenon of female footbinding.[7] Exhibits, catalogs, scholarly articles and books have summoned and analyzed the Orientalist "dreams of butterflies" evoked by the exotic image of frail beauties stepping haltingly through the pages of the Central Kingdom. Fortunately, the brilliant work by historians such as Dorothy Ko has guided this attention in productive directions, underlining how the close study of the practice of binding women's feet in late imperial times can yield valuable information about women's labor, patriarchal values, and complex narratives of desire and resistance (Figure 9.2).[8]

BUTTERFLIES AND PRODUCTIVE BEES

"China is accused of unfairly gaining a foothold in Europe's shoe market," a BBC article proclaimed on June 30, 2005. As a result of an overflow into the European markets of safety shoes made in China, the European Commission opened an investigation into whether China was dumping footwear in Europe. The move followed a series of calls for an investigation by Europe's shoemakers, after an estimated sevenfold leap in China's imports after January 2005. "The EU says imports of shoes from China are up 681% – while prices are down 28% – in the first four months of 2005."[9] These are not just impressive figures, but are also indicators of a paradoxical state of affairs. Prada pumps and Manolo Blahnik's stilettos are global icons of style and fashion. But the shoes that increasingly shape, economically and financially, the present "globalized" world are those belonging to the less glamorous category of illegally made copies. Seventy percent of such shoes – so experts claim – are produced in China. And the country is an important producer also of "Made in China" safety and work shoes for the masses.[10]

FIGURE 9.1 (FACING PAGE): PAIR OF RED SILK "MANDARIN DUCK SHOES" WITH BLUE BINDING AND WHITE SILK MOON GATE, 1900–20. LIKE MANDARIN DUCKS, WHICH LOOK DISTINCTIVELY DIFFERENT AND YET ARE A PAIR, EACH SHOE IS DIFFERENT, BUT PART OF A PAIR. THEY WERE WORN TO SYMBOLIZE MARITAL HARMONY. LOTUS SHOE. BATA SHOE MUSEUM, TORONTO, P02.25. COURTESY OF BATA SHOE MUSEUM.

Yet it would be misleading to imply that feet matter just to increasingly successful Chinese manufacturers or to worried European shoe manufacturers and exporters: mass markets are just one of the conduits through which Chinese footwear is stepping onto the global stage. Lest we become too Eurocentric in our focus, we should note that feet and shoe-wear as objects of both mass and high-end consumption and circulation have begun to matter a great deal to countless Chinese people, including Chinese artists, and old shoes are never out of fashion among hip young artists in modern-day China. The thirty-year-old Peng Wei has indeed made a splash on the contemporary art scene in Beijing by painting shoes using watercolors, a medium tradition-ally reserved for landscape painting.[11] Not surprisingly perhaps, among her watercolors of shoes there are the shoes once worn by women whose feet were bound. For this reason, some have called Peng's paintings "feminist" – something that Peng denies.[12]

It is striking that Peng has chosen to follow the Westernizing Orientalist gaze and turn her admiration for bound feet into paintings (she professes to paint only what she likes), ignoring Jia Baoyu's butterfly dreams. As they are unknown to most contemporary Chinese and Western audi-ences and they do not have – unjustly, perhaps – the marketable sex appeal of lotus shoes, for now the only contemporary representations of these most extravagant boots are very likely to be the ones that are found in specialized dictionaries and manuals. But it is hard to make sense of the complexities of the present without having a good grasp of the past. Let us now turn to his-tory to at least try to begin understanding where these "butterfly dreams" could have come from.

4,000 YEARS OF SHOES

It is not surprising that a country like China, with such diverse customs and styles in terms of its traditional dress culture, would also be characterized by a remarkable variety in footwear.[13] This alone, as Pang Bian writes in his 2001 essay, "justifies its being singled out from other items of apparel to be studied separately as 'shoe culture.' "[14] Indeed, the *Zhou Li* (*The Rites of Zhou*), one of the most influential texts of the Confucian canon, stipulates that people should take off their shoes before entering the house, that shoes and socks should be removed at banquets, and that ministers meeting with the emperor should also take off both shoes and socks. However, bare feet were a taboo on occasions of ceremonial worship. Shoes, of course, in China as well as in many other premodern societies, could show the social status of the wearer, and throughout time com-plex rules and sumptuary laws developed to ensure that certain colors of shoe-wear remained the privilege of the wealthy and the powerful.

Shoes figured as ceremonial gifts and objects in all of the most momentous occasions in the life of premodern Chinese people. Births, engagements, weddings and funerals involved exchanges of shoes; exchanges that mirrored social, hierarchical and economic dynamics. A bride would wear pink or red shoes, while the so-called "longevity shoes," worn by the deceased, had to be blue, black or brown for men, and brightly colored for women (in many cases the same that they had worn on their wedding day). Footwear was also very visible in popular folk practices as, for instance, tokens of devotion and gratitude in temples to statues of Buddha and Buddhist saints. They were in some cases deployed in emergency exorcisms that involved recalling the soul of a scared child back to its original owner, since any type of footwear was so closely associated with the identity of the wearer that the sound of one's shoe sole being banged against the door frame of one's home would immediately be recognized by the wandering soul.

In other situations, shoes could be used as medical therapy. For example, in late Qing China, to rid oneself of a possibly expensive addiction to tea-drinking, all one had to do was to buy a new pair of shoes (a woman's for a man, and a man's for a woman), stuff them full of tea leaves and drink the tea made of such leaves. By the time the leaves had gone, so had the addiction![15] This list could go on extensively. From this very short sample of practices, it appears clear that a brief historical journey through this rich shoe world can yield fascinating and central information about Chinese culture.

Language always offers important insights into the origins of the subject. In classical Chinese, shoes and socks share the same radical, *ge*, which means "animal hide." On the "oracle" bones and tortoise shells used during the Shang dynasty (1766–1100 BC) as divination tools, such a character depicts a whole animal hide, trimmed and stretched out, which would seem to indicate that socks and shoes were partially or completely made out of leather in this period. Shang Chinese would possibly protect their feet by cutting out pieces of animal hide, wrapping them around their feet, and securing them with leather thongs. It is almost unquestionable that the wearing of shoes would also be something related to one's social status. Just as not everyone could have worn Jia Baoyu's "butterfly dreams" in Quing times, only the upper elite would have had the wealth to own the animals from which shoes and footwear could be made in Shang times.

Interestingly, this usage of leather appears to have possibly derived from a Central Asian connection. The most ancient leather shoes in China are a 3,800-year-old pair of boots made from sheep hide, worn by the so-called Loulan Beauty, a mummified female discovered in the 1980s in the ruins of the ancient kingdom of Loulan, in the deserts of the Xinjiang region. The lower and upper parts were sewn together using thick hide threads, in a similar way to the later process of making footwear using bone needles, with animal tendons as thread. Clearly leather shoes and boots would be the ideal choice for the nomadic populations living in the steppes north and southwest of the central plains. Legend wants leather footwear, however, to have been first introduced into the heart of China by King Wuling of the state of Zhao during the Warring States Period (475–221 BC) for military reasons. In 325 BC, threatened by contending states, King Wuling decided to replace his warring chariots with mounted archers. The king dispensed with the traditional loose robes and wooden-soled, flax-fabric shoes normally worn in battle, dressing his cavalrymen instead in tunics, pants and boots modeled on the attire of the northern nomads, thus making his troops among the strongest and best protected of the time. Shoes contributed to the success of warfare.

As for other components of Chinese culture, footwear must be considered alongside geographical and regional divisions. Thus it is quite likely that while China's northern and northwestern people were sewing hide boots with bone needles and hide thread, people in the east were

making straw shoes using bamboo needles and flax thread. Archaeological finds indicate that as early as 5000 BC, the ancient Chinese had learned to make articles of daily use from plant fibers. The principal variation in the form of this footwear was that people in the frigid north wore thick straw boots, while those in the hot, humid south wore straw sandals. Straw footwear was worn by all, whether they were nobles, men of letters or farmers. Along the eastern coast of Shandong province, farmers would wear "straw nests" – boots woven tightly with the stems and leaves of corn leaves. It appears that these materials were most effective in keeping the feet warm and, even today, local farmers still weave this kind of boots for export. In the Shang dynasty, some 3,000 years ago, people learned how to weave silk cloth and color it with mineral and plant dyes. The development of sericulture greatly influenced Chinese shoemaking, and colorful silk shoes gradually replaced straw shoes, especially for the higher ranks of the population. The arrival of cotton also gave commoners a new material for the fabrication of relatively cheap footwear.

A great deal of information about footwear is recovered through archaeological findings. This is particularly true about military apparel, as many dignitaries were buried with their armor or in the company of statues of soldiers meant to protect and guard their eternal rest. From Shang sites, archaeologists have unearthed – on separate occasions – a pair of leather shin guards and a headless, kneeling jade human figure, whose shins show traces of wrapping. According to historical records, before military boots were invented, soldiers wrapped pieces of hide and rattan around their shins for protection, and scholars believe that military boots were developed from these humble beginnings.

The terracotta foot soldiers protecting the grave of Emperor Shihuang of the Qin dynasty (211–206 BC), unearthed outside Xi'an, sport neat stitching on the soles of their footwear, which mirrors that seen on the stitched soles of handmade cloth shoes today. The type of boot worn by Qin Shihuang's archer continued to be used, with few variations, by the military and it was only during the Qing dynasty (1644–1911) that military boots were adapted for civilian wear and became part of the uniform for officials. Boots came in the two styles: pointed or square-toed. The former were for everyday wear, and the latter were for court attendance. The soles of these boots were made from thirty-two layers of cloth and were later used as a model for the cloth shoes worn by the common people, which have since become known as one-thousand-layered shoes. Rumor has it that in the late Qing dynasty, poor people would use layers of paper torn from the pages of the many Bibles distributed in China by Western missionaries, an interesting instance of cross-cultural exchange.[16]

FOOTWEAR AND THE TRANSFORMATION OF CHINA

Paintings, novels, poems and plays provide compelling evidence about the way customs and changes in Chinese shoe culture reflect their close connections with the natural and geographical conditions of China. They manifest social, economic and cultural changes, as well as the likes and

FIGURE 9.2 (FACING PAGE): CHINESE SATIN SHOES WITH SHARP HEEL AND POINTED, UPTURNED TOES, EMBROIDERED WITH FLOWERS IN GREEN, BLUE, IVORY AND PURPLE, C. 1875-95. BATA SHOE MUSEUM, TORONTO, S92.3.AB. COURTESY OF BATA SHOE MUSEUM.

dislikes of rulers and the common people of different periods. With such a long and rich history, it is not surprising that old traditions die hard in China when it comes to foot matters.

In the spring of 2004, the city of Changsha (located in the historically important but geographically remote province of Hunan) hosted a three-day cultural exhibition on Chinese footwear. On display were "more than seventy pairs of shoes representative of various periods of Chinese history." As we can see in the pictures that illustrate this event, part of the appeal of showing the shoes comes not so much from the shoes themselves but from the beautiful young women dressed in "postmodern" Qing attires that – although not historically accurate – were flashy enough to be eye-catching. None of the shoes so interestingly showcased appears to be an original antique, and one can only hope that the pre-Qin shoes listed in the press release would not be so nonchalantly handled by the hostesses depicted in the accompanying photographs. But the point is that these old shoes have traveled far through time, and even after such a long journey, they have managed to retain their appeal.

The 2004 exhibition, although keen to underline historical continuity between old Chinese traditions and a promising industrial future, retained only part of the country's "shoe heritage." It was only in 1998, for instance, that shoe factories in Harbin, the capital of northeast China's Heilongjiang province, stopped production of small shoes for elderly women who had their feet bound in their childhood (Figure 9.3).[17] Another legacy from the past are the so-called "*bu xie*" shoes, very likely the descendants of the shoes sported by Shihuang's foot soldiers. They are at times called "Mao shoes." Because of their affordability and simplicity, they quickly became the shoe-wear of choice of many Chinese revolutionaries. Some have suggested that the shoes have survived because they predate the revolution, and are thus seen as symbols of Chinese – not communist – culture.

These days, on the streets of Beijing and Shanghai, alongside the increasingly fashionable and fashion-sensitive city-dwellers, one can find people from all walks of life strolling about in comfortable shoes, possibly a long way from the butterfly dreams of Jia Baoyu, but not unlike Lu You's wooden clogs in their functionality as well as in their historical "pedigree." Chinese feet do not forget quickly their past, even amidst the imitation Italian leather pumps and Nike sneakers manufactured in Taiwan and in Thailand.[18] This is perhaps the future of the very rich Chinese shoe culture that we have just begun to introduce here, namely a successful mixture of its own complex cultural heritage with global trends and fads, holding onto the comfort of premodern footwear without renouncing, on occasion, the appeal of Prada's latest high-heeled pumps.

FIGURE 9.3 (FACING PAGE): MODERN PRODUCTION FOR TRADITIONAL MARKETS. A BROCADE SHOE WITH AN INSTEP STRAP FOR BOUND FEET, AND STITCHED FELT SOLE. PRODUCED BY THE HONG KONG FIRM BATA PRINCESS, 1970S. BATA SHOE MUSEUM, TORONTO, S79.68. COURTESY OF BATA SHOE MUSEUM.

10.
FASHIONING MASCULINITY

MEN'S FOOTWEAR AND MODERNITY[1]

christopher breward

There is scarcely a young man who enters upon life without being able to furnish him-self with shoes. Nay, most have an opportunity of gratifying their tastes and passions in the purchase of great variety; and I am greatly deceived, if experience does not prove, that much more than half the misery of the world arises either from ill-directed taste in the purchase of shoes, or from the entire want of them. The objects to be obtained in such a dispute are of a most important and substantial character. Religion, patriotism, public and private virtue, pure and fixed principles of taste, intellectual and corporeal refinement, all – all depend upon the choice of shoes.

Crispin Anecdotes: Comprising Interesting Notices of Shoemakers,
Who Have Been Distinguished for Genius, Enterprise and Eccentricity …

Contrary to popular knowledge – which erroneously suggests that masculinity and clothes shopping are irreconcilable states – the acquisition of a pair of good shoes has long been counted among one of the most important considerations under-taken by any self-respecting male follower of fashion. Indeed for most men, regardless of their position on the seriousness of dress, the fitting of the feet in appropriate attire constitutes a commercial transaction deserving of at least their limited attention, if only for those reasons of comfort and value that tend to impinge less directly on the consumption of other items of clothing. The improbably named Reverend Tom Foggy Dribble, in writing "The Street Companion: or the Young Man's Guide and the Old Man's Comfort in the Choice of Shoes" for the *London Magazine* of 1825, certainly held no reservations regarding the status of the man's shoe as an indicator of civilized values, economic well-being and impeccable taste. His robust confidence in the related skills of British producers and consumers is unsurprising, coming as it does in a period when London manufacturers and retailers dictated sartorial rules for fashionable men across the globe.[2] This chapter proposes that the reverend's faith in the moral character of the man's shoe has been sustained across the intervening two centuries, offering a model for aesthetic discernment that stretches beyond the humble realm of the foot to embrace broader issues of taste, modernity and gender.

The original tenets of dandyism, formed from the 1790s onward, focused on the impeccable wardrobe of the English aristocrat, presenting a fiercely controlled style of dressing and behavior that would prove resistant to accusations of effeminacy, profligacy and that unhealthy attachment to surfaces which was associated with the decadence of France.[3] These were practices that might otherwise be used to critique the values of an emergent consumer culture, even when the acquisitive and self-aggrandizing performance of the dandy sometimes appeared to embrace the very same phenomena. Thus, in its mannered disavowal of the vagaries of fashion, the dandy's wardrobe stood as a paradoxical cipher for fashion's spectacular excesses.

Nowhere has this irony been truer than in the long-term status accorded to the unchanging form of the masculine shoe. While the philosophical meanings attached to the complex knotting of the linen cravat or the dense black pile of the velvet swallowtail coat have – like the Brummels and the D'Orsays that sported them – faded into a romanticized past, traditional male footwear maintains a clear connection to the sartorial debates and rhetorical styles of the early nineteenth century. In the delicate balance between function and aesthetics that continues to dictate the pattern of stitching on a black Oxford or the number of eyelets on a brown brogue, there still persists the residue of older discourses on manliness, nationhood and class. Where the hosiery and outerwear of previous generations of men lay revealed as mere temporal fashions, their shoes seem more grounded, immune to the indignities imposed by a shifting sense of fashion but subject to intense deliberation regarding fitness for purpose and occasion.

THE MAN'S SHOES AS MODERNIST "OBJECT TYPE"

Part of the reason for the endurance of the man's shoe as a progressive symbol of aesthetic conservatism lies in the manner through which its forms were celebrated by propagandists for an equally dandified modernism at the opening of the twentieth century. Le Corbusier, writing in his manifesto *L'Art Décoratif d'Aujord'hui* (1925), presented a moral and aesthetic vision that deliberately contested the social value of those feminized and fashion-led items which dominated the displays of the international Paris exhibition of the same year.[4] In a polemic that recalls the renunciatory posturings of the Regency dandy, the rising architect looked to the functional and "innocent" surfaces of utilitarian "industrial" goods as a means of exposing the "shaming" and "dishonest" veneer of the moderne "bric-a-brac" beloved of the housewife consumer.[5] The modernist arbiter of taste critiqued ephemeral modes while fetishizing a myth of durability that still prioritized surface impressions.

Among many suggestions for aesthetic and design reform, Le Corbusier presented five desiderata that find their most potent exemplars in the polished seams and supple leather offered in the modern footwear catalog. His pithy statements provide an entry into further understanding the particular dynamics of the male shoe. Le Corbusier highlighted utilitarian need as a motor for the production of domestic goods:

> Utilitarian needs call for tools, brought in every respect to that degree of perfection seen in industry. This then is the great programme for the decorative arts. Day after day industry is turning out tools of perfect utility and convenience that soothe our spirits with the luxury afforded by the elegance of their conception, the purity of their execution, and the efficiency of their operation. This rational perfection and this precise formulation constitute sufficient common ground between them to allow the recognition of a style.[6]

The idea of clothing as tool had underpinned and smoothed the rise of the English gentleman's wardrobe as a paradigm of civilized taste in the nineteenth century.[7] The utilitarian textiles associated with dressing for the country estate found an easy translation into the style of tailoring associated with Savile Row.[8] And with them the waxed and toughened leather goods of the racetrack or the grouse moor were directly reflected in the craftsmanship put into the gloves and galoshes of the City financier.

To celebrate the elegant cadence of a new shape in toecaps for its own sake ran the risk of inviting ridicule for effeminacy, but when that form could be discussed in terms of its resistance to wear or rain, or the perfection of its construction, then the right of its owner to accrue a reputation for his impeccable style remained unquestioned. Yet the taint of aristocratic taste imbued such objects with the problematic gloss of old-fashioned elitism. Le Corbusier was forced to look to a more self-consciously "modern" and proletarian role model, who could celebrate the bright patina of the mass-produced in as effortless a manner as that in which the old-style milord pulled on his bespoke hunting boots.

> Lenin is seated at the Rotonde on a cane chair; he has paid twenty centimes for his coffee with a tip of one sou. He has drunk out of a small, white porcelain cup. He is wearing a bowler hat and a smooth white collar. He has been writing for several hours on sheets of typing paper. His inkpot is smooth and round, made from bottle glass. He is learning to govern one hundred million people.[9]

Similarly, if the genealogy of the gentleman's shoe lay in the leisured pursuits of the aristocracy, then any claim made on its democratic appeal was fraught with difficulty. Thus from Lenin's embodiment of a banal yet revolutionary modernity, Le Corbusier extended his celebration of utility to an account of the potential of the functional object to free the user from older notions of service and hierarchy. In his third proposition, the adaptability of the demotic industrial product is commended as a metaphor for a utopian vision of social equality:

> The objects of utility in our lives have freed the slaves of a former age. They are in fact themselves slaves, menials, servants. Do you want them as your soul-mates? We sit on them, work on them, use them up; when used up, we replace them. We demand from such servants precision and care, decency and an unassertive presence.[10]

Once again, it is possible to read a surviving variety of dandyism between the lines: the justification for consumption wrapped up in a reverence for unfettered performance. In the eighteenth century, patriotic pamphleteers and caricaturists had often contrasted the well-shod, stockinged feet of John Bull with the naked ankles and callous-inducing clogs of the French peasant.[11] The belligerent freeborn Englishman sported the products of early mass production as trophies of his superiority. Plain speaking, plain living and utterly efficient, the old self-deluded male consumer morphed effortlessly into the new. Le Corbusier's twentieth-century John Bull used the democratizing promises of labor-saving commodities as an excuse to consume. Machine-turned lasts, and uppers put together on sewing machines, had replaced the notion of the bespoke, but the cheaper shoes that resulted offered all-comers the promise of functional and elegant footwear (Figure 10.1).

If, by the 1920s, political reform and internationalism were causing the specter of class strife and the ideal of the nation state to seem slightly outdated as philosophical motors for justifying or condemning the pleasures of consumption, a deeper-rooted misogyny held out as a refuge from which the compromised dandy could play fashion against function and still emerge with footwear unsullied. Le Corbusier certainly made full use of the contrast between plain, functional "masculine" objects and decorative, debased "feminine" ones in his push for a standard of taste that combined the mass-produced with the bespoke in its seeking for modern beauty:

> Trash is always abundantly decorated; the luxury object is well made, neat and clean, pure and healthy, and its bareness reveals the quality of its manufacture. It is to industry that we owe this reversal in the state of affairs: a cast-iron stove overflowing with decoration costs less than a plain one; amidst the surging leaf patterns flaws in the casting cannot be seen. And the same applies generally … this surface elaboration, if extended over everything, becomes repugnant and scandalous.[12]

Here the disavowal of the purely decorative was visceral in its condemnation. Fashion in its purest form is "repugnant" and "scandalous." It is illustrated through recourse to a description of all that is soft and sensuous, nowhere better suggested (for our purposes) than through the juxtaposition of a padded and delicate satin slipper with a sturdy walking boot.

MANFIELD & SONS

LACE BOOTS, Brown

No. 1238	Brown Willow Calf	..	..	..	..	**16/6**
„ 1204	Russet Calf	..	..	..	..	**30/-**

GENTLEMEN'S
STOUT LACE BOOTS
FOR GOLF, &c.

LACE BOOTS, Black

No. 1548	Black Box Calf	..	..	..	**16/6**
„ 1055	Blacking Calf ..	..	..	..	**16/6**
„ 1085	Black Box Calf, Waterproof Soles		..		**25/-**
„ 1103	Blacking Calf ..	..	..	..	**25/-**

HALF SIZES

FIGURE 10.1: CATALOG OF MANFIELD & SONS, NORTHAMPTON: "GENTLEMEN'S STOUT LACE BOOTS FOR GOLF, &C," 1920S. NORTHAMPTON MUSEUMS AND ART GALLERY, BOOT AND SHOE COLLECTION, BS42. REPRODUCED COURTESY OF NORTHAMPTON MUSEUMS AND ART GALLERY.

In a final example, Le Corbusier drew on the rhetoric of the healthy body and the corrupting effects of sexual desire to heighten his sense of terror at the threat posed to a rational universe by the excesses of feminine culture:

> Not only is this accumulation of false richness unsavoury, but above all and before all, this taste for decorating everything around one is a false taste, an abominable little perversion. I reverse the painting; the … shop girl is in a pretty room, bright and clear, white walls, a good chair – wicker work or Thonet … some crockery of white porcelain, and on the table three tulips in a vase … It is healthy, clean, decent. And to make something attractive, as little as that is enough … We assert that this art without decoration is made not by artists but by anonymous industry following its airy and limpid path of economy.[13]

A stress on hygiene joined utility, a celebration of contemporary modernity, democratization, and a rejection of useless decoration on the modernist's agenda for the reformation of popular taste. That these values were explicitly masculine in orientation and implicitly sartorial in character was most clearly communicated in the illustrations selected to accompany the text of *L'Art Décoratif d'Aujord'hui*. In juxtaposition with the more familiar icons of modernism, which included American office furniture, Peugeot automobiles, ocean liners and commercial tableware, Le Corbusier chose images drawn from the world of the gentleman's closet: Hermès luggage, Saderne straw boaters, briar pipes, galoshes and the classic leather shoe. Embodied in the latter objects lay a code for the proper appreciation of the modern commodity, which found its origins not in the promises of Fordism or the hard technology of the industrial workshop, but in an older set of rules and practices engineered for the social display of the "clothes-wearing man."

Representing the commercial application of such practices, the 1907 catalog of John Piggott, a typical gentleman's outfitter trading in the City of London, incorporated in its listing of men's shoe styles all of those desiderata dreamt up by Le Corbusier twenty years later, and similar publications must have inspired the architect in his search for the ideal modern "type-form." Here the discerning consumer could peruse mosquito boots for the tropics, moroccan leather Grecian slippers in black, scarlet or maroon, patent leather Oxfords "for dancing," with low heels and single soles, together with specialized shoes for cricket, tennis, yachting and boating (Figure 10.2). A whole department specialized in footwear for cycling and walking, boasting such specialized items as the new-century cycle shoe with "no unsightly hook or lace." For football the "never miss," "goal kicker" and "sure kick" models ensured that function and appearance elided, while hand-sewn boots "most elegant in style, suitable for town or country wear" accompanied the company promise that "all our footwear is easy fitting, made on the very latest and improved lasts, and fits like a glove."[14]

ADOLF LOOS AND THE MORALITY OF DESIGN

Le Corbusier's enthusiasm for the arcane ephemera of the footwear department was not entirely original. The older Austrian architect, Adolf Loos, had also looked to the masculine wardrobe as a source of inspiration in the formulation of his own creative philosophy, finding in clothing and its relationship to the body a clear metaphor for the social and aesthetic responsibilities of architecture. Indeed, Le Corbusier had reprinted Loos's most influential essay "Ornament and Crime" (which in 1908 had drawn on the surface embellishment of women's fashions and the tattooed bodies of "primitive" peoples for evidence of the "barbaric" effects of pattern), in the first issue of his journal *L'Esprit Nouveau* in 1920. As several architectural theorists have pointed out, Loos believed that male clothing had reached a state of standardization and functional convenience through a process of evolution and the beneficial effects of physical action. This placed it on a more rational plane than the cyclical and corrupting dress of women, whose constant style changes were, according to Loos, driven by the necessity for sexual display.[15] In this sense, "in as much as men's clothing is standardized, it is able to act as a mark behind which the individual is shielded from the increasingly threatening and seemingly uncontrollable forces of modern life (forces that were themselves understood as feminine)." Like modern architecture itself, the male wardrobe was engineered to act as a physical and psychological buffer against the confusing sensations of modernity.[16]

Loos's most explicit debt to men's shoes, in the formation of these ideas, was first worked out in a series of review articles published in *Die Neue Freie Presse* during the summer of 1898. As Le Corbusier's polemic in *L'Architecture* had been partly inspired by the exhibits of a decorative arts exhibition, so Loos's observations arose from his attendance at the Vienna Jubilee Exhibition of the same year. Three preoccupations worked their way through Loos's often short-tempered but constantly witty prose. Firstly, that changes of style in the male shoe could be accounted for in the "natural" processes of evolution. Secondly, that cultural phenomena such as fashion caused the "natural" function of footwear to be compromised. And finally, that the increasing speed of modern life demanded a style of shoe that placed considerations of health and hygiene in paramount position. Under the title "Footwear," Loos flew the motto "*Tempora mutantur, et nos mutamur in illis*: Times change and we change with them. Our feet do the same".[17] At the outset he set up a distinction between the craft of the shoemaker and that of the tailor, the former restricted by the intended function of his wares to produce items that followed the "natural" form of the foot (Figures 10.3 and 10.4), the latter freed to manipulate the given form of the body:

> Of course the form of our feet does not change from season to season. That often requires several centuries, at the very least a generation. A large foot cannot get smaller with the snap of a finger. Here the other clothing artists have it easier … changes can easily be made by means of a new cut, cotton padding and other aids. But the shoemaker must adhere closely to the form which the foot has at the particular moment. If he

THE FIRM FOR FASHIONABLE

MEN'S BOX CALF DERBYS.

Price:
8\11
per
pair.

No. 654.

Page 37.

TAN HIDE DERBY

No. 272.

Price:
6/11
per
pair.

Page 39.

F. DOUGHTY & SONS,

36

Figure 10.2: Page from the catalog of F. Doughty & Sons, London, 1904. Private collection.

FIGURE 10.3 (FACING PAGE): BROWN ELONGATED MEN'S BOOT WITH LEATHER INSERTS AND A COMBINATION OF LACE-UP AND HOOK FASTENINGS. VIENNA, 1890. BATA SHOE MUSEUM, TORONTO, P87.0069. REPRODUCED COURTESY OF BATA SHOE MUSEUM.

FIGURE 10.4 (ABOVE): "BALLY FLEXIBLE." BROWN AND WHITE PERFORATED DERBY SHOE. SWITZERLAND, 1933. BATA SHOE MUSEUM, TORONTO, L87.0020. REPRODUCED COURTESY OF BATA SHOE MUSEUM.

wants to introduce the small shoe, he must wait patiently until the race of men with large feet has become extinct.[18]

Loos also addressed the mechanisms by which the ideal size and shape of foot was arrived at through the sociological demands of changing forms of human activity and the inevitable process of distinction through which one social group defined its power over another. The forces of competition thus gave rise to fashions in shoe size and style, which undercut any rational or biological development. Half crazed though his thesis now seems, it laid out clear parameters for arriving at the supremacy of the modern man's shoe, both in terms of function and aesthetics, and the uncomplicated relationship between the two which Loos identified as the defining paradigm of a successful object:

> But of course the feet of all men do not have the same form at the same time ... What is the shoemaker to do about this? Which type of foot should be his standard? For he will be intent on producing modern shoes. He too wants to be progressive; and he too aspires to acquire the largest possible market for his products. And he sets about it the same way as all the other trades do. He keeps to the foot type of those who have power in society ... All those who thought and felt modern in the last century wore English riding shoes and boots, even if they did not own a horse. The riding boot was the symbol of the free man, who had won a final victory over the buckled shoe, the air of the court, and the glistening parquet floor ... the high heel, useless for the horseback rider, was left behind ... The whole of the following century ... was taken up with the pursuit of the smallest possible feet.[19]

Loos saw, in the frenetic rhythms of contemporary life, the opportunity for reform in the design of men's shoes, a process that could be applied across all facets of material culture. Recalling those images of men that appeared in the fashion plates of nineteenth-century tailoring journals, he recoiled at the effeminate and dainty little pumps that ventured forth from under the pants of otherwise hirsute and muscular models. It would seem that the form of the foot betrayed the enervating lifestyles and decadent attitudes of the European bourgeoisie, hinting at the torpor within. On the eve of a new century it was necessary to look to younger societies and new leisure activities as a means of inculcating a vigor that had been sapped by the demands of fashion.[20]

Although Loos's articles were clearly rhetorical and not to be taken at face value, his overwhelming sense of disgust at the effects of "feminine" culture and female sexuality, together with his willingness to imbue everyday commodities with baleful anthropological insight, threatens to undermine their value as an impartial record of the production and consumption of men's shoes at this pivotal moment in the history of the industry. Loos's direct intellectual descendants in this respect would appear to be those who have positioned footwear as sexual fetish at the expense of any understanding of its role in adjacent fields, as economic product, sociological marker, semiotic sign or indeed as art object.[21] Yet despite their deliberately provocative tone, the 1897 publications find some strong echoes in the concerns of writers from within the shoemaking trades at the time. James Pond, a bootmaker of Norwich (a center for the manufacture of British dress shoes in the nineteenth century), completed "a practical treatise upon the natural care of the feet and their treatment in deformity" a year before Loos's journalism. In its concentration on the hygienic clothing of the feet, the book contributes to a more general discourse on links between health, aesthetics and fashion, which engendered such reforming projects as that pioneered by Gustav Jaeger, and maintained some parallels with those debates on decoration, style and surface that were preoccupying writers on architecture and urbanism in the same period. Like Loos, Pond advocated a theory of design driven by rational utility, which was resistant to the effects of fashion:

> The shape, cut and whole formation of the boot or shoe should be such as to give the best protection and the greatest freedom to all parts of the foot and leg; but fashion, unfortunately, is so mixed up in this question, as in all other questions of clothing, that all endeavours for the comfort of the feet are stifled ... The tailor, dressmaker and hatter may conform to fashion, however ridiculous, without inflicting serious injury upon their customers. This is not the case, however, with the shoemaker, he makes his boots the shape of the last given him, often not knowing, or even thinking about the construction of the foot or leg and its uses.[22]

Besides the effects of fashion, Pond was also worried about the influence that sweated manufacture dictated over standards of finish and an attention to the orthopedic function of footwear. It is interesting that in their fetishization of the gentleman's wardrobe both Le Corbusier and Loos were also attracted to bespoke items, to the handmade and the finely crafted. Here the iconic man's shoe was distinguished from those other reified items of mass production: the porcelain cup or the Thonet chair. Standardized workmen's clothing was overlooked in favor of the products of the traditional tailor or the master cobbler. As far as fitness for purpose was concerned, the individually fitted, hand-sewn shoe was clearly superior to the factory-riveted clog. As Pond concurred:

> There is no doubt that hand sewn bespoke boots and shoes are preferable to ready-made ones as they are more carefully constructed, more pliable to the feet, stronger and more easily repaired ... A riveted boot in whatever form is worse than a wooden bottom or clog. It is rigid, hard and unyielding, and in whatever shape it is made the foot must adapt itself to it ... as they are cheap they are very much worn, causing an enormous quantity of distorted and crippled feet, especially flat feet.[23]

In this manner, through recourse to contemporary debates on physical and moral degeneration among city dwellers, shoe manufacturers were able to promote the cause of the bespoke industry above that of the sweated trades.[24]

If commentators on aesthetic issues relied on the fear of feminization in the field of popular taste as a means of furthering the modernist cause, other interests were best served by focusing on the dire state of the national body. From the soles of the feet upward, critics from the fields of medicine, religion and politics viewed the physiques of men in all walks of life as damaged by the rise of sedentary occupations, by an increased interest in the pursuit of leisure, and by exposure to both the real pollution of urban industry and the polluting effects of commercial culture. Moral and health panics of this nature crossed geographical boundaries, fueling eugenicist research in the United States, Britain and Continental Europe and extending a set of arguments that were already well established in literature pertaining to military strategy from the period of the Boer War through to the advent of the First World War.[25]

It was, then, no coincidence that discussions surrounding the appropriate form of the modern shoe should relate closely to patriotic texts on strategies for the improvement of the physique of conscripts to the armed forces. In 1912 Edward Lyam Munson, a major in the medical corps of the US army, wrote on the design of the military shoe, employing a rhetoric that took civilian concerns regarding health a stage further:

> It is rare to find in civil life a shoe that even approaches the normal foot in shape and contour. Few manufacturers make them, as they are not saleable to the general public, whose choice is swayed rather by considerations of fashion than comfort ... But the soldier at the very outset represents the physically elect of the class from which he comes and is better in this respect than its average; moreover, all his parts, including the feet, undergo development in strength and size under the active life, weight carrying and systematized exercise which it falls upon him to perform.[26]

The panacea for the failings of the civilian shoe designer thus lay in the example set by the soldier's foot and its ideal casing. Beyond its functional prerequisites, which were to provide comfort, support, protection, durability and ceremonial neatness at minimal cost, the military shoe embodied a celebration of fitness, vitality and adaptability which held the potential to reenergize the flagging esteem of the urban office worker as much as it contributed to the success of martial campaigns. Following the First World War, several medical and industrial training texts drew on the expertise of the battlefield, bridging the requirements of the mainstream shoemaking trade and the quartermaster.[27] On a more intimate and private scale, the quiet pride taken by countless demobbed soldiers in maintaining a parade ground polish on the surface of their Oxfords bore testament to the pervasive influence of militarism on the relationship between men and their clothing. In addition to all of this, the proselytizing of Army medical officers remained extraordinarily close to the rhetoric of Loos and Le Corbusier in its fetishizing of function and fear of fashion:

> There can be no question but that of all the protective coverings which the foot soldier wears, his shoes are by far the most important from a strategic standpoint; since upon their shape, durability, use and comfort of fit, pliancy and lightness depends his military

FIGURE 10.5 (FACING PAGE): SHOE MANUFACTURING AT MANFIELD, NORTHAMPTON, C. 1900. NORTHAMPTON MUSEUMS AND ART GALLERY, BOOT AND SHOE COLLECTION, 721024/2. REPRODUCED COURTESY OF NORTHAMPTON MUSEUMS AND ART GALLERY.

efficiency. Next to his armament, the shoe is probably the most important item of the equipment of the soldier. The construction of shoes for civilians is influenced almost wholly by considerations of fashion and style. These are irrational and are changed frequently in the financial interest of the shoe trade.[28]

Military and hygienic concerns were further acknowledged by Loos in his comments on the production of shoes, which also appeared in *Die Neue Frei Presse* in August 1898. Here he championed the cause of his compatriot shoemakers, quoting the English trade press in its assertion that the Austrian footwear industry ranked above all others in the health-giving quality of its product. Loos retained less admiration for compatriot consumers, crediting the rise in deformities of the feet to the willingness of those who could not afford bespoke shoes to patronize the merchandise of "foreign" mass producers in their search for an elusive fashionability. In a ferocious passage of barely concealed anti-Semitism, Loos praised the rational impulses of Austrian craftsmen for setting the nation back on a footing appropriate to the needs of the forthcoming century:

> We Austrians will be able to step out smartly in our shoes in the upcoming century. And good shoes will be necessary in the next century because we are going to be on the march … The ancient Germanic blood still flows in our veins, and we are ready to march forward. We will do our best to help change the world of sitters and standers into a world of work and marching.[29]

MATERIALITY AND MANUFACTURE

Loos's implication that "good" shoes are those that reflect the special talent of the maker ("It is not by chance that the greatest poet and the greatest philosopher to have been bestowed on us by the artisan class were shoemakers"[30]) and the discerning taste of the consumer, leads us into the final area for consideration with regard to the broader meanings of the male shoe. Having focused on aesthetics and function, on the contribution of the dandy, the doctor and the soldier in formulating a metaphorical rule of taste in respect to the modernity embodied in masculine footwear, it only remains for the chapter to assess the ways in which the craft of shoemaking, the circumstances of production, can be read directly from the surface of the product (or, indeed, obscured by it). For ultimately the signifiers of what constitutes a "good" shoe lie beyond questions of style and use. As any shoemaker or retailer would attest, they reside in the literal meeting of leather and thread. The man's shoe is very much the sum of its parts, a physical object whose look, weight, texture and smell bespeak the skill of its maker and point to its intrinsic value (Figure 10.5). The way in which a prospective buyer will "manhandle" his purchase as he raises it from the shop display for closer inspection suggests as much. Textile commodities, pants and shirts that derive their worth from the extrinsic values of fashion, rarely receive such reverential treatment. That shoe manufacturers have always been cognizant of this materiality is clearly evident from the texts of early advertisers. Elias Moses, a pioneering London clothing wholesaler of the mid-nineteenth century, traded on the concrete character of his wares in his evocative promotions:

> Two boots (quite unlike in their style and their leather)
> Were heard very recently talking together.
> It appears, from the facts which the journals record,
> That one was a Wellington fit for a Lord,
> A boot such as very few houses can show,
> With a truly smart Heel and a truly flat Toe.
> The other one differ'd from this altogether:
> As ugly production – a mere waste of leather.
> 'Twas a dumpy, and lumpy and stumpy concern,
> Such as any respectable "trotter" would spurn.
> This queer piece of "craft" (who was all on the rip)
> Was the first who attempted to open his lip.[31]

Moses' efforts at advertising the qualities of his wares came at a moment when the British shoe industry was undergoing a period of profound transition both in the organization of its labor and in the nature of its product. It is ironic that Moses, one of a new breed of wholesaler, should have puffed the attractions of his boots using the language of bespoke tradesmen, for it was precisely the business of entrepreneurs like him to undercut older methods of making to order with ready-made, mass-produced goods at lower prices.[32]

As labor historian James Schmiechen has confirmed, the 1830s and 1840s saw the traditions of an established artisan trade in shoemaking eclipsed by sweated production. Adolf Loos drew on the older myth of the pipe-smoking, clean-shirted, educated cobbler at the end of the century, but in reality by 1849 London shoemakers complained of their lack of work, money and food. Aside from orders from elite consumers, traditional artisans found their professional practice invaded by cheaper female, child and immigrant labor and the bulk of their customers drawn to "inferior" goods. In some respects this "labor aristocracy" had priced itself out of the market. While a reputation for trade union activism had earned shoemakers valuable status and good working conditions in the early nineteenth century, the reorganization of trade in Northampton on the lines of a factory system meant that the newer London retailers could look beyond London manufacturers to source their goods. The revision of trade tariffs in 1826 also opened up contact with suppliers across the English Channel who were willing to supply fashionable French styles at low cost.[33] Moses and his competitors, whose shops grandly answered to the names of Magazine, Depot and Emporium, served a rapidly expanding population, insatiable for the "latest thing," with thousands of pairs of provincial and foreign shoes manufactured under sweated conditions.[34]

Beyond the shifting and fickle tastes of consumers, the actual process of manufacture remained fairly unaltered until fuller mechanization in the 1890s. The first stage in the manufacture of a

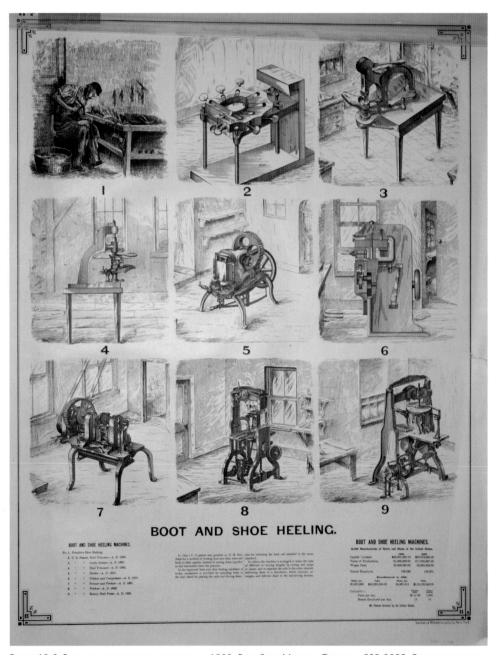

FIGURE 10.6: BOOT AND SHOE HEELING MACHINES, C. 1900. BATA SHOE MUSEUM, TORONTO, S82.0099. REPRODUCED COURTESY OF BATA SHOE MUSEUM.

shoe was "clicking," or cutting out the various parts of the product from the leather. The intricacy of this practice demanded great skill and so was initially least affected by the incursions of sweated and home working. But by the 1860s, the introduction of new cutting tools enabled some division of labor, where several unskilled hands could take on the work previously undertaken by one or two highly trained artisans, instantly increasing the speed of output but undermining an attention to detail. The second stage of production was "closing," or stitching the upper part of the shoe together. The invention of the sewing machine caused this process to be the first to become fully mechanized, so that by the 1890s, both branches of the trade, ready-made and bespoke, relied on machine closing. The third stage of "making" the shoe incorporated the attaching of the sole and heel to the upper around the mold of a last. The first step of joining the insole and upper was a complex maneuver, which relied on skilled handworkers until 1891, when an automatic lasting-machine was patented with female operatives in mind. The fixing of insole and upper to sole was automated thirty years earlier with the introduction of the McKay shoe-sewing machine, enabling up to 600 pairs of shoes to be made by one machine-hand in a working day. The development of heeling machines took longer and this stage continued to be performed by handworkers until the mid-1890s (Figure 10.6). Finally, the finishing of the shoe involved cleaning, lining, accessorizing and packing, a highly subdivided process that had always entailed a high degree of subcontracting and home work, but which nevertheless underwent a massive expansion in scale once the industry had transformed itself to meet a rapid growth in demand.[35]

By the opening of the twentieth century, the classic man's shoe, whether bespoke or ready-to-wear, was a complicated object. In terms of style, its basic look did not differ greatly from the forms of shoe that had attracted consumers more than a hundred years before. It was this supposed "stability" that interested modernist critics. Yet the modern shoe was variously crafted through several industrial processes by hand and machine; it was probably manufactured in parts at separate sites, and it incorporated in its makeup the history of a much altered profession. Despite the accusations of decline that mass production attracted, Edward Swaysland, principal of technical training in Northampton, was able to put a positive gloss on the fruits of his industry in 1905, drawing together those issues of hygiene, functionality and aesthetics that made the man's shoe such a suggestive example for progressive aestheticians. The shoe factories of the English Midlands were some distance, both geographically and intellectually, from the ateliers of Vienna and Paris that framed the writings of Loos and Le Corbusier. But the discipline that Swaysland's trade demanded and the seemingly superior polish of its product opened that obscure amalgam of leather, thread, blacking and tin tacks up to surprising critique and connections, positioning it as a sign for something much more than a simple shodding for the feet.[36]

11.
A DELICATE BALANCE

WOMEN, POWER AND HIGH HEELS

elizabeth semmelhack

Since its emergence as an item within Western fashion, the high heel has been a powerful and mutable signifier conveying disparate meanings. It is a consummate example of artifice, yet over the past four hundred years it has been rationalized and made normative within shifting networks of class, gender and sexuality. In particular, the high heel has become a "natural" feature of female fashion at the nexus of cultural constructions of female irrationality, desire and agency. Rather than exploring the psychosexual and ultimately personal meaning of the high heel, this chapter will endeavor to frame the high heel within cultural terms and explore why it has developed and remained a paramount accessory to received values and traditional power structures and dynamics.

THE RISE OF HIGH HEELS

The appearance of heeled footwear in Western Europe during the late sixteenth century has been firmly established by June Swann's meticulous research.[1] Swann suggests that the addition of pieces of leather, either to the sole of a shoe or inserted directly above the sole for the purpose of repair, is the possible origin of the stacked leather heel.[2] However, given that repairs of this type were not new to late sixteenth-century shoemaking, the question is *why* the heel emerged as an item of fashion at that time. The fact that the English called the new heels "Polony" – Polish – suggests an alternate avenue of inquiry.[3] The inspiration for the heel, as with other examples of fashionable footwear in Europe, may have been the East. The *poulaine,* with its elongated toe reminiscent of Middle Eastern footwear, has been linked to the return of the crusaders, and trade with the Ottoman Empire has been credited with providing the *nalin* as inspiration for the chopine. Yet the range of cultures from which the high heel derived is more complex. The Persians, Ottomans, Crimean Tartars, Polish and Ukrainian Cossacks, and Indian Mughals should all be considered as possible sources for the high heel. Each of these cultures had forms of heeled footwear long associated with male equestrian and military attire; some also featured heeled footwear in female dress (Figure 11.1).

Throughout the sixteenth century, Europeans became increasingly interested in these cultures for a range of political, social and commercial reasons.[4] Trade goods, travel accounts, and diplomatic connections stimulated a greater awareness of the East. Nicolas de Nicolay's *Navigations et Pérégrinations Orientales,* printed in Lyons in 1567–68, is an early example of an illustrated publication that featured detailed information on Near Eastern clothing.[5] The beautiful Tartar riding boot preserved in Livrustkammaren (Stockholm), and thought to have been presented by the Tartar Khan in 1582, provides evidence of a surviving example of footwear as an item of cultural and gift exchange.[6] The swiftness with which the heel became integral to men's European and North American equestrian footwear also suggests a connection to Eastern examples.[7] Although the origin is debatable, it is clear that the heel, albeit sometimes quite modest, had become a symbol of wealth, style and status worn by men, women and children of the upper classes by the early to middle part of the seventeenth century.

By the second half of the seventeenth century, the *high* heel made its debut as the upper classes increased the height of their heels, possibly in response to the incorporation of modest heels into the footwear worn by people of lower social stations. The eye-catching red heels favored by King Louis XIV of France (reigned 1643 to 1715) are the most prominent examples of this shift. During his reign, red high heels, while already an established fashion, became a regulated expression of political privilege: only those granted access to the French court were permitted to wear them (Figures 11.2 and 11.3).[8] The high heel's association with social status remained strong throughout the remainder of the seventeenth century, but gender distinctions became increasingly evident. Men's heels were sturdy or blocky, while women's heels were more tapered and delicate in design, reflecting the cultural preference for a dainty female foot.

FIGURE 11.1: IN THIS
SIXTEENTH-CENTURY
MUGHAL MINIATURE,
POSSIBLY OF A TURKOMAN,
THE FORM OF HEELED
FOOTWEAR FAVORED IN
PERSIA IS CLEARLY SEEN.
REZA JAHNGIR SHAH,
C.1591–92.
© STAPLETON COLLECTION/
CORBIS.

The values ascribed to a small female foot are evident in Charles Perrault's story, *Cinderella*, which debuted in the French court in the late seventeenth century. In the tale, Cinderella's extraordinarily tiny feet are the embodiment of her natural nobility. Her glass slippers transparently confirm this inborn grace and lead to her social elevation.[9] In contrast, her stepsisters' large feet signify their intrinsic lack of virtue. Indeed, the high heel's popularity among women was related to its ability to present the fiction of a diminutive foot by hiding the greater part of the foot under the hem of the wearer's skirts, leaving only the points of the toes visible.[10]

By the early eighteenth century, the high heel was emerging as an exclusively feminine form of footwear and this shift reflected changes in notions of gender. Enlightenment thinkers expounded the ascendancy of reason over the irrational, and within this paradigm, women were contrasted with men as being governed by sentiment rather than intellect.[11] Women's fashion consumption was taken as evidence of their innate irrationality as well as their susceptibility to vice. In response, men's fashion became more restrained, and during this nascence of the suit, men abandoned the high heel.[12] They would not sport high heels for another two centuries, and then in a period of gender, race and sexual "liberation." The move toward greater temperance in men's dress contrasted with women's fashions, which became markedly more ornate as the eighteenth century wore on. The high heel, now exclusively feminine, became one of those luxuries seen as confirming women's natural proclivity toward foolish adornment (Figures 11.4 and 11.5).

HEELS, POWER AND DESIRE IN THE NINETEENTH CENTURY

Mary Wollstonecraft, in *A Vindication of the Rights of Woman* (1792), rejected the contention that women's fondness of dress was inborn and argued that it arose instead, "like false ambition in men, from a love of power."[13] Her observation that women might use fashion to influence men through the exploitation of men's sexual desire, articulated a grave concern. Indeed, as Wollstonecraft was writing, the French aristocracy was in flight, and in popular rhetoric its downfall was directly linked to licentious power wielded by sexually exploitative women. The connections between femininity, sexuality, power and fashion articulated in the eighteenth century continue to inform the meanings of the high heel, one of the few sartorial vestiges of aristocratic and court culture that has currency today.

As the eighteenth century drew to a close, high heels, among other accoutrements of the aristocracy, became objects of scorn. After reaching unprecedented heights in the 1780s, the heel was reduced to only a few millimeters as the upper classes throughout Europe and North America began to conform to the more "restrained" esthetic favored by the rising middling classes. The loss of the high heel also signaled a change in idealized femininity. In contrast to the seemingly unrestrained freedoms of eighteenth-century aristocratic women, the emergent bourgeoisie embraced the Rousseauan ideals of motherhood and female domesticity.[14] The demure, thin-soled footwear favored in the first half of the nineteenth century signaled a rejection of aristocratic excess

FIGURE 11.2: THE HIGH RED HEELS INSISTED UPON BY KING LOUIS XIV OF FRANCE AND HIS RETINUE STAND OUT IN SHARP CONTRAST TO THE DARK, MORE MODESTLY HEELED SHOES WORN BY THE SPANISH. ANTOINE MATHIEU, INTERVIEW BETWEEN LOUIS XIV AND PHILIP IV. LAUMOSMIER, 1660. © GIRAUDON/ ART RESOURCE, NEW YORK.

as well as an embracing of this new domestication of women; such shoes were not designed for sustained outdoor wear (Figures 11.6 and 11.7).[15]

When the heel did reemerge in the middle of the nineteenth century, the bourgeoisie was firmly ensconced and the confinement of "respectable" women was being challenged on many levels. Both those interested in sustaining patriarchal hegemony and those agitating for female enfranchisement sought the benefits that could be gained by increased female participation in the public sphere; the high heel had a role in defining the way in which women might participate. For those who sought to preserve the gender status quo, the foray of privileged women into the public realm, when couched in terms of leisure and conspicuous consumption, was an effective means of advertising the wealth and influence of their households; these women were accessories of male wealth, consumers not producers.[16] The high heels and lavish fashions worn by privileged women were also intentionally reminiscent of eighteenth-century excess and helped to establish their participation in public life as frivolous, undermining the call for female enfranchisement by reviving claims of women's essential irrationality.[17] Indeed, as Veblen would argue, female fashion consumption provided men with the opportunity to flaunt their economic status while simultaneously lamenting the vast sums squandered by wives on their *toilette*.

The presence of privileged women in the public realm also revived arguments concerning the strength and weakness of female virtue.[18] In the second half of the nineteenth century, the presence and the idea of the courtesan and sexual commodification became central to European intellectual and artistic thought. The concept of the courtesan linked female "power" and sexual manipulation. It also illustrated the failure of female agency and provided a warning to those "respectable" women who sought more autonomy. Although wives and daughters were being allowed, even encouraged, to flaunt the family's wealth through extravagant fashions, their actions were proscribed by the specter of impropriety. Despite these admonitions, or perhaps because of them, the commodification of female sexuality became a mainstay of modernity and defined sexual allure was emerging as a goal of fashion. High heels, in particular, became infused with erotic significance.

Manet's painting *Olympia,* which scandalized the public when exhibited in the Paris Salon of 1865, was a blatant image of sexual commodification established, in part, by the presence of contemporary footwear (Figure 11.8). Rather than being a *nude* allegorical figure, Olympia was a portrait of a *naked* prostitute, and it was her fashionable mules that ensured the viewer would perceive her as such.[19] Manet's inclusion of footwear referenced pornography, where shoes were emerging as a standard accessory to the commodified body. Shoes heightened the voyeuristic appeal of the pornographic image through their association with the public realm, the realm

FIGURE 11.3 (FACING PAGE): THIS UPPER-CLASS CHILDREN'S SHOE FEATURES A PAINTED RED HIGH HEEL. IT DATES TO THE END OF THE SEVENTEENTH CENTURY AND MAY HAVE BEEN WORN BY A LITTLE BOY. POSSIBLY FRENCH, 1680–1700. BATA SHOE MUSEUM, TORONTO, P90.201. REPRODUCED BY KIND PERMISSION OF BATA SHOE MUSEUM.

FIGURE 11.4: As fashionable women sought higher and higher heels in the 1770s and 1780s, shoemakers had to experiment with ways of supporting the arch of the wearer's foot. Much like bridge construction, high-heeled shoes from this period often feature innovative arch support. English, 1780–85. Bata Shoe Museum, Toronto, P98.5. Reproduced by kind permission of Bata Shoe Museum.

where the body was hidden from view. Conversely, shoes also provided tantalizing evidence of the private aspects of the female body in public. The two shoes that peeked out from under a woman's dress were proof that the skirted female, although presented as having a single, impenetrable mass below the waist, did in fact have a well-articulated lower half.

Within the public realm, shoes signaled the start of the leg which, as Valerie Steele put it, is "the pathway to the genitals."[20] Whether seen on the street or in the pornographic image, shoes increasingly had the power to signify and eroticize both the public and the private spheres in the second half of the nineteenth century. High heels, specifically, became increasingly eroticized and the higher the heel, the greater the shoe's association with sexuality. This is evidenced by the debut of fetish shoes with exaggeratedly high heels, and by the increasing sentiment that high heels were no longer proper for young girls, a concept that still holds in the West today.[21]

THE HEIGHTS OF EROTICISM: HEELS IN TWENTIETH-CENTURY CULTURE

In the early twentieth century, the high heel's capacity to signify values of the proper and improper, public and private, demure and deviant, increasingly shaped the construction of female status, desirability, and self-representation. For early twentieth-century suffragettes, heels were a means of establishing femininity. Dressed in their best clothes they pounded the pavement in heeled button-boots, or enjoyed athletics such as tennis in feminine high-heeled sports shoes, a means of combating arguments that enfranchisement would defeminize women (Figure 11.9). For post-enfranchisement women after the First World War, it was the high heel's ability to establish not only femininity, but also sexual allure, that became paramount.

The democratization of fashion created by the new postwar consumer culture expanded the high heel's role in competition between women. The most extreme example was the "flapper" who suggested sexual availability by wearing daringly high heels, shockingly short skirts, and makeup such as rouge and lipstick, which until the 1920s had been signifiers of prostitution.[22] The "New Woman," who more consciously appreciated the advances gained by the suffragettes, also attempted to differentiate herself from what Dorothy Bromely, in 1927, termed "the old school of fighting feminists who wore flat heels and had very little feminine charm."[23] She did so by incorporating toned-down aspects of the sexually charged fashion into her own wardrobe. The transformation of signifiers of commodified sex into respectable attire was a trend that would increasingly define women's fashion of the twentieth and twenty-first centuries.

That the high heel, specifically, continued to connote sex appeal is evidenced by a comparison with the fashionable platform shoe of the 1930s and 1940s.[24] When the platform first appeared, it was associated with beachwear and referenced leisure and play, as the chapter in this volume by Stefania Ricci suggests. By the end of the 1930s, prominent shoe designers such as Salvatore Ferragamo had transformed the platform into an item of high fashion.[25] However, despite its currency within *fashion*, the platform had limited *erotic* appeal, if we consider its inconspicuousness in its matching contemporary erotica. Like Manet's *Olympia* and the myriad pornographic images from the 1850s on, pinups of the 1930s and 1940s were frequently displayed in little more than their shoes (Figure 11.10). As the pinup entered into the wider culture during the 1940s, erotic associations of the high heel were further heightened and the high heel's function as a sexual signifier increased. The erotic currency of the high heel is also demonstrated by contrasting images used during the Second World War to marshal Americans to the war effort. Depictions of strong, "sensibly" shod women doing "men's work" urged women to fill positions vacated by soldiers, while spike-heeled pinups were meant to buoy the soldiers' spirits.[26] "Sensible" shoes still imply a lack of sex appeal.

As men reclaimed their civilian jobs at the end of the Second World War, renewed emphasis on female domesticity emerged and women were encouraged to return to the home. Fashion reflected this cultural shift by bringing women's postwar style into greater agreement with the pinup ideals of the war years. The high, significantly more attenuated heel that became important in fashion in the late 1940s reflected this trend, which culminated in the invention of the stiletto in the mid-1950s.[27] By the mid-1950s, cultural icons of femininity and sexuality, whether they were *Vogue* models, television housewives or Hollywood bombshells, were typically represented in stilettos. High heels increasingly became normalized attire for many average women as well (Figure 11.11).[28]

This ultrafeminine fashion brought a renewal of rhetoric concerning fashion consumption as a reflection of women's essential irrationality. In particular, the gait of a woman wearing stilettos was at the core of many representations of women as sexually alluring yet ludicrous. The emphasis placed on the breasts and buttocks when wearing stilettos was enhanced by the swaying of the hips that resulted from walking in them. Images of women precariously balanced atop towering stilettos suggested voluptuousness and vulnerability, as well as foolish submission to fashion. Images such as these became central themes in erotica. *Playboy*, which debuted in 1953 and quickly became one of the most popular magazines in America, often featured humorous cartoons of preposterous, bodacious beauties in excessively high stilettos. More often than not, the centerfold "playmates" wore little more than a pair of stilettos, a trend that has remained unabated.

The stiletto's reign as the essential female shoe was challenged in the 1960s. The "youth quake" ushered in gamine-inspired fashions, complete with scandalously short skirts and low-heeled shoes. The fashionable 1960s female was not so much a voluptuous bombshell as a wide-eyed woman-child for whom high heels seemed excessively "grown-up." For those engaged in the burgeoning women's liberation movement, the high heel was a symbol of oppression, not a means to placate societal fears concerning women's aspirations to equal rights. The artifice of the high heel was also rejected by the "back to nature" elements of the counterculture, which promoted many traditional concepts concerning female sexuality: "barefoot and pregnant" being a literal ideal for some. Although the high heel was abandoned by both the fashion-minded and the socially conscious, its erotic currency remained unchallenged.

FIGURE 11.5: ACHILLE DEVERIA, ONE YEAR AFTER MARRIAGE (UN AN APRÈS LE MARRIAGE), MID-NINETEENTH CENTURY. THIS IMAGE DEPICTS A MOMENT OF DOMESTIC MELANCHOLY IN THE ABSENCE OF A HUSBAND. © SNARK/ART RESOURCE, NEW YORK.

UN AN APRÈS LE MARIAGE.

Composé et dessiné sur pierre par A. DEVERIA
imprimé et publié par C. MOTTE à Paris.

FIGURE 11.6 (ABOVE): THE IDEALS OF FEMALE DOMESTICITY WERE REFLECTED IN THE DELICATE, THIN-SOLED FOOTWEAR FASHIONABLE IN THE FIRST HALF OF THE NINETEENTH CENTURY. THE WHITE PAIR IS ENGLISH, THE BLACK PAIR IS FRENCH, 1840S. BATA SHOE MUSEUM, TORONTO, P81.403 AND P81.170. REPRODUCED BY KIND PERMISSION OF BATA SHOE MUSEUM.

FIGURE 11.7 (LEFT). NINETEENTH-CENTURY NOSTALGIA FOR EIGHTEENTH-CENTURY EXCESS IN FEMALE FASHION EXTENDED TO THE SHOE. THE CURVACEOUS HEEL THAT BECAME A LATE NINETEENTH-CENTURY STAPLE WAS COYLY CALLED A "LOUIS" HEEL AFTER KING LOUIS XV OF FRANCE. BLACK LACE-UP BOOTS WITH ELABORATE HAND-EMBROIDERED DECORATION PRODUCED BY FRANÇOIS PINET, FRENCH, 1880S. BATA SHOE MUSEUM, TORONTO, P91.128. REPRODUCED BY KIND PERMISSION OF BATA SHOE MUSEUM.

The licentious, "no strings attached" disco culture that arose in the 1970s once again brought fashion and pornographic fantasy together. Fashion photography blatantly linked contemporary pornography and the high heel, an essential and established part of the lexicon of erotic imagery, which returned as an important fashion accessory. The high heel, like the libidinous economy in which it was fashionable, reflected established male fantasies rather than sexual liberation or equality. The reintroduction of the high heel in men's fashion at the same time, after a long absence, further reaffirmed rather than redefined traditional gender roles. The fashions of the 1970s, although ostensibly patterned on new androgynous ideals that rose out of progressive social thought, were more a return to male fashions abandoned centuries earlier, or a parody of women's fashion, than an earnest incorporation of feminine styles. Many male rock stars wore extremely high platforms, long hair and makeup to enhance outrageous stage personas. This ranged from camp in the case of Elton John, to pseudo-menacing with Kiss. Their garish artificiality and gender-bending, although represented as transgressive, recalled established traditions of burlesque and cross-dressing, which used parody to reaffirm the "natural" order of male hegemony (Figure 11.12).

PIMPS AND PLATFORMS

The high-heeled "superfly" fashion was also based on traditional constructions of gender roles. Superfly fashions developed in the immediate post-civil rights decade as an expression of African-American hypermasculinity and homosocial enfranchisement. Taking its name from a very popular 1972 blaxploitation gangster film, and modeled on the fashions of the most flamboyant pimps, the style asserted black masculinity through association with the ownership of female sexual commodity. The iconic image propagated by the popular media portrayed a pimp in his thick-heeled platform shoes attended by his stable of anonymous, mincing, spike-heeled women – predecessors of the 1990s "ho." The "pimp strut," ostentatious jewelry, flashy clothes and outrageous high heels were intimidating or ironic, but never feminine. Despite the claims that androgyny and unisex styles marked 1970s fashion, the high heel, whether worn by a man or a woman, reinforced rather than challenged conventional conceptions of gender and sexuality.

By the beginning of the 1980s, men had abandoned all forms of the high heel in favor of the business brogue or the status sneaker as an unprecedented number of women began to vie with men for significant roles in the workplace.[29] "Dress for Success" advised women to wear modest, feminized versions of the male business suit, while the fashion world promoted "power dressing," which travestied the "Dress for Success" suit by infusing it with overt sexuality. In this incarnation, the successful businesswoman was depicted as aggressive, even predatory, both economically and sexually; she wore "killer" shoes with toweringly high stiletto heels. Dominatrix references edged their way into fashion; insinuating professional women were "pros" of a different sort.[30] This tension formed part of the charge of Helmut Newton's photographic strategy, in which the shoe was central.

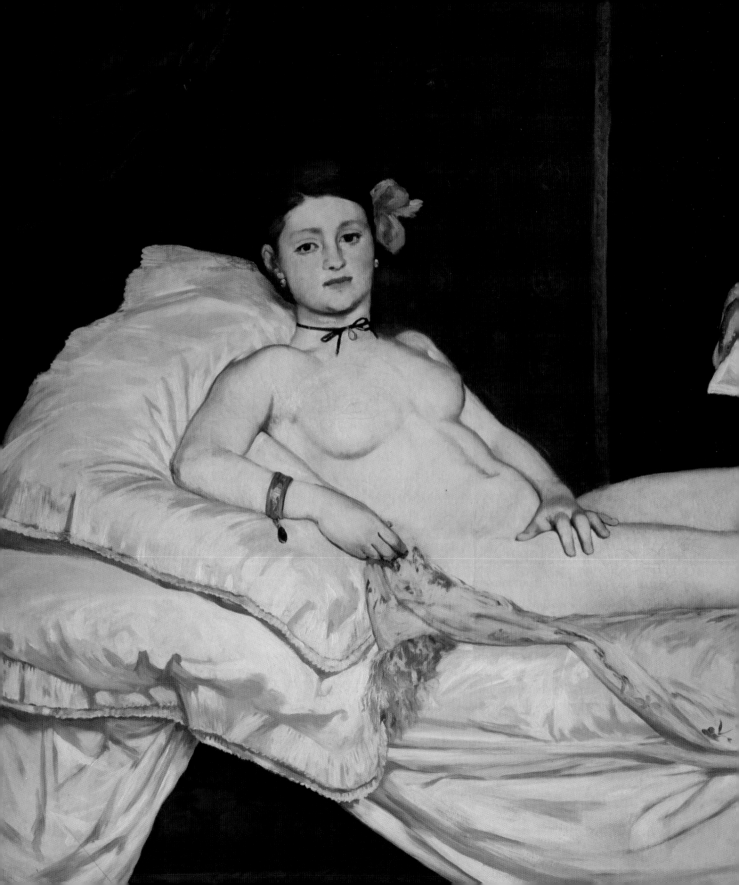

FIGURE 11.8: NAKED EXCEPT
FOR A FEW BAUBLES AND A
PAIR OF MULES, MANET'S
OLYMPIA HAD MORE IN
COMMON WITH EMERGENT
PORNOGRAPHIC IMAGES OF
THE CONTEMPORARY
COMMODIFIED FEMALE THAN
WITH THE LONG-STANDING
CLASSICAL TRADITIONS OF THE
NUDE. EDOUARD MANET,
OLYMPIA, 1863–65.
© COLLECTION OF MUSÉE
D'ORSAY. AKG-IMAGES/ERICH
LESSING.

FIGURE 11.9 (ABOVE): FOR EARLY TWENTIETH-CENTURY WOMEN, HEELS WERE A MEANS OF PROCLAIMING FEMININITY WHILE AT THE SAME TIME ADVOCATING GREATER ENFRANCHISEMENT. FOR EXAMPLE, SPORTS SUCH AS TENNIS WERE ENJOYED IN FEMININE, HIGH-HEELED SPORTS SHOES AS A MEANS OF COMBATING THE ARGUMENTS THAT SUFFRAGE WOULD DEFEMINIZE WOMEN. TENNIS SHOE, AMERICAN, 1920S. BATA SHOE MUSEUM, TORONTO, S89.123. REPRODUCED BY KIND PERMISSION OF BATA SHOE MUSEUM.

FIGURE 11.10 (FACING PAGE): THE HIGH, SIGNIFICANTLY MORE ATTENUATED HEEL THAT BECAME IMPORTANT IN FASHION IN THE LATE 1940S CULMINATED IN THE INVENTION OF THE STILETTO IN THE MID-1950S AND BROUGHT WOMEN CLOSER TO THE IDEAL OF THE SPIKE-HEELED PINUP POPULAR WITH MEN DURING THE WAR YEARS. SKYSCRAPER STILETTOS, AMERICAN, MID-1950S. BATA SHOE MUSEUM, TORONTO, S82.74. REPRODUCED BY KIND PERMISSION OF BATA SHOE MUSEUM.

The linkage between female success and sexual commodification also found expression in the emergence of luxury lingerie as an important commodity in the 1980s. The American lingerie giant, Victoria's Secret, decorated its stores to suggest nineteenth-century bordellos, sold distinctly Edwardian undergarments such as bustiers, and published soft porn catalogs showing lingerie-clad, stiletto-wearing women. This romanticization of late nineteenth-century sexual commodification reflected tensions concerning female social and economic advances; these mirrored the mid-nineteenth century cultural focus on the courtesan, which also arose at a time when many women were calling for greater equality. Arguably, the high heel was now as much a form of lingerie as outerwear. Given its sustained relationship with pornographic image-making, its presence in the business world was thus problematic. For this reason, the average working woman shunned the highly sexualized high heel promoted through fashion and pornographic fantasies and wore low-heeled pumps that were feminine but not overly sexual. These women were ridiculed by the media, which depicted them as frantically running to work in sneakers, clutching their "sensible shoes."

TURNING TRICKS: HEGEMONY AND HIGH HEELS

The 1987 stock market crash triggered corporate downsizing and increased instability in the workplace. The advent of the Internet in the mid-1990s ushered in new economic possibilities. It also introduced a new model of male success, the "wonder boy," which threatened the authority of tenured men. The burgeoning men's movements reflected this insecurity.[31] "Grrl Culture" arose at this time and proponents self-consciously distanced themselves from images of sexually unfulfilled and overworked "pro-choice" 1980s "superwomen." They claimed to exercise power through the exploitation of their natural "power tools," that is to say their breasts and genitals, promiscuous sex, objectification of men, and participation in fashion consumption and display.[32] Parallels between 1990s "Grrl Culture" and 1920s flapper culture, which also arose at a postfeminist moment, are unmistakable, particularly in their use of sexualized fashion to differentiate themselves from women of the previous generation. Debbie Stoller, editor of *Bust Magazine*, wrote in 1999:

> From lipstick lesbians to rouge-wearing riot grrls, today's vampy visionaries believe that it is possible to make a feminist fashion statement without resorting to wearing Birkenstocks 24/7.[33]

By referencing the unisex Birkenstock sandal, Stoller conjures up the "woman's libber" whom she characterizes as being as devoid of femininity as the "low-heeled fighting feminists" of the early twentieth century. The superstar Madonna became the icon of "Grrl Power" because she "dressed like a sex object, but … suggested that the trappings of femininity could be used to make a sexual

FIGURE 11.11 (FACING PAGE): AS MEN RECLAIMED THEIR CIVILIAN JOBS AT THE END OF THE SECOND WORLD WAR, THERE WAS A RENEWED EMPHASIS ON FEMALE DOMESTICITY AND WOMEN WERE ENCOURAGED TO RETURN TO THE HOME. THIS GENERAL ELECTRIC PROMOTIONAL IMAGE FOR A NEW ELECTRIC OVEN DEPICTS THE IDEALIZED WOMAN OF THE 1950S: DOMESTIC, FEMININE AND WEARING HIGH HEELS. © BETTMANN/CORBIS.

statement that was powerful rather than passive."[34] That the path to "power" was through conspicuous consumption, or that fashion consumption and the providing of sexual service were "feminist" statements, seems to have been an unreflected assertion.

LIMOUSINE SHOES

By the late 1990s, shoe designers such as Manolo Blahnik and Christian Louboutin, famous for their toweringly high heels, were elevated to the status of cultural icons. The hit TV show *Sex and the City* made these designer shoes symbols of status, sexuality, and "Grrl Power" (Figure 11.13). The flip side of all this conspicuous consumption of distinctly non-sensible shoes was that it signified economic folly, as the sophisticated *Sex in the City* character Carrie Bradshaw made clear with the line, "I've spent $40,000 on shoes and I have no place to live? I will literally be the old woman who lived in her shoes!"[35] Shoes are central to the puns and innuendo of *Sex and the City*, as the writers and producers realize that they are central to late twentieth-century female experience.

At the turn of the twenty-first century, popular rhetoric equating female sexuality with power was concomitant with the ascendancy of fashion inspired by strippers and sex workers in both haute couture and ready-to-wear markets. Classic stilettos were replaced with more blatantly dominatrix-inspired footwear, and striptease thong underwear replaced elaborate lingerie. Aspiring writers published first-person accounts such as *Stripper Shoes*[36] and *Ivy League Stripper*,[37] housewives practiced striptease aerobics; the terms "bitch" and "ho" came into common parlance. The fashions of the postfeminist flappers who sought to flaunt sexual freedom by wearing spiked heels and rolled stockings which revealed rouged knees insinuating that they had recently performed fellatio, were paralleled by their late twentieth-century great-granddaughters, who expressed their own "power" by wearing T-shirts emblazoned with phrases such as "Porn Star" and footwear referencing streetwalkers (Figure 11.14). High-fashion designers such as John Galliano and Tom Ford blatantly alluded to sexual commodification in their designs. The message of Dolce & Gabbana's 2003 spring/summer line could not have been clearer, with spike-heeled, bondage-referencing sandals emblazoned with the word "SEX" spelled out in gaudy rhinestones.

HIGH HEELS: PATRIARCHAL OR PARODIC TOOLS?

The sexual signifiers being touted as accessories of female power, such as footwear alluding to the sex trade, bring with them a long and complex history of meaning in relation to patriarchy. Fashions explicitly linking women to commodified sex confirm, rather than challenge, male hege-

FIGURE 11.12 (FACING PAGE): CAMPY VERSIONS OF FEMALE ATTIRE SUCH AS EXTREMELY HIGH PLATFORMS, LONG HAIR AND MAKEUP WERE FREQUENTLY USED BY MALE ROCK STARS TO AUGMENT OUTRAGEOUS STAGE PERSONAS IN THE 1970S. MANY MALE FANS ALSO SPORTED HIGH HEELS AT THIS TIME AS WELL. THIS PAIR WAS MADE BY THE TORONTO SHOEMAKER, MASTER JOHN AND, ACCORDING TO THE DONOR, WAS "WORN TO KICK THE SHIT OUT OF GUYS IN BAR ROOM BRAWLS." PLATFORM BOOT, MASTER JOHN, 1973. BATA SHOE MUSEUM, TORONTO, P96.111. REPRODUCED BY KIND PERMISSION OF BATA SHOE MUSEUM.

mony and privilege. This is reflected in the concepts and vocabulary of "pimping" and the trappings of "ho" couture becoming normative rather than radicalizing, despite the attempts by some to use them ironically. For the past four hundred years, the high heel has signified a multiplicity of meanings. It is difficult to attribute the advent of the high heel or its persistent presence in Western culture to primarily personal or psychosexual factors. Neither the trite, essentialist sentiment that women just love shoes, nor the Lacanian theorizing which attributes an essential phallic nature to the high heel, explains its development in the West or its shifts in cultural signification over time. Rather, it is the high heel's centrality to gender construction and related issues of economic and cultural hegemony that are the very core of its enduring presence in Western culture.

FIGURE 11.13 (FACING PAGE): THIS STRAPPY GOLD STILETTO SANDAL WAS DESIGNED BY MANOLO BLAHNIK IN THE MID-1990S AND IS AN EXAMPLE OF HIS "SEXY" AND ARCHITECTURALLY INTERESTING HIGH HEELS. "SIZZLE SANDAL" BY MANOLO BLAHNIK, 1990S. BATA SHOE MUSEUM, TORONTO, S99.32. REPRODUCED BY KIND PERMISSION OF BATA SHOE MUSEUM.

FIGURE 11.14 (OVERLEAF): THE SIMILARITIES, BOTH FORMALLY AND CULTURALLY, BETWEEN THIS PHOTOGRAPH OF A WOMAN COMPETING IN THE "MISS BUCK WILD" PLAYBOY TV EVENT AND MANET'S OLYMPIA ARE STRIKING. CLAD ONLY IN HER HYPERSEXUALIZED STILETTOS AND A BIT OF JEWELRY, THIS TWENTY-FIRST-CENTURY STRIPPER STRIKES A POSE THAT GIVES VISUAL EVIDENCE OF THE PERPETUATION OF THE HIGH HEEL'S CONNECTIONS WITH FEMALE SEXUAL COMMODIFICATION. © BRENDA ANN KENNEALLY/CORBIS.

12.

SHOES AND THE EROTIC IMAGINATION[1]

valerie steele

According to an early version of the Cinderella story, the evil stepsisters cut off their toes and heels to fit into Cinderella's glass slippers, but were betrayed by a trail of blood. In William Klein's satiric film *Qui Êtes-Vous, Polly Magoo* (1965) a professor explains that the hidden meaning of the Cinderella story is "the value of tiny feet and beautiful clothes." He triumphantly concludes: "So there you are: fetishism, mutilation, pain. Fashion in a nutshell." Although this is obviously an exaggeration, many people would be inclined to agree, at least with respect to high heels. High-heeled shoes exert a powerful charm for many people. There is a little of Imelda Marcos in many women, and many men exhibit an almost Pavlovian response to the sight of a woman in high heels. Are they all fetishists? How does hard-core fetishism differ from the widespread enthusiasm for "sexy" shoes and playing "footsie"? This chapter will attempt to explain why the foot and shoe play such an important role in the erotic imagination. Historically, the obvious comparison is with bound feet, a part of the complex Chinese shoe-culture suggested elsewhere in this volume in the chapter by Paola Zamperini.

AN EXAGGERATED EROTICISM

The popular perception of the nineteenth century once focused on the idea of sexual repression, and it was widely assumed that Victorian sexual "prudery" spawned myriad hypocritical perversions. "The campaign to conceal the leg was so effective that by mid-century men were easily aroused by a glimpse of a woman's ankle," wrote historian Stephen Kern in *Anatomy and Destiny*. "The high incidence at this time of fetishes involving shoes and stockings also testifies to the exaggerated eroticism generated by hiding the lower half of the female body."[2] Philippe Perrot also argues that: "In the nineteenth century, female bosoms and behinds were emphasized, but legs were completely hidden, distilling into the lacy foam of underwear an erotic capital, the returns on which could be gauged by the cult of the calf and by the arousal caused by the glimpse of an ankle."[3] Historical analyses of the nineteenth-century fashion often employ an economic trope, and suggest that capitalism exploits the obsession with bodies in order to make new commodities (Figure 12.1).

It is a crude and misleading stereotype to suggest that the long skirts of the Victorians "caused" widespread foot and shoe fetishism. Women's skirts, after all, had been long for centuries – in the "permissive" Paris of the eighteenth century as well as in "prudish" Victorian London. Legs were certainly regarded as being sexually attractive. In *The Fleshly School of Poetry* (1872), Robert Buchanan argued that "sensualism" was spreading dangerously through society:

> It has penetrated into the very sweetshops, and there ... may be seen this year models
> of the female Leg, the whole definite and elegant article as far as the thigh, with a fringe
> of paper cut in imitation of female drawers and embroidered in the female fashion! ...
> The Leg, as a disease ... becomes a spectre, a portent, a mania ... everywhere – the Can-
> Can, in shop windows.[4]

Kern suggests that this is evidence of sexual repression, but it might more logically be interpreted as evidence of growing sexual display or, perhaps, the spreading commercialization of sexuality. There is, moreover, no reason to think that foot and shoe fetishism were more common in the nineteenth century than they are today. Shoe fetishism seems to have emerged, however, in the eighteenth century.

The French writer Restif de La Bretone (1734–1806) was much closer to what we might consider a "true" fetishist. In his novel *La Pied de Fanchette*, Restif described how the narrator stole the rose-colored slippers of his employer's wife, which were so appealing with their little pink tongues and green heels: "My lips pressed one of the jewels, while the other, deceiving the sacred end of nature, from excess to exultation replaced the object of sex." In other words, after kissing one "jewel," he ejaculated into the other. According to David Coward, "[Restif's] daily diaries reveal even more clearly than his stories that he was a shoe voyeur, a shoe stealer, and a shoe collector."[5] He particularly liked very high heels.

The height of shoes, like their more or less small size, has erotic connotations. That most striking shoe of the Renaissance was the Venetian chopine, an enormously high platform shoe that was associated particularly with courtesans.[6] Platform shoes (for men or women) have existed in many cultures where their significance is by no means limited to eroticism. By increasing the apparent stature of the wearer, they can signify high status. When not too high, platform shoes, like the Japanese *geta* examined in the chapter by Martha Chaiklin, can even serve functional

FIGURE 12.1: GERMAN-MADE BOUDOIR SLIPPERS WITH ROUND TOES, BREASTED LOUIS HEELS AND VAMP DECORATED WITH GOLD-COLORED LACE, PRODUCED BY J. FUHRMANN IN BADEN, C. 1875–90. BATA SHOE MUSEUM, TORONTO, P91.18. REPRODUCED BY KIND PERMISSION OF BATA SHOE MUSEUM.

purposes such as raising the wearer out of a muddy street. There is no question, however, that very high shoes inhibit the wearer's movements, a form of "bondage" that some people find erotic.[7] Sometimes even the appearance of restriction is perceived as erotic. In 1992, the House of Chanel sold cork-soled platform sandals with ankle straps, inspiring an article in the *New York Times* in which fashion historian Anne Hollander asked what was so "sexy, perverse and delicious" about this look. Musing about "untold erotic practices," she suggested that an elegant ankle harness presents the foot "as a beautiful slave."[8]

"THE INDESCRIBABLE ECSTASY"

In the seventeenth century, European shoemakers modified platforms to create the high-heeled shoe. In the beginning, high heels were worn by both men and women. As men's fashions became more subdued, however, high-heeled shoes became associated with women. The erotic appeal of high heels cannot, therefore, be separated from their association with "femininity." It is important to stress, however, that women's fashion does not always emphasize the high heel.[9] Shoe fetishists, however, usually have done so.

The nineteenth-century *Englishwoman's Domestic Magazine* offered many testimonials to the high-heeled shoe, including several that explicitly compared the style with footbinding. "One can understand about the torture endured by Chinese ladies … [but] no one will, I think, deny the piquant and graceful effect of the High-heeled shoe."[10] A small, "neat" foot in a "delicate" shoe, giving a "graceful" walk was among the clearest enthusiasm of many *EDM* correspondents.[11] They anathematized the "large, clumsy, heavy" heels of men's shoes, preferring narrow heels, "as high as possible," which gave "a high instep" and "an arched waist."[12] One correspondent insisted that he had "seen fair Parisiennes walk with ease on heels quite three inches high."[13] Notice how the numerology of foot size seems to have been transposed to the size of the heel.

"High heels have succeeded the corset question in the ladies' '*Conversatione*,' will you allow me to express my opinion upon this latter as upon the former subject?" wrote Walter, the unknown author of an extraordinary nineteenth-century erotic document. He liked the "graceful mode of walking" induced by high heels, especially the way they caused a lady to "point her foot." Indeed, he himself had "adopted ladies' boots … [and] gradually increased the height of the heels [to three inches]" (Figure 12.2).[14]

Long before fashion emphasized high heels, fetishists did, and they have consistently advocated heels significantly higher than the fashionable norm. According to shoe historian Mary Trasko, fetishists have always emphasized "the extreme and ignored fashion trends."[15] The term "kink" entered the English language quite early: "The love of high heels is one of our 'kinks,' and I think a very harmless one at that," wrote a correspondent to *London Life* in 1913.[16] Within the fetishist subculture, high heels were second only to corsets in popularity (Figure 12.3). Indeed, high heels, corsets, and cross-dressing formed a common combination. Happy Heels, for example, claimed to have persuaded her husband to wear high heels and corsets while at home.[17] Mr X said that he wore eight-inch heels and a nineteen-inch corset.[18] Submissive Wife endured tight corsets and stilt-like heels to please her husband. Six-Inch Heels also "dress[ed] to please Hubby," but she also claimed to please herself "even more." "I cannot see myself submitting unless I enjoyed it."[19]

Some of the fetishist literature on high heels was obviously fantastic. Heels were getting higher as skirts got shorter, claimed one correspondent to *Photo Bits* in 1910.[20] But the real picture was not that simple. In 1910, this journal published the serial story "Peggy Paget's Patent Paralysing Pedal Props," fetish shoes with eighteen-inch heels and a "stilt" or "prop" under the sole in the front:

> Oh the tap of those "props" and "heels" on the hard floor! Oh, the ecstasy – the indescribable ecstasy that throbbed my every vein as I walked! Oh, the delight – the unutterable delight – that consumed me as the mirrors around the walls reflected my regal height and the erect pride with which I "dotted"![21]

A person wearing such shoes was not necessarily expected to be able to walk. Standing *en pointe* (not unlike a ballet dancer), with arches radically curved, the wearer could barely hobble. A fetish shoe of the latter part of the nineteenth century has an impossibly high heel, which could have been designed to be inserted (like a dildo) into the fetishist's anus. Shoe museums around the world exhibit significant collections of these extraordinary artifacts, which seem to bridge the leather industry from saddlery to footwear (Figures 12.4 and 12.5). Fetishistic pornography often describes how the male is scratched, stabbed, and penetrated by the woman's or transvestite's high heels.

THE SHOE AS WEAPON – AND AS WOUND

In the 1960s heels were high, mannered and fetishistic, even for secretaries and ladies who lunch. "The high-heeled shoe … has become an object of devotion that borders on passionate worship," declared *High Heels* in 1962. Clad in a high-heeled shoe, "the foot becomes a mysterious weapon which threatens the passive male; and he glories in being so conquered." The high-heeled shoe is a "symbol of love" – and also "a symbol of aggression." "It signifies power. It indicated domination."[22] Primitive gender stereotypes are typical of fetishist fantasies: "Nature had decreed that the male is aggressive while the female remains passive. But this situation has been reversed in the past few decades."[23] Although couched in terms of "female equalization," the image of the dominant female probably has more to do with the psychic reality of male-female relations within the fetishist's natal family. "The whole idea of the female wearing high heels is to emphasize her naturally dominant and aggressive personality," wrote one correspondent.[24] "I consider men are real slaves," High Heeled defiantly told *London Life*, adding, "A man should be allowed to choose which kind of shoes he likes."[25]

"The bare foot … holds no secrets!" But once covered, it becomes "mysterious" and "forbidding" – and therefore fascinating. The leather "is like firm, hard skin!"[26] The man who worships high heels "is actually humbling himself before the superior sex." He regards woman with such "awe and reverence" that she seems "untouchable" and he feels grateful to kiss her shoes, finding

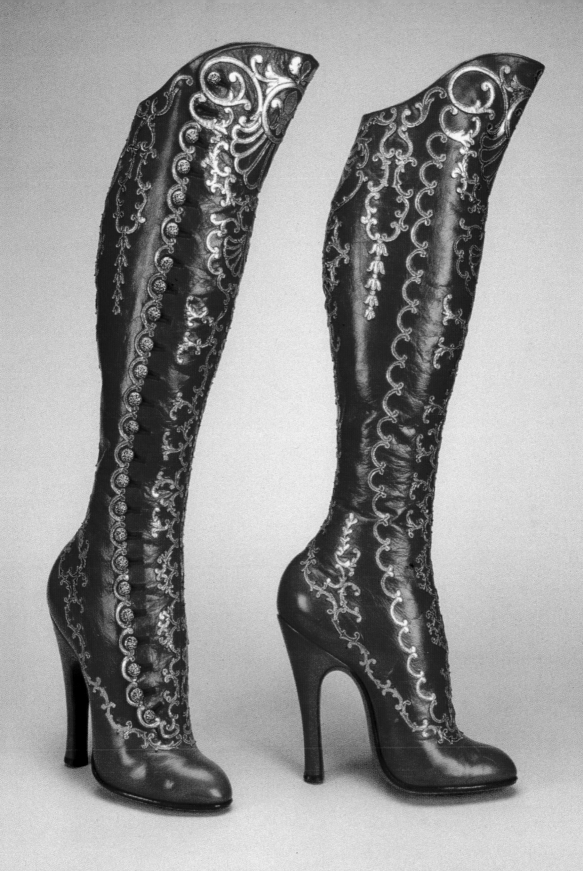

this a satisfying "form of humiliation."[27] There is also the giantess or crush fantasy, which envisions women as huge giantesses crushing tiny, insignificant men underfoot. *Leg Show* includes a number of photographs and drawings of powerful female feet, some naked, others in heels, crushing and squishing everything from bananas to snails and bugs (videos are also advertised, which include "wet, slurpy sound effects"). One particularly striking series of photographs shows a woman's foot in a black, high-heeled shoe being besieged and attacked by dozens of tiny plastic soldiers.[28]

Richard von Krafft-Ebing believed that "the majority – and perhaps all" shoe fetishists were masochists. Mr. X, for example, wanted to "lie at a lady's feet and smell and lick her shoes."[29] Havelock Ellis presented the case of a man whose erotic life focused on women's legs and feet, "exquisitely clothed," and on being "trampled on with utmost severity." C. P. wrote:

> The skirts should be raised sufficiently to afford me the pleasure of seeing her feet and a liberal amount of ankle, but in no case above the knee, or the effects is greatly reduced … The treading should be inflicted … all over the chest, abdomen and groin, and lastly on the penis, which is, of course … in a violent state of erection … I also enjoy being nearly strangled by a woman's foot.[30]

The strangling fantasy that C. P. enjoyed when the foot pressed on his throat suggests some significant connotations. Certainly, the pressure on the penis recalls the pressure of the corset, the constrictions of the tight glove, and so on. C. P. even derived "a strong erection" from seeing grass "rise again" after a woman's "foot has pressed it."[31] He did not like boots, however, and had "an unconquerable aversion to red in slippers or stockings; it will even cause impotence." Attracted by the shoe as a weapon, he was repelled when it symbolized the wound.[32]

Some shoe fetishists, however, are fascinated by physical mutilation. A man from Oregon wrote to the Biz-zarre Club about his interests in "extreme" and "unusual" shoes: "I am a student of shoe design specializing in orthopedic styles for the lame or deformed."[33] *London Life* published a number of letters about the "monopede kink."[34] The photographer Helmut Newton appeared to be evoking this type of fetishism when he shot Jenny Capitan dressed as a "cripple" in a full-leg cast and neck brace, posed in front of an unmade bed in the Pension Dorian, Berlin.[35] "Panty Raid," an example of transvestite pornography, includes a number of fantasies about fetish shoes. When the dominant female "stamped with her dainty but powerfully shod foot, tiny sparks escaped from the stiletto seven-inch heel!" Each shoe also had "an open toe through which peeped a gleaming red nail." Illustrations in shoe fetish magazines often show female toenails as cruel red talons or claws. The captive male in the story was dressed as a woman as punishment: "Bruce nearly gagged when both of his feet were punished as they were inserted into the high arched instep of these white patent leather shoes." The most striking aspect of the shoes was their blatant castration imagery: "The vamp was decorated with an unusual design [reminiscent of Revolutionary French imagery]: a miniature guillotine, glimmering in a rhinestone setting."[36]

FIGURE 12.3 (FACING PAGE): A BEDROOM SHOE MADE OF GOLD KID, LINED WITH RED SILK AND TAFFETA, WITH 4¾ IN. HEELS, 1896. BATA SHOE MUSEUM, TORONTO, P89.14. REPRODUCED BY KIND PERMISSION OF BATA SHOE MUSEUM.

BOOTED MASTER

The shoe is also central to aspects of queer sexuality as explored in the chapter by Clare Lomas, Peter McNeil and Sally Gray in this volume. There are no rhinestones or stiletto heels in pornographic novels such as *Boot Licker*, *Boot-licking Slaves*, and *Booted Master*, but the titles gives a sense of this genre, in which boots symbolize a big penis. Boots with heavy soles and heels that smell of sweat and leather are ultramasculine: "The black leather engineer boot is the boot for men who know that you are what you wear on your feet." A boy must learn to be "worthy of the boots of a man."[37] In *Booted Master*, the tough biker Nino mocks Brian's effeminate shoes: "Sneakers! … You little pussy! … And I suppose you got a pair of red satin panties on under your jeans, too?" Motorcycle clubs, Nino says, have "a dress code just like the dress code that demands a jacket and tie for a man at a fine restaurant, or a certain style to get into Studio 54." He ties Brian up, with a sneaker tied around his genitals, "to teach you about boots." This segues into a scene of licking boots: "They'll be like mirrors … you'll be able to look down and see your peter in 'em." The taste is of "dirt, leather, cum, shit and piss."[38]

"Let me feel your boots around me," a man says. But Brian insists that men who have sex with other men are *not* "queer or gay … They just did it with guys … for fun." Wearing boots is a masculine privilege, for studs only. "You didn't think you could fill my boots did ya, punk?" mocks Nino. Then he is supplanted by a man in cowboy boots of "polished leather with ingrained designs … tall heels and pointed toes." The man also wears "a pair of cowboy chaps still smelling of bull semen and an opened shirt, exposing a muscled chest."[39] Boots can taste like velvet. Slaves lick their masters' heavy black leather boots "like a baby licks a pacifier."[40]

Boots have also been associated with lesbians and stereotypes of lesbian identity. In contemporary Brazil, the word for "dyke" is *sapatao*, which literally means "big shoes." One Brazilian man explained: "The shoe has the connotation of the foot, that the man who has a large foot, he … has a big prick … It's a popular proverb." But "Of all the terms for the dyke, 'army boot' [*coturno*] is the strongest," added another man, "[because] it's the symbol of machismo." A soldier put on "boots that come up to here, a thing to step in the mud with, to go to battle … So it's very much a man's thing! Understand? So, the army boot is a shoe that stands up to everything and is strong." Conversely, the Brazilian slang term for a "femme" lesbian is *sapatilha* (slipper), "because *sapatilha* is the shoe that ballerinas use."[41]

Boots have been strongly correlated with both masculinity and powerful phallic femininity for more than a century. A Susceptible Bachelor wrote to *Englishwoman's Domestic Magazine* that boots, "as emblematic of strength and resistance," were "decidedly masculine." He preferred "delicate curving sandals," although whether for himself or for his ladyfriends is unclear.[42] Nimrod associated booted women with Amazons: "Ladies' riding-boots should be Wellingtons or Napoleons," worn with chamois trousers. Spurs (another enthusiasm for many *EDM* correspondents) should, he argued, be clearly visible.[43] A twentieth-century transvestite reported that he liked the look of women's boots "because it hides ankles (bony and therefore not feminine enough) and emphasizes the calves (flesh)."[44]

FIGURE 12.4 (FACING PAGE): WHITE AND RED "EXHIBITION" BOOT, SECOND HALF OF THE NINETEENTH CENTURY. NORTHAMPTON MUSEUMS AND ART GALLERY, BOOT AND SHOE COLLECTION, BS425. REPRODUCED BY PERMISSION OF NORTHAMPTON MUSEUMS AND ART GALLERY.

A rare case of female fetishism involved a general's daughter attracted by the "shiny riding boots of her father." She chose to marry an ugly old man "just because he wore very high riding boots." "A man clad in boots and sitting atop a horse is the only man," she asserted. Conversely, a man in low civilian shoes was "no man at all in her eyes." She was violently repelled by a man's naked foot, especially the big toe. "She herself preferred to wear high shoes because of the virile and erect appearance it gave her and also because of the *pleasant sensation of being tightly laced in.*"[45]

SHOES AND SEX

"Many close-ups of pretty feet slipping into, in … and out of sexy spike heels," promises an advertisement for fetish videos.[46] The shoe can function as a symbolic substitute for the penis, and also for the vagina into which the phallic foot is inserted. Freud thought that the shoe was frequently fetishized because it was the last (acceptable) thing that a boy saw when he looked up his mother's skirt before his eyes met the horrifying female genitals. But in his book *The Denial of Death*, which won the Pulitzer Prize, Ernest Becker argues that "The foot is its own horror; and what is more, it is accompanied by its own striking and transcending denial and contrast – the shoe."[47] Other body parts also have their corresponding fetish objects. The genitals are veiled by lingerie, the fleshy torso and breasts are armored in corsets, but the foot and shoe form a particularly striking unit. Whereas the foot is a low and dirty "testimonial to our degraded animality," the shoe – made of soft and shiny polished leather with an elegantly curved arch and pointed toe, lifted above the ground on a hard spiked heel – "is the closest thing *to* the body and yet it is not *the* body" (Figure 12.6).[48]

In support of his theory, Becker quotes from a case history in Médard Boss's *The Meaning and Content of Sexual Perversions*. It describes a man who believed that "sexual intercourse is a disgrace for humans."[49] Boss's patient was also repelled by naked feet. He was very much attracted to clothing fetishes, however, particularly ladies' shoes and boots:

> Whenever he saw or touched [ladies' boot and shoes] "the world changed miraculously," he said. What had just appeared as "grey and senseless within the dreary, lonely and unsuccessful everyday, then suddenly drifts away from me, and light and glamour radiate from the leather to me." These leather objects seemed to have "a strange halo" shedding its light upon all other things. "It is ridiculous, but it feels like being a fairy prince. An incredible power, Mana, emanates from these gloves, furs and boots, and completely enchants me." … Naked women or a woman's hand without a glove or especially a woman's foot without a shoe … seemed to be like lifeless pieces of meat in a butcher shop. In fact, a woman's naked foot was really repulsive to him … However, when the woman wore [the fetish] she … grew above the "pettiness and vicious concreteness of the common female" with her "abhorrent genitals" and she was raised into … "the sphere where superhuman and subhuman blend into universal godliness."[50]

FIGURE 12.5 (FACING PAGE): WET-LOOK BLACK COURTS, 1975. LARGE SIZE, POSSIBLY FOR A TRANSVESTITE. UNKNOWN MAKER. NORTHAMPTON MUSEUMS AND ART GALLERY, BOOT AND SHOE COLLECTION, 1982.6.6P. REPRODUCED BY PERMISSION OF NORTHAMPTON MUSEUMS AND ART GALLERY.

There is much to be said for Becker's theory, and yet it overemphasizes the differences between foot and shoe.

Many fetishists are attracted to *both* the body part and its covering. Some work to glamorize the foot with pedicures, creams, and nail polish; others are attracted to "red, swollen, dirty, sweaty" feet.[51] Some fetishists claim to "worship" feet and shoes; others seem to want to punish feet by forcing them into shoes that are "beautiful," but also painful or crippling. One man who likes to "direct the stream of semen … into the opening of the shoe" (a man's patent leather shoe) was severely depressed when he noticed "a light crack in one of the shoes." It was "as if I had seen the first wrinkle in the face of a beloved woman."[52]

Repulsion and attraction alternate. "I even get turned on by the sight of my own feet," declared one man, communicating via the Internet. By contrast a recent biography of the novelist F. Scott Fitzgerald reveals that "the sight of his own feet filled him with embarrassment and horror," and he tried never to let other people see his naked feet. Yet Fitzgerald was sexually excited by women's feet. In a scene from *This Side of Paradise*, he uses the image of a man's ugly feet to symbolize evil and sexual immorality: "The feet were all wrong … It was like a weakness in a good woman, or blood on satin." His biographer argues that Fitzgerald's phobia about feet, "which stick out stiffly and were strongly associated with sex," was related to his belief that his penis was inadequate.[53]

Fetishism, Becker argues, "represents the anxiety of the sexual act," and the fetish itself functions as a "magical charm" that transforms the terrifying reality of "species meat" into something "transcendent."[54] The intense repulsion experienced by fetishists is extreme, like the over-idealization of the cultural fabrications that fascinate them. Yet who would doubt that physical sexuality seems at least a little threatening to almost everyone? Performance anxiety is a male fear, and this may be one reason why fetishism is almost always a male perversion. If a woman is afraid of sex, she may become "frigid," but she can pretend to have an orgasm (if that is regarded as desirable). A man's failure is harder to conceal. So he "hypnotizes himself with the fetish and creates his own aura of fascination that completely transforms the threatening reality." The fetish is "a magic charm."[55]

"In many cases one finds that perverse activity is more freely exercised when certain aesthetic conditions are fulfilled," observed one psychoanalyst many years ago. Just as a man with whipping fantasies insisted on a whip that was exactly the right size, shape and color, so did the shoe and underwear fetishists insist that their objects had to "conform to certain rigid aesthetic laws of pattern, color, line and so on." He added:

> The rigidity of such standards is reminiscent of the severe canons upheld by some critics or exponents of the fine arts. Indeed, if one did not know what was the actual subject matter … it would be very difficult for the hearer to distinguish certain diagnostic discussions of the conditions for perverse sexual gratification from an aesthetic discussion of "good" and "bad" art.[56]

FIGURE 12.6 (FACING PAGE): NAKED LADY SHOE BY RODOLFO AYARO, 1978. NORTHAMPTON MUSEUMS AND ART GALLERY, BOOT AND SHOE COLLECTION, 1982.120.1. REPRODUCED BY PERMISSION OF NORTHAMPTON MUSEUMS AND ART GALLERY.

FIGURE 12.7 (ABOVE): BLACK PATENT LEATHER SHOE WITH SIXTY-TWO RHINESTONES SET IN THE HEEL AND INSTEP STRAP, DESIGNED BY ROSSI MODA FOR YVES ST. LAURENT, 1985–88. BATA SHOE MUSEUM, TORONTO, P88.95. REPRODUCED BY KIND PERMISSION OF BATA SHOE MUSEUM.

FIGURE 12.8 (FACING PAGE): BLACK AND RED PATENT PUMP WITH GOLDEN METAL STUDS, POINTED TOE, BLACK NEOLITE SOLE, BREASTED SPIKE HEEL, 1995. THIS TYPE OF SHOE WAS PRODUCED IN THE 1990S BY M. D. (MATTI DISGRAZIATI - BARKING MAD) SHOE CORP., RUN BY DANIEL RENZI AND MARINO MELOZZI. THE BOOTS ARE DESIGNED FOR THE NICHE MARKET OF STRIPPERS. BATA SHOE MUSEUM, TORONTO, P98.89.A. REPRODUCED BY KIND PERMISSION OF BATA SHOE MUSEUM.

Some psychiatrists suggest that there may, in fact, be a relationship between "creativity and perversion." They argue that "perverts" are especially drawn to art and beauty, and their compulsion to idealize is related to their need to disguise anality. Thus, the fetish object is often both smelly and shiny (Figure 12.7).[57]

Already by the nineteenth century, shiny black leather was especially prized. Krafft-Ebing's *Psychopathia Sexualis* includes several case histories of shoe fetishism. Neglected and maligned as inaccurate and anecdotal, these little stories cry out to be analyzed as narrative texts:

> Case 113. *Shoe-fetishism*. Mr. von P., of an old and honorable family, Pole, aged thirty-two, consulted me in 1890, on account of "unnaturalness" of his *vita sexualis* … At the age of seventeen he had been seduced by a French governess, but coitus was not permitted; so that intense mutual sexual excitement (mutual masturbation) was all that was possible. In this situation his attention was attracted by her very elegant boots … Her shoes became a fetish for the unfortunate boy … He had the governess touch his penis with her shoes, and thus ejaculation with great lustful feeling was immediately induced.[58]

The explanation for the etymology of fetishism given here is extremely problematic. Many men's first sexual encounters involve mutual masturbation while clothed, but they do not usually become shoe fetishists.

"In the company of the opposite sex the only thing that interested him was the shoe, and that only when it was elegant … with heels, and of a brilliant black." These are precisely the characteristics overwhelmingly preferred by shoe fetishists today. When Mr. von P. saw women on the street wearing such shoes, "he was so intensely excited that he had to masturbate … Shoes displayed in shops, and of late, even advertisements of shoes, sufficed to excite him intensely." He was advised to marry, but:

> The wedding night was terrible, he felt like a criminal, and did not approach his wife. The next day he saw a prostitute … Then he bought a pair of elegant ladies' boots and hid them in bed, and, by touching them, when in marital embrace, he was able to perform his marital duty … [but] he had to force himself to coitus; and after a few weeks this artifice failed.

He felt guilty toward his wife, "who was sensual, and much excited by their previous intercourse." But even if he had been willing to "disclose his secret" (which he was not), and if his wife "were to do everything for him, it would not help him; for the familiar perfume of the *demi-monde* was also necessary.[59] This scenario resembles certain twentieth-century accounts – although the modern fetishist-husband often tries to get his wife to go along with his sexual obsessions.[60] The literature on prostitutes indicates, however, that the shoe fetishist is still a recognized type.

FIGURE 12.9 (FACING PAGE): "MAID SHOE," 1980. THIS SHOE WAS DESIGNED BY THEA CADABRA; THE LEGS WERE SCULPTED BY JAMES ROOKE. NORTHAMPTON MUSEUMS AND ART GALLERY, BOOT AND SHOE COLLECTION, 1984.37.2P. REPRODUCED BY PERMISSION OF NORTHAMPTON MUSEUMS AND ART GALLERY.

Foot and shoe fetishism is widely believed to be the commonest type of fetishism existing today.[61] As one publisher put it, "When we started our magazine on sex fetishes, we expected to cover the whole range. But our mail and other feedback quickly told us that the foot and shoe fetishes outnumbered any other fetish group by at least three to one."[62] Pornographic titles include *Foot Worship*, *Foot Torture*, *High-Heeled & Dominant*, *High-Heeled Sluts*, *Spikes Domination*, *Spurs*, *Stiletto*, *Super Spikes* and *Unisex Shoes & Boots*. *Foot Torture* is about a female jogger who is taken to a man's apartment and made to remove her clothing down to her underpants and sweat socks. "After smelling her socks he licks her bare feet, ties them up and places them over the Hibatchi! Then he tickles them and … ."

FOOT WORSHIP

Dian Hanson, the editor of *Leg Show* (one of the best contemporary fetish magazines), warned her readers that there was a "gulf of misunderstanding" between men and women: "Since normal male sexuality intimidates women, imagine what fetishes do to them." When she asked a number of women "if they knew some men were turned on by seeing their feet in sandals, the most common reaction was disbelief. Followed by fear. Some women said that the information made them want to stop wearing sandals, made them afraid to wear sandals." She wanted to reassure women that only the "unbalanced few" needed to be feared; in most cases involving fetishism, the women "had all the power."[63]

For many years, high boots have been the "trademark of prostitutes specializing in sado-masochism."[64] By 1994, Ann Magnuson could joke with the readers of a fashion magazine that designers such as Marc Jacobs had "crossed Emma Pell with Betty Page to come up with … boots that would look smashing with a rubber mac and a horsewhip." Patent leather boots with spike heels were "for the dominatrix in everyone." Wearing these heels, she reported, "I felt a surge of power, knowing that I could lay waste to any man I chose to destroy." She fantasized: "Down on the floor, you worm! I said *now* you worthless CEO!"[65]

In recent years, fashion has frequently emphasized what one fetish magazine called "cruel shoes."[66] As a writer in *Bizarre* put it: "Check out some of these latest fashions and tell us that women aren't getting into that dominant feeling."[67] One professional dominatrix explained that, like her transvestite clients, she had to learn how to walk in five-inch heels, but she preferred them for her work: "It pushed up your ass. Also you can use your high heel as a torture item." Heels also make a woman taller, "which is an advantage over men."[68]

Since exposure implies accessibility, "naked" shoes are also regarded as sexy. Slingbacks are popularly known as "fuck-me shoes" because they present a naked rear view of the foot. Frederick's of Hollywood named one shoe "Open 'n Inviting." "Open to Suggestion" is a "provocative, open-toed pump" that is "sensually punched for a really nude look." According to image consultants, open-toed shoes "encourage men to think of women as a sexual partner rather than as a potential chairman of the board," reported the *Wall Street Journal*.[69] An extra one-sixteenth of an inch reveals the crack between the toes, which apparently can remind men of other kinds of cleavage or, perhaps, other "slits" in the female body. Or as Ann Magnuson reported, "The shoe lewdly exposed my toe cleavage in a display vaguely reminiscent of some meat by-product at my local butcher's shop."[70]

The foot is perceived as a surrogate body, whose different parts can be exposed. Glamorous evening pumps have a "low-cut throat line," reports Frederick's. A "vampish fantasy" highlights a split vamp, open toe and ankle strap. The great shoemaker Salvatore Ferragamo once designed a satin shoe with the vamp "cut away to show the instep in precisely the same fashion as Dior's neckline." He also designed a shoe with a clear "crystal" oval inserted in the sole. When the wearer held her foot at a certain angle, other people could see the bottom of her foot.[71] "Exotic" is another key tem in the Frederick's of Hollywood vocabulary: "Exotic leopard print on sensuous fur." It may explicitly evoke "exotic" sex practices: "A high-stepping sandal in exotic leather in alligator print provokes his desires." A snakeskin sandal is "SSS-insational" (note the accent on *sin*). Bondage is also erotic: "A sexy ankle strap twists seductively around your shapely leg." One sandal had a "captivating 'cage' back" while another features a "sexy chain strap." Certain materials catch the eye: "Patent leather shines seductively day or night" (Figure 12.8).[72]

The popularity of certain fetish objects is not random. There are cultural and historical reasons why certain items of clothing are often chosen as fetishes. High heels are strongly associated in our culture with a certain kind of fashionable and sexually sophisticated woman, which is why they are favored by prostitutes and cross-dressers. According to the magazine *High Heels*, "Flat is … a dirty word! And you'll find nothing 'flat' in this issue of *High Heels* except the tummies of the models – who wouldn't be caught dead in 'flats,' who all have *full* bosoms, *curvy* torsos, *round* hips, *lithe* legs and … *high heels*."[73] Many characteristics commonly associated with feminine sexual attractiveness are accentuated by high-heeled shoes, which affect the wearer's gait and posture. By putting the lower part of the body in a state of tension, the movement of the hips and buttocks is emphasized and the back is arched, thrusting the bosom forward. High heels also change the apparent contour of the legs, increasing the curve of the calf and tilting the ankle and foot forward, thus creating an alluringly long-legged look. Seen from a certain angle, a high-heeled shoe also recalls the female pubic triangle.

Many women also love shoes and avidly collect them. Yet this female enthusiasm seldom parallels the specifically erotic practices of male shoe fetishists (such as licking shoes) or even the visceral response of ordinary fetishizing men (women seldom have an involuntary orgasm when they see a man in nice shoes). Nor do women seem to have the fantasies associated with male shoe fetishists (such as the giantess squishing little bugs). Nevertheless, shoes certainly provide tactile stimuli for women. As Ann Magnuson put it:

> The bones in my ankle cracked … and my Achilles tendons bent backwards … Hobbling down the avenue, I became acutely aware of … my body. My breasts jutted forward, while my back was severely arched. My ass felt bigger than a Buick, and my thighs, or rather my *flanks*, swung back and forth like a couple of sides of beef … Are these shoes disempowering? Do they enslave us? Are we rendered helpless by wearing them? The answer is yes! Yes! Of Course! What other point would there be in wearing them?[74]

The heels also made her feel "mythically omnipotent," while the difficulties involved in wearing them decreased with practice.

"DOTTING" ON SHOES – IMPRINTING IN THE MIND

Whereas men seem to "imprint" early in their lives on certain types of shoes (such as stiletto-heeled pumps), women apparently respond more consciously to the cultural construction of shoes as objects of desire. Their interest in particular types of shoes is often related to the current fashion. Already in the 1960s, Yves Saint-Laurent showed thigh-high crocodile boots, and Mary Quant designed corset-laced boots. In the 1970s, English and Italian fashion shops such as Biba and Fiorucci showed high platform shoes. The 1980s saw fantasy shoes, such as Thea Cadabra's "Maid Shoe," and classic styles, such as pink satin evening mules by Manolo Blahnik (Figure 12.9). The 1990s witnessed a revival of all of these period styles and especially the 1950s stilettos, the classic "bitchy" shoes. The spread of downtown gay male style has also become increasingly conspicuous at the highest level of fashion: from Versace's bondage gladiator boots to Chanel's triple-buckled leather combat boots, which resemble the ones worn by motorcycle cops (except for the entwined letter "C" stitched on the toes). Avant-garde designers such as Vivienne Westwood and Jean-Paul Gaultier have been notably inspired by fetish gear (Figure 12.10). Westwood designed platform shoes so high that the model, Naomi Campbell, fell down on the runway during her show. Gaultier mines all the kinks – from rubber boots to weird creations with multiple spikes.

Fashion writer Holly Burbach once wrote an essay, "Shoe Crazy," asking why so many women loved shoes. Freudian theories may "account for the thrill some men get out of the shoes women wear," she argues, but they fail to explain "the thrill *women* get." As she put it, "No woman with a normal, healthy shoe drive would content herself with a closetful of phallic symbols."[75] The shoe combines masculine and feminine imagery on many levels, from the stiletto heel penetrating the fetishist's body to the foot sliding into an open shoe. Pornography frequently labels the woman in high heels a slut, thus positioning her as an accessible sex object (if she wears prostitute shoes, then she's asking for it.) Conversely, the discourse in women's fashion magazines focuses on the fantasy that men will worship at the feet of a beautiful woman. Equally important is the role shoes play in the creation (and violation) of gender stereotypes: "I adore girls in heels," said fashion photographer Mario Testino. "They can play and wear high heels, and we can't." High heels are "the ultimate symbol of womanhood," declared journalist Frances Rogers Little. And Testino agreed, "It's the one thing that differentiated men from women."[76] The shoe is a complex and primary marker of gender difference, a complex messenger that can trick, bewilder or allure.

FIGURE 12.10 (FACING PAGE): PAIR OF BLACK PATENT LEATHER SUPER ELEVATED PLATFORMS WITH LARGE METAL SPIKES ATTACHED AROUND THE CIRCUMFERENCE OF THE THROAT AND DOWN THE CENTER BACK, PRODUCED BY VIVIENNE WESTWOOD, 1993. BATA SHOE MUSEUM, TORONTO, P.04.8.AB. REPRODUCED BY KIND PERMISSION OF BATA SHOE MUSEUM.

13.
SEX AND SIN

THE MAGIC OF RED SHOES[1]

hilary davidson

The enduring potency of red shoes, both as real items of footwear and as symbol and cultural force, has fascinated people of different cultures in very diverse ways. The "power" of red shoes is not recent. The prestige of red heels in seventeenth- and eighteenth-century European courts is well known. Subsequently, red shoes have taken on other charges. This chapter will focus on Hans Christian Andersen's fairy tale, *The Red Shoes* (1845).[2] This literary work created symbolic associations which have become part of everyday cultural "usage" today. The power of Andersen's fairy tale lies in its capacity to "dematerialize" red shoes by replacing their physicality with a symbolic meaning. This infusion of meaning into an object is a significant example of how dress and shoes are far from trivial and trivializing affairs. It established a template for the way in which red shoes were appreciated and comprehended in the twentieth century, especially by women (Figure 13.1).

The understanding of red shoes proposed by Andersen was not just the result of a literary imagination. The writer was informed by precise ideas and concepts related to red footwear that had been developed in the period before he wrote his story. The peculiar psychological intensity of red shoes must also be further examined by considering Andersen's life and personality. The Danish author's neurotic self-obsession remained a constant feature of his literary production. Many of the features included in *The Red Shoes* have a psychological endurance in contemporary culture. Andersen's concepts of sexuality,[3] mobility, magic, and gender are here traced through time by considering red shoes from the mid-nineteenth century, the time he wrote his famous tale, to the present day. Are "red shoes" simply red-colored footwear? Is the symbolic potential necessarily "readable" from the physicality of red shoes, or is it in the context of wearing that interpretive meanings are generated? Rarely worn by men today, why do red shoes continue to carry so much charge, especially for contemporary women, from novelists to consumers?

THE SYMBOLISM OF RED SHOES

Red shoes synthesize multiple and ambiguous social codes. The meanings and conflicts around the combination of a color and footwear are highly charged as a cultural marker. The color red represents life and fertility in European and Asian traditions, but it also has associations with danger, war and death. Red is the color of the extremes of humanity, strong emotions, magic and religious experiences. Anthropologist Claude Lévi-Strauss notes how in these "diametrically opposite" states, the color assumes a unique ambivalence, as it can be regarded as either positive or negative.[4] The highest ranks of the Catholic Church wear red vestments, but it is also the color of red-light districts, scarlet women and the Devil. The ambivalence between love and war, magic and religion, nobility and vulgarity, creates fundamental tensions in the use of this color.

This chapter also associates red with the concept of passion, a cultural sentiment character-ized by erotic desire as well as obsessive urges, spiritual exaltation and suffering. A "red shoe" con-joins a highly charged color and a form that is also not entirely "innocent." As Julia Pine explores in her chapter in this volume, the very form of shoes presents associations around the body, identity and sexuality. Shoes retain the imprint of the wearer's foot, and their hollow shape can indicate a vessel for identity, a substitute for the self. This intimacy of body and spirit has caused many superstitious traditions to develop around footwear. Numerous chapters in this volume, including those by Tunde Akinwumi, Sue Blundell and Martha Chaiklin, explore this dimension. In both Eastern and Western cultures, shoes are both "crude" markers and more nuanced indica-tors of female genitalia, in contrast with the phallic foot.

By combining two potent and ambiguous elements, red shoes assume complex symbolic power. Historically, red shoes conveyed authority, wealth and power, linked to the status-enhancing cost of red dyes such as madder, kermes, cochineal and lac.[5] Red shoes were the pre-rogative first of Roman senators, and later solely of the emperor. Popes have worn red since the thirteenth century, while both Edward IV and Henry VIII were buried in red shoes as emblems of their monarchical power. In the seventeenth century, Louis XIV wore red heels on his shoes as a symbol of the divine right of the king. As argued by Elizabeth Semmelhack in this volume, this style filtered down, through imitation, to the aristocracy of both sexes and by the eighteenth century it had become a sign of aspirational fashionability. The cost and quality of shoes made of fine, red morocco leather meant that they were status symbols. By the late eighteenth century, romantic Orientalism transmuted this material into Turkish-style slippers, favored as informal wear for gentlemen of means into the twentieth century.

DEVELOPING THEMES: RED, SHOES AND SIN

Hans Christian Andersen was the first author to make use of red-colored shoes as a literary device, but it should be acknowledged that Jakob and Wilhelm Grimm had used the concept in a slightly different manner within their collection of stories (1812–15), published during Andersen's childhood. Their version of Snow White ends with the wicked stepmother dancing in red-hot iron shoes. In his youth, Andersen may have absorbed elements of a Danish oral tradition from his grandmother; shoes feature in much folkloric literature. *De Rode Skoe* (*The Red Shoes*) was published in Denmark in 1845, within the third and final part of Andersen's book *Nye Eventyr* (*New Tales*). It recounts the story of a poor but pretty girl named Karen, who receives a pair of red shoes on the day of her mother's burial (Figure 13.2). An old lady passing the funeral in her carriage feels sorry for the bereaved girl and adopts her, educating and providing for her, and also burning her clumsy red shoes. The guardian then allows Karen a pair of shining red shoes for her confirmation, as she cannot see their color due to poor eyesight – introducing the notion of deception in a garment. At the service, Karen "thought of nothing except her red shoes"[6] and she chooses to wear them to church the following Sunday. Meeting an old soldier outside, who calls them "pretty little dancing shoes," Karen starts dancing, and cannot stop until she removes the shoes.

The image is that of an orgasmic experience. Later, Karen wears them to a ball instead of nursing her elderly charge, and the shoes make her dance out of the safety of town and into the forest. She cannot stop dancing, for the shoes are stuck to her feet. In the churchyard, Karen meets an angel who curses her; she will dance forever as punishment "until the skin … clings to your bones as if you were a skeleton." Karen dances night and day until the executioner mercifully cuts off her feet, and the shoes dance away with them. On wooden feet she goes to church, where the shoes appear in front of the door to bar her way. Karen then works at the parsonage until her prayers are truly repentant. The angel returns in benediction and her soul flies to heaven on a sunbeam.

The rather gruesome story alters in translations. The version cited here relies on two translations by Danes: Hersholt (1949) and Haugaard (1993). Earlier translations sanitized the tale,

one interpreter suggesting that Andersen could not have possibly meant the conclusion. The tale's disturbing tenor must also relate to the writer's life. Hans Christian Andersen was a self-proclaimed narcissist, childishly obsessed with himself and how others viewed him, with a "desperate craving for affection and praise."[7] Stories such as *The Ugly Duckling* and *The Steadfast Tin Soldier* are in part expressions of the author's sense of social isolation. Such was his egotism that it is reasonable to believe that his characters work through his emotional state. *The Red Shoes* is more than a famous national fairy tale, but a highly charged autobiographical work.

One autobiographical link to the structure of *The Red Shoes* is Karen's preoccupation with her shoes during her confirmation. Andersen received his first pair of boots for his own confirmation in 1819, and was so concerned with their shine and creak that he could not keep his mind on the service.[8] All aspects of Andersen's life reveal how the famous red shoes form a vehicle for personal concerns. Elias Bredsdorff underlines that the writer was a man of "deep and apparently irreconcilable contrasts" whose writings are profoundly concerned with dualism.[9] Rather like the mixed meanings of redness, Andersen was characterized by his friends as a troubling and complex mix of vanity and humility, self-confidence and insecurity, gratitude and bitterness, nervousness and intrepid feelings.

Significantly, Andersen was born the only son of an Odense shoemaker in 1805, and like Karen, he grew up in poor circumstances. The family's one-roomed cottage served as home and workshop. Although many of Andersen's tales feature inanimate objects as protagonists, such as a darning needle or a top, his acquaintance with the materiality of shoes was direct and intimate; it had formed an integral part of his childhood. Their appearance in his tale indicates a personal relationship between the shoe's nature, the material memories of Andersen's childhood, and the economic and cultural circumstances that this object – the shoe – suggested to him. To him, shoes are not glorious or beautiful, as so many chapters in this anthology attest, but rather sinister and mesmerizing. Wullschlager, a recent Andersen biographer, notes that other Andersen tales connect the feet and the human soul: *The Little Mermaid* (1836); *The Girl Who Trod on a Loaf* (1859).[10] In all cases, Andersen's use of the shoe connects sexuality, magic and gender in a negative construction.

ANDERSEN AND FEMININITY

Andersen's mother was a kind, loving, but uneducated woman who grew up in extreme poverty. She was simplistically pious and superstitious and raised her son in fear of the dark and of churchyards.[11] Karen's encounter with the angel in a graveyard at night conveys a particularly horrifying moment in Andersen's mind. His maternally fostered religious faith was based on a firm belief in divine providence. In contrast, the writer's father was a critical believer who questioned dogmatic tenets, rejected much of institutional Christianity, and encouraged young Hans Christian to do likewise. These domestic spiritual conflicts appear in *The Red Shoes* through tensions between magic and religion. When the old soldier appears the first time, his red beard suggesting infernal connections, he taps the shoes on the sole and tells them to "stay on [her] feet for the dance." On the second occasion, he repeats his charm-phrase "What beautiful shoes for dancing," causing the shoes to become mobile. When the girl disobeys again, and her red shoes dance her "out through the city gates and into the dark forest," the soldier repeats the phrase a third time, the number known to activate enchantment; Karen is condemned to the dance forever. When the shoes revisit Karen in order to bar her entrance to church, she identifies them as reminders of her "sins," pride and disobedience. Her final redemption is gained through "God's own mercy" and in heaven "no one asked her about the red shoes."[12] Andersen sets up the paradigm of red shoes as magical, but from a destructive, pagan magic that underlines the wearer's sinful state.

Andersen's other significant use of red shoes is in *The Snow Queen*, written and published only four months before *The Red Shoes* in December 1844, and shows how the motif had been developing. When little Gerda is looking for her playmate Kay, taken by the Snow Queen, she offers the river her new red shoes. They float back to shore, so she stands in a boat to throw the shoes further out. The boat drifts, the shoes follow, and her adventures begin. When the children eventually return, they are grown, and in love. Like *The Red Shoes*, footwear marks a transformative journey, but because Gerda sacrifices her shoes "that were her dearest possession"[13] she is rewarded, unlike Karen. Simply put, while Gerda is a "good" girl, Karen is a "bad" one, and their attitude toward their shoes determines the outcome. This association has proved to be an enduring cultural idea, with red shoes denoting women who transgress against acceptable feminine norms. In the twentieth century the transgression is frequently sexual, a modern theme that still reflects one of the author's inner divides.

FROM SIN TO SEX: THE COLOR OF EROTICISM

Speculation on the nature of Hans Christian Andersen's sexuality began at the beginning of the twentieth century.[14] He loved and desired women, and had intimate, loving friendships with men, but apparently never consummated a physical relationship with either sex. His diaries reveal an underlying fear of sex, both the act itself and its possible consequences, made more complex by the fact that his maternal aunt ran a brothel. It is therefore not surprising to find that a divided sense of eroticism is present at all times throughout *The Red Shoes*. The mirror tells the pubescent Karen: "You are more than pretty, you are beautiful."[15] This is both a marker of vanity but also of the girl's consciousness of her desirability. Her choice of red shoes, the color of passion, as shoes for the physical pleasure of dance, suggests that Karen's later punishments are as much for "normal sensuality" as willful disobedience.[16] Gerri Reaves considers the executioner's act of cutting off the red shoes as a castration that "desexualizes" Karen.[17] Her wearing of the shoes is a form of overt sexuality. The wild physical movement of her enchanted dancing is a form of uninhibited bodily expression inappropriate for a respectable girl.

The parable of succumbing to desire corresponds with Andersen's experience of his mother's own youthful lapse. Her first child was an illegitimate girl six years older than Hans Christian, named Karen-Marie. Raised by her maternal grandmother, she haunted Andersen as "an emblem of degradation, ignorance and poverty," the product of sin who herself may have become a prostitute.[18] As he became successful, Andersen's fears that this half-sister would emerge to shame him increased. She visited him in Copenhagen in 1842, three years before publication of *The Red Shoes*. After receiving her letter announcing her arrival, Andersen's diary records: "A terrible night, sensuous thoughts and despair mockingly filled my mind."[19] His story reflects exactly these divided reactions, suggesting it functions in part as a literary exorcism of his internal turmoil. The choice of the same name cannot be coincidence from a writer acutely conscious of his psychic landscape. Both the story-Karen's self-destructive actions and the shadow of sister-Karen's potential taint serve to underline his crafting of a negative association between uncontrolled female sensuality and red shoes.

The low status of Andersen's family background was something he perpetually tried to rewrite. He courted patronage, as Karen did with her wealthy guardian, seeking recognition from the cream of Danish society. Andersen's disastrous youthful attempts to become a professional stage performer and his subsequent social climbing suggest further nuance for his tale. Karen takes a journey of transformation effected by her footwear, from "thick wooden shoes that chafed her ankles until they were red" – like those Andersen wore in his youth – back to a pair of humble and numb wooden feet, a warning against hubris.[20] It is an expression of the author's fear that he, too, could fall from fame to obscurity at any time.

Celebrated throughout Europe at the time, and in receipt of a royal pension, Andersen continued to be plagued with chronic insecurity. In the story Karen sees the princess of the land wearing neither train nor gown but "splendid red morocco shoes"[21] as the visible sign of royalty. When buying her confirmation shoes, Karen chooses "a pair of red leather ones like those the princess wore," which had been made for a count's daughter but did not fit. Karen literally steps above her station into aristocratic shoes inappropriate even for her guardian's status. The retributive dance occurs in this pair of red shoes, suggesting anxiety for Andersen that some later event would likewise strike him for rising from social oblivion to a position within a court. Andersen endowed his red shoes with the physical mobility of dance and the tense climb of social aspiration. The shoes themselves are agents; markers of bodily change and sensual awareness, motors of social ascendancy, and finally chains of punishment.

SYMBOLIC LEGACIES: RED SHOES IN THE TWENTIETH CENTURY

Republished in 1849 and 1863 in Denmark, Andersen's stories were considered suitable for both adults and children. The bowdlerized versions disseminated to other languages, especially English, devalued their nuance and relegated them to the nursery. During Andersen's lifetime, *The Red Shoes* did not achieve international fame. Some of the psychosexual suggestion of the tale was easily overlooked, as red shoes were still common wear for upper-class children and as informal dress. More palatable tales without such harsh moral warnings as the finale were preferred.

Andersen's red shoes as open-ended symbol subsequently took an even more unpredictable path. The influence of the theme "red shoes" has an afterlife apart from the obvious literary allusion. The development of psychological analysis in late nineteenth-century *fin de siècle* culture swiftly encouraged new psychosexual readings of the shoes.

Changes in the production of shoes also led to new interpretations of "red shoes" (Figure 13.3). Synthetic aniline red dyes appeared in 1868, and their price fell substantially between 1880 and 1910. An increase in the availability of red footwear for the public followed, dispersing what had once been seen as a rare and expensive artifact. Other meanings for red shoes emerged, dependent upon context. Therefore in Proust's novel *The Guermantes Way* (1922), set at the very end of the nineteenth century, the Duc de Guermantes admonishes his wife with: "You've kept on your black shoes! With a red dress! Go upstairs quick and put on red shoes."[22] The scene hinges on the characters of the couple revealed by this potential faux pas. Their friend Swann is present; he has come to tell them he is dying, yet their priorities are for social appearance.

These Proustian shoes echo Andersen's former themes of selfishness and the anxiety of social conformity. There were other more detailed cultural expressions that directly utilized the Danish work to develop the theme of frenzied movement. In 1899, in London, the Alhambra Theatre presented *The Red Shoes*, a "Grand Spectacular Ballet in Four Tableaux and Five Scenes" based on "Hans Andersen's Pretty Story."[23] The story was moved to Russia, where village girl Darinka succumbs to the Spirit of Temptation and steals "pretty scarlet shoes" from the church. What is significant about this early reinterpretation is that it foregrounds the element of dance, connecting all parts of the story through that medium.

The connection between red shoes and dance was thus established quite early. Brightly colored shoes were popular in the dance-crazed 1920s and 1930s, but the cultural expression with the most impact is undoubtedly the 1948 film *The Red Shoes*, starring Moira Shearer. The character she plays is "Vicky," a rising star in the Ballet Lermontov, whose signature role is that of Karen, in a ballet based upon Andersen's tale. In this reworked version, Karen sees the red shoes in a shoemaker's window; a vision tempts her to try them on. They magically jump onto her feet and do themselves up. She wears the red shoes to a carnival, and then is forced to dance to a shadow world. The now demonic shoemaker reappears as the dream world turns darker and the dancing becomes more frenetic. After dancing in a ragged state at the town ball, she asks a priest for mercy. He refuses, but after a hellish dance with the shoemaker, Karen manages to remove the shoes and dies in the priest's arms. The shoes, ominously, return to the shoemaker's window in a pristine state. These shoes are sinister.

Within this balletic storyline, Vicky is forced to choose between becoming a great dancer, or remaining with her husband. The red shoes are representative of two supposedly irreconcilable obsessive passions: love and art. The film deploys red ballet shoes throughout to emphasize the iconic symbol that set the central theme. The Boot and Shoe Collection at Northampton Art Gallery and Museums holds an unworn pair of red ballet shoes made for the film by Freed of

London, suppliers to the Royal Ballet (Figure 13.4). Unremarkable in themselves, we can now view these slippers as indicators of how the red shoe now far exceeds functions of status or feelings of delirium. The discrepancy between the multiple pairs that had to be made for filming and the single example focused on in the screen vision underlines how a mundane leather and satin object has become a highly charged artifact. The red shoe now had a significance far beyond a blocked ballerina slipper and its historical evolution as a high-status leather color.

The 1993 Kate Bush album, *The Red Shoes*, took up aspects of Andersen's cultural legacy and explored their meaning acoustically and in terms of a type of New Romantic videoscape (Figure 13.5). Bush drew ideas from the film, rather than directly from Andersen, and stresses the cinematic charge to her audience by including red satin ballet slippers *en pointe* on the album cover. In a deft reading, Erin Mackie notes that these resemble "bloody stumps," and that dancers *increase* their bird-like mobility after this visual "amputation" of the foot.[24] Within the lyrics, Bush uses the red shoe motif to trace a journey through feminine emotional experience, losing and regaining love, passion and a sense of self. The accompanying film *The Line, the Cross and the Curve* clarifies this interpretation. Issues of individual women's agency or movement through a lifecycle match the theme of the physical journey and mobility of red shoes in Andersen's original model.

MAGIC SLIPPERS AND WAYWARD FEET

Even more famous than balletic red shoes are the iconic pair that featured as Dorothy's ruby slippers in *The Wizard of Oz* (1939). Once again, to secure filmic continuity many pairs were made, of which five are known to survive. They now command astonishing prices at auction: US$666,000 in a sale in 2000.[25] Film buffs know that these slippers were not originally red. The studio changed the shoe color from silver to ruby in order to exploit the new, expensive medium of Technicolor. Although a connection to the Andersen fairy tale is not proven, surely it relates, as *The Wizard of Oz* makes striking parallels. A young, insecure and yearning Dorothy, so ably played by Judy Garland, is whisked away from an isolated home via the magic red shoes that she cannot remove from her feet. Helped by a higher power (the Good Witch of the North) to return home, Dorothy helps others on her way – her famous composite companions the Scarecrow, Tin Man and Cowardly Lion, each of whom represents a flawed (because incomplete) emotional and ethical state. Unlike Karen, Dorothy famously remarks that "There's no place like home," embracing rather than rejecting her upbringing in the heartland of the United States. As a heroine, she is more Gerda than Karen.

Red shoes have become such a tenacious and malleable symbol that they are put to many uses. Numerous recent examples link red shoes with dance and freedom, from avant-garde to queer. Shoemaker Manolo Blahník designed a pair of red satin shoes in 1986 entitled "Martha," evoking twentieth-century expressive dance pioneer Martha Graham. His sketch for these low pumps includes the crossed ribbons typical of ballet slippers, unfurling like a force unto themselves.

FIGURE 13.2 (FACING PAGE): RED SILK SHOES WITH POINTED TOE, C. 1822–31, PRODUCED BY CHARLES SKINNER OF LONDON. THE RIBBONS HELD THE FRAGILE SHOE ON THE FOOT, PERHAPS MAKING THEM SUITABLE FOR DANCING. MODERN BALLET SLIPPERS ECHO THE PRACTICAL DETAIL. BATA SHOE MUSEUM, TORONTO, P85.104.AB. REPRODUCED BY KIND PERMISSION OF BATA SHOE MUSEUM.

FIGURE 13.3 (FACING PAGE): WOMEN'S SHOES IN SINUOUS FIN-DE-SIÈCLE CURVES MAKE A VISUAL IMPACT THROUGH THE BOLDNESS OF THE ANILINE COLOR, A RICHNESS HIGHLIGHTED BY THE JET BEAD EMBELLISHMENT. COURTESY OF BATH AND NORTH-EAST SOMERSET COUNCIL, MUSEUM OF COSTUME, BATMC I.10.158+A.

FIGURE 13.4 (ABOVE): THE ALCHEMY OF CINEMA TRANSLATED THE PRACTICAL NATURE OF MOIRA SHEARER'S RED SATIN BALLET SHOES (VISIBLE IN THE TOE BLOCKING AND PLAIN INNER CONSTRUCTION) INTO AN ICON. PRODUCED BY FREED OF LONDON. NORTHAMPTON MUSEUMS AND ART GALLERY, BOOT AND SHOE COLLECTION, 1996.24. REPRODUCED BY PERMISSION OF NORTHAMPTON MUSEUMS AND ART GALLERY.

As a tale featuring the shoe and the dance, *The Red Shoes* provides a continuing basis for choreographers to explore this theme. In the last twenty years, at least four ballet or modern dance productions have adopted the theme of red shoes. Italian group Lenz Rifrazioni created the most recent, *Scarpette Rosse,* in 2005 to honor of the 200th anniversary of Andersen's birth.

The meaning of red shoes is now extended well beyond a Freudian framework of parental obsessions and sexual uneasiness. The very success of red shoes in popular culture has produced meanings that are not only more positive in nature, but also more widely embedded in international cultural symbolism. The website <www.redshoes.com> is the virtual shopfront of a US dance footwear store, while red ballet slippers remain a "very popular choice for dance aficionados."[26] A recent novel for young adults, *Dancing in Red Shoes Will Kill You* (2005), offers an explicit reminder that Andersen's darker perspectives also remain potent. Contemporary fashion design also plays with the charge of red shoes. In 2004 Dutch fashion designers Viktor & Rolf sent models down the catwalk wearing high, curvy red shoes, whatever the color of the outfit. Here the shoes were positive coded marks of female agency; the pair design strong but feminine clothes, and cite intelligent, iconoclastic women, such as the actress Tilda Swinton, as muses. The Australian designer Akira Isogawa has used red socks for a runway parade: here they can evoke the joy of red shoes, the use of colored socks in Japanese footwear, and also indicate that shoes are an expense that an emerging designer needs to avoid.

The benevolent use of the ruby slippers in *The Wizard of Oz* model, as well as the camp charge of the whole film and its iconic actress figure Garland, now permit them to suggest meanings that are not dark in the Andersen mold, but rather uplifting. They appear in forms as diverse as a lipstick name, an artisan chocolatier, an online feminist magazine, a car license plate, a lunchbox, and jewelry. In contemporary culture, any pair of red shoes that sparkles with sequins, glitter, or rhinestones now connects to the Garland ruby slippers (Figure 13.6). Ironically, they now represent Andersen's model of escape and emotional frenzy, as post-liberation society has made these values positive, not socially bankrupt. It is for this reason that the ruby slipper features so often in gay and queer imagery. Giant ruby slippers held on masts, a part of an "Imelda Marcos" fan club, have been the lead float of the Sydney Gay and Lesbian Mardi Gras parade. As a gay icon, they appear in advertisements for London's 2004 Pride Festival after-show party at the nightclub, Ruby; "Ruby" is the name of contemporary Sydney's most popular trance DJ.

Red shoes are not just important for the queer screen. Andersen's red shoes became a symbol for women who deviated from conventional social behavior. In the twentieth century, red shoes became naturally associated with wayward women who exhibited overt sexuality. The red shoes that sex symbols Marilyn Monroe and Jane Russell wear in *Gentlemen Prefer Blondes* (1953) for their famous dance number are elegant and glamorous, but the pair are calculating gold diggers (Figure 13.7). Monroe had in her personal wardrobe a distinctive pair of red shoes by

FIGURE 13.5 (FACING PAGE): KATE BUSH'S BALLET SLIPPERS ARE SHOWN FROZEN IN THE ACT OF DANCE, PROMINENT AGAINST A SURREAL LANDSCAPE. THE LOOSE RIBBONS AND TORN STOCKING SUGGEST DISORDER AND DANGER. ALBUM COVER. KATE BUSH, THE RED SHOES, 1993. COURTESY EMI RECORDS.

Salvatore Ferragamo made around the time of this film.[27] Auctioned at Christie's in New York in 1999, these scarlet satin stilettos, encrusted with rhinestones, had belonged to the century's most seductive woman, whose life can be construed as taking turns as tragic as Karen's. The director of a modern ballet version of *The Red Shoes* now even calls the theme "The Marilyn Monroe story."[28] Apart from the allure of sexuality, the lyrics to many songs present other versions of "negative" red-shoe women. Mississippi John Hurt sang of an unfaithful wife who while her "husband's goin' away," is "raring to go, got red shoes on [her] feet" as early as the 1920s.[29] A mother "long gone with her red shoes on"[30] abandons her baby in a disturbing lullaby, while Tom Waits's heroine is running away on a dark night, wearing "red shoes by the drugstore" while awaiting her lover.[31] The red shoes are evidence of the women's sexual motives and urge to flee.

Jungian psychologist Clarissa Pinkola Estes has presented an analysis of red shoes, which is negative, within her best seller *Women Who Run With the Wolves* (1993).[32] Using myth, folk and fairy tales to reclaim the principle of feminine wildness, she argues that red shoes represent a psychologically devalued life, creating addictions. Estes presents a Magyar-Germanic version of an old woman's tale known as "The Red-Hot Shoes of the Devil" or "The Red Shoes," and she claims that Andersen's version is a retelling, without citing a source. It is significant that this best-selling book by a psychologist indicates the way that red shoes have become available to be presented as archetypes of feminine self-identity, while emptying out their historical evolution. This trend is replicated in a self-help book by Susan Kavaler-Adler, *The Creative Mystique: From Red Shoes Frenzy to Love and Creativity* (1997).[33]

POSITIVELY MODERN, POSITIVELY RED

Structuralist literary analysis used the fairy tale as the basis for uncovering social meaning and cultural understanding by studying their reiteration and constituent parts. Positive readings of red shoes emerged subsequent to the publication of texts such as Marie-Louise von Franz's *The Interpretation of Fairy Tales* (1970) and Bruno Bettelheim's *The Uses of Enchantment* (1976).[34] It was also possible to identify the beneficial agency of sexuality, mobility and magic within female lives. The strength of Andersen's template is that red shoes can be accorded both positive and negative symbolism depending on cultural setting and politics. Despite the complex struggles and readings of the *femme fatale* of the late nineteenth century, and the "New Woman" of the 1920s, it was not until the liberation politics of the 1960s and 1970s that the red shoe metamorphosis would be possible. With a corresponding increase in female-authored works, feminist rereadings and ficto-criticism, women could write with force about what they thought of wearing red shoes. Numerous women writers of fiction around the world contacted the editors of this anthology with excitement when they read that "red shoes" would be included.

The will to rebadge the red shoe is indicated in the establishment, by Velva Lee Heraty, of the international fundraising organization "The Red Shoes Club." Heraty states that the very idea

FIGURE 13.6 (FACING PAGE): THE RUBY SLIPPER ELEMENTS OF RED AND SPARKLE MAINTAIN THEIR POWERFUL ALLURE EVEN IN MASS-MARKET, FLAT-HEELED SHOES. THE BALLETIC FRONT BOW LINKS THEM WITH ANDERSEN'S DANCING RED SHOES. SHELLY'S SHOES, LONDON, SUMMER 2005. AUTHOR'S PHOTOGRAPH.

of wearing red shoes made her want to live again after the tragic loss of her daughter. She describes the club's members thus:

> You love red shoes because you know that before Dorothy and beyond Marilyn red shoes have become both a symbol and a universal icon … that echoes magic, adventure, passion, confidence and sass. Here's to all red shoe women everywhere.[35]

Heraty's reference to the impossibly good-hearted Dorothy links the ruby slippers to positive and transformative values.

CONCLUSION

The Red Shoes of Andersen's original tale are complex and conflicting symbols. Apparently a moral warning against selfishness, pride and vanity, they also engage with older meanings about class aspiration, prestige and insecurity. Andersen's legacy was to develop and strengthen the "power" that red shoes already possessed from their expensive color and form, and from their sacred, courtly and absolutist pre-nineteenth century use. To this combination, Andersen also brought the type of writing that could only emerge in the nineteenth century of Baudelaire, Symbolists and sexology.

Vivid accounts of wildly passionate behavior and untrammeled female sexuality and mobility made possible by a pair of red shoes reflect some of Andersen's own personal contradictions. While his red shoes can be read as negative in their linking of the female with danger, magic and conceit, Andersen created a mythology for red shoes that had much greater potential for reworking. With the development of new meanings for ballet, for women's movement and for women's autonomous sexual behavior, the red shoe became part of a cultural contest. In researching this chapter, no response has been neutral. The breadth of these reactions demonstrates how the cultural values of red shoes remain incredibly significant. How ironic that in the bicentenary year of Andersen's birth, the red shoe, perhaps more than any other shoe in this volume, has the power to incite passionate controversy, attachment and desire.

FIGURE 13.7 (FACING PAGE): DESIGN ELEMENTS COMMON IN "FETISH" SHOES ARE ALREADY PRESENT IN MONROE'S 1950S SHOES, A HERBERT LEVINE DESIGN OF SHINY RED LEATHER, STILETTO HEEL, SHARPLY POINTED TOES, AND BUCKLE DETAIL. BATA SHOE MUSEUM, TORONTO, P96.160.AB. REPRODUCED BY KIND PERMISSION OF BATA SHOE MUSEUM.

14.

BEYOND THE RAINBOW

QUEER SHOES

clare lomas, peter mcneil and sally gray

Men say that they don't particularly care how they dress, and that it is little matter. I am bound to reply that I don't believe them and don't think that you do either.[1]

Oscar Wilde on tour in North America, 1882

A GAY SHOE?

Two women writers, one man, and queer shoes. We have been asked many times what a queer, gay or lesbian shoe is. Most of our readers will be familiar with the notion of gay and lesbian subculture, which emerged in the post-1945 Western world. Within the counterculture of the 1960s and 1970s, men and women used their dress choices to challenge reductive characterizations about what it meant to desire a same-sex partner. Many women shunned conventional stereotypes of delicate femininity. Many men wished to overturn the late nineteenth-century psychological typing of the effeminate man, and turned to ultramasculine or butch clothing drawn from working-class, sporting and vocational dress. Contemporary culture provides evidence of a very specific relationship between sexual identity and shoes.

The importance of footwear in "gay culture" is not a recent phenomenon. Gay and lesbian histories have confirmed the centrality of dress codes in the establishment and consolidation of politics and subcultural groupings. It is striking how many oral history studies, which have been undertaken, with great impact, with women and men of interwar Britain and North America, point to the significance of shoes. Of particular relevance to this chapter is the changing historical conception of male and female homosexuality and related stereotypical representations, from the effeminate male "pansy" and female "invert" of the early twentieth century, to the overtly masculine "macho man" of the 1970s, and more complex ideas of lesbian appearance and identity. Gay Liberation politics, after the 1969 Manhattan events known as "Stonewall," had the effect of overturning some of the homophobic ideas about duality that had emerged from late nineteenth-century sexology. This is in striking contrast to the evidence, from oral history interviews, of how powerful these binaries were for men and women seeking to live out partially or openly queer lives in the interwar period in countries such as the United States. Our chapter argues that an assessment of "queer shoes" brings to the fore some of the gender distinctions that emerged in the twentieth century. Same-sex desire is not just a question of subcultural codes of mutual recognition and sexual attractiveness. It shapes "ways of looking" beyond homosexual and homosocial contexts, thus making the study of queer shoes central to understanding general shoe culture.

The history of oppression, and consequent secrecy, of differently inflected sexualities has meant that gay men and lesbians have evolved not only coded clothing *practices* by which they might recognize others with a similar sexual orientation or interest, but also a nuanced vocabulary for *reading* dress. This chapter is concerned with both of these aspects, recognition and performance. Being gay or lesbian does not "show" in the same way as race. For this reason, gays and lesbians have evolved "signs of gayness, a repertoire of gestures, expressions, stances, clothing and even environments that bespeak gayness."[2] For men we will particularly explore interwar soft and colored shoes, followed by the hypermasculine shoes of the 1970s. For women, we explore ideas of freedom and movement, and the polarities of comfort and extreme stylization that characterize media ideas and real life experience for lesbians.

QUEER SHOES FOR THE GAY GUYS

An overview of queer dress is in many ways an overview of fashion studies of the past twenty years. Feminist historians were among the first to note the significance of clothing codes, firstly in women's dress and later in men's dress.[3] Their interdisciplinary approach positioned dress within sociology and gender studies. Intersections between feminist scholarship, film theory and queer theory have provided highly nuanced ways of looking at and seeing the invested body. Considerable attention has been paid to the sophisticated skills required to effectively read another's performative adornment practices. These skills are nowhere more developed than at "the edges of cultural boundaries," of which "divergent" sexuality is one.[4]

The relationship between identity, dress and subcultures has been a subject of academic interest since the 1970s.[5] Such scholarship has explored how dress and adornment play a part in the formation of subcultural – including gender and sexual – identity for both individuals and groups. The significance of such research rests on the shift from "essence" or interiority to "play" that now characterizes many parts of contemporary society, in particular youth culture. "Identity" as Simon Thrift observes, "comes from the outside, not the inside; it is something we put or try on, not something we reveal or discover."[6]

Since the 1990s, scholars have further explored the intersection between fashion and gender identity.[7] As underlined by Reina Lewis, "Whatever the attitude to fashion, dress as a marker of identity is hugely significant in the everyday lives of lesbians and gay men." She adds that:

> Clothes function as a marker of recognizability to other gays or as a method of passing
> … Moreover, as consumers of each other's appearance, there is a pleasure to be had in
> recognizing and being recognized. For these reasons, clothes have an importance in the
> lives of lesbians and gays – whether or not they consider themselves fashionable …[8]

It was fashion, along with a parade of bodily gestures and subtle, nation-specific codes, which permitted queer men and women to identify and seek each other out in the period before venues were safe, legal and beyond blackmail. Shaun Cole's recent research on the relationship between gay men's dress and masculinity suggests a "traceable" fixed gay identity for the period from the aesthetic movement of the 1880s (the Wildean moment) through to the 1990s, assessing how gay men have used their clothes to attract sexual partners.[9]

AS LIGHT AS PAPER

Soft shoes for men indicate perhaps more clearly than any other piece of design a conjunction between ideas of class, gender and (homo)sexuality. By "homosexuality" we do not mean the history of same-sex practices in all its facets. Rather, we adopt a definition that argues that in the last third of the nineteenth-century, urban structures, subcultural groupings and the attention of the law, medicine and the media brought the notion of the "homosexual" into being. The term itself emerges within sexology of the 1870s, the trial of poet and writer Oscar Wilde in 1895 defining specific tropes of homosexual identity later widely used in the twentieth century.

Oscar Wilde was an aesthete, embodying principles of the aesthetic art movement not only in his dress but his mannerisms.[10] He liked the fancy dress of Prince Rupert for balls, and a version of French bohemian costume of the 1830s for day. That was the attire parodied by *Punch* and by Gilbert and Sullivan in *Patience*, and it was the type of costume worn by Wilde when he embarked on his North American lecture tour of 1882. Riding on a wave of *Punch*-driven publicity, his lectures on taste caused a sensation from New York to Nova Scotia. Wilde preferred both variety and historicism in shoes, affecting a type of low-cut evening pump with silver buckles and black silk stockings for his first New York lecture held at night. At breakfast interviews he wore "low patent leather pumps" and in Omaha "leather gaiters faced with yellow cloth."[11] In San Francisco, for daywear he wore dun-brown pants and highly polished pointed shoes, with yellow gloves and a buttonhole of heliotrope, a brightly foliated daisy and a tuberose.[12] Wilde also underlines the significance of color for an alternative male wardrobe. He frequently discussed the importance of pastel tones – "The dress of the future … will abound with joyous color" in order to effect color harmonies at odds with what he perceived as the hideous philistinism of utilitarian society.[13] As Lord Henry put it in *Dorian Gray*: "Sin is the only real colour-element left in modern life."[14] Wilde's transition from freedom to imprisonment was described with reference to clothes, including the "loose shoes" that replaced "the cut of the low shoes of the latest mode."[15]

In the interwar period, gay men took up different strands of the possibilities offered in aesthetic movement dressing. The Wildean aesthetic ideas of historicism, color and a type of faux-aristocratic refusal provided a vocabulary of choice and expression. The most potent image of interwar gay male subcultural style was the soft suede shoe. This shoe was such a significant marker because it was about sexuality and even vocation. George Chauncey's study draws on evidence given to the Kinsey Institute by Thomas Painter, who in the late 1930s and early 1940s noted particular dress codes for homosexual men including "green suits, tight cuffed trousers, flowered bathing trunks and half-length flaring top coats" as well as flamboyant accessories. Significantly, he noted that suede shoes were "practically a homosexual monopoly."[16]

In Britain too, it seems that suede shoes became an indicator of "inverts" in the interwar period. Terence Greenidge's 1930 book, *Degenerate Oxford?*, tells of the two types of student at university: the athlete and the aesthete. He wrote that:

> Oxford Romanticism is responsible for the mass production of effeminate men
> … wearing rather brightly coloured coats, cut short and very tight in the waist,
> their grey flannel trousers will be of a conspicuously silver hue and flow loosely,
> their feet will be shod with gay suede shoes. They will speak with artificial voices
> of a somewhat high timbre, also they will walk with a mincing gait.[17]

The role of footwear here appears to be part of an overall performance to communicate what was then considered a deviant sexuality. Oral testimonies corroborate the idea that suede shoes could indicate sexual inclination. Trevor Thomas, a museum worker, stressed that people who attended private parties – one of the main meeting places at a time of few clubs and bars – were not "outrageously obviously gay people … you all wore dark suits, three piece, very quiet shirts."[18] Nevertheless, Thomas "became known as the man who wore suede shoes."[19]

The blue suede shoes signaled the queerness of a male homosexual wearer in a closeted world but only to those who had the key to that code. Blue suede shoes signaled to other like-minded men that the wearer was interested in having sex with men or being included in a homosocial world. He could simultaneously signal this information while "passing as straight" to those not in the know. He could therefore avoid violence or arrest in circumstances in which homosexuality was illegal or subject to random attack. Shoes, like other aspects of dress, adornment and grooming are therefore a crucial part of the way sexualities are expressed and communicated.

By the 1950s, the suede shoe was such a striking marker that in commenting on interior design as a coded "queer profession," Ashley Hicks noted of his famous father, David: "My father starting his career three years before, was afraid that he might be 'branded for life with the suede shoes, mauve tie image which I loathed.' "[20] Here Hicks points to a configuration of class: many upper-class queer men also shunned such obvious signs, which they perceived as degrading of their social standing.

With the greater adoption of casual wear and the emergence of very distinct urban subcultures, queer identity had become more complex and divided. As informal items of dress and the new North American and Italian leisurewear entered the male repertoire, it became more difficult to typecast a piece of clothing as outrageous. Peter Robins, describing 1950s fashion, recalled:

> The fashionable dress in the early fifties was … grey flannels – jeans weren't in vogue in those days – grey flannels and sports shirt with sleeves turned up and if you didn't want a tie you wore a cravat and you invariably had to have brown shoes or brown suede shoes … There was no seriousness in it because … a lot of normal people used to wear brown suede shoes and grey flannel trousers and cravat."[21]

The research of subcultures, which has predominantly recorded male and heterosexual experiences, expels the belief that it was only homosexuals who were interested in their dress and their appearance.

Historicism in men's shoes also provided opportunities for queer men to experiment with alternative but socially acceptable appearances. Cecil Beaton's neo-Edwardianism is well known, with a wasp waist, long coat and bespoke shoes. Less well known is the dress of Bunny (Neil) Roger, a wealthy heir and dress designer of the same era.[22] Bunny's shoes – black and white leather and suede brogue ankle boots, patent leather boots, side-buttoned ankle boots with faux spats by Poulsen, Skone & Co. suggest the way in which an extreme attention to a narrow cut and elegant streamlining might point to a fashion consciousness almost fetishistic in its detailing. His dressing also indicates the impossibility of ascribing dandy appearance to gay men; a dandy might just as well be a man using his sharp appearance to attract women. Cohen notes, in her essay on Virginia Woolf and dressing, "Both fashion and queerness depend on marking distinctions between *and* couplings of ordinariness and deviance."[23] The difference generally lies in the detail or the mode of wearing. Later in life, Bunny's wardrobe extended to the fancy dress of an amethyst catsuit accompanied by Asian-style slides. Bunny and his brother Sandy also once hosted a party for New Year which appeared in *The People* as a "fetish party": men in high heels and bondage straps dragged their wives on chains. "While Sir Alexander [Roger] exploded, Lady Roger merely remarked 'I wonder how that man managed to walk in those high-heeled shoes all night.' "[24]

Ironically, a "soft" shoe such as the deck shoe had, by the 1980s, taken on completely different connotations. With its suggestion of masculine sporting prowess and casual nonchalant air, it became the shoe of choice for male college students in the United States and Australia. But the shoe is always about more than the style or form: a brown deck shoe meant something very different to a blue and white one. Whilst watching television, a friend recently described the male presenter as being "light on his loafers." Further inquiry confirmed that it was the presenter's sexuality that was being noted. Shoes are clothing objects animated by actions, choices and performance, as well as part of cultural idiom and social understanding used to describe or entertain someone's sexual choices.

LICK MY BOOT

Urban, social and economic history point persuasively to the Second World War as the watershed moment that permitted the establishment of large and viable gay subcultures. Subcultures arose in denser cities, often in port localities where the flux of travel was more accentuated. Many men and women had experienced homosocial environments and friendships during the war and as they were demobilized in the large port cities such as San Francisco and Sydney, some did not return to the families they had left behind. Living alone outside marriage also required particular types of real estate; the small "bachelor flat," for example, was an innovation of this period. The coincidence of a new wave of bohemianism, revived artistic circles proud to be liberal and accepting, and the availability of low-rent accommodation led to inner-city areas becoming more markedly "queer."

Cultural identity and its codes are not fixed entities lying outside of history and culture. Styles that can be can be politicized in a queer context can also be depoliticized and repoliticized as circumstances change – the blue suede shoes being a case in point. Cultural forms do not have fixed meanings as people make sense of them in different ways according to the time, place and circumstances of reception. The evolution of the Gay Liberation movement and notions of gay pride, involving both men and women, led to a different kind of communicative semiotics particularly evident among gay men in North America.[25] A set of public stereotypes based on conventional male imagery – cowboy, construction worker, motorcyclist, cop – were developed as the basis of a gay male "look," which embodied established male sexual fantasies of hypermasculinity and virility.[26] The cowboy boot had appeared in kitsch gay pornographic art of the 1950s by Quaitance and Tom of Finland. In the 1980s, the Timberland boot became an index of gay urban cool, but as Richard Martin noted, worn by gay men partly unlaced, producing the effect of "their tongues – more phallic symbolism – flapping out."[27]

Hal Fischer's 1977 publication, *Gay Semiotics*, based on a series of photographs taken in his neighborhood of Castro Street and Haight Ashbury in San Francisco, California, suggested that "The gay culture's new visibility has exposed a subculture developing its own myths, cultural heroes, stereotypes and sign language … And since gay men needed a method to communicate sexual preferences, a sexual semiotic was developed."[28] Initially tracing archetypal images rooted in myth, such as the cowboy, Fischer documents how such images were subverted and utilized by the gay community. The cowboy or biker, for example, an image rooted in heterosexual mainstream culture, could be easily adapted into modern-day dress of jeans, flannel shirt and boots, and was acceptable in mainstream culture as a masculine mode, while simultaneously asserting "gayness" (Figure 14.1).[29]

Judith Butler's important work on performative gender formation has given fashion scholars a fertile framework for looking at queerly inflected cultures of adornment. Butler suggests that queer-invested practices, such as drag and other "parodic practices," for example cross-dressing and lesbian butch/femme identities, expose and subvert gender-essentialist culture and unsettle the idea of the existence of a "true gender identity."[30]

Eve Kosofsky Sedgwick uses the terms "camp performative" and "camp recognition" in a discussion of (particularly) gay male dressing and looking. "Camp performative" relies on an ironic reading of a "stable set of codes" to which a range of (both knowing and ignorant) responses is possible. The gay men of the late 1970s, wearing male construction workers' boots, plaid shirts, Levi 501s and a set repertoire of hypermasculine hair and facial hairstyles were engaging in Sedgwick's "camp performative." The early adopters of this North American "clone" fashion trend were able to be both recognized by those "in the know" and at the same time able to "pass" as straight by the adoption of a conventionally accepted masculine look which could be (for a time at least) "misread" by straight observers. This queer-inflected looking has been particularly highly developed in urban gay male settings.[31] The insistence on seeing "clothes as performance" can be seen, as Richard Dyer observes, as an "act of queering" which adopts a conventional set of masculine imagery that is then worn with irony.[32] One can therefore experience, in one male homosexual setting, a range of modes of reception of dress which includes all of the following: "identification with, desire for, and parodies of masculinity"[33]

FIGURE 14.1 (FACING PAGE): "HARD SELL," TOPPER FOOTWEAR ADVERTISEMENT, GAY NEWS, LONDON, NO. 50, P. 9, N.D. (RAN BETWEEN JUNE 1972 AND APRIL 1983). THE CAPTION READS: "MANUFACTURERS OF CLOTHES, AFTERSHAVE, LIQUOR AND NOW EVEN BOOTS AND SHOES WILL GO TO ANY LENGTHS IT SEEMS TO SELL THEIR PRODUCT. AND IF THAT MEANS PROMOTION OF THE KIND SHOWN IN OUR PHOTOGRAPH ABOVE, THEN WE'RE ALL FOR IT! THE PARTICULAR BRAND OF FOOTWEAR, SO AESTHETICALLY (AND MODESTLY) ARRANGED IN THIS PUBLICITY SHOT, COMES FROM TOPPER, OF CARNABY STREET, SHAFTESBURY AVENUE, AND KINGS ROAD, LONDON." © TERRY LAMBERT. COURTESY CLARE LOMAS.

Hard sell

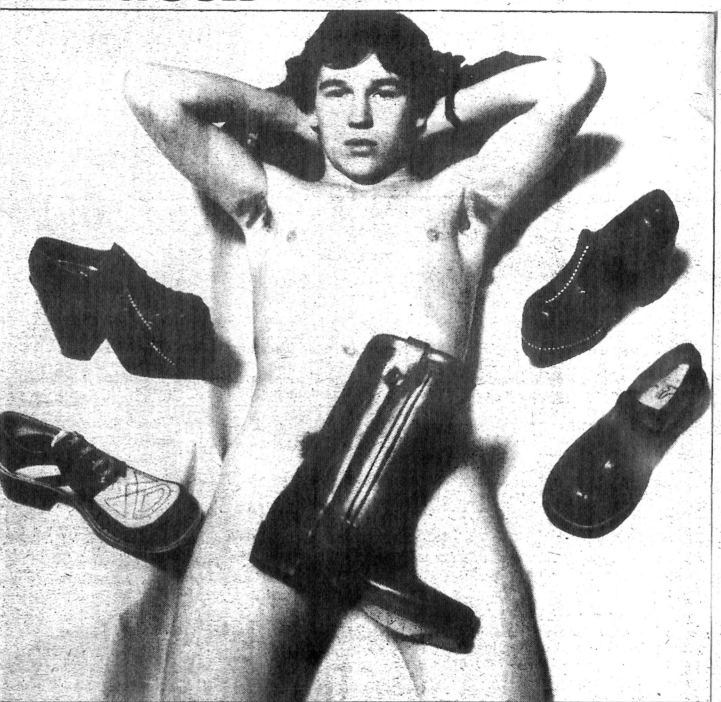

LONDON: *Manufacturers of clothes, after-shave, liquor and now even boots and shoes will go to any lengths, it seems, to sell their product. And if that means promotion of the kind shown in our photograph above, then we're all for it!*

The particular brand of footwear, so aesthetically (and modestly) arranged in this publicity shot, comes from Topper, of Carnaby Street, Shaftesbury Avenue, and Kings Road, London.

FIGURE 14.2: VITA SACKVILLE-WEST AT MEREWORTH CASTLE, 1958, PHOTOGRAPHED BY CECIL BEATON. BROMIDE PRINT. REPRODUCED BY COURTESY OF THE CECIL BEATON STUDIO ARCHIVE, SOTHEBY'S.

LESBIAN IDENTITY

For lesbians, not legally acknowledged in the United Kingdom until changes to legislation in the 1980s, the struggle to define a suitable identity in the early twentieth century involved appropriating and subverting elements of both masculine and feminine dress. Class privilege always guarantees certain protections and the public face of lesbianism was certainly articulated through wealthy protagonists. From the painter Gluck (Hannah Gluckstein) to the queer married writer Vita Sackville-West, from Marion Barbara Joe Carstairs (Queen of Whale Quay, one of the world's richest women) to Marlene Dietrich, women, clothes and a highly charged sexual ambiguity were never out of the public eye. The 1920s was an extraordinary queer moment. Feminist scholarship has identified this decade as a key decade of struggle in the area of sexuality. As Rolley notes, the sex reform of the 1920s and the assault on the "spinster" type went hand in hand with a new focus on intimacy and heterosexual intercourse.[34]

In the 1920s, British *Vogue* was run by two lesbians, Dorothy Todd and Madge Garland, later sacked by Condé Nast for their extreme articles on the architecture of Le Corbusier and fashion notes such as "What spinsters are wearing" to signal their sexual proclivity.[35] The trial and banning of Radclyffe Hall's 1928 novel, *The Well of Loneliness*, drew enormous attention to Hall and her lover, Lady Una Troubridge. Their polarized dress and mannered appearance might be perused in *Tatler* or *The Queen*. As members of the wealthy upper class, Hall and Troubridge lived in relative freedom, defining themselves with reference to "science" and Havelock Ellis's systematic definition of homosexuality, which argued that sexual inversion was congenital. Hall wore low-heeled lace-ups, which signaled participation in public space but might also suggest country life. Troubridge, on the other hand, wore evening pumps and fabrics of great beauty and delicacy.[36] They were a sartorial template of a noble, pseudoscientific theory and seem to have played on this stance.

Other Englishwomen, such as Vita Sackville-West, were photographed in clothing styles that signaled their seriousness of purpose. One of the great garden designers and plantswomen of the twentieth century as well as a writer, Sackville-West designed and wore, from about 1931 until her death in 1962, an extraordinary pair of custom-made gardening boots that combined utility, country life and a decidedly determined bent. With canvas uppers lacing all the way to the knee, they accentuated her height in breeches, and a pair of secateurs or dagger-like knife for weeding was thrust into the top (Figure 14.2). Pearls accompanied the ensemble. On her lecture tour to America in 1933, Sackville-West's appearance was described in the type of detail previously afforded to Wilde:

> Wearing a brown felt hat of masculine design and unpressed brim, Miss Sackville-West
> bore out in appearance her theories of independence for women. She wore a woollen
> ensemble of blue, including a Slavic shirtwaist, cerise earrings and glass beads of similar
> value or colour. Her brogues included thong lacings to the calf of her leg …[37]

There is a poignant photograph of these two-tone boots lying empty, unlaced, on a fringed chair at Sissinghurst; without their owner they look impotent, unable to be occupied by anybody else.[38] Gertrude Jekyll, the other genius of Arts and Crafts garden design, is also commemorated by a superb oil painting of her gardening boots, now in Godalming Museum.[39] These shoes indicated the seriousness of these women's mission to transform taste and society through a pursuit that might be undertaken by all women. Jekyll had resisted posing at all, as "I think ugly people had better not be painted," and Nicholson painted the boots while waiting for her.[40] Unlike the Van Gogh boots mentioned in Julia Pine's chapter in this volume, Miss Jekyll's boots sit up pertly and defiantly, ready for their wearer to take charge. They are not the shoes of drudgery.

BOOTS OF LEATHER, SLIPPERS OF GOLD

The emergence of a lesbian community in Buffalo, New York, from the 1930s to the 1960s, is documented in the evocatively titled book *Boots of Leather, Slippers of Gold* (1993).[41] This groundbreaking study revealed that the identities of butch/femme lesbians have always been problematic and questioned by those who were concerned that their identity as a couple was merely a parody of the heterosexual norm. Nonetheless, at a time when so-called deviant sexuality was criminalized and medically listed as a psychiatric illness, forming an identity by appropriating existing gender roles, dress and behavior was a highly significant form of resistance.

In the 1940s, a time when women wearing pants was becoming more socially acceptable due to their wartime working roles, butch lesbians used shoes to underline their position. One participant in the oral history project, Leslie, stressed this significance by noting that to go with her pants it was vital to have "the most masculine-style shoes you could find, flat shoes, like Oxfords."[42] Another participant, Piri, claimed that on one occasion, wearing women's shoes with men's clothes prevented her from being arrested:

> I've had the police walk up to me and say, "Get out of the car." [I say] "I'm drivin'."
> They say get out of the car; and I get out. And they say, "What kind of shoes you got
> on? You got on men's shoes?" And I say, "No, I got on women's shoes." I got on some
> basket-weave women's shoes. And he say, "Well you damn lucky." Cause everything else
> I had on were men's – shirts, pants. At that time when they pick you up, if you didn't
> have two garments that belong to a woman you could go to jail …[43]

Similarly, "femme" or ultrafeminine identities could be underlined through a choice of footwear, notably high heels: "They would wear high heels and makeup and have their hair done in the highest fashions of the day."[44]

In Britain, a similar dress style was appropriated by butch and femme lesbians. Margaret, born in 1927, describing butch lesbians, recalled:

A lot of them used to dress in very tailored suits. A lot of women used to have their hair all Eton chopped and Brylcreemed down and they'd wear tailored jackets and skirts and lisle stockings and brogue shoes. And some would wear ties but not a lot of women wore trousers then."[45]

However, the lines between dress indicating sexual deviancy and affiliation to the emerging sub-cultures were blurred for women as well as men. Vicky, born in 1939, reminisced:

I suppose I always was a bit butch. I was the only one at college to have a drape blazer and a DA haircut. I was a Teddy girl. I wore suede shoes with crepe soles. I had a blue suede pair. I think grey was my favourite colour, I had a very pale grey coat with a black velvet collar. And we used to wear a high neck, like a shirt, but not a shirt because women didn't wear shirts then."[46]

Second-wave feminism of the 1960s and 1970s highlighted women's clothing and appearance precisely because clothing and accessories are such a visible form of gender and sexual identification. There was a split in the women's movement, the strands of which Elizabeth Wilson termed "authentic" and "modernist." The "authentic" strand rejected the objectification of women and saw feminized dress as a form of oppression.[47] The "modernist" strand recognized clothing as part of a postmodern form of play and supported the idea of women participating in feminine activities, such as wearing makeup, skirts and high heels. The insinuation was that to be supportive of the women's movement you had to reject such female accoutrements, however it appeared that the alternative was to follow an equally stifling dress code, and these tensions have never fully been resolved.

It was during this climate that some women, enraged by sexist advertising campaigns, voiced their disapproval of posters where women were displayed as objects for heterosexual men, by spraying graffiti on billboard advertisements. One example, recorded by Jill Posener in her collection of photographs *Spray It Loud* (1982), is of a billboard poster for Pretty Polly hosiery.[48] The poster depicts a large speckled egg to the right of the image. The eggshell is cracked as if at the moment of hatching with a pair of female legs protruding from the egg. The feet are clad in high-heeled mules, which are decorated with pale feathers, with more feathers floating down to the bottom of the image. Above the legs is the advertiser's tagline: "Legs as soft and smooth as the day you were born." Wittily spray-painted onto this image, under the main tagline, is the slogan: " ♀♀ Born Kicking! ♀♀ ," clearly subverting the image so it will be read as a lesbian feminist critique of modern patriarchal society.

During the 1980s, in the UK, following the influence of second-wave feminism, mainstream womenswear and styling did become more masculinized. By the early 1990s, there was a blurring between lesbian dress styles, popularized by the mainstream press as "lesbian chic," and the sexually ambivalent apparel worn by "Riot Grrls," which later crossed over into mainstream

FIGURE 14.3: "BLUNDSTONE BOOTS. THE WAY THINGS SHOULD BE," VIZ MAGAZINE, SPRING/ SUMMER 1993. THIS IMAGE SHOWS THE BLURRING BETWEEN LESBIAN/BUTCH AND FEMME STEREOTYPES AS WELL AS THE RIOT GRRLS SUBCULTURE. COURTESY CLARE LOMAS.

BLUNDSTONE BOOTS
THE WAY THINGS SHOULD BE

fashion (Figure 14.3). This style consisted of mixing what had previously been identified as femme items with butch items of dress, such as knee-length floral or pastel-colored dresses worn with thick socks and big black boots, often Dr. Martens, Caterpillar or Blundstone (Figure 14.4).

This blurring of lesbian identities with mainstream fashion has meant that some identifying codes associated with dress are no longer clear-cut. The painting *Erect* (1992), by the artist Sadie Lee, can be interpreted in a variety of ways. On one level the image depicts two young women, seated; one is wearing a jacket, pants and boots, the other is wearing a dress and shoes. One arm of each woman is around the other, indicating a bond of friendship. Those with knowledge of the artist might know that this image is a portrait of her and her lover. Those without this specific knowledge may still decode the image and recognize that the positioning of the arms and hands symbolizes a stronger bond than mere friendship. The clothing – one woman wearing pants and boots and the other wearing a dress and court shoes – when read together indicates the women's lesbian identity. It appears here that the shoes are the exclamation mark underlining the women's sexual proclivity.

SHOES AND THE CITY

While "queer" is sometimes used as an interchangeable term with "lesbian and gay," ideas of "queer" extend beyond same-sex attraction and sexual activity. As David Halperin puts it, "queer" need not be grounded in any stable sexual identity but acquires its meaning from oppositional relation to the norm."[49] It "describes a horizon of possibility [which] … cannot in principle be limited in advance."[50] "Queer" as a strategy is thus a different type of identity politics, as it denies the notion of a stable essential identity that needs to be "uncovered."

An incident from the HBO television series *Sex and the City* will serve as a coda to our chapter on queer shoes. In the episode in question, Carrie Bradshaw's silver Manolo Blahnik stilettos are stolen from the shoe pile at the entrance to a heterosexual baby shower at which the guests have been requested to remove their shoes in order to protect the floors of the suburban family home. After her hostess fails to be concerned about Carrie's loss of an expensive and much-loved pair of shoes, Carrie, back in Manhattan, takes a good hard look at the hetero-normative social rules which say that marriage and babies are a cause for endless celebration and gift-giving, while single womanhood is neither cause for celebration nor an attractor of gifts. To redress this imbalance, Carrie issues an invitation to her upcoming "marriage to myself," as she puts it, and nominates Manolo Blahnik as the "wedding register" store. In this way, the writers of the episode position the silver stilettos as an emblem of a more expansive and "queerer" world.

In another episode, a key character – not Samantha, the most libidinal, but the rather discreet Charlotte – socializes with a group of hip, moneyed "power lesbians" "who know the secret to invisible makeup."[51] When she is questioned about what is so attractive about this group, even though she doesn't "go there" sexually, she wistfully and ironically comments on her envy for their great shoes: expensive, impractical high-heeled shoes. Indicating how fashion is always implicated in power dynamics, gay activists such as Peter Tatchell have recently condemned the focus in the gay community on haircuts, dress and body as part of the "dehumanizing" of the community. North American gay activists struggle constantly with the political dilemma of whether gays and lesbians should appear as good citizens and thus be more likely to be afforded their legal rights, or alternatively that they should refuse to conform. Fashion – and shoes – are still on the front line of sexual politics.

FIGURE 14.4: DR. MARTENS BOOTS. BATA SHOE MUSEUM, TORONTO, P95.34. BY KIND PERMISSION OF BATA SHOE MUSEUM.

15.
MADE IN ITALY

SALVATORE FERRAGAMO AND TWENTIETH-CENTURY FASHION[1]

stefania ricci

"Made in Italy" is one of the most recognized "labels" in present-day global fashion. It is a reassuring mark of design, creativity and quality, yet its history is rather recent, developing only in the second half of the twentieth century. It coincides with a period of Italian economic development and design culture: the Vespa, Cinquecento car, Alessi's appliances and Barilla pasta designed by Giugiaro, but also Valentino glamor and later Armani austerity. The list of "design icons" seen as quintessentially Italian is as long as the variety of meanings associated with the notion of "Made in Italy." The link with fashion, however, was evident from the very beginning of Italy's ascendancy to a global design leader. The Anglo-Saxon expression "Made in Italy" was first used in 1951 within the first fashion runway parades of postwar Italy. It was created as an overall expression in order to identify a wide range of Italian products and used to convey ideas of quality and creativity, especially for foreign buyers and markets. The development of Italian fashion in the following fifty years relied on the fame of the wider concept of "Made in Italy."

One must recognize, however, that "Made in Italy" emerged in the Fascist period when, catalyzed by isolation and economic difficulties, Italy was able to develop an autonomous language of style. After the Second World War, other factors facilitated this process. The Marshall Plan, commencing in spring 1947, aimed to repair the physical damage of war and to start a new economic cycle through the imitation of American industrial strategies. It faced, however, the particular context of a country in which material resources were minimal but the skilled workforce was prominent.[2] These topics are considered here in the context of the life and work of Salvatore Ferragamo, shoemaker and shoe designer, whose contribution to both Italian and world fashion stretched from the late 1920s to the early 1960s (Figure 15.1). Ferragamo came to symbolize a matrix of Italian skill, taste and design that cohered to form a recognizable international fashion identity.

1951: THE YEAR ITALIAN FASHION WAS BORN

The original runway parades held in Florence in 1951 were followed during that decade by a series of complementary and competing events. *L'alta moda* (high fashion), as it came to be known in Italy, was also on show in Rome. A series of smaller gatherings was taking place in Bologna, Milan, Turin and other Italian cities, promoting specific subsections of the Italian fashion system such as leather goods, the *alta moda accessori*. American magazines such as *Footwear News* heavily publicized Italian footwear during those years by showing the frequent footwear runway shows taking place there. The material and cultural vibrancy was matched by the general development of the Italian economy during the 1950s and early 1960s. In 1950, the Italian shoemaking sector exported shoes worth just over 200 million lire; four years later its export was 2.3 billion lire.[3] Such an enormous expansion was possible only through the complete restructuring of traditional shoemaking firms. Many *laboratori artigianali* (artisans' workshops) were transformed overnight into integrated businesses, creating the original nucleus of the small- and medium-sized businesses that are still producing the most recognized Italian brands in the world.

The prodigious results of the 1950s came after two decades of debates in the specialist press and fashion magazines and a series of private, public and professional initiatives devoted to the promotion of Italian fashion. Their failed interwar mission was to publicize the "originality" of Italian fashion and in so doing, to create a separate identity for it, distinct from the well-known and long-established notion of Paris/French fashion. In the difficult interwar period Italian fashion attempted to assert its "personality," especially by denying that it was imitative of French ideas. At the center of such initiatives was Giovan Battista Giorgini. From 1923, Giorgini worked in Florence as a buyer for large American chains and department stores. He possessed detailed knowledge of production and for more than ten years was the motor of the Florentine fashion runways. Giorgini's own problem (selling to the American market) reflected a more general issue for Italian producers. There was cultural resistance on the other side of the Atlantic to buying Italian fashion; the *Bel Paese*, as Italy was known, was, in American minds, a cliché of poverty, spaghetti, olive oil and low-cost products. Giorgini was conscious that there was much more to sell, especially in terms of high-quality leatherwear. Production was carried out by specialized artisans, whose skills were possibly unique, but whose capacity to promote their products within a clearly identifiable "style" was totally absent.[4]

Americans, but also French couturiers, had become keen buyers of Italian accessories well before the Second World War. They were supplied with buttons, bags and shoes produced in hundreds of small workshops scattered in Italian towns both in the north and south of the country. Italian leatherwear, in particular, was well known for its centuries-old tradition starting with the medieval urban guilds and continuing to the 1930s and 1940s, with small workshops producing high-quality goods. These artisans kept their skills alive by passing down the trade from father to son and through the protection of productive specialization. Often these occupations were carried out only in one town, or in one area by a socially homogeneous group of producers.

For these producers, quality – rather than style or design – was imperative.[5] This was a problem, rather than a strength, for Italian fashion. The artisanal identity did not match with any image of "class" or "prestige" for Italian products. High fashion had, however, according to Giorgini, all the potential to create a bridge between the artisanal, the artistic and the commercial worlds. There was a need to feed into the media world – especially the wide screen's actors and actresses – in order to capture the attention of journalists, the international press and, through them, the wide transatlantic markets. Italian "elegance" had to be the centerpiece of a strategy that was not only cultural, but also commercial and economic.

Florence was seen as the only Italian city with the potential to rival Paris as a showcase for Italian fashion. The Tuscan capital was still enjoying an artistic renaissance born out of the war period, when it had been a much safer place for artists than Paris or Berlin.[6] Art, it was claimed, was in the very "genetic code" of the city, its beauty, *buon gusto* (good taste) and artistic culture noted since the Quattrocento. Giorgini's real achievement was his success in attracting to Florence the large American buyers such as I. Magnin of San Francisco, Bergdorf Goodman and Saks of New York, and Henry Morgan of Montreal, as they were on their way back from the Paris parades (rather like the Grand Tour in reverse). Giorgini staged, in his own house, what appeared to be an impromptu setup, but which was in reality the result of the entrepreneur's deliberate strategy. Both American buyers and journalists seemed to appreciate the formal beauty of Italian fashion, as well as the quality of materials and techniques, comfort and a unique versatility of use or function. In the following years similar events followed, all orchestrated by Giorgini, who used his knowledge of fashion together with the artistic beauties of Florence to attract foreign buyers. He created the idea that the "Italian Style" was first of all a way of living, rather than a way of appearing. Culture and art were supporting this claim and creating a notion of "Made in Italy" in which aesthetic vision and quality were joined in a unique ensemble.[7]

FIGURE 15.1 (FACING PAGE): SALVATORE FERRAGAMO WITH HIS SHOEMAKERS IN THE 1930S. REPRODUCED BY KIND PERMISSION OF THE FERRAGAMO ARCHIVE.

FERRAGAMO AND THE AMERICAN DREAM

Many of the fashion designers that Giorgini employed in his first Florentine runway show of 1951 were young and mostly unknown outside small national circles. The exceptions included Sorelle Fontana, well known within postwar Italian high fashion, and the famous Emilio Pucci, then an emerging stylist of ready-made clothes. Giorgini could also rely on an international name for the category of "accessories": Salvatore Ferragamo (Figure 15.2). He willingly joined Giorgini's initiative and produced all of the footwear used in the show. It was on this occasion that Ferragamo produced, for the evening wear of Emilio Schubert, one of the most famous shoes of the twentieth century: the sandal with "kimo," a leather or satin stocking to match the color of the dress. The idea for this shoe came from a long journey to the Orient undertaken by Ferragamo the previous year. Ferragamo was particularly inspired by the traditional Japanese sandal *tabi*, usually worn with white cotton socks, as described in Martha Chaiklin's chapter in this volume. The idea for the "Kimo" is also in line with a widespread attitude of 1950s fashion – especially in Italy – to use the same garment in different occasions or situations. This was defined by the press as a "*trasformismo alla Fregoli*" (from an early twentieth-century actor famous for his camouflage), that is to say an ability to change visual appearance, which filtered from the catwalk to the boutique and accessories, to reach here its highest level of expression.

Ferragamo also represented the Florentine component of Giorgini's vision. His firm was based in the Palazzo Spini Feroni in Via Tornabuoni, in the elegant center of the city. From the late 1920s, Ferragamo, more than anyone else, represented the high-fashion end of footwear in Italy. This had been a booming sector since early in the twentieth century and was composed of dozens of small artisanal businesses that produced high-quality footwear, such as Gatto and Dal Co' in Rome and Savoia in Milan. Their names, however, remained essentially a local and national phenomenon. Similarly, the sportswear and small leather goods produced by Gucci in its workshop in Lungardo Guicciardini in Florence were known at the end of the 1940s only by a selected clientele of locals and a few international travelers in search of exclusivity. They rarely appeared in fashion magazines and were totally ignored by the large American department stores.

Figure 15.2 (below): Sandal "Kimo" by Salvatore Ferragamo, 1951. Reproduced by kind permission of the Ferragamo Archive.

Figure 15.3 (facing page): Salvatore Ferragamo with his clients' lasts, 1955. Reproduced by kind permission of © Locchi.

This brief summary of Italian fashion in the late 1940s and early 1950s should serve as a background for understanding the achievements of Ferragamo. His success was exceptional in several ways and has been explained mainly by referring to his peculiar training, complex international links, personal stamina and unique capacity to communicate with the public (Figure 15.3). This chapter will demonstrate how the professional and personal story of Salvatore Ferragamo is important not only for its unique features, but also for the many elements that it shares with the lesser known but important producers, designers and "fashion makers" who consolidated "Made in Italy" around the world. Some of the elements of Ferragamo's success belonged to a common trait of innovation and originality and were widely shared by large parts of the Italian fashion system. The story of Ferragamo, before and after the Second World War, is typical of the complex nature of Italian footwear manufacturing, born out of artisanal traditions and destined to become one of the country's leading economic sectors.

SALVATORE FERRAGAMO

Salvatore Ferragamo was born in 1898 in Bonito, a small village in the province of Avellino in the south of Italy. He was the son of a peasant family with little means. In his autobiography he claimed that he produced his first pair of shoes when he was just nine years old, for the first communion of his sister – a type of visionary experience perhaps? His early exploits led him to an apprenticeship with a local shoemaker, and on to continue his training in Naples, a center famous for its high-quality and "artistic" footwear production since the eighteenth century.[8] Other shoemakers who in the 1950s started brands that eventually became famous at a global level, trained in the same geographic area where Ferragamo completed his apprenticeship. This was the case with Mario Valentino, whose father Vincenzo was the owner of a workshop in the Piazza delle Mure Greche, Naples, which produced very expensive footwear.

In 1914, when Salvatore Ferragamo was just sixteen, he decided to join his elder brothers in the United States. He was one of the hundreds of thousands of poor peasants and unemployed people from the south of Italy forced to migrate to the Americas in search of work. It was in these years that the so-called "American dream" became one of the major cultural constructs in the Italian public imagination. Little is known of Ferragamo's inner motivations, apart from the familial links, for emigration. He was a clever young man for whom migration was not the only chance to earn a living, but a way to improve his creative and cultural potential. He knew that the US footwear industry was the most technologically advanced in the world and that it would allow him to further his knowledge of the sector well beyond the limits of Italy. On landing in New York, Ferragamo quickly found a job in a shoe factory in Boston where the popular "Queen Quality" brand was produced. He was impressed by the speed and efficiency of the American system, rather than the final quality of the product. It was not just a problem of mass production. Queen Quality produced at a higher standard than the average American quality, but the final result was a type of shoe that was heavy and clumsy in its construction, when compared with the artisanal production of an Italian shoemaker.

Salvatore Ferragamo was not only an acute observer, but also a man of action. As soon as he had completed his analysis of the footwear production system in the factories of the industrial eastern US, he convinced his two brothers and sister to move to Santa Barbara in California, where the film industry was well under way. Here Ferragamo envisaged that he could find the right customers for luxury handmade shoes. The family opened a small, bespoke shop and Salvatore attended evening courses on anatomy at the local university, where he hoped to improve his knowledge of the relationship between footwear and the body. His dream was to produce shoes that were not only aesthetically beautiful but also characterized by high standards of comfort and functionality. The American experience, both in the industrial eastern US and in the glamorous West Coast, remained the two most relevant factors shaping Ferragamo's professional life and influencing the entire concept of "Made in Italy."

The first chance to acquire customers among the actors on the silver screen came via Salvatore's brother, who was employed by the American Film Company as a stage assistant; he commissioned Salvatore to make a pair of cowboy boots. Within just a few months, Ferragamo's shop had become one of the favorite stores of film directors and divas of the silent cinema. Ferragamo become the shoemaker to Pola Negri, Mary Pickford and her sister Lottie, Gloria Swanson and Mae West (Figure 15.4). They wore his shoes not only on film sets, but also in the glamorous streets of Los Angeles. Ferragamo was well known for his women's shoes, but in his early days he also produced men's shoes for films and for selected customers such as his friend Rodolfo Valentino. When, in 1923, the film industry moved to Hollywood, Ferragamo followed and opened an elegant and spacious store called the Hollywood Boot Shop on the aptly named Hollywood Boulevard at the crossing with Las Palmas, one of Hollywood's busiest areas. It was in these years that Ferragamo produced footwear for the films of Cecil B. De Mille, James Creuze, David Wark Griffith and Raoul Wash, including classics such as *The Ten Commandments* (1923), *The Covered Wagon* (1923), *The White Rose* (1923), and *The Thief of Baghdad* (1924).

In the 1920s, Hollywood was immersed in a magic atmosphere: partly dream, partly the incarnation of the ephemeral illusion that characterized the American film industry of the time. The very distinction between set and real life was blurred in a way never experienced before. The modern notion of the visual media as the conveyor of gender, social and cultural models came into being through the integrated media and marketing efforts of the cinema industry. Fashion was no longer a game of small urban elites and the printed media. Hairstyles, makeup, clothing, and also attitude and social behavior, were influenced by the Hollywood divas, whose poses and choices could reach as far as Europe, forcing even Paris to work in synchrony with Hollywood.[9] The Roaring Twenties were a period of experimentation not only in art, but also in fashion. As skirts became shorter and shorter, shoes claimed the center stage. New leather tanning systems allowed the production of novel colors, as well as techniques of painting and printing leather, for instance metallic and pearl tones. Shoes could now appear very different from older types, both in aesthetic terms and in their versatility. Versatility was in turn tied to new modes of living promoted in magazines and within film culture.

Southern Pacific

ARGONAUT

Chateau Art
Studios
L H
4

BACK TO ITALY: FAILURES AND SUCCESS

Ferragamo's early training in the United States allowed him to experiment with new production techniques, also to create shoe models without the limitations on cost and raw materials that he would have faced in Italy – Salvatore Ferragamo was in a very special position when compared to shoemakers in Italy and in Europe. However, the United States did not offer a specialized workforce trained in the production of handmade shoes, which Ferragamo needed for the expanding US market. He was now retailing his shoes not only through his Hollywood store, but also through large departments stores such as I. Magnin of San Francisco and Saks of Fifth Avenue in New York. So in 1927, Ferragamo decided to return to Italy and chose Florence as the new headquarters for his international business, where he had a highly qualified but cheap workforce.

Florence was well known as a center for the production of leather goods such as gloves, bags, suitcases, linings and the famous Florentine multicolored and tool-engraved leathers. But even so this does not explain why an international shoemaker from the south of Italy would have chosen Florence – where he had no particular business, family or personal ties – as the main location for his business. Florentine shoemakers were probably as good as the traditional producers in regions such as Umbria and Marche (both in the central southern part of the country), but could not rival the refined production of the major urban centers of Campania, the southern region where Ferragamo came from, or Sicily – where there was an established tradition in shoemaking dating back generations. Florence, however, was the Mecca of international tourism: its allure did not confine itself just to art, but extended into the artisanal production of a range of unique consumer goods from embroidery to lace, straw hats, expensive glass and metal products. To relocate to Florence was a statement of distinction and quality as well as of global influence.

From an international point of view, Florence was an anomaly. Larger European metropolises such as London, Paris and Berlin produced fashion and trends, but did not possess a concentration of skills for the manufacture of products of the highest quality. This explains why foreign buyers, especially from the other side of the Atlantic, were in those years creating connections with Florentine producers, and used middlemen such as Giorgini to provide them with luxury products that were not always considered fashionable. During his American years, Salvatore Ferragamo had acquired an in-depth knowledge of the American market, especially in terms of taste. Florence was thus the perfect set to develop his creativity by inventing the contemporary myth of the Renaissance *bottega*, a place where artists operated, where ideas were molded into shapes, and where modern masterpieces (*capolavori*) were produced. Ferragamo was perhaps one of the first to understand the power of a message that combined high-quality artisanal products with the historic and artistic past of the city. The very act of buying a Ferragamo shoe was not only a fashion statement, but also an act of appropriation of the cultural and artistic tradition of Florence.

FIGURE 15.4 (FACING PAGE): SALVATORE FERRAGAMO ON A HOLLYWOOD FILM SET. PHOTO: © ALINARI.

Ferragamo brought with him to Florence a new wave of creativity, and major international links; he combined the American philosophy of "industrial" production with the Italian tradition of handmade products; he reshaped the figure of the shoemaker as the expert in one of the production stages. He also introduced the American concept of shoe variety, based not only on large choice of sizes, but also on different widths with custom-made adaptations. Importantly, Ferragamo was also the inventor of new technical devices such as the *cambrione*, a metal shank that supported the arch of the foot (Figure 15.5). Traditionally, the *cambrione* had been made of thick leather or similar materials. This and many other inventions made the shoe an object of experimentation for shapes, materials and colors. His use of color was unique. Not only did he use the entire palette, but he combined unusual colors with more traditional ones. The result was highly innovative, as in the use of straw plaits (normally used in the production of hats) for shoe uppers (Figure 15.6) or the adoption of the famous lace of Tavarnelle for the most refined products.[10]

Ferragamo was a man of his times and was widely influenced by new trends in the visual arts, architecture and design. As one of the emerging new industrial designers, Ferragamo "invented" by starting from strict functional needs and by adapting form to function. Design and notions of contemporary art were fused. The Futurist Lucio Venna, for instance, was the artist in charge of the first Ferragamo advertising campaign and designer of the famous Ferragamo logo used on the instep of all shoes. Modernism was everywhere at the core of the brand's creative process. While conceiving the "*pezzo unico,*" the individual "masterpiece" of Renaissance inspiration and the artistic artifact of modernist quality, he was also investigating mass production and taking patents of invention on each applicable idea. Multiplicity and industrial concerns were always combined with artistic creativity. Recently, 400 patents of "invention, ornament, utility" that were registered by Ferragamo from the 1930s to the 1950s, have been discovered in the Archivio di Stato in Rome. These are a unique body of sources for the study of the relationship between creativity and technical knowledge (Figures 15.7 and 15.8).[11]

Ferragamo's creations of the 1920s and early 1930s are unique for the decoration of the shoe uppers and for their use of strong and deep colors, sometimes with monochrome effects or in multicolored patchworks that combined fabrics and colored leather. This particular use of color has been attributed to a combination of the deep colors reminiscent of the south of Italy and Ferragamo's fascination with Mexican folklore, acquired while in California. The chromatism of Giotto in the early Renaissance was mixed with the philosophy of color as dynamism, inspired by twentieth-century Futurism. Curvy uppers were combined to form geometric patterns inspired by the abstract art of the 1930s. At the same time, Ferragamo was heavily indebted to traditional Florentine craft production. He was inspired by products as varied as the wrought iron decorations of buildings and railings to the small mosaics used in goldsmithing. He was also inspired in the production of "classical" and "oriental" shoes by the recent archaeological discoveries: the well-known Tutankhamun's tomb in Egypt (opened in 1923) and the Villa dei Misteri in Pompeii, discovered in 1927.

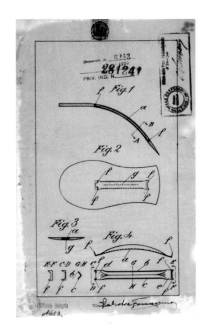

FIGURE 15.5: PATENT OF INVENTION FOR "A SYSTEM TO STRENGTHEN THE SHOE THROUGH THE USE OF A CURVED METALLIC BLADE WITH LIFTED BORDERS TO PROVIDE FURTHER RESISTANCE," N. 281241, JANUARY 1931. ARCHIVIO DI STATO DI ROMA.

Ferragamo's creative emphasis was not just artistic. On the one hand he used ornament as a device to personalize artifacts; on the other hand, he developed a fluid or organic understanding of function and product design. In the early 1930s, he patented some of the major inventions in the history of footwear. These include a system for the sewing of soles with invisible stitches; different methods for cutting hides in order to produce entire uppers; and leather decoration through processes of abrasion of the skin.

Ferragamo's invention covers a long period from the late 1920s to his death in 1959, with a major gap in the years 1934–37. This was a dark period for Ferragamo and high-quality footwear production in general. The economic crisis, starting in the United States in 1929 and reaching Europe in the early 1930s, was accompanied by major managerial problems for Ferragamo's firm. In 1933, Ferragamo did not possess the financial backing to patent his inventions; business was slowing down and he was forced to close his workshop in Via Mannelli. Bankruptcy was unavoidable. However, this setback was faced as a challenge: Ferragamo rented a workspace in Palazzo Spini Feroni in Via Tornabuoni, at the very heart of Florence; he energized foreign export – especially to the United States – and tried to avoid the mistakes made in the previous decade. He also shifted his market target from the New World to the Continent, making his brand known in Europe and in Italy in particular. *Il calzolaio delle dive* (shoemaker to the stars), as he was called in the United States, became, in the 1930s, a prominent brand in Italy. By 1938, Ferragamo's efforts had paid off: he bought Palazzo Spini Feroni, where he opened a major shop on the ground floor and a workshop on the first floor. In the same year, he opened two new branches in the smart Via Condotti in Rome and in Old Bond Street in London.

FERRAGAMO: ARTIST AND ARTISAN

Since the mid-1930s, Ferragamo's main concern had been "form." This is not surprising, as "form" is one of the major themes of Italian design of the period between 1930 and 1960. There is a kind of "architectural" influence in most shoes produced by Ferragamo in this period: symmetry, balance, the details of construction and the relationship between weight and measure. These are symbolized in the cork platform shoes, one of Ferragamo's best-known creations, patented in 1937 (Figures 15.9, 15.10 and 15.11), two years before platform shoes became an international fashion and assumed an iconic symbolism for the late 1930s. The platform shoe was not simply a "fashion innovation." It was conceived in terms of function, as it raised the heel and provided a more stable support for the arch of the foot. This was also a solution to a problem of raw materials. In 1935 Mussolini had invaded Ethiopia and the United Nations had placed sanctions and embargos on Italy. The steel that Ferragamo had used for the *cambrione* was now impossible to buy.

This period of austerity and penury was taken by Ferragamo as a challenge. The platform allowed the "artist" to make use of a wider surface, on the uppers and across the platform heels, for decoration. Several variants of the platform model were produced: the platform shoe with a separate heel; the classic all-in-one platform sole and heel; the platform made with pressed, rounded layers that were chiseled, painted, or decorated with small glass mirrors inspired by ancient mosaics, or with brass grids patterned with flowers and gemstones. Inspiration came from furniture, domestic objects, architecture such as the New York Chrysler Building, rather than from fashion itself. Some of the creations were inspired by Surrealism, such as the rhinoceros horn shape or the exaggerated high heels reminiscent of the costume of Greek tragedy or the chopines of the Renaissance. All of these were in synchrony with similar ideas in France, for instance the work of Elsa Schiaparelli, the fashion designer and friend of Salvador Dalí, but also the work of Christian Bérard and Jean Cocteau (Figure 15.12). Ferragamo and Schiaparelli met for the first time only after the Second World War. Their mutual synergy derived from the pages of fashion magazines and through communal clients such as Claudette Colbert and Marlene Dietrich, defined by Ferragamo as "the possessor of the most beautiful legs, ankles, and feet in the world."[12]

The economic sanctions against Italy led to a series of measures developed to substitute new materials for imported raw materials, and to reduce the use of energy. The stimulus was not just to change ornamental decoration, but also to experiment with new technologies. For example, Ferragamo created heels by sewing together wine bottle corks; he also invented several leather substitutes. Inventions followed one after the other: heels made of transparent Bakelite, replaceable wooden soles of glass imitating car wheels and yarn bobbins (Figure 15.13). His experimentation with "poor" materials shows how luxury is not dependent on the raw material used, but on an idea conjoined with quality of workmanship. This is a modern idea of luxury. Flax, straw,

FIGURE 15.6 (FACING PAGE): SANDAL WITH WOVEN RAFFIA UPPER AND CORK PLATFORM BY SALVATORE FERRAGAMO, 1938–40. REPRODUCED BY KIND PERMISSION OF THE FERRAGAMO ARCHIVE.

FIGURE 15.7 (LEFT): PATENT OF INVENTION GRANTED TO SALVATORE FERRAGAMO, N. 6961, 1930. ARCHIVIO DI STATO DI ROMA.

FIGURE 15.8 (RIGHT): PATENT OF INVENTION FOR "SHOES WITH LIFTED HEEL BUT WITHOUT A SEPARATE COMPONENT...," N. 354889, DECEMBER 1937. ARCHIVIO DI STATO DI ROMA.

wool, and cellophane (from candy wrappers) were used by Ferragamo to create shiny effects, pleats, and other aesthetic solutions, which were adopted in the same years by producers of Italian consumer goods such as Ars Luce, who made lampshades of similar materials.

Ferragamo's creative efforts were widely publicized by the Fascist regime within the mass media and the specialist press. For the regime, Ferragamo's success was even more important, as he had a notable international profile. Ferragamo himself was well aware of the importance of his persona as the incarnation of his business venture. Rather than presenting himself as a "great entrepreneur," Ferragamo proposed a notion of artisan-artist by having his picture taken at the shoemaker's stool, in the process of creation, not dissimilar from a sculptor.[13] At the end of the war, when Florence was still peripheral to the fashion circuits, Ferragamo was keen to associate himself with VIPs, from queens to aristocrats and actresses, who were "immortalized" by a photographer while Ferragamo measured their feet in his richly frescoed Florentine palace. Virtually all of the stars were shot proudly in this genre, which of course recalled the flattering model of Cinderella and also showed off the stars' delicate stockinged feet to the media; Marlene Dietrich, in particular, had very small and unblemished feet.

With the end of the Second World War and the reopening of commercial barriers, Ferragamo was able to consolidate his position at an international level. Perhaps more than anyone else, he represented postwar Italian fashion and design. In 1947 Ferragamo invented an upper made with only one continuous transparent nylon wire, creating an "invisible" sandal. This allowed him to win the Neiman Marcus prize in Dallas, the "fashion Oscar," which he shared with Christian Dior. Inspiration came this time from a fisherman on the banks of the Arno, who Ferragamo saw using a transparent fishing line. The "invisible sandal" (Figure 15.14) was such an international success that Ferragamo took out several patents (for its construction; for its use of materials; and for the heel with a chiseled "F" for Ferragamo).

In the postwar years, the study of "form" was increasingly conceived as the balance between function and multiplicity of use. Ferragamo considered heels and soles to be the two key elements of the architecture of the shoe. In 1946, Ferragamo patented a shoe sole for children, which prevented torsion of the foot and was provided with one of the earliest nonslip devices. This was followed, in 1952, by a décolleté high-heeled shoe, which was visually stunning as the foot arch used the upper's leather, thus limiting the sole to the small heel and the front part of the shoe. This model of the "gloved arch" is well known for its flexibility and beauty.

A few years later, Ferragamo's attention was directed again to the use of metal structures, especially for the sole. Although the material was rather rigid, it allowed an unprecedented comfort and a neo-baroque decorative exuberance created by the use of chiseled and engraved motifs. The pinnacle of Ferragamo's experimentation with metals was surely his most precious model: an eighteen-carat golden sandal commissioned by an Australian client. This was created in collaboration with the goldsmiths of Ponte Vecchio in Florence, and is one of the clearest examples of the continuous relationship between modern Italian design and the ornamental repertoire of the decorative arts. This mix of innovation and recovery of tradition was the strongest message of Ferragamo's strategy at that time. By the mid-1950s he was already playing with "retro" Art Nouveau decorative themes, by creating heels with steel structures partially inspired by the ephemeral architecture of universal exhibitions and by the funicular arches used in Gaudì's architecture. At the same time, however, one can see the influence of organic architecture of the 1950s: the "shell sole," for instance, was adopted within a variety of models, from *bottines* to dancing shoes. The "shell sole" was inspired by the American Indian *opanke*, a moccasin with a sole that covers the heel and becomes part of the footwear upper. The foot is contained and "caressed" by the wrapping curves of the sandal, in a way not dissimilar to Arne Jacobsen's "egg chair" of 1956.[14]

AN INDUSTRIAL FUTURE?

During the 1950s, Ferragamo had to face competition from other Italian and international high-class shoemakers, and the difficult demands of increasingly sophisticated customers with access to mass media. These are the reasons why, although maintaining a craft-based production system, Ferragamo differentiated his production to include less expensive products: "Ferragamo Debs" and "Ferrina Shoes," for instance, were machine-made and produced entirely in England. Similarly, he started producing handbags, and printed scarves inspired by the artistic artworks of major Italian towns; and in 1959 he gave his name to a small collection of sport and casualwear produced by Lord and Taylor and designed by Ferragamo's younger daughter Giovanna (Figure 15.15).

The death of Salvatore Ferragamo, in 1960, demanded a restructuring of the firm's organization. His wife Wanda (born in 1921) and his six children continued to manage the firm, each covering an aspect of production or a commercial area. Salvatore's eldest daughter, Fiamma (1941–98), continued her father's creative mission by managing the footwear design department. Under

Figure 15.9 and 15.10 (facing page) and 15.11 (above): Platform sandals by Salvatore Ferragamo, 1938. Reproduced by kind permission of the Ferragamo Archive.

Figure 15.12 (left): "Arcobaleno" black suede shoes with weave-like embroidery by Salvatore Ferragamo, 1935. Reproduced by kind permission of the Ferragamo Archive.

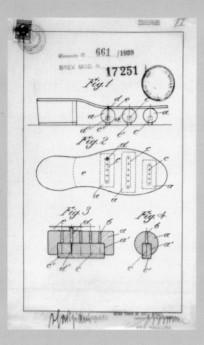

FIGURE 15.13: PATENT OF INVENTION FOR "FRONT PART REPLACING THE SOLE, MADE WITH THREE GALATITE CYLINDERS, GLASS AND SIMILAR MATERIALS," N. 17215, 1940. ARCHIVIO DI STATO DI ROMA.

Fiamma's direction, most production processes became mechanized. This was considered a necessary choice in order to increase production while maintaining relatively low prices. In the 1950s, Ferragamo turned out 350 pairs of shoes a day, all produced by hand by 750 employees; in the 1960s, the firm manufactured 2,000 pairs of shoes a day, most of which were produced in small factories in the regions around Florence and Naples. The firm continued to ensure quality and creativity by creating new models and prototypes.

Ferragamo is one of the major examples of the trajectory from small, artisanal production to light industry that was taken up by many other Italian firms in the 1960s and 1970s. The role of fashion has generally been overshadowed by the success and recognition of object-design firms such as Alessi. A degree of "industrial" spirit was present as early as Ferragamo's "American dream" years and technological innovation was always prioritized as a major development strand for his firm. "Beauty and function," as well as "artisanal and industrial" are important dualities within Ferragamo's (and by extension Italy's) twentieth-century economic development. Since that February day in 1952 when Giorgini recruited his friend Salvatore Ferragamo in a campaign to create the idea of "Made in Italy," the *Bel Paese* has fostered a myth of quality, good taste and innovation. The artisanal spirit of the medieval and Renaissance period has survived, ironically by using the production and communication tools of modern industrial societies. Here modernism, with its focus on the theme of originality and identity, has provided an important bridge between cultures of making and "product development." Shoe fashion's role cannot be underestimated in this shift.

Figure 15.14 (above): Sandal "Invisible" by Salvatore Ferragamo, 1947. Reproduced by kind permission of the Ferragamo Archive.

Figure 15.15 (right): Kid and crocodile décolleté shoe by Ferragamo, 1958–59. Reproduced by kind permission of the Ferragamo Archive.

16.
STYLE THROUGH DESIGN

FORM AND FUNCTION

giovanni luigi fontana

THE FASHIONABLE SHOE

The stylistic and technical aspects involved in the making of a shoe are often overlooked by consumers, who are more interested in appreciating the aesthetics and fashionability of the product. Footwear is born out of a combination of a practical as well as a theoretical understanding of the properties of materials, production techniques, and design issues. Shoes are firstly "imagined" – conceptualized, often on paper, studied, planned and finally made. This distinction between material production and the immaterial imagination of shoes has allowed the attribution of meaning to these artifacts, a topic widely discussed throughout this book. This is part of a process which is here reconsidered as the "conceptualization of shoes – soles and uppers; at the same time gradually assigning them particular and changing meanings – religious, social, ethical, sexual – until these make up an integral part of their actual existence as autonomous 'foot masks'."[1]

This chapter charts the rise of shoemaking as an intellectual as well as a practical occupation by analyzing the role of stylists and designers in the evolution of this sector. Footwear, it is argued, is "the result of a complex and well-organized project, in which the stylistic and technical elements of shoe development overlap with economic and commercial aspects."[2] The relationship between "costume" and "fashion" is central to the understanding of how shoes are created.[3] In the case of twentieth-century Italy, the fashion system of the "Made in Italy" concept created specific effects on the organizational structure of shoemaking and allied sectors.[4] These topics will be investigated in the concluding part of this chapter through the case of the high-quality shoes produced, since the late nineteenth century, in the area between Padua and Venice better known as Riviera del Brenta (Figures 16.1, 16.2 and 16.3).[5] The chapter will use surviving artifacts to underscore its argument.

FROM SHOE STYLES TO THE SHOE STYLIST

Many chapters in this volume have touched upon the idea of creativity in shoemaking. The very myth of the shoemaker-*célèbre* considered in the final chapter by McNeil and Riello, is just one way of popularizing a notion of shoe production in which the "mental" creation is central. If this often means invoking ideas of exceptional craftsmanship, luxury and exclusivity, the opposite can be said about the professional figure of the shoe "stylist" (Figure 16.4). The transition from hand-made and bespoke to fully mechanized production of footwear during the late nineteenth and twentieth centuries has created the need for complex managerial and planning tools. The "stylist" emerges as a skilled expert in charge of the transition of shoes from concept to material object.[6] During the last fifty years in particular, shoe stylists have increasingly acquired the role of fashion designers and product managers. It is part of their task to qualify and personalize models, thus increasing their value for consumers. Their professional profile is now seen as more than plain "styling." The stylist performs a critical part in the marketing strategy of manufactured goods, increasingly based on product innovation rather than simple price competitiveness.[7]

The emergence of the shoe stylist has coincided with the development of a modern consumer economy in which fashion no longer coincides with mere notions of material quality, luxury and exclusivity. Fashion is now a mass phenomenon – culturally and socially defined (Figure 16.5). It is "the adoption of certain clichés, models, objects and colors; aiming at a constant absorption by the market of inexpensive products which become quickly obsolete."[8] Although the media gives a lot of space to fashion as an élite phenomenon – the Paris runway shows, supermodels and extremely refined products – it is the "fashion market," characterized by mass consumption, "fast fashion," short lifecycles of products, and often exaggerated stylistic content, that is central in the economic and social lives of most of us. Present-day society is "not any longer influenced by fashion as created in the great workshops of haute couture and handed down, through traditional

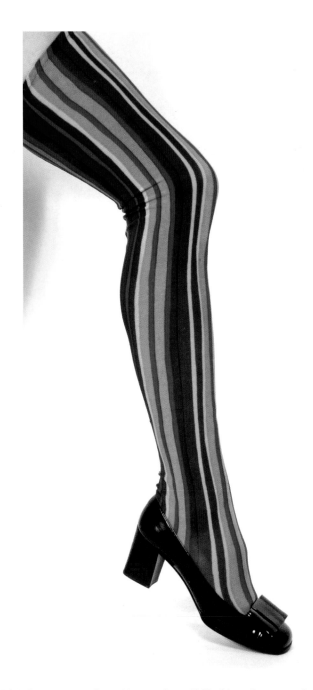

FIGURE 16.1: COLLANT-BOOT BY ROGER VIVIER FOR DIOR, 1960S. MUSEO ROSSIMODA, STRA, VENICE.

channels, from the highest and most representative social ranks to masses of consumers, but rather by a fashion increasingly intended as freedom of expression and individuality, evading every attempt not only of predetermination, but to a great extent, of forecast as well."[9] Production materials and technologies, rather than creativity and exclusivity, characterize the economic feasibility of fashion.

This is not a static context. The very profile of the stylist has changed dramatically over the last few decades. At the highest point of "Fashion" in the 1980s, stylists were often called on to simply carry out a job of product embellishment, without coming into close contact with production and distribution networks. This was particularly problematic for shoe stylists. They have profound knowledge of the anatomical structures of the foot, of workmanship and processes, and of specialized materials and technologies (Figure 16.6). They also need to carefully control the main variables affecting the price, such as the waste of materials, the cost of seaming, and the difficulty of assembling primary and secondary components.

In a context of continuous product innovation and high obsolescence of models, the shoe stylist is in charge of constantly reinventing products, production and the overall shape of the sector according to the needs of the market. The footwear manufacturing industry has to anticipate other lines of clothing and apparel by several months and eventually synchronize itself with the main tailoring lines. Stylists are in charge of "following" and more often "forecasting" fashion by interacting with creators and designers: "They suggest proposals to them in order to obtain reactions or general indications to compare with the previous year's fashion."[10] This process allows manufacturers to set guidelines for the planning of new models, which are continuously revised and modified. The final result is the creation of a prototype to be subjected to a concluding test run of aesthetic accomplishment and market feasibility.[11]

The role of the shoe stylist has changed again in recent years. In Europe, the very concept of fashion has been transformed with the end of a period of "exaggerated" consumption that had led to an overevaluation of stylistic features against the intrinsic quality of products. Fashion is no longer seen only as the stride for "modernist innovation," but also as the reinterpretation of previous influences – a reminiscing about fashions of the past. Consumers now privilege quality over quantity. They have acquired greater consciousness of products and needs and require greater quality, superior comfort, and most of all, more functional products. This has led companies to reconsider the devising and planning of products (Figure 16.7). The innovation of fashion products has therefore been brought back onto a more mundane terrain, in which the "stylistic history" and "product identity" of a company play a substantial role in creating products that are recognizable by the company's targeted consumer group.[12]

FIGURE 16.2 (FACING PAGE): SANDAL WITH SUSPENDED HEEL, DESIGNED BY KARL LAGERFELD FOR FENDI, 1990S. MUSEO ROSSIMODA, STRA, VENICE.

FIGURE 16.3 (ABOVE): PLATFORM SHOE MADE OF PLEXIGLASS BY ROSSIMODA FOR ANNE KLEIN, 1990S. MUSEO ROSSIMODA, STRA, VENICE.

FIGURE 16.4: THE FIRST STAGE OF THE WORK OF A SHOE DESIGNER. PAPER MODELS ARE CUT IN THE PATTERN DEPARTMENT OF A SHOE FACTORY IN THE RIVIERA DEL BRENTA, LATE 1970S. REPRODUCED BY KIND PERMISSION OF A.C.RI.B.

Thus, a more collegiate and coordinated action has replaced the stylist's individual role, enabling different ideas and experiences to be developed in projects that are coherent within the business environment – local, national and global.[13] In this context, research and development have acquired growing relevance in shoemaking and designers have gone from being simple producers of ideas to being able to develop a project in which all elements – stylistic, technical and marketing – are present and appropriately valued. In the shoe manufacturing sector, as in all other sectors related to fashion, creatives – although expressing themselves in the most stylistically advanced and most innovative ways – must always meet market and production requirements, evaluating and using all available information before starting the actual planning and layout of a fashion product. In a market economy, stylistic planning is not solely the result of pure and simple creativity, but the result of the effort of an interfunctional group, rigorously coordinated, aware of the problems related to the industrial nature of the product, and attentive to the technical and production aspects related to its making and marketing.[14]

Fashion designers, besides possessing a strong aesthetic sense, a sharp spirit of observation, an intuitive "sensibility" and the necessary capacity to translate thoughts into things, must also be able to develop ideas that are original and suited to the specific requirements of the market (Figure 16.8).[15] For this reason, designers must associate commercial skills with technical and stylistic ones; they need to maintain a continuous relationship with the sale network and the distribution structure of the firm, assuring themselves of a constant and up-to-date flow of information. Of course, close contact with the wider "fashion world" is essential. As observed by Morlacchi, this part of the production process rests on:

> a delicate and often intangible relationship between stylistic sensitivity and market reality. First of all, designers must be good at interpreting information regarding trends and

tastes; improving their research and observation skills, sorting out offers, determining the best ones, thus stimulating the production of new ideas. Moreover, they must have an operational technique of their own, which, applied at the moment an idea originates, allows the efficient manufacturing of the product, thereby making its purchase easier.[16]

Such operational techniques are the research and knowledge of the characteristics of different materials; the study and creation of the structural elements of a shoe (molds, soles, heels); and the development of their creative skills for the qualification and characterization of products. Key figures in the structural fabric of the shoemaking industry, designers "must enable the industry to match aesthetics and rationality, production aspects and commercial reality."[17] Theirs is an "applied art," strongly linked to production and function. For these reasons, designers have to keep in mind the distinctive characteristics of the company they work for, particularly the technical qualifications and the operational capacity of the firm.

MASS FASHION, NICHE MARKETS

Consumers are often unaware of the way fashion has transformed the organization of production in many sectors in most world economies in the last half-century. The above-mentioned "fashion industries," in particular textiles and clothing, shoes, leather goods and several allied trades such as ribbons, lace and accessories, are strongly influenced by the rules of fashion. Fashion – such an ethereal word – accounts for the way in which such products are traded and sold, but also planned and manufactured. The story of the period since the end of the Second World War has been a tale of conflict between the inconstant behavior of fashion (the "folly of fashion") and the rigidity of production systems based on traditional concepts of Fordist mass production, vertical integration of production and little flexibility in production.

One of the challenges of fashion for the industrial system of production has been the rising importance of "seasons." Garments and accessories are no longer influenced just by climatic conditions; the idea of the season is now the renewed expression of taste – collective and personal – at precise points in time. The continuous stream of creativity born out of "collections" (spring, summer, fall and winter) is a response to the built-in obsolescence of fashion goods. These conditions are at the origin of the distinctively atypical production system governing the shoemaking industry. This industry, similarly to others operating in the fashion business, is characterized by an extreme fragmentation of production.[18] The strong manual component and complex division of labor is coupled with low technological complexity of production and low capital requirements to enter the sector. This makes shoemaking a prolific terrain for small and medium-sized businesses, ranging from traditional artisanal manufacturing to technologically sophisticated firms servicing niche markets.

These elements are particularly visible in the evolution of the Italian shoemaking sector, from the success of "Made in Italy" in the 1950s to the present-day trends in that country. While the advent of mechanized production systems after the Second World War, mass production and direct distribution created a market of low-cost standardized products, especially after 1960, the emergence of a fragmented and variable demand for high-quality products could be better satisfied by small and medium-sized firms. These firms were better prepared to respond to complex consumer needs, as they profitably combined technical versatility and the use of ad hoc knowledge and experience in flexible production.[19] This was the formula adopted by many Italian shoemaking companies after the Second World War, translating an artisanal mentality into the search for technological opportunities for a varied, personalized and high-quality production.[20]

In the 1950s and 1960s, the Italian shoemaking industry reflected a social structure characterized by two distinct consumption models based on different levels of income. A small but wealthy class of customers preferred highly personalized, handcrafted footwear, while a larger and less affluent class bought standardized machine-made shoes. This implied a dual structure of production: the shoemaking industry produced high volumes for the lower part of the market, while a myriad of small craft workshops produced for the higher end of the market. During the 1970s, however, profound cultural, social and economic changes in the Italian peninsula led to the emergence of new demands in clothing. Footwear was at the forefront of such changes as the concept of the "seasonal collection" came to identify the sector (Figure 16.9).

Small craft firms, in opposition to traditional industrial production, responded well and often structured change in the consumer market. They switched their production from bespoke to small series – rather than large, standardized ones – thereby responding with stylistically innovative products to the new needs. These craft workshops came to represent a production world that discovered "a stylistic vein and a great will to change."[21] An increasing number of small companies opted for niche production – shoes made with great care in a choice of leather and finishes, and produced in a limited number – making the "fashion factor" a fundamental attribute of their products. This was possible thanks to the specialized skills of their workforce, a high number of craftspeople and designers capable of interpreting market trends and often of imposing Italian fashion trends on foreign markets.

This new model of production organization flourished as fast as the growing market for medium-quality, fashionable Italian shoes. By the late 1970s, it had imposed itself over other types of production organization, either craft-based or industrial-based: "the niche market of shoes made with a high stylistic content spread until it became the predominant part of the market."[22] This has been explained, on the consumer side, through the concept of "homologating differentiation" of the late 1970s and 1980s: the rise of "designer labels" that attributed exclusivity while creating group identities among the wearers of such brands (Figure 16.10). In the case

FIGURE 16.5: BALLERINA-TOPOLINO (BALLERINA-MOUSE) SHOES BY MARK JACOBS, SPRING-SUMMER COLLECTION 2006. MUSEO ROSSIMODA, STRA, VENICE.

FIGURE 16.6 (OVERLEAF): COVER OF THE *MANUALE DI CALCEOLOGIA PER LA SCUOLA MODELLISTI CALZATURIERI DELLA RIVIERA DEL BRENTA*, PUBLISHED BY THE CONSORZIO CENTRO VENETO CALZATURIERO IN THE EARLY 1990S. THE MINIATURE SHOES ON THE COVER ARE WORKS BY ARTIST PIETRO MARTELLO.

CAL

Per la Scuola Mo

MANUALE DI
CALZATUROLOGIA

...sti Calzaturieri della Riviera del Brenta

CONSORZIO
CENTRO VENETO
CALZATURIERO

of footwear, brands emerged from the names of shops, boutiques and shoe stores, especially those located in city centers. Often they were not linked to any specific "style," but to the "autonomous and spontaneous creativity of some businessmen; entrepreneurs and technicians who, following the rising demand, transformed themselves into stylists."[23]

Creativity, style and quality are the characteristics that define the birth and development of the most important footwear "districts" in Italy.[24] Such areas, specializing in the production of footwear, propose a unique relationship between design, innovation and an in-depth knowledge of products and markets. The choice of products as well as the marketing strategies adopted strongly influenced the structure and shape of local production systems. Industrial districts such as those specializing in the production of footwear emerged as a grouping of manufacturing activities, normally small and medium-sized companies producing similar types or similar qualities of products. The demise of large, vertically integrated companies (with the entire production system under one roof), meant the multiplication of actors carrying out different stages of the production cycle, producing parts, catering for specific markets, or working on allied productions.[25] It is not rare to find a shoemaking district with medium and large producers, small manufacturing companies, artisans and service enterprises.[26]

At the beginning of the 1980s, the articulation of demand fully developed across different social classes and levels of income, amplifying a phenomenon that had interested the elite and medium markets in the previous decade. A new market structure came into being. The rise of the "fashion product" weakened the position of traditional shoemakers, especially those who had specialized in bespoke. In the 1980s it was the designer name, rather than the exclusivity of little-known master shoemakers, which increasingly characterized large segments of the market (Figure 16.11). The average consumer almost rejected any product devoid of stylistic features. Self-presentation and lifestyle brands became signifiers of success. Clothing and accessories, in particular, became important sources of social recognition. The production of "fashion goods" could only be organized on an industrial scale in order to satisfy a booming demand. The interweaving of different types of firms became even more complex.

This was the decade of "yuppiedom," a lifestyle that can appear now simplistic, but which played on a complex internal contradiction: "As a matter of fact, those who bought designer shoes thought to set themselves apart from the mass; yet, at the same time, they followed the trend of their peer group, thereby increasing the number of its members and homogenizing it more and more."[27] This mechanism fed itself until the end of the 1980s, when an unfavorable economic situation in Italy and on international markets reduced the appeal of the "Made in Italy" format.

FIGURE 16.7 (FACING PAGE): THE WORKING SPACE OF A SHOE DESIGNER. REPRODUCED FROM *MAESTRI CALZATURIERI DELLA RIVIERA DEL BRENTA. 7 SECOLI D'ARTE, STRA, 1993.*

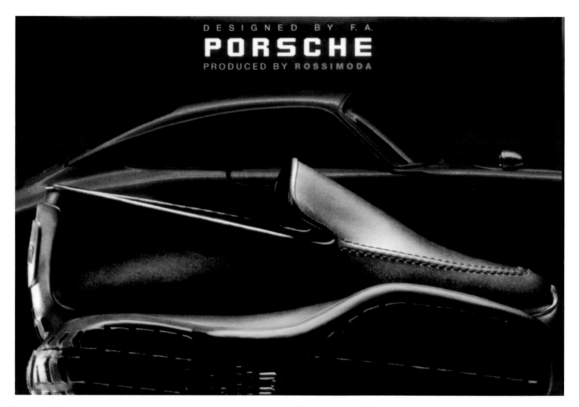

FIGURE 16.8: "PORSCHE, MODEL GT," 1978. REPRODUCED FROM *CALZATURE D'AUTORE. ROSSIMODA. 50 ANNI PER LE GRANDI FIRME*, FIESSO D'ARTICO, VILLA FOSCARINI ROSSI, 1997. © ROSSIMODA.

A revision of consumer models in the early 1990s to embrace a more careful, eco-friendly and responsible attitude toward consumption produced a crisis for the Italian shoe.

The early 1990s were a period of major revisions of established stylistic and production processes in footwear manufacturing in Italy. Consumers were now requesting more sophisticated and nuanced products.[28] The stylistic and innovative features of shoes were now more or less taken for granted by consumers. Much more importance was now given to the finishes, the overall functionality of the shoes and to the relationship between cost and quality. Of course, the interest in brands and designer labels was not fading, but consumer choices were now increasingly guided by personal taste, the need for self-satisfaction and a closer scrutiny of the price tag. Hence the need for shoe designers to adhere more closely to those basic concepts that had rendered them recognizable to consumers. Brands were no longer bought because of their social significance to others, but because of the correspondence between the values and ideas represented by the brand and those supported by the consumer (Figures 16.12 and 16.13). Italian shoemaking has not achieved, in last two decades, the same level of growth as in the previous two. The golden age of "Made in Italy" (post-1950) and the Italian shoe, with Milan runway shows and frenzied spending, could not continue forever. Consumers too have "matured." Today they require a product that is stylish and aesthetically pleasant, without devaluing practicality and worth.[29]

THE RIVIERA DEL BRENTA

The final part of this chapter will concentrate on one of the most important areas of shoe manufacturing in Italy: The Riviera del Brenta, an area between Padua and Venice in the northeastern part of the country. The Riviera explains the relationship between the concentration of production activities and the historical trajectory of an area of "shoe export."[30] The Riviera indicates how districts come into being and develop through specific entrepreneurial behaviors and know-how. They are proactive entities that interact with widespread changes in society and the economy, and with the values, attitudes and behaviors of the population.[31]

The very essence of the Riviera district is the existence of local manufacturing skills that made it possible to develop a modern manufacturing industry. These were the skills of local cobblers and shoemakers, which through a strict master-apprentice learning process, were preserved from the famous shoemaking tradition of the early modern Venetian republic. Despite the change in the economic structure of the area since the end of the eighteenth century, such skills survived and flourished locally, until at least the end of the following century. But as in the case of Ferragamo illustrated by Stefania Ricci in this volume, traditional skills remained dormant until they interacted with a different production context, such as North American mechanized shoe manufacturing. In 1898, Giovanni Luigi Voltan set up a factory, following a period of training in the United States. This was to become one of the most important footwear business-es in early twentieth-century Italy and a model for many local shoemakers to follow (Figure 16.14).[32]

Voltan was responsible for the spreading of skilled knowledge, a new industrial culture and important managerial skills. The business also created a network of relations between people and enterprises, which fostered the overall growth of the shoemaking industry in the region. The workforce was trained in the latest technologies, thus acquiring skills that were later employed in the setting up of other industrial undertakings. The story of many workers was a shift from self-employment in small shoemaking workshops to the modern footwear factory. Once trained, they returned to their workshops and transformed them into small and medium-sized industrial undertakings. This is the origin of an industrial district: a process of cyclical setting up of new business structures.

The first wave of entrepreneurial activity followed the expansion of the consumer market at the end of the First World War (Figure 16.15). Many former employees continued to set up their own businesses also in more difficult times, such as during the economic crisis of the 1930s and the period of high unemployment at the end of the Second World War. During the 1950s and 1960s, the industrial-artisanal nucleus of the Riviera district grew larger and larger because of increasing domestic and international demand for Italian footwear (Figure 16.16). The Riviera del Brenta benefited in particular from its very location, as it was close to the major European markets and easily accessible. The cohesiveness and self-perpetuation of the district, across sever-al generations, was possible thanks to a process of codification of skills and knowledge. This was the period of the rise of the stylist as a "creator" of shoes and the district was able to train this new generation through the Ottorino Tombolan Fava Shoe Design School. Founded in 1923 as a vocational school for the training of craftsmen and later shoe designers, it was the first of its kind in Europe.[33]

By the early 1950s, the footwear industry of the Riviera del Brenta was able to satisfy a var-ied and changeable demand for high- and medium-quality shoes. Their production policy was essentially consumer oriented in a way that was not dissimilar from what their fathers had done for individual customers. An increasing share of the market for Italian shoes was taken by foreign customers (Figures 16.17 and 16.18). The district soon specialized in the production of footwear for European markets (especially Germany) and later for extra-European countries, in particular the United States. The importance of foreign markets played an essential role in fostering cooperation – rather than competition – within the district, leading to joint ventures, shared promotional

FIGURE 16.9 (FACING PAGE): LATE 1960S ADVERTISEMENT OF THE RIVIERA DEL BRENTA SHOES. "MODA DELLA RIVIERA DEL BRENTA. SCARPA, CIN-TURA, E BORSA BY MENIN, FIRENZE." © A.C.RI.B. REPRODUCED FROM GIOVANNI LUIGI FONTANA, *100 ANNI DI INDUSTRIA CALZATURIERA NELLA RIVIERA DEL BRENTA*, STRA, A.C.RI.B., 1998, 281.

Graziose combinazioni scarpa-borsa-cintura di Menin.
Original combinations of a Shoe, Handbag and Belt
produced by Menin.
Trois originales parures, chaussures-sac-ceinture, de Menin.
Originelle Kombinationen, Schuhe, Tasche, und Gürtel
von Menin.

*Moda sulla
Riviera del
Brenta*

Yves Saint Laurent
chaussures

FIGURE 16.10 (FACING PAGE): ADVERTISEMENT FOR CHAUSSURES BY YVES SAINT-LAURENT. REPRODUCED FROM *CALZATURE D'AUTORE. ROSSIMODA. 50 ANNI PER LE GRANDI FIRME*, FIESSO D'ARTICO, VILLA FOSCARINI ROSSI, 1997. © ROSSIMODA.

FIGURE 16.11 (ABOVE LEFT): THE HIGHEST OF FASHION: SHOES BY YVES SAINT-LAURENT, 1990–92. REPRODUCED FROM *CALZATURE D'AUTORE. ROSSIMODA. 50 ANNI PER LE GRANDI FIRME*, FIESSO D'ARTICO, VILLA FOSCARINI ROSSI, 1997. © ROSSIMODA.

FIGURE 16.12 (ABOVE RIGHT): SHOE PRODUCED BY RENÉ CAOVILLA, 1990. REPRODUCED BY KIND PERMISSION OF COLLEZIONE CAOVILLA, STRA.

materials and other communal strategies to secure export markets. Local firms organized joint exhibitions in Stra and Padua; and participated together in international events such as trade fairs in Bologna, Milan, Düsseldorf and in Central and Eastern Europe. A further step was undertaken in 1962 when the Association of the Riviera del Brenta Footwear Manufacturers (A.C.Ri.B) was founded, followed by the Consortium of the Riviera del Brenta Footwear Masters in the 1970s, and the establishment of a Technological Center in the 1980s.[34]

The importance of foreign markets and the shared investment in cultural, didactic and entrepreneurial institutions balanced competitiveness and cooperation and marked the way toward a general specialization of the Riviera del Brenta in the production of high-quality women's shoes, produced in small batches.[35] The success in the production of highly fashionable products has been possible thanks to the skilled workforce, and to craftsmen and designers endowed with creativity and imagination who are able to interpret market trends and often impose the Italian style on foreign markets through their own models. The success in womenswear was replicated in men's and children's footwear and, since the 1970s, extended also to include increasing shares of the Italian footwear market (Figures 16.19 and 16.20).[36]

During the 1980s and the 1990s, the production model adopted by the Riviera del Brenta faced moments of crisis as well as a need for adaptation, yet always managed to preserve its competitiveness and to continue its own success.[37] The irony of Italian production is that the artisanal family tradition might seem to foster conservatism, but the reality of Italian economic organization is such that responsiveness to fashion change as well as to shifting consumer outlooks can be effected there with great success. The Riviera del Brenta is now concentrating its efforts on a smaller but higher quality market compared to the 1970s. The area produced 11 million shoes a year at the end of the 1970s, but in the middle of the 1990s it commanded a much higher turnover (nearly double) producing just 8.5 million shoes a year. Firms are now producing 200–250 new models each season and produce from 10 to 10,000 pairs of each model (Figures 16.21 and 16.22).[38] A hundred years after the start of the Riviera del Brenta as a shoemaking area in the late nineteenth century, the district has nearly 900 firms (half of which produce shoes and half of which specialize in the distribution, service and accessories trades). It gives work to 13,000 people and produces 13 percent of the total Italian production of footwear, the great majority of which (87 percent) is exported.

CONCLUSION: FORM, FUNCTION AND FOOTWEAR

Footwear is a key feature of clothing and has been central to fashion history. The relationship between shoes and fashion is the field of action of the stylist. The job of a stylist is to conceive a shoe that maximizes functionality, highlights symbolic value and satisfies economic requirements.

Figure 16.13 (top): Shoe produced in the Riviera del Brenta in the early 1990s. Reproduced from *Calzature d'Autore. Rossimoda. 50 anni per le Grandi Firme*, Fiesso d'Artico, Villa Foscarini Rossi, 1997. © Rossimoda.

Figure 16.14 (center): Men's short shoe produced by the Calzaturificio Giovanni Luigi Voltan, Stra, Riviera del Brenta, Italy, c. 1930. Calzaturificio Giovanni Luigi Voltan Collection.

Figure 16.15 (right): Women's shoe made of kid and plastic, by Calzaturificio Polato, Riviera del Brenta, Italy, 1923. © A.C.Ri.B. Reproduced from Giovanni Luigi Fontana, *100 Anni di Industria Calzaturiera nella Riviera del Brenta*, Stra, A.C.Ri.B., 1998, 138.

Figure 16.19 (top) and 16.20 (center): Women's shoes, 1970s, produced in the Riviera del Brenta. © A.C.Ri.B. Reproduced from Giovanni Luigi Fontana, *100 Anni di Industria Calzaturiera nella Riviera del Brenta*, Stra, A.C.Ri.B., 1998, 300.

Figure 16.21 (right): An "airy" creation by Rossimoda, 1985. Reproduced from *Calzature d'Autore. Rossimoda. 50 anni per le Grandi Firme*, Fiesso d'Artico, Villa Foscarini Rossi, 1997. © Rossimoda.

And as fashion is always mutating, so the work of the stylist is neverending – it is defined only by dynamism. In the modern production world, as seen in the case of the Riviera del Brenta in Italy, shoe designers and stylists operate within a complex production world, exploring new organizational solutions and testing new markets. The stylist is a central link between fashion, technological progress and a variety of distributive channels. New challenges are ahead of us and the shoe stylist is now becoming a "fashion co-coordinator" rather than a designer. His/her task is to mediate between fashion as conceived by the *Maisons* and the manufacturing requirements of production. History is central again, as the stylist has to be conscious of the historical evolution of fashion, the dynamics of market over time and the physical, material, but also "mental" properties of shoes.[39] To the stylist, the shoe is also an intellectual domain.

FIGURE 16.22 (FACING PAGE): FENDISSIME, 1994. REPRODUCED FROM *CALZATURE D'AUTORE. ROSSIMODA. 50 ANNI PER LE GRANDI FIRME*, FIESSO D'ARTICO, VILLA FOSCARINI ROSSI, 1997. © ROSSIMODA.

17.
SOLE REPRESENTATION

SHOE IMAGERY AND TWENTIETH-CENTURY ART

julia pine

One of my latest pictures represents a pair of shoes. I spent two long months copying them from a model, and I worked over them with the same love and the same objectivity as Raphael painting a Madonna.

Salvador Dalí, 1942[1]

While imagery of clothing, especially that of the unworn or disembodied garment, is frequently employed in twentieth-century Western art as a metaphor for the missing subject, it is shoe imagery that holds a particularly prominent place in avant-garde and postmodern art of the twentieth century. Indeed, many of the most influential artists of this period have chosen the pump, boot, sneaker or slipper either as a subject or medium: Salvador Dalí, René Magritte, Meret Oppenheim, Andy Warhol, Yayoi Kusama, Roy Lichtenstein, Allen Jones, Jim Dine, and Robert Gober among them (Figure 17.1). Here we ask why it is that one lowly and seemingly insignificant object has maintained such a vivid presence, appearing with surprising frequency in numerous media and critical practices.

ART AND THE LOWLY SHOE

A significant part of the fascination for the shoe among major twentieth-century artists surely stems from formal considerations. As sculptural objects, shoes provide a multitude of plastic, perspectival and dynamic possibilities, something that any shoemaker or designer will confirm. Perhaps more effectively than a disembodied pair of pants or gloves, empty shoes, which can retain their shape on or off the foot, also readily indicate bodily stance – are they standing, lying down, jumping? – and locomotion, further underlining a human presence and narrative possibilities. This is also true of other mundane objects that appear in art as canonical forms: the top hat, walking cane, or bicycle. But while these items have been naturalized in the esteemed tradition of "high" art, the shoe's presence seems pronounced precisely because we sense that it does not really belong within that domain. Indeed most of the shoe imagery used in twentieth-century fine art practice is rooted in the "low" media of commercial and popular culture, emerging from advertising, product design, strip comics, caricature, erotic art and fashion merchandising (Figure 17.2). From this purview, the shoe's stubborn, often cloddish presence always seems to announce its status as an interloper, an uncouth visitor from elsewhere, a shrill or ill-mannered commoner determined to infiltrate an elegant party. As art historians Kirk Varnedoe and Adam Gopnik suggest, we recognize the presence of the shoe in art as "a comic motif that [is] also the announcement of a particular kind of modern energy. *In your face.*"[2]

From this perspective, the shoe's assertive appearance in art is always disturbing because it disrupts the binary between so-called high and low forms of visual culture. This is no small load to bear, for, as Varnedoe and Gopnik suggest, "the story of the interplay between modern art and popular culture is one of the most important aspects of the history of art in our epoch."[3] It is, they claim, "central to what made modern art modern at the start of this century, and it has continued to be crucial to the work of many younger artists in the last decade."[4] Taking advantage of the self-conscious "outsider" status of shoes, artists have employed this loaded device in a variety of ingenious forms. These include conceptual, aesthetic and political critiques prominent throughout the twentieth century, foregrounding issues of subjectivity, sexuality, gender and consumption. Needless to say, when we arrive in a gallery to find an unworn shoe, translated from its lowly and humble lot on the foot or floor, staring back at us from a canvas or plinth, *in our face*, we encounter an already culturally charged object, transformed within the parameters of fine art production.

THE TRUTH ABOUT VAN GOGH'S BOOTS

In his influential essay of 1935, "The Origin of the Work of Art," German philosopher Martin Heidegger queries the nature of art and the connotational function of objects as they appear in paintings: "What and how is a work of art?" he asks, and "What is at work in the work?"[5] To illustrate his argument, Heidegger chose one of eight different pictures, produced by Vincent Van Gogh, of pairs of worker's boots, examples that the philosopher interpreted as belonging to a peasant woman. "From the dark opening of the worn insides of the shoes the toilsome tread of the worker stares forth," he writes, "in the stiffly rugged heaviness of the shoes there is the accumulated tenacity of her slow trudge through the far-spreading and ever-uniform furrows and richness of the soil."[6]

Heidegger interpreted Van Gogh's subject matter as revelatory; to him the boots signified the beauty and nobility of the worker's being. "The art work lets us know what shoes are in truth," he suggests. "Van Gogh's painting is the disclosure of what the equipment, the pair of peasant shoes, *is* in truth ... If there occurs in the work a disclosure of a particular being, disclosing what and how it is, then there is here an occurring, a happening of truth at work."[7] Heidegger positions Van Gogh's image of peasant boots, then, as a sort of vicarious portrait of the soul of the implied human subject; the "disclosure" of a distilled essence of his highly idealized conception of a peasant woman. Ironically, as art historian Meyer Schapiro points out in his 1968 critique of Heidegger's essay, these "truthful" boots did not belong to a peasant woman at all, but were worn by the artist himself.[8] What this projection suggests is that, when it comes to interpreting subject matter in art, the constructs of "truth" or "disclosure" are duly culturally coded.[9]

Although Heidegger was writing about a late nineteenth-century work of art, his analysis may have been informed by the currency of Dada, New Objectivity and Surrealist art of the 1920s and 1930s in using representations of disembodied clothing drawn from the print culture of modern life. Within mass-market advertising and popular culture, cartoons, caricatures and promotional materials proliferated. Images of plumped-up shirts and bloomers devoid of the human body were infinitely more popular, creating a dialogue between the present clothing and the absent human. This quality intrigued many avant-garde artists, who were also drawn to the imagery of shoes, recognizing this artifact as a powerful cultural indicator. For example, in Western popular iconography we can generally agree that, like Van Gogh's clodhoppers, a pair of work boots broadly signifies "the worker," while a pair of black stiletto pumps is metonymic of an attractive and sexually receptive woman. Drawing on this and other popular associations of the shoe motif, footwear appears most frequently in fine art contexts roughly within three themes. The first is that of the comic/parodic, often in the service of social critique; the second is that of the sexual and psychological, particularly in relation to popular understandings of psychoanalytic theory and the work of Sigmund Freud; the third relates to the consumerist model of late capitalism.

FUNNY FEET: SHOES, COMEDY AND SATIRE

The comic strand of shoe imagery in modern and contemporary art traces its lineage to popular visual culture as it developed in the early modern period. Indeed, while signs shaped like shoes and boots often hung outside shoemaker's shops for the purpose of identification and advertising in eighteenth-century England, early prints show how representations of these objects also became comic devices and could be indices of celebrities or political figures. Art historian Diana

FIGURE 17.1: ANDY WARHOL, GOLDEN SHOE "MARGARET TRUMAN," 1956. © ANDY WARHOL FOUNDATIONS FOR VISUAL ARTS/SODRAC (2006). PRIVATE COLLECTION, VENICE.

Here's to Love.
May it's wing never
lose a feather, till your little shoes,
and my little shoes, sit under the
bed together !

FIGURE 17.2: AN EARLY TWENTIETH-CENTURY EXAMPLE OF SHOES LITERALLY "STANDING IN" FOR THE MISSING SUBJECT. ANONYMOUS, HERE'S TO LOVE, C.1910. POSTCARD. PRIVATE COLLECTION.

Donald writes that the prints of the period reveal "a relish for emblems … their symbols are newly born creations of the *argot plastique* of the streets, the common language of crowd ritual, woodcut broadsides and cheap ballads."[10] In the 1760s, for example, the image of a boot was widely employed to represent the British Jacobin leader Lord Bute, who was appointed prime minister of Great Britain under George III for the years 1762 and 1763. Noting the visual conflation of the boot with the unpopular figure's surname, Donald stresses the semiotic power of this motif, noting that "the jackboot symbol of Lord John ("Jack") Bute, attained universal currency and was used … with an almost cabalistic sense of potency" (Figure 17.3).[11] A bawdier version of this conceit appears in an anonymously executed caricature which features the Dowager Princess of Wales suggestively grasping the spur and implying a liaison with the enormous Bute/boot.

In the nineteenth century, images of unworn or emphatic footwear became stock comedic devices, appearing with frequency in print media such as British *Punch*. While in European and Asian cultures, big feet and sloppy or oversized shoes have always signified vulgarity, peasantry and poverty, by the end of the century, as Varnedoe and Gopnik suggest, in American print culture the foot and shoe device, in particular the outsized one, "moves from the margin to the center and becomes … a motif that suggests the jaunty, dandified syncopation of modern life – a world of kicks and turns and flying leaps."[12] "By the early twentieth century," they continue, it had become standard iconography in the American comic milieu, as "more of a clown's big shoe, an exaggerated "adult" feature, that … makes us laugh at the absurd contrast between the grown-up appearance and the infantile comportment."[13] Tracing this motif from Mickey Mouse to characters in the work of the "underground" cartoonist Robert Crumb, Varnedoe writes that the giant foot and shoe was "one of the most pervasive images in America," and indeed, it became so hackneyed that it sank "to the lowest reaches of gag-a-day comics so that, by the early fifties, the work of the hack cartoonists was labeled by their condescending colleagues simply as 'big foot' style."[14]

Varnedoe and Gopnik note the influence of the "big foot" style in the work of a number of US-based artists, most notably that of painter Elizabeth Murray, and especially in the later work of Philip Guston, influenced by pop art, whose gritty, cartoony style features endless representations of outsized, upturned, worn-out shoes. "For Guston," write Varnedoe and Gopnik, the "image of the upturned sole and the cobbled shoes … became a symbol at once of protest and of exhaustive surrender."[15] Noting the artist's choice of crude imagery, they claim that "Guston insisted that this was a base level of truth – that real souls could only be found in foot soles, and that shoe leather offered an uncompromising, glamourless image of lived experience … for him, too, it is a symbol of death."[16]

In the early twentieth century, the shoe was used in a more acerbic fashion in German Dada collages. Legs, boots and shoes were such a popular motif, with resonances of dynamic modernity and social turmoil, that it is almost unusual to find a Dada collage of the 1910s and 1920s *without* an image of a shoe. Berlin-based Hannah Höch, for example, seemed to celebrate the dynamic aspects of modernity and female emancipation through leg and shoe imagery in many of her collages, which featured multiple cutouts of dancing, leaping and "joyous" women's legs. Raoul Hausmann, Höch's partner and colleague, on the other hand, used the device as one of implied force and disrespect, "stepping" on the head of the offending party in his collage *The Art Critic* of 1919–20, where a boot finds itself nestled on the forehead of the unsavory titular personage. In other Hausmann works, such as his photomontage *Dada-Cino* of 1920, a boot appears gratuitously in a jumble of words and pictures snipped from newspapers and magazines, perhaps reflecting the chaos of Weimar-era Germany as well as the "visual overload" of burgeoning advertising and urban imagery.

SEXING THE SHOE: FOOTWEAR, FEMINISM AND THE FETISH

Being so well suited to collage as a medium, footwear also appears frequently in assemblage works, a type of sculpture constructed from everyday objects, made popular by the Surrealists in the late 1920s and 1930s. Perhaps the most striking of these is by Meret Oppenheim, entitled *My Governess* (Figure 17.4). Executed in 1936, the same year as her famous *Luncheon in Fur* (better known as the *Fur Cup*), this simple but poignant construction consists of a pair of white women's pumps, trussed with string like a Christmas goose and "served" on a silver platter. Considering that the somewhat androgynous Oppenheim was one of a handful of female artists working in the notoriously masculine Parisian Surrealist milieu, it is tempting to read this simple object metonymically, as "woman bound," perhaps with personal references, as much as being a general metaphor for woman's oppression. This holds particular relevance for Oppenheim's work, as a year after she created *My Governess*, she wrote, "I felt as if millennia of discrimination against women were resting on my shoulders, as if embodied in my feelings of inferiority."[17]

Clearly following in this tradition is a more recent work by the bespoke shoemaker and "shoe artist" Gaza Bowen, based in Santa Cruz, who, from 1986 to 1992, produced a number of feminist-inspired shoe assemblages. One of these, her *Shoes for the Little Woman* of 1985, is a vivid plastic concoction cobbled from detergent bottles, scouring pads and kitchen utensils (Figure 17.5). Like Oppenheim's assemblage, it too addresses the problems of domestic servitude and constructs of femininity. Both works relate to the notion of female performativity, brought into dialogue in 1929 by the English psychologist Joan Riviere in her paper "Womanliness as Masquerade." In it, Riviere reviews the essentializing or naturalizing model of femininity, which she compares to a mask, and writes that for women, "The capacity for self-sacrifice, devotion, self-abnegation expresses efforts to restore and make good … what has been taken from them."[18]

While Bowen and Oppenheim use the imagery of the high heel to position in discourse the subjects of gender and gender performance, such an approach is only made possible by the sexual connotations the high-heeled shoe has accrued as visual shorthand for "woman" and sex itself. Since the *fin de siècle*, when feet, ankles and legs were the focus of much erotic attention, the high-heeled shoe became a popular emblem of the erotic, although as Freud noted, the symbolism of the shoe as a sexual vessel or vagina traces its origins through many centuries, and has deep roots

A WONDERFUL SIGHT.

FIGURE 17.3: ANONYMOUS, A WONDERFUL SIGHT, ETCHING ON LAID PAPER, 1762. CARICATURE SATIRIZING LORD BUTE, THE HIGHLY UNPOPULAR SCOTSMAN MADE PRIME MINISTER OF GREAT BRITAIN IN 1762. KING GEORGE III, REPRESENTED BY THE DOG, IS BEING LED BY TWO TARTAN-WEARING SCOTS, WHILE THE BOOT ON HIS HEAD INDICATES THE INFLUENCE OF BUTE, WHOSE NAME PUNS ON THE WORD "BOOT." PHOTOGRAPH SUZANNE MCLEAN. BATA SHOE MUSEUM, TORONTO, P83.97. REPRODUCED BY KIND PERMISSION OF BATA SHOE MUSEUM.

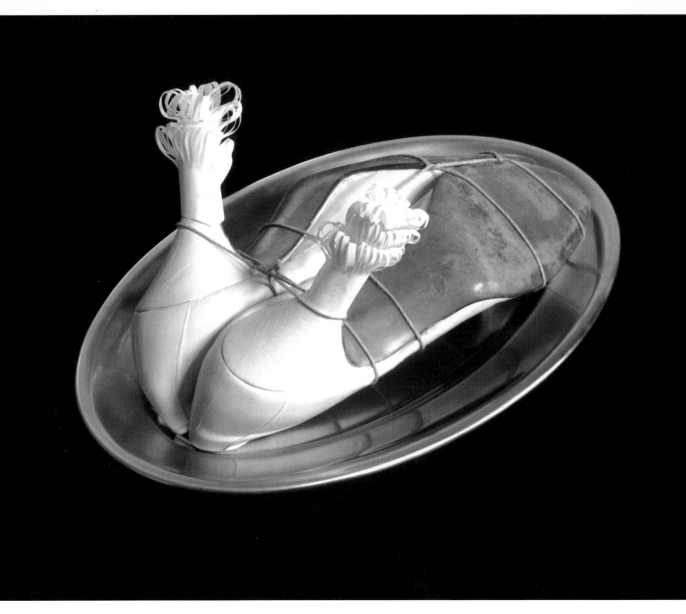

Figure 17.4 (above): A resonant surreal object suggesting narratives of consumption, restraint and female performance, by the maker of the famous *Fur Cup*. Meret Oppenheim, *My Governess*, 1936. © Prolitteris (Zurich)/SODART (Montreal), 2005. Photograph courtesy of Moderna Museet, Stockholm.

Figure 17.5 (facing page, top): Gaza Bowen, *Shoes for the Little Woman*, mixed media, 1985. A shoemaker as well as a conceptual artist, Bowen's shoe sculptures combine her technical knowledge of footwear with a feminist sensibility. Image courtesy of Gaza Bowen, © Gaza Bowen. Collection of Norton Family Foundation.

Figure 17.6 (facing page, below): Anonymous, Homemade "Penis Shoes," German, c. 1930. A Weimar era send-up of the sexual symbolism of the high-heeled shoe. Image courtesy of Mel Gordon.

in mythology and folklore.[19] This is perhaps most neatly delineated in the Cinderella story, where the search for "perfect fit" positions the heroine's slipper as an index of emotional and sexual compatibility.[20]

In the modern era, shoe imagery has also proliferated within erotic and pornographic print media. In countries such as Germany, France and England, a specialized genre of "fetish" erotica developed and seems to have been exported from Europe to North America around the period of Second World War.[21] This work was published for practitioners of erotic cross-dressing, sado-masochism, bondage and discipline; those interested in body modification, tattooing and piercing; and object, clothing and footwear "fetishists" or "enthusiasts," to use the preferred nomenclature.[22] This material helped to create what cultural theorist Benedict Anderson calls "imagined communities," codifying and developing sexual clothing styles within the fetish enclave.[23]

Some of the enthusiast genre's best works were published anonymously, for example the ink drawing *Homemade "Penis Shoes"* executed in Berlin in the 1930s (Figure 17.6). With a pert row of penises atop a spindly, black, strappy sandal, it articulates, with graphic aplomb, the sexual symbolism of the high heel. Women's footwear features prominently in German interwar avant-garde art, as it does in the work of the New Objectivity artist Rudolph Schlichter, himself a self-confessed and "pronounced shoe fetishist."[24] Similar to Schlichter's work, an interest in fetish erotica is also evident in the prints and drawings of the Surrealist artist Hans Bellmer. Although famous for his dismembered and reconfigured dolls, he also created a number of works on paper featuring boots and concupiscent scenarios invariably including tangles of well-shod and stockinged legs, high-heeled shoes being carried away in hot-air balloons, or boot-shaped openings in brick walls.

No artist borrows as heavily from the genre of fetish art than the British pop artist Allen Jones, whose work of the 1960s and 1970s is saturated with highly eroticized images of legs, stockings and stilettos. Perhaps this is most notable in his dark and saucy *Shoe Box*, a portfolio of seven lithographs and a sculpture produced in an edition of 200 in 1968. *Shoe Box* consists of a black PVC-covered box containing layers of material. The first of these is a cobalt blue plastic film, upon which the word "Exotic" is embossed. This is followed by a last made of brushed aluminum, in the *en pointe* ballet position, accompanied by a stand to which it is to be attached. Below are seven monochromatic lithographs of shoes, some of which directly reference postwar American "kink" magazines such as *Exotique* and *Bizarre* (Figure 17.7). As the box requires opening, the sculpture assembling, and the prints uncovering and handling, Jones impishly creates an interactive piece that vicariously draws the viewer into an erotic milieu. As such, he playfully turns a connoisseur's perusal of prints into an intimate tactile encounter with the trappings of shoe fetishism.

The more perverse implications of the shoe are articulated particularly vividly in the obsessive productions of the Japanese artist Yayoi Kusama, who frequently uses empty shoe imagery in her work, such as *Suitcase, Shoes* of 1963, a virtual orgy of men's and women's footwear stuffed

FIGURE 17.7: JOHN WILLIE (JOHN ALEXANDER SCOTT COUTTS), COVER OF *BIZARRE*, VOL. 12 (1953).
BIZARRE WAS A NORTH AMERICAN "FETISH" MAGAZINE. THIS ISSUE PROMISES SOMETHING OF INTEREST
FOR THOSE WITH A PENCHANT FOR FOOTWEAR. © BIZARRE PUBLISHING COMPANY.

with phallic fabric forms (Figure 17.8). In both Kusama's and Jones's work, the conflation of "fine art" and crude sexual fetishism also slyly suggests a connection between two modes of "fetish": the erotic "worship" of objects such as the shoe, the article most commonly associated with sexual fetishism, and the "fetishization" or "overvaluation" of the art object itself. The latter points to the concept of commodity fetishism as outlined by Karl Marx, where the "products of the human mind become independent shapes, endowed with lives of their own," which Marx describes in terms of the "fetishistic character which attaches to … commodities."[25] Indeed, as early as 1920, the Surrealist writer Georges Bataille made a similar analogy between the art object and the erotic object of desire, quipping in the avant-garde periodical *Documents*, "I defy any lover of modern art to adore a painting as a fetishist adores a shoe."[26]

By the late 1920s, Salvador Dalí appears to have taken up Bataille's challenge, and to become familiar with Dalí's oeuvre means to experience repeated encounters with the artist's pronounced interest in shoes. Disembodied pumps, espadrilles and brogues reappear in a surprising number of media throughout Dalí's works, in prints, collages, assemblages and oils, as the artist toyed with the iconographic, aesthetic and plastic possibilities that these objects yielded. Dalí avidly read Sigmund Freud, who wrote on shoe fetishism in *Three Essays on the Theory of Sexuality* (1905), and later in an essay entitled "Fetishism" (1927). As such, it is difficult to interpret Dalí's *Surrealist Object*, an assemblage he constructed in 1931, as anything more than a parodic schema of the Freudian formulation of fetishism. Dalí's description is an important element of the piece, and in keeping with the pseudosexological aspect of the work, he explains its functioning in semi-clinical language:

> A woman's shoe, inside which a glass of milk has been placed, in the middle of a paste ductile in form and excremental in colour. The mechanism consists of plunging a sugar lump on which an image of a shoe has been painted, in order to watch the sugar lump and consequently the image of the shoe breaking up in the milk. Several accessories (pubic hair stuck on a sugar lump, small erotic photo) complete the object, which is accompanied by a box of sugar lumps for spares and a special spoon, which is used to stir the grains of lead inside the shoe.[27]

Similar in tone to Dalí's dip into the dynamics of fetishism is an article written by Surrealist writer Tristan Tzara, entitled "D'un certain automatisme du gout" ("Concerning a Certain Automatism of Taste"), which appeared in the Surrealist journal *Minotaure* in 1933.[28] In it, Tzara muses upon the erotic implications of fashionable hats. To illustrate the text, the American Surrealist artist Man Ray submitted photographs of models wearing "suggestive" head coverings, three of which were designed by the Paris-based couturière Elsa Schiaparelli.[29] Perhaps this treatise gave impetus to what is perhaps the most amusing of Dalí's shoe-inspired works, a collaboration he produced with Schiaparelli for her winter 1937–38 collection, known simply as *The Shoe Hat*. This felt cap was designed to look like a high-heeled shoe wedged upside down on the wearer's head, and was in keeping with other whimsical designs Schiaparelli had devised, including

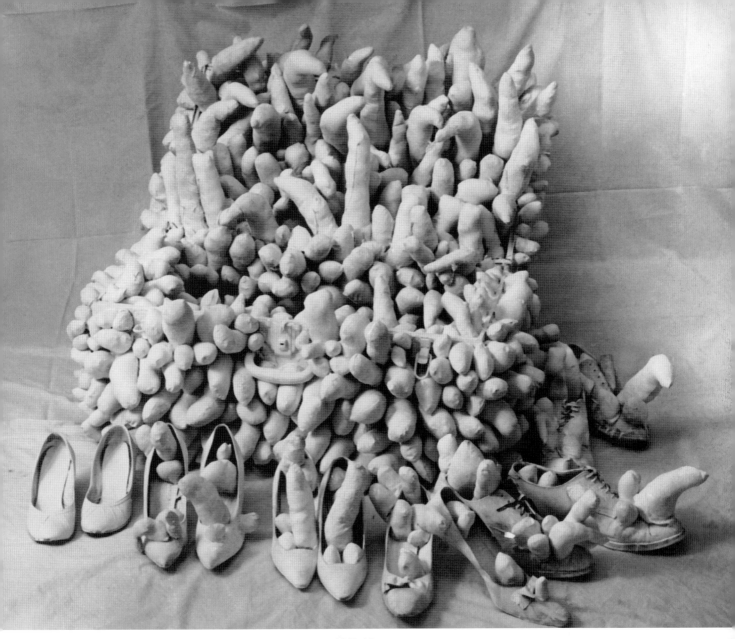

Figure 17.8: Yayoi Kusama, Suitcase, Shoes, mixed media, 1963. Multiple patterns and a proliferation of objects are typical of Kusama's work from the 1960s. Image courtesy of and © Yayoi Kusama.

those in the shape of mutton chops and inkwells. Although the hat was most frequently produced in black, another version, with a Schiaparelli signature shocking pink velvet heel, rather loudly proclaimed its phallic implications. This is especially so when paired, as it is in a photograph of Dalí's wife Gala, with another Schiaparelli-Dalí collaboration: a simple black dress and jacket embellished with bright red lipsticked lips, another device clearly evoking genital symbolism.[30]

THE UNCANNY UNDERFOOT

More recently, Freud's writings have been revisited by art historian Hal Foster in his influential book *Compulsive Beauty* (1993). Foster maintains the importance to the Surrealist sensibility of a phenomenon Freud termed "the uncanny," which the psychoanalyst examined in detail in an essay written in 1919. According to Freud, "the uncanny" involves "the return of a familiar phenomenon (image or object, person or event) made strange by repression." He writes:

> Our analysis of instances of the uncanny has led us back to the old, animistic conception of the universe. This was characterized by the idea that the world was peopled with the spirits of human beings; by the subject's narcissistic overvaluation of his own mental processes; by the belief in the omnipotence of thought and the technique of magic based on that belief.[31]

This "return of the repressed," or underlying animistic conception of matter, is perhaps a useful tactic for approaching what is probably the most famous of the Surrealist images involving shoes, René Magritte's *The Red Model* of 1935. In it, a pair of man's boots seems to be caught in a transitional state between foot and foot covering. This anthropomorphic quality is also, of course, a precondition for sexual fetishism, which implies the object possesses a magical or sentient quality, replacing, as it does, the human as the sexual object. *The Red Model* also evokes Heidegger's analysis of the peasant's boots, which, through "disclosure" reveals the "truth" of the wearer's "being." Indeed, Magritte seems to have taken Heidegger's analysis to its most literal visual conclusion. The "uncanniness" of this hybrid object is mystified within Magritte's own comments, when he explains that "the problem of shoes demonstrates how the most barbaric things pass as acceptable through the force of habit. One feels … that the union of a human foot and a leather shoe arises in reality from a monstrous custom."[32] This idea connects us to other writers in this volume, those dealing with the fairy tale or the strangeness of shoes.

Intimations of the uncanny are characteristic of Surrealist art but this sensibility appears more recently in the work of contemporary American sculptor and installation artist Robert Gober, whose installations often feature artificial body parts thrusting out of walls or dangling from mundane household objects. Gober is an openly gay artist, and his work is frequently interpreted as addressing issues of sexuality and sexual identity. In particular, his incorporation of delicate and

FIGURE 17.9 (FACING PAGE): ROBERT GOBER, UNTITLED, BEESWAX AND HUMAN HAIR, 7.6 x 6.7 x 19 CM, 1992. FASHIONED FROM DELICATE ORGANIC MATERIALS, THIS OBJECT CREATES AN UNEASY TENSION BETWEEN THE CHILDLIKE AND THE ADULT. PHOTOGRAPH GEOFFREY CLEMENTS, COURTESY OF THE ARTIST AND MATTHEW MARKS GALLERY, NEW YORK.

organic materials such as human hair and wax, and his use of unlit candles and holes bored through body parts, might be read to engage with the notions of loss, corporeality and disease, and hence his work is often read in terms of the AIDS crisis. Perhaps one of the artist's most disturbing objects is the diminutive *Untitled* of 1992, a small child's strap shoe made of translucent yellow wax, inside which sprout coarse, adult-textured hairs (Figure 17.9). Similar to many Surrealist objects, this is a profoundly unsettling piece, although one that evokes social anxieties specific to the late twentieth century. Gober's uneasy conflation of delicate youth and adult masculine virility intimate the problems of the increasingly early sexualization of children and widespread concerns regarding issues of pedophilia. Perhaps, too, he evokes the metaphoric infantalization of adults in an increasingly "dumbed down" American cultural landscape.

TREADS AND TRADEMARKS

The subjects of sexual symbolism, fetishism and psychology held considerable currency in the earlier part of the twentieth century when it came to the matter of shoes in art. Meanwhile, the postmodern era engages with what might be considered more characteristic preoccupations, reflecting the rise of the "youth market" and "consumer culture." References to both are loudly articulated in pop artist Roy Lichtenstein's bombastic oil on canvas work, entitled *Keds*, of 1961 (Figure 17.10). Executed in his trademark "comic book" style, the work, which spans almost three by four feet, mimics the dynamic presentation of advertising, and quite literally embodies the *in your face* "kick" of the then-emerging teenage culture, signified in 1950s and 1960s America by the "high-top" sneaker. In case we miss the artist's insistence on the corporate presence in the title, *Keds*, which is the brand name of an existing American shoe company, Lichtenstein adds a very visible copyright symbol in the bottom right of the work, further underscoring an increasing conflation between high and low art forms, and between mass-produced graphic imagery and the unique, "one-off" art piece.

The contemporary German photographer Andreas Gursky makes reference to the power of the brand and corporate encroachment in his 1996 work *Prada I*, a large-format photograph of a mid-1990s visual merchandising display in a Prada shop (Figure 17.11). But while Lichtenstein's *Keds* reflects, and perhaps even celebrates, the energy and excitement of modern advertising and adolescence, Gursky captures a somber, minimalist-inspired consumer moment, as each pair of shoes stands glibly at attention to be carefully and reverentially perused by the viewer. Like *Keds*, and also Jones's *Shoe Box*, *Prada I* brings into question not only formulations of the fetishization of the art object and the branded consumer product, but by inferring comparison of the art gallery with the high-end boutique, it throws into question the role of the curator, gallery, gallery-goer and art market as well. If we draw upon Heidegger's technique here of

FIGURE 17.10 (FACING PAGE): ROY LICHTENSTEIN, KEDS, OIL AND PENCIL ON CANVAS, 123.2 x 97.5 CM, 1961. AS WITH HIS BETTER-KNOWN COMIC BOOK IMAGERY, HERE LICHTENSTEIN TURNS TO CONTEMPORARY ADVERTISING GRAPHICS FOR INSPIRATION. © ESTATE OF ROY LICHTENSTEIN. IMAGE COURTESY OF THE ROY LICHTENSTEIN FOUNDATION.

"reading" the shoe as a form of "truth at work," then *Prada I* offers up a rather sobering form of disclosure.

SHOES WITH VIEWS

Gursky's cool and sterile *Prada I* is a far cry from Van Gogh's rough and earthy peasant boots, executed more than a century earlier. While Van Gogh's boots may have seemed, to viewers in the Dutch painter's day, a perplexing choice for the subject of a painting, in the current pluralist atmosphere, the empty shoe seems as likely an object as any other for incorporation in an installation, assemblage or painting. What the comparison of the two works suggests, however, is the extraordinary diversity of this sartorial motif, which draws on contemporary visual culture, popular understandings of psychology, and an engagement with discourses relating to sexuality, gender identity and corporate encroachment. Perhaps more than any other artifact, the shoe in art points to the overvaluation or "fetishization" of the art object itself, underscoring, by way of contrast, fine art's role as an indicator of "high culture" in terms of objects "magically" imbued with personality. As Marx wrote, regarding the fetishism of commodities, it demonstrates "a life of its own."[33] Clearly, it would seem that in twentieth-century Western art there are certain discourses and sensibilities that need to be addressed, "truths" that need to be "disclosed," raspberries that need to be blown, or points that need to be made, which can only adequately be articulated through an image of an empty shoe.

Figure 17.11: Andreas Gursky, Prada I, c-print, edition of 6, 145 x 220 cm, 1996. Gursky captures the minimalist fashion aesthetic of the mid-1990s, and suggests the conflation of high-end clothing with fine art as much as it points to the commercial ethos of the art market. © Andreas Gursky/SODRAC (2005). Courtesy Matthew Marks Gallery, New York.

18.
LIMOUSINES FOR THE FEET

THE RHETORIC OF SNEAKERS

alison gill

Now the Adidas I possess for one man is rare
Myself homeboy got fifty pair
Got blue and black 'cause I like to chill
And yellow and green when it's time to get ill
Got a pair that I wear when I play ball
With a heel inside makes me ten feet tall
My Adidas and me close as can be
We make a mean team my Adidas and me.

"My Adidas" by Run DMC

I am a sneaker fan and not a collector. I love them as something to enjoy and wear. People think I'm crazy, I wear my Bathing Apes, Jeremy Scotts, Micro Pacers and don't worry if they get messed up.

Ben Pruess, Director of Sport Heritage, Adidas, interviewed in *SneakerFreaker*, 5

Sports shoes – commonly called sneakers or trainers – are well-known objects of avid consumer spending. The release of a new model is able to invoke a passion among consumers so intense that they will spend large amounts of money and effort to acquire it. This is no "consumer madness" or irrational desire. A case must be made for fuller understanding of the powerful "rhetoric" of the sports shoe and the meanings it assumes for its owners, whether fans or collectors, wearers or nonwearers. As a powerful sign of performance and aesthetics, an encasement of the foot that marries functional and fashion features, each sports shoe can be an expression of skill, speed, power, fitness, sporting history, attitude and style. For those with a passion for collecting and wearing trainers and sneakers, the particular rhetorical language of the sports shoe is significant in constructing new notions of wearing. The terms "sneakers," "trainers," "runners," "kicks," or "shits" are all important indicators of the attitude with which they are worn. In addition, these sports shoes take "command" of certain places in everyday life via their complex branding strategies.

ON RHETORIC AND TRAINERS

Design theorist Richard Buchanan argues for a wider understanding of the "rhetoric of products." Products are vehicles of argument and persuasion: they communicate notions of value, meaning and style, and foster fantasy, intimacy and desire with their potential consumers.[1] The transformation of the casual sports shoe or sneaker into the performance- and lifestyle-enhancing "trainer," after 1975, is a preeminent example of a global product that is iconic of lifestyle values. The trainer is also a measure of the persuasiveness of the niche marketing methods that have been applied to products and consumer groups for over thirty years.[2] As a measure of rhetorical power, the sports shoe is now so integral to everyday life – both athletic and recreational – and universally ubiquitous, that it is able to seduce, communicate with, and situate the identity of consumers. This is done without necessarily commanding a great deal of reflection on the part of the consumer (Figure 18.1).

This chapter sets out to explore the communicative rhetoric of the trainer – its powerful hold on cultural meaning – in the contemporary cultural setting of a so-called postindustrial global economy.[3] It will involve various key developments in the design and market positioning of sports shoes in the last three to four decades, as well as analyzing a selection of the messages that marketing encodes for these shoes and their related activities. Therefore the "rhetoric of trainers" will be approached via the promotional and designed language of advertising; the personal significance awarded to sports shoes by consumers and wearers in biographies, conversation, anecdotes and literature; and finally the cultural significance of sports shoes noted by cultural theorists and material culture scholars. Particular emphasis is given to the multifaceted processes that design the meanings of sports shoes in order to investigate their place as "vehicles of argument and persuasion."

GLOBAL ICON AND THE DEMOCRATIZATION OF SHOES

In the 1970s, American sneaker companies such as B. J. Goodrich (P. F. Flyers), Dunlop and Converse, which had produced unchanged models for decades, were challenged by emerging marketing-driven firms such as Adidas, Puma, New Balance, Onitsuka Tiger, Reebok and Nike. These newer firms not only promoted more specialized shoes for individual sports, but also began updating their models annually. The notion of planned obsolescence was artfully refined by a new, foreign breed of company through the combination of production innovation, introduction of new materials, offshore production and hefty advertising budgets. The humble casual shoe called a sneaker was transformed from a staple item of youth dress and leisure culture into an "icon" of global marketing power. The previously generic sports shoe was segmented into categories of trainers and sports shoes for leisure, running, basketball, aerobics, cross-training, skateboarding, football, cricket, tennis, hip hop and dance-party culture, according to different lifestyles and subcultures. It was at this stage that some version of the trainer became essential equipment for contemporary living.[4]

There are three aspects to the rhetoric of trainer marketing that have helped to embed them in the consciousness of consumers and allowed them to gain their cultural hold. If we examine the belief that choosing the right pair of shoes is the first step in committing to a program of exercise, the first rhetorical construction is the message that the technical features of shoes can assist and enhance performance. This is the rhetoric of progressive, performance-enhancing technology that has come direct to the consumer from high-tech, biomechanical and space-industry studies within shoe-testing "laboratories." The trainer thus takes up the interwar utopian ideas promoted within the emergence of modernist industrial design. The advertising message is that the consumer will directly benefit from a brand that is, as the Adidas phrase goes, "committed to [performance-enhancing] shoe technology."[5]

Secondly, performance enhancement became particularly seductive when promoted alongside the rhetoric of bettering the self, physically and psychologically, which was central to the cult of fitness and health spearheaded by the jogging and aerobics trends of the 1970s. Health and fitness became synonymous with enhanced attractiveness and success. Consequently, the sports shoe was not only positioned as a key agent to performance enhancement, but also to goal-oriented health and fitness activities tailored to a notion of an improved self. "You can run to become a better runner. Or you can run to become better" – claimed a recent Nike advertisement. The same company's slogan from 1977 reminded consumers that "There is no Finish Line," thus underlining that the runner was committing to a lifetime pursuit of self-improvement.

Thirdly, if we return to the exercise of choosing the "right" shoes for a sporting activity, one quickly realizes how integral aesthetics and image have become in choosing the "right" shoes. Sports shoes are a key component of the "equipment of style" of most sporting activities and include clothes, body contour, skin condition and hairstyle. The aesthetics of sports shoes have also become an integral detail of many fashionable "looks" and lifestyles, played both on and off the court or sports field. The rhetoric of lifestyle image emerging from the promotion of fashion and sportswear labels has persuaded consumers to see sports shoes as an indicative part of an overall lifestyle image and "fashioned look." The "rhetorical" dimension underscores the fact that these looks are complete with messages about the values and attitudes implicit in their successful reuse and reconstruction. Therefore, while the aesthetics of the sports shoe could be said to respond to the broader seasonal dynamics of the fashion industry, the sports shoe has been an influential presence in a fashion industry that looks to the street and gym for sources of inspiration, and seems to have led the introduction of sportswear features into many ready-to-wear lines and collections. The branding rhetoric of sports shoes is a compelling mix of performance, self-identity, and aesthetic concerns.

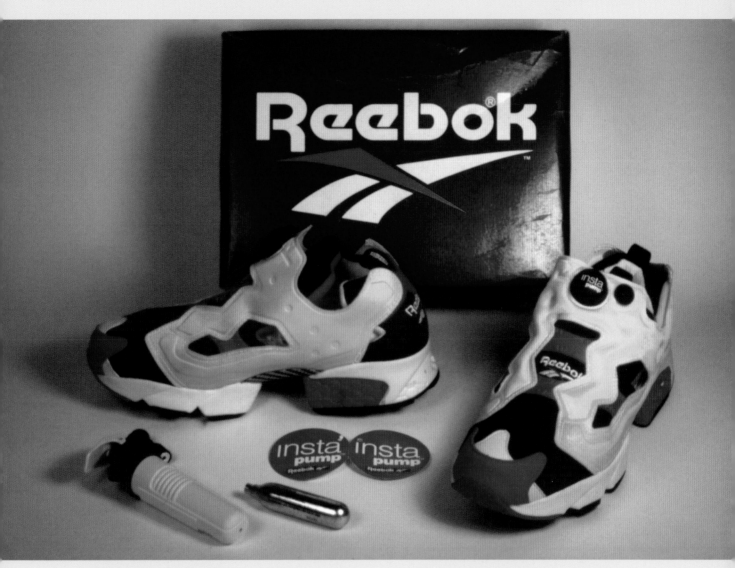

FIGURE 18.1: PAIR OF REEBOK RUNNING SHOES – INSTA PUMP – WITH ROUND TOE, YELLOW, RED AND BLACK UPPERS, BLACK AND WHITE SYNTHETIC RUBBER SOLE, AND RED AND WHITE SYNTHETIC RUBBER HEELS, 1995. BATA SHOE MUSEUM, TORONTO, P95.117. REPRODUCED BY KIND PERMISSION OF BATA SHOE MUSEUM.

FROM HUMBLE BEGINNINGS TO THE GLOBAL RISE OF THE TRAINER

Before exploring marketing forces, the origins of the sports shoes in the canvas and rubber-soled sneaker that was an offshoot of American and British rubber and tire production, and its formative place in the postwar youth psyche, need to be indicated. In Britain and America, parallel developments in the vulcanization of rubber – later applied as a strengthening bond between a canvas upper and a rubber sole – enabled the production of a lightweight croquet shoe, in 1876,

FIGURE 18.2: SPORTS SHOES WITH COTTON CANVAS UPPERS, AND RUBBER SOLES WITH WEDGE SHAPES. PRODUCED BY KAUFMAN, TORONTO, 1956–60. BATA SHOE MUSEUM, TORONTO, S92.24. REPRODUCED BY KIND PERMISSION OF BATA SHOE MUSEUM.

by Britain's New Liverpool Rubber Company. "Sandshoes" and "plimsolls" were available for use in lawn sports and as children's footwear in the late nineteenth century. While the word "sneaker" seems to have been registered by North American etymologists by 1870, to refer to the quiet sounds emanating from "shoes with canvas tops and India rubber soles," the term would have generally applied to a range of sandshoe and tennis shoe variants produced by small rubber or shoe companies in America until their 1892 merger into the US Rubber Co.[6]

Keds (a white canvas shoe with a blue label) were released in 1916 as the consolidated product of the US Rubber Co., becoming a popular shoe for children and teenagers. A year later, the second eventual mainstay of the American sneaker market was released in the model of the Converse All Star.[7] America assumed "ownership" of the sneaker concept as the uniform of youth and was able to make maximum use of the much older Goodyear company's 1839 patent for vulcanized rubber, which made possible the canvas and rubber design.[8] The centrality of the sneaker in the postwar dress codes of American youth – a well-laundered informal combination of jeans or skirt and pressed shirt – and the promotion of its consumption alongside democratic participation in sport, dance entertainment, school and after-school leisure activities, cemented the position of Keds, the All Star and another model, the P. F. Flyer (produced by B. F. Goodrich), in American youth culture (Figure 18.2).

From the 1920s to the 1970s, the All Star grew in popularity alongside the growing interest in basketball as a professional and amateur sport, and was sold in sporting goods stores as such. Like Keds, P. F. Flyers and Spalding shoes, which dominated department store sales, All Stars were also purchased for comfort in exercise and for recreation of a general nature. By 1955, Converse was claiming that the All Star was the number-one-selling shoe in America, largely because it appealed to children, teenagers, men and women, cutting across formerly separate shoe markets. As the benefits of physical exercise or sporting activity for good health were increasingly promoted in the industrialized world, and the building of sporting and leisure facilities was integrated into the reconstruction of cities in postwar Europe, sports shoes became a requisite for after-work and after-school recreational activities.

SHOES OF THE GODS

The modern Olympic movement had already revived a wide interest in athletics and the heroic nature of sport. In Europe, two shoemakers produced athletic and sports shoes – Britain's Joseph Foster from 1900 and Germany's Adolf Dassler from 1926. The companies established respectively by these men – Reebok and Adidas – would become leading players in defining the applications and meaning of sports shoes internationally, and later eclipse American domestic sneaker producers. For example, the domestic market for American-produced rubber-soled sneakers was affected by a series of tariff changes after 1966, allowing imported athletic shoes to gain a larger percentage of the market. Initially, it was the infiltration of German-manufactured Adidas products into the market that signaled the change to domestic sneaker production after 1966, but later the various parts, models and brand names produced in Asia by companies including Nike and Reebok, flooded the American market. The tariff debates around sports shoes were a small-scale forerunner of the auto wars of the 1970s over the impact of cheap Japanese cars on the American car industry.

LIMOUSINES FOR THE FEET

In the 1960s and 1970s, advertising began a dramatic transformation of the sports shoe, from object of comfort and function into a lifestyle commodity – an extension of the personality, tastes and interests of the wearer. Converse coined the phrase "limousines for the feet" to describe the added value of fame, prestige and star status associated with their shoes through endorsement by professional basketball players. As early as 1923, "Chucks" became the signature shoe of the player Chuck Taylor. By the mid-1970s, Converse had signed endorsement deals with the likes of Julius "Dr. J." Erving, an NBA star player, whose story of personal transformation captured the imagination of New York youth. As print advertisements began to feature individual athletes, spectators' interest in various sports began to extend to recognition of the players' shoe choices and even the attitude with which shoes were worn by these new stars.

The new product identities crafted for the shoes via an association with professional sportspeople were highlighted by annual product releases and a wide choice of colors and materials. It was possible for consumers to differentiate themselves through their purchases. However, at the same time market competition was increasing. The popularity of the canvas Converse and Pro-Keds models on basketball courts began to be seriously challenged by Pony, Nike and Adidas models, which offered leather, suede and nylon mesh uppers, low- or high-top designs, and a wide selection of color combinations. The majority of professional players moved to the more expensive and more supportive leather models such as the Adidas Pro model (1965) and Adidas Superstar (1969), Converse All Star Pro models (1970), Nike Blazers (1972) or the Puma Clyde (1972) in suede, thus opening up a significant aspirational divide between the canvas-wearing adolescent and/or amateur, and the professionals of the ball tournaments. In addition, audiences began to make distinctions between preferred on-court models and off-court favorites, often ahead of advertising, which needed to adjust to consumer response.

Bobbito Garcia's *Where'd You Get Those?: New York City's Sneaker Culture 1960–1987* (2003) recounts that Puma Clydes, while originally a popular suede model with professional basketball players when released in 1972, became, by the mid-1970s, a preferred non-canvas alternative for New York off-court or street wear, available in a plethora of two-color combinations. Film director Seth Rosenfeld, interviewed by Garcia, remembered that "Clydes were the perfect sneakers to sport with anything … Lee jeans … We'd also rock AJs … they were gabardine and polyester pants, a variation of the double-knit pants of the generation before us. They were dress pants, but we wore them with Clydes cuz they looked so hot."[9]

Accordingly, by the late 1970s, Puma had adjusted its advertising to address its two potential markets – "basketball players" and "casual wearers" – knowing very well that it was the latter category that was peaking, exemplified in their print advertisement featuring star Knicks player Walt "Clyde" Frazier in his super-slick, off-court attire of dark suit and fur coat. As street wear, Garcia observes that "the Clydes" challenged the canvas models such as the Pro-Ked "69ers" and the Converse All Star in staying power for street wear, as they remained an immensely popular shoe choice for hip-hop and fashion-conscious youth, particularly throughout the 1980s.[10] The words "cool," "hot," "butter" or, in New York specifically, "shits," were used to describe what particular and often changing models represented for their wearers, as they also reflected some sense of the values – whether fashionable style, professional credibility, dreams of fame, or attitude – incorporated into the meaning of shoes through promotional advertising, player endorsements and consumer response.

The forced shift of sports shoe companies from "production-minded" to "marketing-minded" concerns in the face of aggressive competition from newcomers Nike, Tiger, Reebok, Puma and Adidas started in the early 1970s and came to maturity twenty years later.[11] The measure of this is the priority given to advertising budgets and the skilled crafting of the phenomenon of the brand-name athletic shoe. According to Tom Vanderbilt, "from 1950 to 1990, or from P. F. Flyers to the Reebok Pump, global ad spending had risen from $39 billion to $256 billion, a third faster than the expansion of the world economy."[12] Between 1985 and 1993, for example, Nike's annual advertising budget swelled from $20 million to well over $150 million.[13] Different branding strategies were developed. The Converse All Star, Keds and P. F. Flyers pioneered the construction of a simple brand name and identity for their canvas sneakers around continuity of supply to American youth. The All Star pioneered, from 1923, the notion of an athlete's signature shoe. Nike honed, from 1985, the tethering of the sale of a product to fans' dreams about athletic prowess.

In Michael Jordan's Air Jordan brand identity – based around his exceptional in-flight moves toward the basket – Nike managed to project sports fans' compelling desire to see and enjoy greatness in athletic performance around their Air Jordan shoe. Since the Jordan advertisements of 1985, Nike CEO Phil Knight has managed to assemble a promotional pantheon of beloved athletes representing the cream of different sports. Into this compelling mix with universal appeal, Nike has added a fundamental dimension to their advertising, based on the technical innovation of shoe models promoting high performance and personal technology (Figure 18.3). Thus, the shoes worn by sporting legends have taken on an abiding interest for enthusiasts, in a way similar to car models, airplanes and electronics. Marketing has been central in this "transformation" of the sports shoe. In the mid-1980s, for instance, Reebok took the lead in American sporting shoe sales away from Nike (for a short period while the Air Jordan phenomena took root) by spearheading the aerobics trend and promoting a shoe specifically for women, thus defining a distinctly female domain of the fitness revolution in shoeing an army of jumping, hopping and skipping women in a white leather sports shoe.

The companies behind these major marketing innovations have assumed a high-profile status as leaders in the global economic market place. Two terms have been used to refer to the iconic impact of the sports shoe on global economics: the "sneakerization of the economy" and the ascendance of "soft goods." "Sneakerization" refers to the multiplication of inexpensive goods such as sunglasses, accessories and sports shoes in highly segmented markets with a rapid turnover, playing on the power of brand identity. In the case of sports shoes, this has been made possible by the production of shoe parts and their assembly in cheaper Asian economies, where companies have established complex webs of manufacturing and distribution across multiple countries. In the 1970s and 1980s, manufacture was initiated in Japan, South Korea and Taiwan, until rising wages and production costs brought about moves to China, Vietnam and Indonesia.

Sports shoe production companies are more appropriately called neo-Fordist in organization because they still rely heavily on large-volume production, assembly-line organization, and low-skilled and low-waged labor, yet they have a subcontracting network and production partnerships that make them akin to other post-Fordist organizations.[14] According to Maria Eitel, Vice President of Corporate Responsibility for Nike, their shoes are produced in 900 factories across 55 countries, by about 700,000 workers.[15] The majority of these factories are not owned by Nike and the company's current emphasis on marketing the product has led to a corporate redefinition: as Eitel states, "As a company we're a design and marketing company," thus hiding their involvement in production.[16] Executives of other companies have followed suit in proclaiming that they are "shoe marketers," not shoe manufacturers.[17]

The sports shoe is an example of "soft goods," a term that articulates the ascendancy of marketing over production concerns as the key to growing profit. The reconstruction of businesses that were structured around long production runs into flexible manufacturing relied on marketing strategies that would move the fast-changing products. In this highly competitive period from the 1970s to the 1990s, when the production and marketing of sports shoes was played out in high gear, the product obtained true global reach and was established across a range of price levels, so that the less wealthy could afford a cheaper alternative to the leading brands. As the phrase "limousines for the feet" reflects, the general direction of the sports shoe market was to establish desire for a high-performance sports or athletic shoe that was akin to the market relationship of a four-wheel drive or sport utility vehicle to other cars. As Vanderbilt writes, "large, loaded with impressive but rarely used options, a statement less of need than desire."[18]

PROGRESSIVE DESIGN: THE ROLE OF PERFORMANCE-ENHANCING TECHNOLOGY

Sports shoe design is a marrying of protective materials and functional features to an aesthetic outer surface that connotes skill sets, strength, power and individuality. High-performance shoes are realized through the research and testing of biomechanical engineers, physiologists, textile material technicians and sportswear designers who are aided by computer-modeled design and production. Due to the global size and competitive nature of the sports shoe market, companies have invested heavily in the research and development of lightweight and high-performance shoes for various terrains and purposes. Much of the corporate terrain of the high-performance sports shoe has been defined by intensely competing economic and global players such as Nike, Reebok and Adidas, whose fights have been likened to the Coca-Cola and Pepsi marketing wars. The promotional rhetoric of these high-flying manufacturers tells audiences that the performance-enhancing equipment of the professional sporting elite is now democratized for everyday wear. The trickle-down pace of innovations from high-end performance shoes built for world-class athletes, to the average consumer, is determined by material, labor and distribution costs. The promotional materials serve to reiterate the notion that these shoes are built on an authentic core of athletic expertise and that technological research is made available to all. The outcome has left the average person owning at least one pair of trainers, but also a sense that these shoes possess capacities far above their own.

Since the first nylon mesh upper was introduced into the basketball market (where canvas, leather, and suede encasings reigned) by the Adidas Shooting Star in 1970, for purposes of lighter weight, research and development has seen the introduction of new synthetic materials. There are meshes, elastics, polyurethanes, rubbers, composite foams, latex; new fastening and support systems, improved cushioning and sole technology, and the cross-fertilization of innovations across all sports. While high-profile examples such as Nike Air technology have focused the public imagination on mid-sole cushioning systems, the pace of change in design is dazzling across all zones of the shoe – uppers, mid-soles, lasts, and surface traction of soles. Vanderbilt observes that the industry is structured by a twin form of planned obsolescence attuned to the dual aesthetic and performance concerns of design. If the aesthetic of the shoes does not go out of style first, the technology will probably be eclipsed by the following year's innovation.[19] He notes that industry's seasons have accelerated to four a year, rather than the former two, and recounts the pressure to produce new products in each shoe category every ninety days.[20]

Nike's Air technology is one of the most well known of the running shoe cushioning inventions, as it compartmentalizes pressurized air (the ultimate free anti-material) in the sole in order

FIGURE 18.3: PAIR OF NIKE AGASSI SNEAKERS WITH BOX AND SOCKS, MID-1990S. BATA SHOE MUSEUM, TORONTO, P98.84. REPRODUCED BY KIND PERMISSION OF BATA SHOE MUSEUM.

to make a high-technology support system for reducing knee and ankle strain due to shock of impact.

The innovation of see-through or window compartments in the soles of the shoes successfully captured the imagination of the consumer beyond the running market, and the industry has seen a series of designs that unveil the mid-soles and their support technology, anticipating developments in other design fields such as the iMac computer and its transparent casing. A trend for promoting a shoe's technological innovations started early for Nike, with the famed waffle sole design of the early 1970s, inspired by coach Bill Bowerman's waffle iron, to deliver better traction on the athletic track. Following the successful marketing of Air technology, Nike Shox set new standards in terms of promotional brochures with technological specifications and claims, and provided a new, spring-based column cushioning system, not unlike the approach to shock absorbers in Formula One racing cars.

While each of the big corporate players has been responsible for popularizing zones of the sports shoe industry – Adidas and their football shoes, Reebok and the aerobics shoe and Nike and the running shoe – all have mobilized armies of wearers, seemingly as reliant on their shoe technology as they are committed to fitness. Nike has been ahead of its time in the promotion of high-performance shoes for mass audiences by harnessing the power of athletic excellence and timely performances of elite figureheads. Nike has been successful in terms of sales volume and has created "intoxicating" messages about athletic dreams of greatness, notwithstanding the fact that statistics reveal that only twenty percent of performance shoe wearers use them in sporting pursuits.[21] This harsh reality does not consider that the majority of wearers connect with the comfort of performance features and a brand image of athletic integrity produced by Nike's association with elite sportsmen and women. There is evidence, however, to suggest that the serious running market prefers the more low-profile ASICS and Brooks brands.

KEEP-FIT TRAINERS: A MATTER OF SELF-IMPROVEMENT

The fitness boom of the 1970s spearheaded the incorporation of high-performance shoes into everyday life, and is probably more responsible for the mass consumption of running shoes and trainers than any single breakthrough technology. A product of intersecting medical and holistic health discourses and burgeoning industries of physical science and sports medicine, the phenomenal growth in the gym and fitness industries since the 1970s has meant that every form of exercise, dance and relaxation has been commodified into an hourly session. These industries advocate that the self can be reconfirmed through a commitment to training a new, more authentic form for itself called the trim body, now a social norm. Exercise, dance and relaxation were promoted as part of an accelerating set of routines and practices that claimed to deliver self-improvement, enhancing not just ability, but also self-esteem, attractiveness, body shape, health, well-being, work performance, lifestyle image and ultimate social acceptance.

In addition, the commitment to keeping fit and trim worked in conjunction with a new sartorial awareness and desire for a look of health, well-being and informality that could be created through tracksuits, gym accessories, and the footwear that became known as cross-trainers. Extending into the late 1980s, the Olivia Newton-John anthem *Let's Get Physical* encapsulates an era of celebrity-endorsed exercise programs for home and gym, and branded gym clothing and accessories that prescribed a need for a cross-trainer – a hybrid shoe designed for durability, support and flexibility across fitness activities such as running, walking, aerobics, weight-training, basketball and leisure etc. Within this context, we can understand the marketing influence of the professional athlete as a model of fitness who signifies celebrity and integrity, a respected figure who practices an authentic self-reconstruction for a vocation. In sum, even if one was not using shoes for fitness or a program of exercise, the health and fitness revolution led to a renewed commitment to all forms of recreation and leisure, as part of a balanced working life, for which a trainer shoe was required.

The late 1980s cross-trainer of the Nike Air and Air Max generations was a sturdier and feature-laden addition to the market position already carved out by the relatively lightweight running shoe for jogging, and women's aerobic shoes such as the Reebok Freestyle and the Pump, required to cushion the repetitive impact of aerobic routines. With the rise of the cross-trainer, the minimal cushioning of former styles was quickly superseded by models that included a lightweight, strong upper, elaborate cushioning and support technologies (such as outlined above), and a robust and wider sole, designed to enhance the normal (and correct any abnormal) motion of the foot. In parallel with the swelling presence of these limousines in everyday life, the trainer's outsoles became increasingly elaborate compositions of synthetic polymers of varying patterns, densities and colors, to cushion and support the action of the foot within. Within this composition of the outsoles, it became essential to build in the brand name and logo as a component feature, as well as on the surface of the upper and the patterns of the undersole (Figure 18.4). Logos and trademarks such as the three stripes (Adidas), Nike's dynamic tick (Swoosh), the Puma ribbon, the Onitsuka tiger (ASICS), and the Converse star have not been immune to redesign. As a fundamental part of the corporate strategy of branding, the repositioning is used to condense and adjust the desired image of athletic integrity by symbolizing dynamism, power and speed.

FASHIONABLE COLLABORATIONS: THE TRAINER, SPORTSWEAR AND FASHION

As the high-performance features of the trainer were taken up as essential equipment for everyday living, the gap between sportswear and fashion – once defined in opposition as functional uniforms versus stylish clothing – has been closing. This has been achieved both in the work of high-profile collaborations between fashion designers and sportswear companies, such as Stella McCartney with Adidas in 2005, and by more general trends that have seen many collections include garments that are more ready-to-run than ready-to-wear. The trainer, first used by Vivienne Westwood on the catwalk in the 1980s, has introduced both a sports aesthetic and new performance materials to the fashion industry and fashion audience. It is in keeping with a contemporary lifestyle that is perhaps more sedentary (as urban) than in the past, but also structured toward the desire for distinct sessions of active recreation and leisure. Many fashion collections have now learned to *equip* the fashionable body not only with comfortable, lightweight shoes descended from the trainer, but also ensembles of lightweight performance fabrics made into workout and leisure clothes, including Velcro tab fastening systems and stretch-fit concepts developed in tandem with trainers.

When hip-hop culture became a source of fashion ideas in the mid to late 1980s, the spotless, untied sneaker was consolidated as a must-have style icon to finish a look consisting of oversized jeans and tracksuits. The Adidas shell-toe classic was immortalized by Run DMC's 1986 hit song "My Adidas," the trainer functioning as a statement of black identity and empowerment. In Run DMC's case, it was an expression of pride from the black, ball-playing youth of Queens, New York; a "transporting symbol" as termed by Steven Langehough, an escape route from poverty and invisibility.[22] Extending much further than hip-hop culture, the effect of this meeting of a sportswear aesthetic, music and dance culture with a brand-name black style consciousness was to consolidate the idea of a trainer's (and other sneaker alternatives') key place in many other popular fashion ensembles, sport or cultural trends and youth identity statements. For example, the ensemble of the grunge anti-fashion aesthetic emanating from the Seattle music scene in the 1990s, consisting of dressed down jeans, T-shirt and well-worn sneakers, became a uniform worn by bands such as Sound Garden and Nirvana and their fans, and enabled a revival of the Converse One Star sneaker, which was immortalized by Nirvana frontman Kurt Cobain's suicide in a pair of Converse sneakers.

FIGURE 18.4: PAIR OF NIKE SNEAKERS WITH ROUND TOE, WHITE AND NEON YELLOW SOLE OF MOLDED SYNTHETIC MATERIAL. PRODUCED IN SOUTH AMERICA, 1989. BATA SHOE MUSEUM, TORONTO, S89.186. REPRODUCED BY KIND PERMISSION OF BATA SHOE MUSEUM.

The trainer has commanded an influential place in runway shows both as a part of ready-to-wear collections – a key sign of an informality affecting contemporary dress generally – and as an indicator of urban and subcultural attitudes deciding fashion trends. It has been a new site for designers' attentions, as some have turned to customizing shoes in collaboration with leading brands – the "designer sports shoe." For example, Junya Watanabe customized Nike Vandals for Comme des Garçons' military wear collection (2004).[23] "Collabs" is the new term for bringing both high-profile and more underground fashion designers and shoe companies together in order to generate new aesthetics and new models across fashion and sportswear. These collaborations are extensions of the long-standing practice or street art of *customizing* trainers – an outlet for fantasy and measure of sneaker passion – which generates exhibitions, magazines and websites, and is fed back into the research and development of major companies via the findings of "cool hunters" who identify street trends.

CONCLUSION AND POSTSCRIPT ON THE REHTORIC OF LIGHTNESS

The last three decades of trainer marketing have witnessed the added value of high-performance technology, motivational messages about life-changing fitness, and fashionable collaborations that have ensured a central place for the trainer in the leisure industries and image-driven dynamics of contemporary life. Design-technology innovations wished to build into shoes a host of high-performance features derived from biomechanics and athletic studies, and to market the notion of supporting and improving on nature – cushioning, cradling, spring-loading. The latest design development is to return to the foot itself, marking the disappearance of the feature-laden ostentation and corrective technology of the trainer in favor of a light, encasing shell celebrating the ergonomics of the foot. This development has been several years in the making, as fashion shoes have been shedding any excess bulk in trainers, possibly inspired by the simplicity of old-school styles, and moving in the direction of a cross between a sneaker, a trainer and a slip-on fashion shoe. Sports shoe designers and podiatrists have signaled a direct change in paradigm over four years, away from the notion of controlling the motion of the foot, to allowing the subtle movements of the foot to occur and feed this information back to the brain.[24]

Again seeming to lead the field of product and idea, Nike have put the name "Free" to their latest running shoe. This counters the well-cushioned, over-technical trainer with a shoe that provides a running experience which is said to be like running barefoot. Allowing one's feet to take the load, the aim of the Free trainer is to strengthen and tone the foot, tendons, ankles and toes. Adidas were using this concept seven years ago with their "The Feet You Wear" tagline, which promoted a cradling, cross-trainer basketball shoe endorsed by ball-player Kobe Bryant, which was said to be styled on his near-perfect feet. Now there is an even more concerted effort to promote the concept of a totally uninhibited foot, throwing out the notion of synthetic overpadding, and delivering a more authentic notion of lightness. Rather than having to adhere to historical forms of manufacturing, materials and making, the contemporary trainer promises a shoe culture that is so appealing because it can be presented and understood as "advanced" and "natural" simultaneously. It is for this reason that the trainer, and its business shoe variants incorporating translucent cores, are viewed by consumers as the ultimate shoe liberation, but one which requires constant monitoring and updating, hence purchasing.

THE MALE CINDERELLA

SHOES, GENIUS AND FANTASY[1]

peter mcneil and giorgio riello

OF COBBLERS AND LITTLE WOMEN

To the cobbler: from the Little woman around the corner.[2]

This was a peculiar card sent by the well-known London dress designer Norman Hartnell to the even more celebrated London shoe designer Rayne. The camp irony of the message is intertwined with serious "style politics." As the message implies, both men were well known in the "fashion village" of 1930s London. However, the message subtly plays on the fact that the two men's privileged social positions were once servile occupations. Hartnell's card also deploys a celebrated queer weapon – camp. The shoe is an object that frequently verges on the borders of kitsch and camp.

As underlined by Julia Pine is this volume, the very mundanity of the shoe was of interest to the avant-garde, notably Dada and Surrealism, in the 1920s and 1930s. This aspect of shoes was well recognized by Andy Warhol, both in his torn paper and fabric collages of the 1950s and 1960s, and his 1980s' Gold Dust series. It was also a theme revisited by feminist artists and craftspeople of the 1980s and 1990s. It became omnipresent in the 1990s in camp pop performances of fashion excess (*Absolutely Fabulous*) and in fictionalized metropolitan sex lives (*Sex in the City*). The woman's shoe as a kitsch bauble and vulgar, anti-modern excess, is always hovering around the edges, a point carefully assessed by Christopher Breward in a chapter on modernity included in this volume. The photographer of shoes for contemporary publicity often abstracts them: it is said of Guy Bourdin that his shoots for Charles Jourdan are "famous for sublimating the product to the point of obscurity."[3] If the "intellectual purist" is suspicious of shoes, fashion per se is even more so. Shoes remain the Cinderella of fashion.

Queerness, camp and kitsch feminine behavior are just some of the salient aspects of the complicated nature of shoes. Several chapters have touched upon the contradictions arising from the mysterious character of such objects. The cultural and social complexity of shoes is at once intellectually constructed and the result of their physical nature. A coat, a hat or a dress can be turned inside out and their constructions can be observed and studied. By contrast, the shoe would have to be dismembered in order to understand its inner workings. Certain shoe designers have played with this ambiguity (Figure 19.1). It is perhaps for this reason that shoes remain one of the least understood components of modern dress. This is true for both the brogue and the stiletto, which still cannot be made in fully mechanized processes, as well for as the designer sneaker, whose structure and inner workings are not evident from the exterior.

This book is conscious of the clash between the trivialization of shoes and their rather opaque and difficult "personality." If this book fell in the trap of "over-reading" shoes, historians know that the problem is quite the reverse. Fashion, stylistics, dressing and sartorial choices in the past were not incidental to everyday life: they *were* everyday life. However, the trivial nature of shoes remains more than a passing feature. This is probably due to a certain rigidity of modernist thought and design practice, as well as the rationalist impulse of the second half of the twentieth century. This is true more than ever in the contemporary world in which the media structure popular understandings of history. The irony of the postmodern world is that despite the rhetoric of multiple and shifting identities, readings of objects are perhaps more shallow than ever before. Veiled in Disney-like forms, the past is often presented to us as "an eternal present" full of similitudes and similarities across time. Our study of shoes, which refutes the idea that Marie Antoinette was "just like" Imelda Marcos, nonetheless encountered enormous difficulties in sifting through a wide range of simplistic literature on the topic of shoes.

The dumbing down of fashion (and shoes as its "greatest degeneration") is even more remarkable if we consider its recent invention. The twentieth-century conception of eighteenth-century life was very much formulated through the nineteenth-century rococo revival, which

privileged certain aspects of court life and dress. Writers such as the Goncourt brothers used the idea of rococo luxury and the role of the artist to critique the utilitarianism of mercantile Paris of the 1860s. This definition of luxury revolved around the world of women, and tended to forget that the eighteenth-century consumer was as likely to be an interested male. The details of eighteenth-century life, such as the form and workmanship of women's shoes – for example the famous pink mules in Boucher's *Portrait of the Marquise de Pompadour* – were described with poetic intensity by these nineteenth-century apologists of hedonism and aestheticism. That shoes and gloves might be so imbued with allegorical, decorative and monetary value in the past was evident to any nineteenth-century connoisseur examining great shoes, which were collected for these as well as purported historical reasons (Figure 19.2). Other great nineteenth-century novelists and philosopher-poets recognized and acted upon the social importance of fashion and fashionable behavior.[4] Shoes are an object and an idea. In writing about dress, Marcel Proust emphasized the significance of clothes: "The complication of their trimmings, none of which had any practical utility or served any visible purpose, added something detached, pensive, secret, in harmony with the melancholy which Mme Swann still retained." Proust evokes, better than anyone, that dressing was about an idea: "One felt that she did not dress simply for the comfort or the adornments of her body; she was surrounded by her garments as by the delicate and spiritualized machinery of a whole civilization." Dress to Proust might disclose a secret intention; "suggestions of the past blended with the person of Mme Swann the charm of certain heroines of history or romance."

The writers of this volume would probably concur that the shoe occupies a particular place in the repertoire of attitudes to fashion. If fashion is trivialized as both artifact and social force, then the shoe is even more likely to be condemned as evidence of waste, or fetishized; recall that it was Marie-Antoinette's shoe, not her dress or headdress, that was meant to have been saved from the guillotine.

Part of the continuing appeal of the Jean-Honoré Fragonard's iconic painting *The Happy Hazards of the Swing* is quite apart from the libidinal aspects of the image and the rococo vortex into which the woman swings. She is in the act of kicking off her shoe, a metaphorical and literal release. Representing both abandon and orgasm, her shoe is a light indoor mule, not the type of shoe necessary to protect the foot outdoors. As Jennifer Milam notes of the iconography here, the tossed shoe is emblematic of female abandonment to passion; the unshod foot of lost virginity.[5] As shoe historians underline, such indoor shoes were often made by a separate workmen's guild and were in some ways not really "shoes" (*souliers*). The feminine object is thrown into the sky and assumes a supernatural character that sets it apart from earthly, common shoes. "High heels create artifice. It's the way you walk," writes Blahnik.[6] The soft, fragile ladies' shoe becomes at once part of the realm of "imagination" and "residual" of a mundane nature that it attempts to obliterate. It is within this conundrum that the "great" shoe designers of the nineteenth and

FIGURE 19.1 (FACING PAGE): A MYSTERIOUS SHOE: A SHOE WITH STOCKINGS OR STOCKINGS WITH SHOES? RED STILETTO SHOE WITH RED LACE SHAFT AND BACK ZIPPER CLOSURE, PRODUCED BY HERBERT LEVINE, 1959. BATA SHOE MUSEUM, TORONTO, P.93.35.AB. REPRODUCED BY KIND PERMISSION OF BATA SHOE MUSEUM.

FIGURE 19.2 (FACING PAGE): BLUE VELVET LATCHET-TIE SHOES OWNED BY LADY STANHOPE, C. 1660. NORTHAMPTON MUSEUMS AND ART GALLERY, BOOT AND SHOE COLLECTION, 1994.279.1. REPRODUCED BY PERMISSION OF NORTHAMPTON MUSEUMS AND ART GALLERY.

FIGURE 19.3 (ABOVE): GOLD SHOES, 1920S. THE SHOE BECOMES A SEMI-PRECIOUS OBJECT. NORTHAMPTON MUSEUMS AND ART GALLERY, BOOT AND SHOE COLLECTION, 1967.81.14P. REPRODUCED BY PERMISSION OF NORTHAMPTON MUSEUMS AND ART GALLERY.

twentieth centuries, from Pinet to Perugia, from Ferragamo to Blahnik, have elevated shoemaking to the artistic pinnacle by pursuing Fragonard's lost pump, at the service of ladies, rather than men (Figure 19.3). Ironically, both Ferragamo and Blahnik began their careers by making men's shoes: Western cowboy boots for the former; men's saddle shoes for the latter.

The Cinderella myth is also linked to the relative status of women's feet: "Gloria Swanson's feet will never age," notes Ferragamo wistfully in his autobiography.[7] "The face and figure may show the telltale signs of advancing years; the feet remain youthful and beautiful."[8] Women's stockinged feet do have a resemblance to shoe lasts in the black and white photography of his era. That the custom shoemaker must handle them gently relates them also to Christian rites of supplication (here we must confess to our readers that we are good Catholic boys). Both Ferragamo and Blahnik write in ecstatic tones of the beauty of the undamaged foot, a foot uncorrupted by civilization – and bad shoes. Ferragamo's favorite foot was Mary Pickford's: "The joints inside her feet are like those of a baby … they are the most perfect feet in the world."[9] Blahnik prefers the feet of Sicilian youth worn smooth by walking barefoot in sand.[10]

THE MAKERS OF LIGHTNESS AND TRANSPARENCY

Both genders wear shoes, but they have developed different relationships with them. The most celebrated shoe designers of the twentieth century have helped to shape this gendered rhetoric and have focused their energy mostly on women. The height of the heel and the possibility of ornament in women's shoes are seen as providing more creative impetus to design as well as better profit. Again, this is an important shift that must be historically contextualized. For many centuries, shoes used to be about class as well as about gender. Most essays included in the first part of this book refer to this point. During the twentieth century, class and gender in shoes merged into a notion of "classed gender." And this gender was female; she was served her expensive shoes in surroundings of hushed luxury where the men were either subservient assistants or mere visitor-chaperones (Figure 19.4).

We owe to Benstock and Ferriss's edited volume, *Footnotes: On Shoes* (2001), many insights on the gendered (read "female") psychological side of shoes. *Shoes: A History from Sandals to Sneakers*, however, has pursued several lines of enquiry on the understanding of shoes. This has been necessary as we have tried to unravel time-embedded practices, culturally specific meanings and historical contingencies in the use of footwear. From the very functional aspect of women's shoes, this book has moved to discuss socially constructed notions of gender relations as negotiations of material artifacts. References have been given to the eroticization of the female foot in Europe as well as in Asia, and to the very specific affinity between footwear, design and ornament in the twentieth century. If the social and cultural have been central to our analysis of the "gendered shoe," the connection – as well as little-known interstices – between the psychological and the aesthetic has been an additional subject of concern in this volume.

Figure 19.4: A. Guillaume, At the Shoe Shop, 1927. Private Collection. © Snark/Art Resource, New York, ART183190.

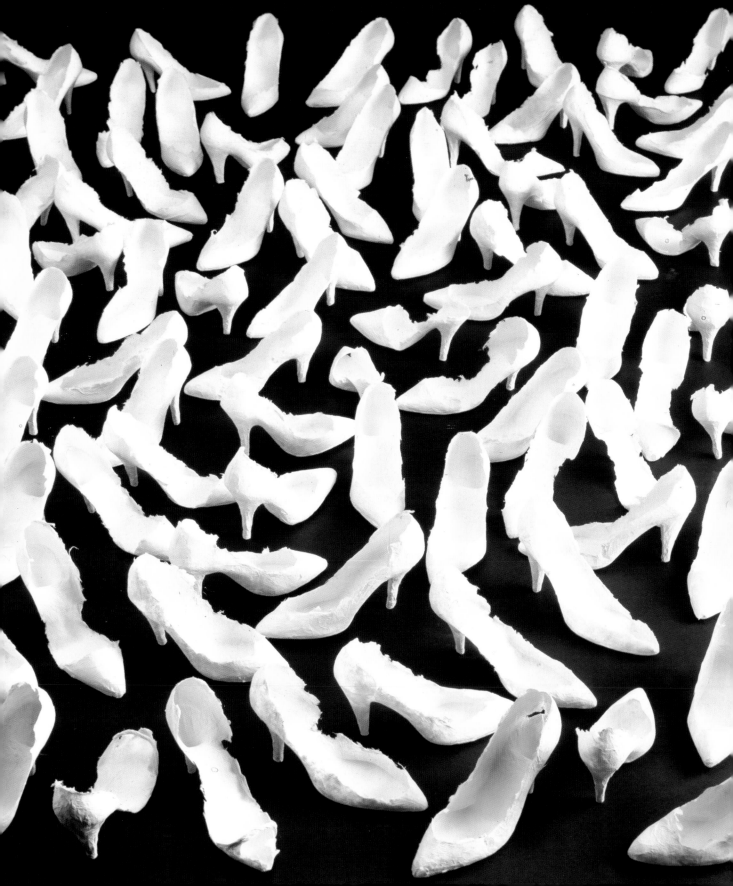

Perhaps the best-known case of such a match from heaven between the mental-emotional aspect of shoes and their visual and aesthetic nature is the "myth" of invention and inventiveness that surrounds shoes. The shoe designer as an artist is not only linked to the making of unique pieces, but also to the creation of ideas that transcend the physical nature of shoes (Figure 19.5). Salvatore Ferragamo's autobiography underlines the completely abject and socially unacceptable position of a cobbler in a small Italian village in the 1910s: "To be a shoemaker was a disgrace; it would bring the family into disrepute."[11] The low status of the shoemaker before the notion of high-fashion design is something that has been underplayed by the subsequent generation of shoe designers.

Whereas Ricci's chapter in this volume points to a network of patents, innovations and a determined strategy, Ferragamo underlines his narrative with a model of impossible struggle, faith in vocation and God, and the vagaries of the shoemaker. Ferragamo's claims that his specially designed shoes could cure cripples, infantile paralysis and elephantine obesity in society ladies where doctors had failed, suggest that he is transferring some of the hagiographic power of St Crispin to himself.[12] Many of the famed shoe designers of the twentieth century transcended their lowly family trade to become famous: Elizabeth Semmelhack's recent catalog lists André Perugia (1893–1977), who was the son of a cobbler; Charles Jourdan (1883–1976), a cutting-room foreman by day; and, more recently, Jimmy Choo (1961–), designer of shoes for Princess Diana among other stars, another success story who is descended from a family of shoemakers in Penang.[13]

Another of the narratives in Ferragamo's life, as accounted by Stefania Ricci, was his strife to create an "invisible" shoe, an act of fusion between foot and footwear, between nature and artifact. Lightness has been an unlikely point of strength, even for mass-produced sneakers in the late twentieth century. Nike's Air Jordan shoes, examined by Alison Gill, show us the promise of nearly superhuman athletic qualities, a reality far removed from the rubber and other synthetic materials that make the sports shoe.

The "rhetoric of lightness" in shoe fashion, particularly for women, has been carefully approached by distinguishing different historical contexts. The sandal-like Roman and Greek shoe adopted in neoclassical dress of the late eighteenth and early nineteenth centuries, was inspired by notions of nudity and purity and a new vision of light, "limpid" clothing as a fantasy that attempted to go beyond the limitations of standard forms. The dream was a shoe that was not encumbering, but spoke of freedom and liberation; hence the sandal for women, the flat slipper and the soft boot for men. It is interesting to note how this "rhetoric of lightness," as examined in Peter McNeil and Giorgio Riello's chapter, is actually quite different from its original concept in ancient Greece as explained in Sue Blundell's analysis. The symbolic and practical meaning of shoelessness, rather than of light shoes, was paramount in the construction of gendered and class identities in the ancient world.

FIGURE 19.5 (FACING PAGE): AS LIGHT AS PAPER. WHITE STILETTOS, INSTALLATION BY SUSAN CUTTS, 2001. THE ARTIST PLAYS WITH THE IDEA OF LIGHTNESS TO CONSTRUCT AN ARTWORK IN WHICH SHOES ARE SIMILAR TO DOVES. REPRODUCED BY KIND PERMISSION OF SUSAN CUTTS.

The narrative of the great *belle époque* and early twentieth-century shoe designers continued the idea of a shoe that appeared weighty in terms of historical allusion and material value, but which seemed weightless to lift, touch and wear. From the early work of Ferragamo in the 1930s to the more mainstream shoe fashion of the 1960s, lightness was achieved through the use of transparent plastic, invisible yarn and glass. The myth of the "glass shoe" is achieved through the invisibility of the support that then reshapes the body. This is beautifully illustrated by a clear vinyl boot with a solid vamp decorated with silver rhinestones, produced by Rayne in the early 1960s. The translucency of "plastic shoes" borrowed the theatricality and ideas from the cinema of the 1930s, mixing "camp" glamour, the visibility of the wearer and the invisibility of the shoe (Figure 19.6).

THE HORROR OF HEAVINESS

The history of shoes reveals that the past distinction between utilitarian and "disposable" shoes evaporated in the twentieth century. By disposable shoes we mean the type of ephemeral shoe that features in eighteenth- and early nineteenth-century erotic art depicting indoor or fantasy spaces and including mules and slippers (Figure 19.7). A trope of eroticism such as the mule gradually disappeared as a male garment and became associated with women. This does not mean that men's feet became de-eroticized; simply their appeal was more strictly linked to the "rhetoric of heaviness," from the military boot to the sado-macho boot of Tom of Finland. While men's shoes continue to rely on traditional materials such as heavy leather, preferably black, women's shoes have been the terrain of continuous experimentation, from "poor" materials such as canvas and rope to plastics, stones, metal wires, even recycled textiles and fabrics. If high-quality men's shoes pride themselves on the long-standing tradition of their makers, and models unchanged for decades, women's shoes are at the forefront of contemporary design practice.

This book indicates that men are very concerned with how they are shod. Yet the shoe museums and the extant objects prioritize women. This has been a difficult problem for a book whose aim is to provide a coherent analysis accompanied by visual support. Apart from a few striking examples, men might almost not exist in the shoe museum. The ordinary nature – or perhaps better to say the normative nature – of men's shoes makes them unremarkable objects to collect. Women's shoes, on the other hand, have all the right features to become collectors' items. Although we have insisted on designer wear and the importance of the shoe with provenance (the "unique" piece), women's shoes are collected also for other reasons. They are often tokens of memory and are left by mothers to daughters. Nineteenth-century wedding slippers survive in their thousands and are carefully preserved in old chests for generations to come. Other shoes are kept because of their inherent beauty or because of their decoration. A splendid pair of women's shoes such as the garnet silk boots with wheat-colored silk embroidery, produced by the famous Pinet in Paris in the late 1860s, suggests a possible avenue of analysis of women's shoes that is not inspired by innovative

FIGURE 19.6 (FACING PAGE): CLEAR VINYL BOOT WITH SOLID VAMP AND TOPLINE BAND DECORATED WITH SILVER RHINESTONES. PRODUCED BY RAYNE, LONDON, 1961–65. BATA SHOE MUSEUM, TORONTO, S97.125.AB. REPRODUCED BY KIND PERMISSION OF BATA SHOE MUSEUM.

"design," but by the pleasure of reiterating traditional decorative fields and iconography familiar to their wearers (Figure 19.8).

This book ends with a plea for further study on men's shoes. Curators and scholars have so far investigated men's footwear in relation to production issues, in particular the arrival of mass production in the late nineteenth and early twentieth centuries. The chapter by Alison Matthews David has made use of the vast collection of men's military boots at the Northampton Boot and Shoe Collection and relevant examples of high-design men's shoes have been included in Christopher Breward's chapter. The Musée International de la Chaussure in Romans, France, owns several exceptional pieces of menswear by companies such as UNIC, which need further study, in particular asymmetrical shoes and shoes that experimented with color and materials in the 1930s and 1940s.

Sneakers and a new breed of mixed sport-casual shoes present a challenge to established gendered notions of footwear. From the height of Dolce & Gabbana shoes to cheaper "youth brands," men's shoes are experimenting with a more innovative vocabulary of design solutions and materials, and are increasingly indulging in ornamentation, embellishment and conspicuous decoration. The decline of traditional men's shoemaking in British shoe centers such as Northampton has recently been captured in a film with the provocative title of *Kinky Boots* (2005), to signify how the demise of men's shoe production can only be replaced by less strict gendered notions of shoes both in consumption and production. Northamptonshire-based artist, Guy West, proposes in his *Absolut Stiletto* an eroticized shoe that plays on substitution (the red last instead of the main body of the shoe and a blade instead of the heel). The last, symbol of the very action of making, is now transformed into a concept: the idea of the shoe (Figure 19.9).

MALE CINDERELLAS

The idea of the shoe designer is so striking because it is the reversal of the iconography of the humble artisan, the cobbler or simple maker. Rather than being painted in the rustic surrounds of a simple cottage, with wicker birdcage, lasts, awls, measuring sticks and other tools of the trade, the male Cinderella – now proudly defined as a "designer of shoes" – is more likely to be styled in a Beatonesque fantasy among the baroque birdcages that featured in postwar fashion salons. Shoes are transposed to the polite environment of the exclusive boutique (Figure 19.10). Vivier, for example, was shot sitting on a verdant lawn, his shoe creations scattered around him like a jeweled carpet of paradise. Vivier for Dior often echoed or reproduced the fabric worn in the dress and wrap. This was not "modern" dress; it was "prescribed" dress, in which the shoe had to match the bag.

The rhetoric of strictness and "fantastic folly" surrounds the shoes of Yanturni – a real shoe mystery if there ever was one. Clearly a master mythmaker, Yanturni (1874–1936) was believed to have been a type of moonlighting museum curator, working in the Cluny Museum of the Middle Ages by day, and somehow crafting shoe gossamer of antique lace and crushed velvet by night. Alas, the myths and superstitions of shoe lore have a hard life thanks to the patient research of curators

Figure 19.7: Colored lithograph of young woman rising from bed with maid putting her slippers on her feet by Achille Deveria, c.1827–35. Bata Shoe Museum, Toronto, P.80.1560. Reproduced by kind permission of Bata Shoe Museum.

such as Marie-Josèphe Bossan and Elizabeth Semmelhack, who can pride themselves on having resolved the mythic nonsense that surrounds the great mystery of shoemaking. New research indicates another spelling for his name – Pietro Yantorny – and his origins as a shoemaker from the age of twelve.[14]

That it has taken so long for research to be conducted on Yanturni indicates the status of the shoe in fashion history: Ferragamo complained of the lack of attention paid to footwear within the costume history available in his day in his autobiography: "There were few examples shown, because it is a subject sadly neglected by the historians of fashion."[15] Ferragamo's autobiography included a dust jacket designed to underscore his ascendancy; it depicted a young boy at a cobbler's bench, his face cradled on the worktop in desperate tiredness. Ferragamo was no exception to a rule that wants all famous shoe designers to be born out of the "art of shoemaking." This is the type of art expressed through the vocabulary of craft, of familial traditions and secrets passed down from father to son (surely not from mother to daughter). Common in the lives of so many famous shoe designers of the twentieth century is also the happy-ending story of rags to riches: from shoemaking as an underappreciated artisanal occupation to success, fame and luxury, notwithstanding occasional downfalls, as in the case of Ferragamo. If fathers and grandfathers provide the right background in terms of skills, understanding of materials and customers, the twentieth-century shoe designer is often portrayed as a man of exceptional charisma, inventiveness and experimentation. Each of them is unique. They are all stars that will never shine again.

The very vocabulary of art is embodied in the frequent cross-references between designers, forming schools, movements and periods. It is not surprising to find that museums privilege "great" shoes, which generally means women's shoes of innovative form and texture (Figure 19.11). The analogy with sculpture is not hidden but rather foregrounded: that Jourdan trained as a sculptor is cited as evidence that shoes indeed are a type of art. Shoes are not art, but it is precisely the realm of art that continues to be evoked, with form and materials, by the great contemporary innovators such as Blahnik.

Various explanations are advanced for Blahnik's greatness. One is that he is a sculptor, hence the significance of the 1970s platforms, types of Donald Judd for the feet. Another explanation for Blahnik's success is that he makes women beautiful, and appear rich. As Patsy commented in the English television series *Absolutely Fabulous*: "These women with skeleton-like legs, walking in their Manolo Blahniks [and] wearing trenches down Sloane Street."[16] However, this is a general claim made for many shoe designers. Others point to a poetic dimension: "He is the Proust of shoes. Ugliness makes him bleed," states André Leon Talley (Figures 19.12 and 19.13).[17] All Blahnik shoes are named so that they are both "artworks" (sometimes autographed by the designer where the name cannot be rubbed off) and individual "personalities." Might he not be great because he resolves one of the debates of twentieth-century design: the relationship between

FIGURE 19.8 (FACING PAGE): GARNET SILK BOOTS WITH WHEAT-COLORED SILK EMBROIDERY PRODUCED BY PINET, PARIS, LATE 1860S. BATA SHOE MUSEUM, TORONTO, P.95.80.AB. REPRODUCED BY KIND PERMISSION OF BATA SHOE MUSEUM.

fashion object and ornament? Blahnik attempts to fuse the body with ornament in a new way. Tendrils seem to grow out of the legs, recalling the black and gold "Serpent" shoes designed by Ferragamo for Esther Ralston, "with golden scales painted as lifelike as I could make them, writhed halfway up her beautiful legs."[18] This is more apparent in the drawings than the product. Perhaps a part of the appeal of Blahnik is also the issue of the faux "bespoke"; many of his shoes appear very individual but are in fact produced in batches, not dissimilarly from Mannerist Madonnas crafted in their hundreds by famous Cinquecento artists with the help of their pupils. This is the individuation and endless novelty remarked upon by the fashion theorist Gilles Lipovetsky.[19]

Blahnik continues the tradition of allusion – historical, literary and mythological. Various forces are credited by those who enthuse about him, ranging from a love of Italian film to the photography of Cecil Beaton. His drawings reveal a type of poetic dimension – a metamorphosis between the vegetable, mineral and animal world – in which shoes are alchemical and mysterious. The rhetoric is similar to that of the fashion world of the nineteenth-century *demi-monde*, but the women's sexuality is not. In twentieth-century fashion, the sexual charge and attention to fashion associated with *demi-monde* culture seems to have been transferred to the 1950s model of the couturier such as Dior, and this intense personal interest in the maker of the shoe persists within shoe fashion.

Contemporary advertisers frequently present working women as modern-day Cinderellas, as in the case of a 2004 women-only credit-card campaign in Singapore directed at the working girl surrounded by her shoe wardrobe. The idea of Cinderella at the ball can also be evoked more subtly, as in the case of a pair of jewel-like shoes for a gala, remarkable for the integration of the detailing of satin, kid, and *diamanté* (Figure 19.11). Women are perhaps not so interested in John Galliano, but they like his clothes and bags, whereas the idea of Jimmy Choo or Manolo Blahnik creates both a frenzy of media copy and intense after-dinner conversation in cities as diverse as Kuching and Sydney. That characters such as Carrie in *Sex and the City* maintain that they can run in their Blahniks, continues to underscore the notion that great shoes are about beauty and lightness. Numerous women asked, while we were writing this book, whether women really can race in Blahniks. We doubt it; designers such as Louboutin state that women do not need to run anyway. Certainly the rise of the stiletto would seem to be a reversal of the rejection of feminine types elaborated by Chanel and her flat pumps, which were produced within a strict *chromatisme Chanel* of very limited colors.[20]

STEPPING OUT

The editors of this volume always wanted to "step out" in high heels. We do this with a very special white mule with "birdcage" stiletto heels now at the Bata Shoe Museum (Figure 19.14). It

FIGURE 19.9 (FACING PAGE): ABSOLUT STILETTO BY NORTHAMPTONSHIRE-BASED ARTIST GUY WEST, 2000. REPRODUCED BY KIND PERMISSION OF GUY WEST.

FIGURE 19.10 (FACING PAGE): LE MIGNON PETIT SOULIER: MODÈLE DE PERUGIA. POCHOIR PRINT, 1924–25. BATA SHOE MUSEUM, TORONTO, P.95.72. REPRODUCED BY KIND PERMISSION OF BATA SHOE MUSEUM.

FIGURE 19.11 (ABOVE): PAIR OF COURT SHOES IN BLACK DUCHESSE SATIN WITH FINE SILVER KID EDGE TRIM. THE VAMP IS DECORATED WITH A "BOW" FORMED ON THE TWO DIAMANTÉ-ENCRUSTED BALLS. THESE SHOES WERE PRODUCED IN THE EARLY 1950S BY PERUGIA FOR PRINCESS LILIAN OF BELGIUM, SECOND WIFE OF THE FORMER KING LEOPOLD III. BATA SHOE MUSEUM, TORONTO, P.04.34.AB. REPRODUCED BY KIND PERMISSION OF BATA SHOE MUSEUM.

Figure 19.12 (facing page): "Camata" gold court shoe by Manolo Blahnik. This shoe has a clear sculptural plastic form with restrained but evident decoration. Northampton Museums and Art Gallery, Boot and Shoe Collection, 2002.20. Reproduced by permission of Northampton Museums and Art Gallery.

Figure 19.13 (above): Gold mule by Manolo Blahnik, 1988. Northampton Museums and Art Gallery, Boot and Shoe Collection, L.571.7. Reproduced by permission of Northampton Museums and Art Gallery.

summarizes the idea of the downtrodden and isolated shoemaker, accompanied by his bird-companion, transformed to the international and erudite shoe designer, which our authors have considered in this book. The shoe also plays with the idea of the encasement of the female owner, and the possibility of new, transparent, open futures for fashion.

There is a photograph of Ferragamo peering through the crystal sole of one of his shoes, like a lens in a camera. Surely here he becomes the male Cinderella, who both creates and confirms magical identity: "No, it will not break as you walk," the caption reads.[21] Ferragamo imagined a shoe future in which there was a wardrobe of shoes "which is one shoe … She will be able to buy the uppers in any style and design and she will own a wardrobe which might otherwise have been far beyond her purse."[22] How ironic that such a "foundation shoe" and uppers has not been realized for the type of elegant day and evening wear imagined by Ferragamo; but that it has more or less been realized for the youth trainer market. The tool of the computer holds perhaps the greatest challenge to traditional shoe forms. Industrial designer William Tu's idea for a convertible/collapsing woman's shoe plays with the notion of the coquettish fan as well as employing a contemporary heel that contracts with six options to become a flat shoe for daywear (p. 425). Perhaps the tension of shoes for the future will be between the pull of conservatism – the high-heeled decorative shoe fit only for a princess-lady "so that every woman may be shod like a princess and a princess like a fairy queen"[23] – and the reality of a society which more and more espouses endless novelty, speed and change.

Figure 19.14: Pair of white mules with "birdcage" stiletto heel and birds, c. 1955–60, made by da Creazoni-Mariorty Anacapa, worn by a lady in the mid-1950s. She bought them as a novelty one summer and wore them "quite a bit until all her friends had seen them." Bata Shoe Museum, Toronto, S.95.48.A-D. Reproduced by kind permission of Bata Shoe Museum.

NOTES

Preface

1. Every effort has been made to contact copyright holders of images reproduced in this volume. If any copyright holders have not been properly acknowledged, please contact the publisher, who will be happy to rectify the omission in future editions.

Introduction: A Long Walk

1. Bilger, "Sole Survivor."
2. Wendy Parkins suggests that "dress is a situated bodily practice." Parkins, "Introduction," 5.
3. Johnson and Lennon, "Introduction," 2 and Barnes and Eicher, "Introduction," 1.
4. Perkins Gilman, *Dress of Women*, 46.
5. Solnit, *Wanderlust*, passim.
6. Jones, "Empty Shoes."
7. Sokoll, *Essex Pauper Letters*, 152.
8. Badouin, *De Calceo Antiquo*.
9. Gay, *Trivia*; Mercier, *Tableau*; Mercier, *Nouveau*; Rétif de la Bretonne, *Nuits de Paris*.
10. Goldsmith, *History of Little Goody Two-Shoes*.
11. Perrault, "Cinderella" and Andersen, "Red Shoes."
12. Diderot, and d'Alembert, *Encyclopédie*; Garsault, *Art du Cordonnier*.
13. Volumes inspired by Garsault were published also in the early nineteenth century by John Rees and the French bootmakers (father and son) Francou. Rees, *Art and Mystery of a Cordwainer*; Francou, and Francou, *Art du Bottier*.
14. Andry de Bois-Regard, *Orthopædia*; Sokosky, *Coup-d'Oeil sur les Imperfections de la Chaussure*; *The Art of Preserving the Feet*; Camper, *Abhandlung über die beste Form der Schuhe*. Camper's book was first translated into English as an appendix to another important work on the history of footwear by James Dowie published in 1861. Dowie, *Foot and Its Covering*.
15. *Crispin Anecdotes*. Anecdotal tradition has survived into the twentieth century with the publication of *The Romance of the Shoe* by Thomas

Wright in 1922, where the lives of distinguished shoemakers (turned poets or inventors) is intertwined with the history of shoemaking and shoe manufacturing in Britain and the progress of the "gentle craft."
16. Brown, *Sixty Years' Gleanings from Life's Harvest*.
17. Devlin, *Boot and Shoe Trade of France*; Devlin, *Shoemaker (Part 1)*; Devlin, *Shoemaker. The Guide to Trade (Part 2)*; Devlin, *Critica Crispiana*; Devlin, Contract Reform.
18. Thompson and Yeo (eds), *Unknown Mayhew*.
19. Hall, *Book of the Feet*.
20. Hall, *History and Manufacture of Boots and Shoes*.
21. Horlock, *A Few Words to Journeymen Shoemakers*; Sensfelder, *Histoire de la Cordonnerie*; Ratouis, *Théorie et Pratique de la Fabrication et du Commerce des Chaussures*; Ratouis, *Histoire de la Cordonnerie*.
22. Greig, *Ladies' Old-fashioned Shoes* and Greig, *Ladies' Dress Shoes*. Another interesting early twentieth-century book is Redfern's *Royal and Historic Gloves and Shoes*.
23. The Boot and Shoe Collection at Northampton Art Gallery: <www.northampton.gov.uk/site/scripts/documents_info.php?categoryID=1482&documentID=142>
24. The Musée International de la Chaussure – Romans: <www.villeromans.com/rubrique.php3?id_rubrique=64>
25. The Bata Shoe Museum:
26. The Deutsches Ledermuseum: <www.ledermuseum.de/index.html>
27. The Museo del Calzado: <www.sho.es/museo/>
28. The Ferragamo Museum:
29. Museo della Calzatura Bertolini di Vigevano: <www.comune.vigevano.pv.it/culturali/calzatura.html>. See also *Dalla Parte della Scarpa*. Museo della Calzatura dell'A.C.Ri.B. at Dolo near Venice: . The Marikina Shoe Museum, 10 miles south of Manila in the Philippines, was perhaps the most striking of them all, as it showed the collection of 3,000 shoes formerly belonging to Imelda

Marcos. The museum has recently closed. Torres, "Marikina Shoe Museum," unpublished paper courtesy Peter McNeil and Gerry Torres.
30. Wilson, *History of Shoe Fashions*; Brooke, *Footwear*; Swann, *Shoes*; Ledger, *Put your Foot Down*; Swann, *Shoemaking*; Grew and de Neergaard, *Shoes*; Swann, *History of Footwear*.
31. Rossi, *Sex of the Foot*; Steele, *Fetish*; Fontana, *100 Anni di Industria Calzaturiera*; Steele, *Shoes*; McDowell, *Manolo Blahnik*; Benstock and Ferris, *Footnotes*; Bossan, *Art of the Shoe*; Cox, *Stiletto*.

Chapter 1. Beneath their Shining Feet

1. The term "classical" is generally used to refer to the period 500 to 330 BC. Most of the evidence I shall be citing comes from this period. During this time, "Greece" consisted of hundreds of independent city-states, of which Athens was culturally one of the most active. Most of the visual and literary evidence for footwear comes from Athens. The evidence that exists for other states suggests that the styles and symbolism of Athenian footwear were to be found elsewhere in the Greek world.
2. A. A. Bryant's article, though written in 1899, is an invaluable catalog of the footwear terms used in Greek literature, and the contexts in which they appear. Bryant, "Greek Shoes." Katherine Morrow's book of 1985 provides a detailed chronological analysis of changing styles in the footwear that is represented in Greek sculpture. Morrow, *Greek Footwear*.
3. Some iron frames for wooden soles, and occasionally the wooden soles themselves, have been found in tombs of the sixth and fifth centuries BC.
4. Where particular vase paintings are referred to in the chapter, they appear in the Notes under the name of the city in which the collection is held (or the name of the city and of the museum, where there is more than one), and the catalog number. The best source for further information on these pieces is the Beazley Archive, at <www.beazley.ox.ac.uk>. If a painting

is illustrated in Kilmer, *Greek Erotica*, this is indicated in the note.
5. Plato, *Symposium*, 174A.
6. Xenophon, *Constitution of the Lacedaimonians*, 2.3.
7. Hence, for example, *lakonikai* or "Spartans," good-quality shoes or boots which were normally red in color, may actually have been exported from Sparta. See Aristophanes, *Wasps*, 1158–62, where an Athenian who is being forced to wear *lakonikai* complains that he is being made to tread on enemy soil.
8. Plato, *Republic*, 369D.
9. Plato, *Symposium*, 221E.
10. Lysias, *Speeches*, 24.20.
11. Diogenes Laertius, *Lives of the Philosophers*, 2.122.
12. Bryant, "Greek Shoes," 72.
13. Xenophon, *Hellenica*, 2.3.31.
14. Xenophon, *The Education of Cyrus*, 8.2.5.
15. Herodotus, *Histories*, 1.155.
16. Aristophanes, *Women Celebrating the Thesmophoria*, 253–68.
17. Aristophanes, *Women in the Assembly*, 74–5, 319, 345 and 508.
18. Pollux, *Vocabulary*, 7.86 and 7.92.
19. Demosthenes, *Against Conon*, 54.34.
20. Thucydides, *Histories*, 1.6.
21. Aristophanes, *Knights*, 319–21.
22. Oxford 1967.305. See Kilmer, *Greek Erotica*, R545.
23. See Homer, *Iliad*, 14.186 and *Odyssey*, 1.96.
24. Homer, *Iliad*, 2.42–6, 10.21–4.
25. Aeschylus, *Agamemnon*, 944–6.
26. Iamblichus, *Protrepticus*, 21.
27. See for example Munich 2646 and Florence 3949.
28. See Berlin 2286, and Florence 73749.
29. See Wurzburg 490, side A; Florence PD266, side A; New York, Metropolitan Museum of Art 96.18.131, side A; Vienna 2150, side B.
30. For example, Athens, NAM 1659; Boston 95.1402; New York, Metropolitan Museum of Art 19.192.86; London, British Museum E774; and Petersburg, Hermitage 179. See Oakley and Sinos, *Wedding in Ancient Athens*, 67 (figs. 30 and 31), 68 (fig. 35), and 76 (fig. 44).

31. Säflund, *East Pediment*, p. 87 (fig. 42), and pp. 105–7.

32. Burkert, *Lore and Science*, 172, 177–8; Ogden, "Controlling Women's Dress," 214.

33. Callimachus, *Hymns*, 6.124–5.

34. Morrow, *Greek Footwear*, 3–22 and 185–8.

35. See <www.elsevie.gr/Elsevie HomeEN/services/history>.

36. Chrysostom, *Homily*, VIII on I *Timothy*.

37. See Richter, *Korai*, figs. 364–5, 375–6.

38. Xenophon, *Treatise on Household Management*, 10.2.

39. Aristophanes, *Lysistrata*, 42–8.

40. Aristophanes, *Lysistrata*, 414–19.

41. Athenaeus, *Banquet of the Sages*, 568a.

42. Clement of Alexandria, *Paedagogus*, 2.11.116. A terracotta vase in the form of a sandal with the injunction "follow" on its sole has also been found in Lower Egypt, dating from the second century BC (the Graeco-Roman period). See Elderkin, "Hero on a Sandal," 385.

43. See, for example, Paris, Louvre G13; Orvieto 585; Florence 3921; and Milan A8037. See Kilmer, *Greek Erotica*, R156A, R486B, R518B (ii), and R530. See also a lost cup illustrated at R490 A & B.

44. On shoes besides washbasins see Munich 2411; Syracuse 20065; and Paris, Louvre G291. See Kilmer, *Greek Erotica*, R454 I. On shoes underneath couches where there is sexual activity see London, British Museum E68 (*Greek Erotica*, R514B); Paris, Louvre G81 (*Greek Erotica*, R495); Florence 73749 (*Greek Erotica*, R493A and B); Boston 95.61 (*Greek Erotica*, R223A).

45. See Paris, Louvre G549 and L60.

46. Once Berlin (East) 2272. In Kilmer, *Greek Erotica*, R77.

47. See Amelung, "Rito," 115–35; Brelich, "Monosandales," 469–89; Deonna, "Monokrepides," 50–72; and Edmunds, "Thucydides," 71–5.

48. Pindar, *Pythian Odes*, 4.75–77, 96.

49. Thucydides, *Histories*, 3.22.

50. See Gazda (ed.), *Villa of the Mysteries*, color plate 1.

51. Vidal-Naquet, *Black Hunter*, 64, 69–70.

Chapter 2. Sumptuous Shoes
This chapter has been translated from Italian by Giorgio Riello and Peter McNeil.

1. Orme, *Medieval Children*, especially pp. 73–5.

2. For useful analysis of the archaeological evidence for shoes, see Grew and De Neergard, *Shoes and Pattens*.

3. See Cosentino, *Osteoporosi e Invalidità Motorie*.

4. Fiorentioni Capitani and Ricci, "Considerazioni sull' Abbigliamento," 53.

5. Muzzarelli, *Guardaroba Medievale*, 192–204, in particular p. 194.

6. Mariacher, "L'Arte dei Calzolai a Venezia," 36.

7. "Sfiorano la terra solo con la punta dei piedi quando indossano le scarpe allungate sulle punte." Eiximenis, *Estetica Medievale*, 73.

8. Eiximenis, *Estetica Medievale*, 73.

9. Vianello, "Storia Sociale della Calzatura," 627–34.

10. Muzzarelli, "Le Leggi Suntuarie."

11. Muzzarelli and Campanili (eds), *Disciplinare il Lusso*.

12. Muzzarelli (ed.), *La Legislazione Suntuaria*.

13. Muzzarelli (ed.), *La Legislazione Suntuaria*, 214.

14. Muzzarelli (ed.), *La Legislazione Suntuaria*, 409.

15. Muzzarelli (ed.), *La Legislazione Suntuaria*, 131. The law established the same fine for producers and consumers in order to prevent the former ignoring the law in search of an easy profit.

16. Ottavini and Maria (eds), *La Legislazione Suntuaria*, 182.

17. "Di drappo con passamano di seta o filosello del medesimo colore senza alcun altro ornamento." Ottavini and Maria (eds), *La Legislazione Suntuaria*, 194.

18. Muzzarelli (ed.), *La Legislazione Suntuaria*, 329 and 330.

19. Muzzarelli (ed.), *La Legislazione Suntuaria*, 333 and 335.

20. Polidori Calamandrei, *Le Vesti delle Donne*, 96.

21. Similarly, in 1313 the shoemakers of Reggio Emilia asked the chief of the city (*Capitano del Popolo*) to provide a precise model that could be adopted to measure all shoes produced in the city, and that such a model should be sculpted and displayed in a public place where everyone could see it. *Liber Grossus Antiquus Comunis Regii*, vi, 157–59.

22. Ottavini and Maria (eds), *La Legislazione Suntuaria*, 832.

23. "Fuit reformatum quod unicuique liceat portare planellas ad sui libitum quo ad altitudinem." Ottavini and Maria (eds), *La Legislazione Suntuaria*, 1075.

24. Butazzi, "Un Paio di Pianelle."

25. Butazzi, "Un Paio di Pianelle," 340.

26. *Kodansha. Enciclopedia del Giappone.*

27. Orsi Landini and Niccoli, *Moda a Firenze 1540–1580*, 143–45.

28. Levi Pisetzky, *Storia del Costume*, ii, 282–83.

29. Vianello, "Storia Sociale della Calzatura," 644.

30. Castiglione, *Il Libro del Cortegiano*, l.I, XL, 88.

31. Tertullian, *De Cultu Feminarum*. For an English translation see: <www.tertullian.org/works/de_cultu_feminarum.htm>

32. "Gloria in vestimenti, in pianelle alte, in rete, in gabioti, in capilli, in annele…e altre vanità." Biblioteca Comunale Ariostea, Ferrara, S. 15 III 9: Bernardino da Feltre (attributed), "Confessione Generale Molto Utilissima."

33. "Facto ornamenti de donna vani come é la coda, scarpe rossi, pani frapati e rechamati." Bellotti (ed.), *Interrogatorio Volgare Compendioso et Copioso*, 161.

34. Exceptions were made for the footwear worn by the powerful. In Venice, for instance, where elegance was more important than moral obedience, the Doge's shoes were red, as they were henceforth for most monarchs and court members throughout Europe.

35. Levi Pisetzky, *Il Costume e la Moda*, 171.

36. Piponnier and Mane, *Se Vetir au Moyen Age*, 87.

37. Burgelin, "Abbigliamento."

38. "Portare calighe da soldato, massimamente se lunghe, spettando questa maniera di calzari principalmente ed esclusivamente agli uomini. Posto pure che le calighe non fossero troppo lunghe, non per questo si possono concedere alle donne calzari militareschi per ornamento delle tibie, giacché… le donne devono mostrare maggiore umiltà ed onestà degli uomini." Giovanni da Capestrano, *Degli Ornamenti*, 63.

39. Giovanni da Capestrano, *Degli Ornamenti*, 66.

40. Levi Pisetzky, *Storia del Costume*, ii, 145–46.

41. Kybalova, Herbenova and Lamarova, *Enciclopedia Illustrata della Moda*, 116.

42. Kybalova, Herbenova and Lamarova, *Enciclopedia Illustrata della Moda*, 116.

43. Fabrics were another important material used in the manufacturing of footwear, and expensive examples were often embroidered or inset with precious textiles.

44. Archivio di Stato di Bologna, reg. perg. 11 c: "Callegari, Statuti 1340–46."

45. Tosi Brandi, *Abbigliamento e Società*, 119–23.

46. Grew and De Neergard, *Shoes and Pattens*, 102.

47. Tosi Brandi, *Abbigliamento e Società*, 121.

48. Albertani, "Lo Statuto di Bolzano del 1437," 84.

49. Levi Pisetzky, *Storia del Costume*, ii, 375.

50. "Vel aliqui facientes vel vendentes scarpas vel calzarios."

51. In medieval monetary systems, the *lira* was composed of *soldi*. Up to twelve *denari* made one *soldo*.

52. Levi Pisetzky, *Storia del Costume*, ii, 487.

53. Pertegato, "Tecniche di Lavorazione," 347–54.

54. Butazzi, "Un Paio di Pianelle," 343.

55. "I stenti e le bugie sono communi a loro, come a tutte le sorti di genti che serva ad altri, perché oggidì i lavori vanno con tanta fraude che malamente s'abbattiamo in uno che voglia dire il vero." Garzoni, *La Piazza Universale*, 1346.

56. "D'ornamento a tutto il mondo in generale, perché tutti compariscono lesti e garbati con un bel par di scarpe in piede, o siano alla spaguola o alla napolitana o alla savoina, over

con un par di pianelle o di zoccoli belli, come s'usa a' tempi nostri." Garzoni, *La Piazza Universale*, 1346.

Chapter 3. Courtly Lady or Courtesan?

1. Ruskin, *St Mark's Rest*, 211–23.

2. Selvatico and Lazzari, *Guida Artistica e Storica di Venezia*, 99; Ludwig and Molmenti, *Vittore Carpaccio*, 281–2.

3. It has been determined that the painting was originally a pendant to *Hunting on the Lagoon* (J. Paul Getty Museum, Los Angeles). The Torellas' coat of arms seems also to indicate that the two women were members of that noble family. On Ruskin's interpretation of this painting, see Schuler, "Courtesan in Art," 210–12. On the subject of the titling of this painting, see Polignano, "Maliarde e Cortigiane," 5–23.

4. Polignano, "Maliarde e Cortigiane," 14.

5. Extending Riegl's use of iconography from emblem to sign, Panofsky distinguished between the primary meaning of the discarded wooden pattens as protective footwear and the secondary or iconographic meaning, Panofsky's "disguised symbolism," as evidence of sacred ground. See Hall, *Arnolfini Betrothal*, 106–12.

6. Linda Seidel argued that Giovanni's discarded pattens are a sign that he had entered the bedchamber, about to consummate the marriage. Hall, *Arnolfini Betrothal*, 103. Whereas Panofsky drew a link between discarded wooden pattens and God's command to Moses from the burning bush to remove his shoes on sacred ground, Hall argues instead that they signal "clothing of estate" or high status (Hall, *Arnolfini Betrothal*, 106–12). He describes their use at the court of Philip the Good as "apparently an honorific accoutrement with a value inversely proportional to their cumbersomeness and lack of purpose when worn indoors, although it is amusing to contemplate the clatter that must have accompanied the passage of these courtiers through the ducal residence." Hall, *Arnolfini Betrothal*, 111.

7. The word *zoccola* is derived from a cross between a diminutive of the Latin *sorex* (rat) and the Italian *zoccolo*.

8. Ruskin wrote the following Hogarthian view of the role of the artist: "I suppose him to have been commissioned to paint the portraits of the two Venetian ladies – that he did not altogether like his models, but yet felt himself bound to do his best for them and contrived to do what perfectly satisfies them and himself too ... It may be, however, that I err in supposing the picture a portrait commission. It may be simply a study for practice gathering together every kind of thing which he could get to sit to him quietly, persuading the pretty ladies to sit to him in all their finery, and to keep their pets quiet as long as they could, while yet he gave value to this new group of studies in a certain unity of satire against the vices of society in his time." Ruskin, *St Mark's Rest*, 211.

9. Ruskin, *St Mark's Rest*, 213.

10. Roche, *Culture of Clothing*, 144.

11. Barni and Fasoli, *Italia nell'Alto Medioevo*, 299–301 and 818; Cecchelli, *Vita di Roma nel Medio Evo*, 810.

12. See Butazzi, "Un Paio di Pianelle," 338–9 and Archivio di Stato di Venezia, "Atti diversi," manuscripts, b. 134, n. 5 bis, cc. 11v–12r.

13. See Butazzi, "Un Paio di Pianelle," p. 340. Historians of costume are still debating the origins of this fashion. Traditionally they have been located in the Middle East, where the Turkish women used a "bridge" form of shoes called *kubkab* at the baths. This idea could have been imported into Europe by the Venetians, who called them *patiti*, which may then have become chopines. Other historians believe instead that these shoes were originally invented in Spain, where there was an abundance of cork, the material mostly used for the soles. On this subject see Vianello, "Storia della Calzatura," 642–3.

14. See Vianello, *Arte dei Calegheri*, 18–21.

15. On this topic see Muzzarelli's chapter in this volume.

16. Butazzi, "Un Paio di Pianelle,"

338–9; and Muzzarelli, *Guardaroba Medievale*, 96.

17. Frick, *Dressing Renaissance Florence*, 184.

18. Cited in Levi Pisetzky, *Storia del Costume in Italia*, iii, 85.

19. Cited in Levi Pisetzky, *Storia del Costume in Italia*, iii, 82.

20. Levi Pisetzky, *Storia del Costume in Italia*, ii, 146.

21. Jacopone da Todi is cited in Malabarba, *Ai Piedi di una Donna*, 17.

22. Cited in Urbani De Gheltoff, *Di una Singolare Calzatura*, 7. For the Florentines' *pianelle*, see Calimandrei Polidori, *Vesti delle Fiorentine*, 96.

23. Muzzarelli, *Inganni delle Apparenze*, 172 and 180–1.

24. This law has been published in *Intorno alla Acconciatura del Capo*. A similar law forbidding shoemakers to sell shoes taller than an "arm" was promulgated in Florence in 1384. See Levi Pisetzky, *Storia del Costume*, ii, 146.

25. Anderson, "Chopine," 38.

26. Casola, *Viaggio a Gerusalemme*, 100–1.

27. Cited in Davis, "Geography of Gender," 33–4.

28. Cited in Levi Pisetzky, *Storia del Costume in Italia*, ii, 284.

29. Calamandrei Polidori, *Vesti delle Donne Fiorentine*, 96.

30. Anderson, "Chopine," 38.

31. Vecellio, *Habiti Antichi et Moderni*, 146.

32. Reproduced also in Levi Pisetzky, *Storia del Costume in Italia*, iii, fig. 31.

33. *Venetian Woman with Movable Skirt*, Metropolitan Museum of Art, New York: Elisha Whittelsey Collection, The Elisha Whittelsey Fund, 1955 (55.503.30).

34. Garber, *Vested Interests*.

35. *Portrait of Woman as Cleopatra*, The Walters Art Museum of Baltimore, Maryland, 37.534.

36. Vecellio, *Habiti Antichi et Moderni*, 97.

37. Vecellio, *Habiti Antichi et Moderni*, 100, 130 and 138. Indeed, when Fabrizio Caroso published his dance manual called *Nobiltà di Dame* (1605, a revised

edition of the original manual printed in 1581), he added instructions for using chopines that were one and a half handspans tall, but nevertheless explained how to move the feet while walking in order to give the impression that they were instead a more modest three fingers thick, thus implying that this was the limit for a true lady (*dama*). See Caroso, *Nobiltà di Dame*, 75–6.

38. Laughran, "'Infecting Souls and Sickening Bodies."

39. Timmons, "Habiti Antichi et Moderni," 28 and 30.

40. The citation accompanies the engraving *Image of the Women at Home*, but Vecellio explains in the description that they were actually courtesans at home. Vecellio, *Habiti Antichi et Moderni*, 143. On the problems of distinguishing between courtesans and prostitutes, see Ruggiero, *Binding Passions*, 32–48.

41. Garzoni, *Piazza Universale*, ii, 1346 and notes.

42. Moryson, *Itinerary*, iv, part 1, 172.

43. Evelyn, *Diary of John Evelyn*, 227–8.

44. Romano, "Gondola as a Marker of Station," 360.

45. See the collection of anecdotes and laws preserved in the Biblioteca of the Museo Correr, "Codice Gradenigo," n. 189, c. 84r.

46. Vianello, *Arte dei Calegheri*, 20–1.

47. Biblioteca of the Museo Correr, "Codice Gradenigo," n. 189, c. 86v.

48. See de Limojon de Saint Disdier, *Ville et la Republique de Venice*, 303. For Richard Lassels see Davis, "Geography of Gender," 35.

49. Davis, "Geography of Gender," 36.

50. Squicciarino, *Vestito Parla*, 87.

51. Chojnacki, "Power of Love," 158–9.

52. Davis, "Geography of Gender," 36.

53. For Tarabotti's *Antisatira* see Levy Pisetzky, *Storia del Costume*, iii, 373.

Chapter 4. Walking the Streets of London and Paris

A version of this chapter appeared in *Fashion Theory*, 9 (2) (2005) as "The Art and Science of Walking: Gender, Space and the Fashionable

Body in the Long Eighteenth Century."

1. Benstock and Ferriss (eds), *Footnotes*.

2. Silverman, "Fragments."

3. Ribeiro, "Fashion in the Eighteenth Century."

4. Brewer, *Common People and Politics*; *English Satirical Print*; Duffy, *Englishman and the Foreigner*.

5. Ogborn, *Spaces of Modernity*; Ogborn, "Georgian Geographies?"; Brewer, "Lights in Space"; Ogborn and Withers, "Introduction."

6. Stobart, "Shopping Streets"; Stobart, "Culture Versus Commerce."

7. Solnit, *Wanderlust*, 177–81.

8. Bills, "William Powell Frith."

9. Gay, *Trivia*. This was no longer the case at the end of the eighteenth century, when both Rétif de la Bretonne and Mercier investigated the urban fabric of Paris by walking through the city. Rétif de la Bretonne, *Nuits de Paris* and Mercier, *Tableau de Paris*.

10. Borsay, "Rise of the Promenade"; Corfield, "Walking the City Streets."

11. Von la Roche, *Sophie in London*.

12. Bedarida and Sutcliffe, "Streets," 385–6.

13. Brewer, *Pleasures of the Imagination*, 56–68.

14. Rendell, *Pursuit of Pleasure*, 21–4.

15. Gowing, "Freedom of the Street"; Marriot, "Spatiality of the Poor."

16. Roche, *Culture of Clothing*, 53.

17. Chrisman, "Émigration à la Mode."

18. Campbell, *London Tradesman*, 218; de Garsault, *Art du Cordonnier*, Rees, *Art and Mystery*.

19. Bossan, *Art of the Shoe*, 51–7.

20. *Nouvelle Encyclopédie*, 217. The *Nouvelle Encyclopédie* of 1824 was an updated version of Garsault's 1767 text and as such it included a clog overshoe which by that time was mostly out of fashion.

21. Harvey, *Men in Black*. For a critique on the longue durée see Kuchta, *Three-piece Suit*.

22. Silverman, "Fragments," 139.

23. Perrot, *Fashioning the Bourgeoisie*, 70–3.

24. Boucher, *History of Costume in the West*, 305.

25. *Monthly Magazine*, October 1806.

26. Ribeiro, *Dress in Eighteenth-Century Europe*; Steele, *Paris Fashion*.

27. Garsault, *Art du Tailleur*, 31; Crowston, *Fabricating Women*, 24–73.

28. Ribeiro, "On Englishness in Dress," 15–17.

29. *The Life of the Right Honorable Charles James Fox*, 18.

30. Rauser, "Hair, Authenticity," 101–2.

31. McNeil, "Fashion Victims," ii, plates.

32. Smollett, *Travels*, 120.

33. *The French Dancing-Master*.

34. *The Baboon A-la-Mode*, 4.

35. Straub, *Sexual Suspects*, 62–3.

36. "Character of a Macaroni," *The Town and Country Magazine*, vol. IV, May 1772, 243.

37. McNeil, "Macaroni Masculinities."

38. Fine and Leopold, "Consumerism."

39. Richardson, *Pamela, or, Virtue Rewarded…*, vol. II, 122.

40. Moritz, *Journeys of a German in England*, 61.

41. Burke, *Fortunes of the Courtier*, 124–32.

42. Hughes and Hughes, *Georgian Buckles*.

43. Merrick, "Commissioner Foucault," 297.

44. *Appeal From the Buckle Trade of London*, 2.

45. Riello, "La Chaussure à la Mode," 107–9.

46. Ashelford, *Art of Dress*, 176–7.

47. Ledger, *Put Your Foot Down*. 101–43; J. Swann, *Shoemaking*, 15.

48. Riello, "Chaussure à la Mode," 116 and Riello, *Foot in the Past*, ch. 7.

49. Vaughan, *Essay Philosophical and Medical*, 28.

50. Vaughan, *Essay Philosophical and Medical*, 91.

51. 15 December 1785, 19.

52. Vigarello, *Concepts of Cleanliness*.

53. Feher et al. (eds), *Fragments*; Herdt (ed.), *Third Sex Third Gender*.

54. Entwistle, *Fashioned Body*.

55. Cit. in Ribeiro, *Fashion in the French Revolution*, 132.

56. Vaughan, *Essay Philosophical and Medical*, 45–6.

57. *The Art of Preserving the Feet*, 196.

58. *Crispin Anecdotes*, 11.

59. Breward, *Fashioning London*.

60. Rousseau, *Emile*, 405.

61. Roche, *Culture of Clothing*, 38.

62. *Almanach des Modes*, 154–5.

Chapter 5. War and Wellingtons
A warm thank you to Sue Constable at the Northampton Boot and Shoe Collection for her generosity and invaluable assistance with this project. Thanks also to Giorgio Riello, Peter McNeil, Hilary Davidson, Barbara Burman, Jonathan White, Jackie Clarke, the staff at Stratfield Saye, and Major Beresford of the Royal Hussars Museum, Winchester.

1. Balzac, "Théorie de la Démarche," 175.

2. Rolt, *Moral Command*, 87.

3. *The Soldier's Companion*, n.p.

4. Any music played by military bands was in marching tempos and drum majors were instructed to make sure they kept perfect time with a metronome. Myerly, *British Military Spectacle*, 74.

5. Kipling, *Complete Verse*, 378.

6. Matthews David, "Decorated Men," 20.

7. Wells was the son of a shopkeeper and spent his childhood in an underground kitchen: "So that, when I looked out of the window, instead of seeing – as children of a higher upbringing would do – the heads and bodies of people, I saw their under side. I got acquainted indeed with all sorts of social types as boots simply, indeed, as the soles of boots; and only subsequently, and with care, have I fitted heads, bodies, and legs to these pediments." Wells, *Misery of Boots*, 1–2.

8. Dowie, *Foot and its Covering*, 167.

9. Clements, *Marc Isambard Brunel*, 52.

10. Thornton, "Brunel the Bootmaker," 2.

11. Summerville, *March of Death*, 115.

12. Clements, *Marc Isambard Brunel*, 52.

13. For drawings of Brunel's shoemaking machinery see Mounfield, "Early Technological Innovation," 133.

14. Rabinbach, *The Human Motor*.

15. Northampton Boot and Shoe Collection, 1955–56.1 Other caches of boots have been discovered in this way. For example, images of the Ripley Cache feature on the website of the University of Southampton Textile Conservation Centre <www.concealedgarments.org>.

16. Dowie, *Foot and its Covering*, 164.

17. Lemire, *Dress, Culture and Commerce*, 11.

18. Alison Matthews David, "Cutting a Figure."

19. Scott, *Gender and the Politics of History*, 99.

20. Luchet, *Art Industriel*, 379.

21. Luchet, *Art Industriel*, 209.

22. Luchet, *Art Industriel*, 160.

23. See Maynard's *Fashioned from Penury* for a discussion of the effects of badly sized shoes on both the navy and Australian convicts alike.

24. See Russell's *Russell's Despatches*, and Lambert and Badsey, *War Correspondents*.

25. Dallas, "Soldier's Duty," cited in Kerr, Pye, Cherfas, Gold and Mulvihill, *Crimean War*, 102.

26. *Daily Mail*, January 26, 1855, cited in Dowie, *Foot and its Covering*, 167.

27. Devlin, *Contract Reform*, 13.

28. Baudens, *Military and Camp Hospitals*, 23.

29. Rabinbach, *The Human Motor*, chs. 8 and 9.

30. Munson, *Theory and Practice of Military Hygiene*, 48.

31. Hacking, *Taming of Chance*, 105–14.

32. Runting, *First Aid*, 4.

33. Swaysland, *Boot and Shoe Design*, 8.

34. The Northampton Boot and Shoe Collection holds an unparalleled collection of these sealed pattern First World War boots, including boots produced for several Allied nations.

35. The term "Derby" is still used for a lace-up boot or shoe and is more informal in style than the Oxford.

36. "A chrome tan was substituted for the vegetable tan, with the result that leather could be produced in a month, whereas formerly it took a

year." Anonymous, "60,000 pairs of Army Boots a day," *The Times*, September 16, 1915, 5.

37. Munson, *Theory and Practice*, 90.

38. Special correspondent, "England in Time of War. XII Northampton Boots and Billets," *The Times*, January 2, 1915, 3.

39. The OED defines trench foot as a painful condition of the feet caused by prolonged immersion in cold water or mud, marked by swelling, blistering, and some degree of necrosis.

40. Imperial War Museum, Manuscript 02/43/1: "Stevens."

41. Craik, *Uniforms Exposed*, 21–50.

42. Matthews David, "Decorated Men."

43. *The Whole Art of Dress*, 56.

44. Zacharie, *Surgical and Practical Observations*, 81.

45. Zacharie, *Surgical and Practical Observations*, 85.

46. Myerly, *British Military Spectacle*, 27.

47. Devlin, *Boot and Shoe Trade*, 45.

48. Although Wellington defeated Napoleon on the battlefield, twenty years later French boot and shoe imports outperformed British manufacture of Wellington boots in the marketplace. See Devlin, *Boot and Shoe Trade* and Riello, "*La Chaussure à la Mode*."

49. Wellesley and Steegman, *Iconography*, ix.

50. "Fancy Costume and the Regimentals of the Army," *Gentleman's Magazine*, May 1828, 7.

51. It is outside the scope of this chapter to explore the "domestication" of the Welly, but it seems to have lost its martial connotations when made from rubber rather than leather. The Rubber Growers' Association, *Rubber and Footwear*.

52. Breward, *Fashioning London*, 21–48.

53. Longford, *Wellington*, 131.

54. Hesketh-Pritchard, *Sniping in France*, 33.

55. Webb-Johnson, *Soldiers' Feet*, 2.

56. Webb-Johnson, *Soldiers' Feet*, 8.

Chapter 6. The Perils of Choice

1. A wedding shoe dated 1812, now in the Danvers (MA) Historical Society, bears two different labels, one added by the maker ("particularly made for retailing by Warren Perkins, Reading"), the other by the Boston retailer ("made in particular for Josiah Vose's shoe store").

2. While pattens and clogs were available early on and rubbers after 1825, none of these were fashionable. For warmth in a carriage, stylish women wore overshoes of velvet or of knitted wool, sometimes lined with fleece and trimmed with fur.

3. Trollope, *Domestic Manners*, 300.

4. Flint, "Travellers in America," 289.

5. Trollope, *Domestic Manners*, 300, in an editorial note quoting the Cincinnati *Mirror and Ladies' Parterre*, August 13, 1832.

6. See McNeil and Riello, "Art and Science of Walking."

7. Front-lacing nankeen boots bound with green silk, c. 1805–1815, said to have been worn by Sally or Betsy Nichols, daughters of a wealthy merchant of Salem, MA. Peabody Essex Museum, catalog #123,580.

8. Riello, "*La Chaussure à la Mode*."

9. "Chit-Chat upon Watering-Place Fashions," *Godey's Lady's Book*, July 1850.

10. Zakim, "Sartorial Ideologies." See also Zakim, *Ready-Made Democracy*.

11. Sand, *Story of My Life*, 203–4.

12. *Harper's New Monthly Magazine*, April 1856, 714.

13. "Editor's table," *Godey's Lady's Book*, January 1843, 56.

14. *Demorest's*, Spring-Summer 1883, 71.

15. "Editor's table," *Godey's Lady's Book*, January 1843, 57.

16. "Dress in Rural Districts," *Godey's Lady's Book*, September 1849, 228.

17. "Dress in Rural Districts."

18. Mrs. A. M. F. Annan, "The Cheap Dress," *Godey's Lady's Book*, September 1845, 89.

19. *Godey's Lady's Book*, July 1857, 196.

20. *Godey's Lady's Book*, February 1860.

21. Saguto, "The Wooden Shoe Peg," 8–9, quoting J. Leander Bishop, *A History of American Manufactures From 1608–1860* (Philadelphia, 1868, reprinted by Johnson Reprint Corporation, N.Y. & London, 1968), vol. 2, 509.

22. Blewett, *We Will Rise in Our Might*.

23. "Shoe Shopping – the Congress Boot," *Godey's Lady's Book*, August 1848, 119–120.

24. "Street Shoes," *Shoe and Leather Lexicon*, 1916, 62.

25. "Over-Styling and Over-Capacity," *Shoe Retailer*, January 20, 1923, 63.

26. "The Retailer as Style Arbiter," *Shoe Retailer*, September 15, 1923, 46.

27. *Ladies' World*, December 1899, 27.

28. *Shoe Retailer*, June 1900, 33.

29. "Now for Tennis Shoes," *Shoe Retailer*, May 1900, 34.

30. For a catalog of mid- to late twentieth-century "tribal styles," see Polhemus, *Streetstyle*.

Chapter 7. Purity, Pollution and Place

1. Rice cultivation also began in Japan during the Yayoi period.

2. *Mono-i-gutsu* were worn by mounted archers. *Tsuranuki* still had the fur attached and were generally replaced by *waraji* after the Kamakura period (1185–1333). Hunters and other professional groups sometimes wore leather shoes with iron spikes, also called *Tsuranuki*, because they were derived from the *tsuranuki* worn by warriors.

3. Yanagita, *Meiji Taisho*, 28.

4. Takekoshi, *Economic Aspects*, vol. III, 171.

5. Sadler, *Short History*, 5.

6. Seiki, *Art of Japanese Joinery*, 8.

7. Coaldrake, *Way of the Carpenter*, 9–10.

8. Nitschke, *From Shinto to Ando-Studies*, 35.

9. Quoted in Koizumi, *Dōgu to kurashi*, 186.

10. The original saying was based on the story of Daoist Immortal chokaro (chang-kuo-lao), who could produce a magic horse out of a gourd, which would travel great distances in a single day. Chokarao is also remembered for resisting the corrupt administration of Chinese Emperor Xuan-zong in the eighth century.

11. Kitagawa, *Morisada mankō*, vol. 5, 27. Another story is that *koma-geta* were popularized by a prostitute named Fuyō in the employ of Hishiya Gonzaemon. De Becker, *Nightless City*, 195–6.

12. De Becker, *Nightless City*, 141.

13. When wearing *sōkai* or in certain indoor situations, Zen monks still wear the pocketless style, which are known as *bessu*.

14. Yamakawa, *Women of the Mito Domain*, 43.

15. Kitagawa, *Morisada mankō*, vol. ii, 276, 279–80.

16. Another example of the belief that *geta* had protective properties was that it was thought that by writing on them in ink, the wearer would be protected from foxes.

17. Akita, *Geta – kami no hakimono*, 93–7.

18. De Becker, *Nightless City*, 146.

19. A pleated, split, skirt-like garment worn over a kimono.

20. *The Pillow Book*, 262.

21. Rodrigues, *João Rodrigues's Account*, 186–7.

22. Boxer (ed.), *True Description*, 56.

23. Rodrigues, *João Rodrigues's Account*, 146.

24. Doeff, *Recollections*, 81.

25. Kitagawa, *Morisada mankō*, v, 17–18, 31.

26. Smith, "Japanese Village," 13.

27. Inui, *Edo no shokunin*, 78.

28. Deerskin was the preferred leather for the manufacture of footwear and it became a significant item of import in early modern Japan.

29. Meijlan, *Japan*, 60.

30. Donoghue, *Pariah Persistence*, 26.

31. *Jinrin kinmo zui*, 234.

32. McClain, "Space, Power," 62, 71–2.

33. Price, "History of the Outcaste," 22–3.

34. *Me no yugamitarukara, kokochi ashiya*. "Nanaju ichi ban shokunin utaawase," in *Edokagaku Koten Sosho*, vi, 55, 69.

35. Buraku kaiho kenkyūsho (ed.), *Buraku mondai jiten*, 507–8.

36. Buraku kaiho kenkyūsho (ed.), *Buraku mondai jiten*, 14. An apocryphal story tells us that they were invented by tea-master Sen no Rikyu (1522–1591). *Setta* became popular as a casual shoe in the seventeenth century.

37. Terajima Ryōan, *Wakan sansai zue*, vol. V, 187–8.

38. Sasaki and De Vos, "Traditional Urban Outcaste," 135.

39. Kitagawa, *Morisada Morisada mankō*, ii, 279.

40. Nishiyama et al., *Edo gaku jiten*, 674.

41. *Edo hitorimono annai* (1810), reproduced in *Edo gaku jiten*, 675–96.

42. Hiroshima-shi rekishi kagaku kyōiku iinkai (ed.), *Geta-zukuri*, 4.

43. For instance Hatsu, a village in Chikuzen province, Kyushu, with a population of about 460 in 1766, had a footwear shop. See Kalland, *Fishing Villages*, 72, 83.

44. Ihara, *Scheming World*, 127.

45. Rossi, *Sex Life of the Foot*, 16.

46. "Nanaju ichi shokunin utaawase," 68.

47. Aston, *Shinto*, 248.

48. Seigle, *Yoshiwara*, 78.

49. *Seifūzoku*, iii, 36.

50. Kitagawa, *Morisada mankō*, vol. V, 33–4. Some authors claim heights of up to two feet but no evidence has been found to support this claim. See also Andrea Vianello's chapter in this volume.

51. The wooden piers that supported the foot bed.

52. De Becker, *Nightless City*, 30, 201.

53. Yamamoto, *Hagakure*, 80.

54. Ikku, *Shank's Mare*, 23.

55. Yasumi, *Ryokō yōjinshū*, 21, 66.

56. See Kitagawa, *Morisada mankō*, ii, 284–5.

57. Ikku, *Shank's Mare*, 132–3. Yaji brags that he can make them last longer than his leggings, and when questioned how, jokes, "Because I always ride."

58. Shioda, *Hakimono*, 159.

59. Thunberg, *Travels in Europe*, 272.

60. Griffis, *Mikado's Empire*, vol. II, 468.

Chapter 8. Interrogating Africa's Past

1. Clarke, *Travels and Explorations*, 243–4; Millson, "Yoruba Country," 586; Burton, *Abeokuta*, 107 and 134; Lander, *Records of Captain Clapperton*, 195 and 212; May, "Journey in the Yoruba," *passim*.

2. Lloyd, "Osifekunde of Ijebu," in P. H. Curtin (ed.), *Africa Remembered*, 264 and 278; Lloyd, "Osifakorede of Ijebu," *Odu*, 62.

3. The limited sources in this area include: Wass, "Yoruba Dress," and Akinwumi, "Persistence and Change."

4. Akinjogbin, *Milestones and Concepts*, 3; Smith, *Kingdoms of the Yoruba*, 10.

5. Bascom, "Early Historical Evidence."

6. Akinwumi, "Commemorative Phenomenon," 23–35.

7. Willett, *Ife*, 105–6, notes on plates 6, 10 and color plate III.

8. Burton, *Abeokuta*, 134.

9. Adéòyè, *Asa Ati Ise Yoruba*, 218.

10. Adéòyè, *Asa Ati Ise Yoruba*, 218.

11. Lander, *Records of Captain Clapperton*, 195.

12. Isichei, *History of Nigeria*, 91.

13. For the trade route of brass in Nigeria, Shaw and Adepegba trace it differently, from northern Nigeria via northeastern Yoruba country to Ile-Ife and Ijebu, where much of this material was used for creating artworks and royal paraphernalia including sandals. Shaw, "Note on Trade"; Adepegba, *Yoruba Metal Sculpture*, 56.

14. Usman, "Aspects," 178.

15. Crowder, *Story of Nigeria*, 12.

16. "Kano Chronicle," iii, 109–11; Adamu, *Hausa Factor*, 59–60.

17. Adams, *Remarks on the Country*, 218–19.

18. See the chapter by Andrea Vianello in this volume.

19. Adams, *Remarks on the Country*, 92.

20. *Iwe Iroyin*, October 4, 1862.

21. Whitford, *Trading Life*, 97, 114.

22. The word *bata* is an indigenous Yoruba word for "footwear." *Bata* was not derived from the worldwide Czechoslovakian brand Bata (i.e. Bata Shoe Co.).

23. The bark of *bata epogi* left imprints that made beautiful surface patterns, especially on sandy ground in the Yoruba coastal area.

24. Adéòyè, *Asa*, 218.

25. Ladele, Mustapha, Aworinde, Oyerinde and Oladapo, *Akojopo*, 202; Adéòyè, *Asa*, 218. *Patako* were worn during the rainy season to protect their feet from mud.

26. Personal communication: Mr Ola Famude, 65 years old, 45 Falodun Street, Makoko, Lagos, July 16, 2004.

27. *Patako* produced a "pa-pa-pa" sound when worn and left imprints of even more beautiful patterns on the ground than those mentioned for pod and bark sandals. Field interview: Chief J. O. Malomo, 76 years old, the *Agbayewa* of Ilesha, Oke Padri Street, Ilesa, November 17, 1987.

28. Cited in Lloyd, "Osifakorede," 62.

29. De Negri, *Nigeria*, 50.

30. Labi, *Asante Kings*, 7.

31. See Thompson, "Divine King," 228; Fagg, *Yoruba Beadwork*, Drewal and Mason, "Beads, Body and Soul," 24.

32. Ogunba, "Crowns," 250.

33. Ogunba, "Crowns," 250.

34. Drewal and Mason, "Beads," 22.

35. Thompson, "Divine King," 242.

36. See Lander and Lander, *Niger Journal*, 317; Willett, *Ife*, 106–8; Fage, "Some Remarks," 346.

37. De Veer and O'Hear, "Gerhard Rohlfs," 259.

38. Lander, *Records of Captain Clapperton's*, ii, 13, 184–5.

39. Kalilu, "Leather Work," 109, 111.

40. Lloyd, "Osifekunde," 264.

41. Kalilu, "Leather Work," 111.

42. Clarke, *Travels*, 243.

43. Adediran, "The 19th Century Wars," 349.

44. Adediran, "The 19th Century Wars," 351.

45. Johnson, *History of the Yorubas*, 265.

46. Johnson, *History of the Yorubas*, 265.

47. Johnson, *History of the Yorubas*, 263–5.

48. Akinyele, *Iwe Itan Ibadan*, 138–40.

49. Adediran, "The 19th Century Wars," 356.

50. The elite included Reverend J. A. White in 1852 and Bishop James Johnson in 1883 respectively. CMS, CA2/087: "James White, Journal Quarter, 1852," 13; Echeruo, *Victorian Lagos*, 38; Ayandele, *Ijebu of Yorubaland*, 23–4.

51. Oduyoye, *Planting of Christianity*, 262.

52. Ayandele, *Ijebu*, 23–4; Oduyoye, *Planting of Christianity*, 263.

53. Atanda, *New Oyo Empire*, 229.

54. Interview with R. A. Akunyun, age 82, tailor, Apinni Quarters Oyo, February 21, 1981.

55. Interview with Mrs Victoria Popoola, age 78, Iporo ake, Abeokuta, December 9, 1987.

56. Personal communication with Mr. Ola Famude, Makoko, Lagos, July 16, 2004.

57. Hurlock, "Sumptuary Law," 300–3.

58. Atanda, "Fall of Old Oyo"; Smith, "Little New Light."

Chapter 9. A Dream of Butterflies?

1. Dabing and Jinbo (eds), *Zhongguo*, 79.

2. Yongshen, *Tangshi xuan*, 66.

3. Menglong (ed.), *Xingshi hengyan*, 250.

4. Xueqing, *Honglou meng*, 627. The translation here is slightly modified from David Hawkes's translation, *The Story of the Stone*, Penguin, 1977, ii, 401.

5. Dabing and Jinbo (eds), *Zhongguo*.

6. See, just to mention one of the most recent studies of this tendency: Kraus, *Party and the Arty*.

7. See for example: Fan, *Footbinding*; Jackson, *Splendid Slippers*; Ko, "Body As Attire"; Levy, *Chinese Footbinding*; Steele, *China Chic*; Wang, *Aching for Beauty*.

8. Ko, *Every Step a Lotus*.

9. Story from BBC News: <http://news.bbc.co.uk/go/pr/fr/2/hi/business/4636675.stm> (June 30, 2005). As Adam Minter writes, it could be "a measure of the conservative nature of China's art establishment that shoes painted in a medium typically reserved for mountains and waterfalls can be considered radical."

10. Adidas, the German sportswear giant, just to mention the most recent case of copyright infringement of shoe-wear in China, has recently launched a lawsuit against three Chinese companies for intellectual property rights violations, seeking three million yuan in compensation. See <www.tribuneindia.com/2005/20050901/biz.htm>. See also <www. english. epochtimes.com/news/4-10-17/23816.html>.

11. See <www. cityweekend.com. cn/en/beijing/features/200_22/

12. See <www. cityweekend. cn/en/beijing/features/2004 _22/ Cover_PengWei> (November 11, 2004).

13. There are countless very useful publications about traditional clothing and footwear and their changes at the turn of the twentieth century. Some key texts are: Finnane and McLaren (eds), *Dress, Sex and Text*; Harrison, *Making of the Republican Citizen*; Roberts (ed.), *Evolution and Revolution*; Steele and Major (eds), *China Chic*.

14. Pang Bian, *China Today*, 2001, 2, <www. chinavoc.com/life/focus/ shoeshistory.asp>.

15. Renchun, *Lao Beijingde chuantai*, 178–9.

16. Garret, *Traditional Chinese Clothing*, 25.

17. Beijing, Xinhua Agency, October 18, 1998.

18. See <archives.cnn.com/2000/ ASIANOW/east/08/03/china. shoes.ap/>.

Chapter 10. Fashioning Masculinity

1. I am grateful to the editors of the current volume and to the editors (Shari Benstock and Suzanne Ferriss) and publishers of the Rutgers University Press volume *Footnotes: On Shoes* (Rutgers University Press, 2001) for allowing the re-publication of this chapter in a revised version here.

2. Breward, *Fashioning London*, 21–47.

3. Moers, *Dandy*.

4. Troy, *Modernism and the Decorative Arts*.

5. Sparke, *As Long as it's Pink*.

6. Le Corbusier, *Decorative Art*, xxiii.

7. Kuchta, *Three-Piece Suit*.

8. Breward, *Hidden Consumer*, 24–75.

9. Le Corbusier, *Decorative Art*, 7.

10. Le Corbusier, *Decorative Art*, 8.

11. Donald, *Age of Caricature*.

12. Le Corbusier, *Decorative Art*, 87.

13. Le Corbusier, *Decorative Art*, 90.

14. *John Piggott, Outfitter's Catalogue*, 99–106.

15. Lehmann, *Tigersprung*, 155–8.

16. Wigley, *White Walls*, 90–1.

17. Loos, *Spoken into the Void*, 55.

18. Loos, *Spoken into the Void*, 55.

19. Loos, *Spoken into the Void*, 55.

20. Loos, *Spoken into the Void*, 56–7.

21. Rossi, *Sex Life of the Foot and Shoe*, 101–14.

22. Pond, *Foot and its Covering*, 17.

23. Pond, *Foot and its Covering*, 18–20.

24. Anderson, *Kafka's Clothes*.

25. Bourke, *Dismembering the Male*.

26. Munson, *Soldier's Foot*, 35–9.

27. Sewell, *Resume on Weak and Tired Feet*.

28. Munson, *Soldier's Foot*, 34.

29. Loos, *Spoken into the Void*, 61.

30. Loos, *Spoken into the Void*, 61.

31. Moses, *Fashion's Favourite*.

32. On Elias Moses see Chapman, "Innovating Entrepreneurs."

33. Riello, "*La Chaussure à la Mode*."

34. Schmiechen, *Sweated Industries*, 9–12.

35. Schmiechen, *Sweated Industries*, 29–31.

36. Swaysland, *Boot and Shoe Design*, 8 and 39.

Chapter 11. A Delicate Balance

1. Swann, *History of Footwear*, 96.

2. Swann, *History of Footwear*, 96. In "Seventeenth-Century Shoes," Swann also suggests that the covered heel derived from the chopine.

3. Swann, "Seventeenth-Century Shoes," 96. Although Swann points out that they were called "Polony" in English, she does not investigate the connection beyond stating that she has not found a link. However, Poland was of cultural and political interest to European countries at the time and Poland's proximity to the Cossacks, Crimean Tartars and the Ottomans, as well as the influence of those cultures on Polish dress, gave Poland an air of Eastern exoticism.

4. For example, in the 1590s the Papacy, the French and the Hapsburgs initiated diplomatic relations with the Cossacks, in the hope of commencing a campaign against the Ottomans.

5. An earlier example is Coecke van Aelst, *Turks in MDXXXIII*.

6. Swann, *History of Footwear*, 94.

7. It has also been suggested that the heel may have arisen as a modification of the exclusively female style of footwear, the chopine. However, by the late sixteenth century, chopines held strong negative gender associations; the women who wore them, and the chopines themselves, were frequently the subject of derision. Therefore, the transformation of the chopine into a man's accessory seems unlikely. See also Andrea Vianello's chapter in this volume.

8. Swann, "Seventeenth-Century Shoes," 97.

9. Some have suggested that glass (*verre*) is a mistranslation of fur (*vair*). However, scholars agree that Perrault intended the word "glass."

10. Lyon, "Big Feet."

11. See Steinbrügge, *The Moral Sex*.

12. On the "great male renunciation" in the late seventeenth and eighteenth centuries, see Kutcha, *The Three-Piece Suit*; Harvey, *Men in Black*.

13. Wollstonecraft, *Vindication*, 23.

14. Jones, "*Coquettes* and *Grisettes*."

15. See in particular McNeil and Riello, "Art and Science of Walking."

16. Veblen, *Theory of the Leisure Class*.

17. The term "Louis heel" dates to the 1860s, but referenced the eighteenth-century court of Louis XV.

18. Clayson, *Painted Love*.

19. Olympia is depicted wearing a pair of fashionable indoor mules which reference both eighteenth-century and contemporary fashion in their design.

20. Steele, *Shoes*, 18

21. For a detailed analysis of the topic of fetish see Steele, *Fetish* and her chapter in this volume.

22. Peiss, *Hope in a Jar*.

23. Dorothy Bromley as quoted in Todd, "*New Woman*," 33.

24. "Platform" in this chapter is defined as a high, contiguous sole that is flat at the bottom with no indication of a heel. High heels, on the other hand, may feature thick platform soles, but the heel must be distinguished from the sole.

25. See Stefania Ricci's chapter in this volume.

26. The most famous pinup of the Second World War, purportedly owned by one out of every three enlisted men, was of Betty Grable in a bathing suit and heels. At the same time, Vargas girls wearing nothing but high heels were emblazoned on planes and other military equipment. During the war years, women favored platforms over the sexy shoes of soldiers' dreams. Perhaps the platforms, fabricated of unrationed materials and flamboyantly fashionable yet not overly erotic, were a remedy for wartime deprivations.

27. The success of the stiletto was, in part, due to the technological advances of war. Prior to the Second World War, the materials generally used by shoemakers limited the height of a heel. Wood, the most frequently used material for high heels, often snapped under the weight of the wearer despite attempts to reinforce the heels with metal pegs. By the 1950s, the search for a strong material led some shoe designers to make use of metal technology to develop the steel heel. Lightweight, thin, and able to sustain great pressure, the new steel stilettos allowed heel heights to soar.

28. Wright, "Objectifying Gender."

29. An exception is the high-heeled cowboy boot of the "urban cowboy," which signaled rugged individualism in the United States.

30. Cox, *Stiletto*, 126.

31. Robert Bly's "mythopoetic" reclamation of masculinity in his 1990 book, *Iron John*, explicitly linked the crisis in masculinity to the shifts in employment and gender roles.

32. Lipps, "Thanks for the Mammaries," 10–11.

33. Stoller, "Untitled," 42.

34. Stoller, "Untitled," 45.

35. *Sex in the City*, episode 64.

36. Bartlett, *Stripper Shoes*.

37. Mattson, *Ivy League Stripper*.

Chapter 12. Shoes and the Erotic Imagination

1. The author would like to thank Oxford University Press for allowing the republication of part of chapter four of *Fetish: Fashion, Sex and Power* (1996) with some revisions and updating.

2. Kern, *Anatomy and Destiny*, 2.

3. Perrot, *Fashioning the Bourgeoisie*, 11.

4. Buchanan, *The Fleshly School of Poetry* (1872), quoted in Kern, *Anatomy and Destiny*, 82.

5. Coward, "Sublimation of a Fetishist," 100.

6. See Andrea Vianello's chapter in this volume.

7. Rossi, *Sex Life of the Foot and Shoe*, 149.

8. Anne Hollander, quoted in Grimes, "Chanel Platform," 8.

9. Baynes and Baynes (eds), *Shoe Show*, 46.

10. "Harmonie," *Englishwoman's Domestic Magazine*, June 1, 1869, 327.

11. "Robin Adair," *Englishwoman's Domestic Magazine*, September 1, 1870, 190.

12. "High Heels" and "Fred," *Englishwoman's Domestic Magazine*, September 1, 1869, 167.

13. "Robin Adair," *Englishwoman's Domestic Magazine*, December 1, 1870, 377.

14. "Walter," *Englishwoman's Domestic Magazine*, January 1, 1871, 62.

15. Trasko, *Heavenly Soles*, 74.

16. *London Life*, June 10, 1933, 22.

17. "Happy Heels," *London Life*, May 31, 1930.

18. Mr. X, "The Cult of the High Heel," *Photo Bits*, March 25, 1910.

19. "Six-Inch Heels," *London Life*, April 15, 1933, 44–5.

20. *Photo Bits*, June 2, 1910.

21. "Peggy Paget's Patent Paralysing Pedal Props," *Photo Bits*, May 14, 1910.

22. *High Heels*, January 1962, 7–11.

23. *High Heels*, January 1962, 7–11.

24. *High Heels*, February 1962, 37.

25. "High Heeled," *London Life*, May 31, 1930.

26. *High Heels*, January 1962, 9–10.

27. *High Heels*, January 1962, 8–9.

28. *Leg Show*, September 1994, 16, 78–81.

29. Krafft-Ebing, *Pscyhopathia Sexualis*, 172–5.

30. Quoted in Havelock Ellis, *Studies in the Psychology of Sex*, 33–4.

31. Havelock Ellis, *Studies in the Psychology of Sex*, 34–5.

32. Havelock Ellis, *Studies in the Psychology of Sex*, 34–8.

33. Photocopy in Fetish file, Kinsey Institute.

34. *London Life*, May 13, 1933, 22.

35. *Helmut Newton*, image 36.

36. "Panty Raid," in Carslon Wade, *Panty Raid*.

37. *Booted Master*, 8 and 5.

38. *Booted Master*, 15–17, 19 and 41.

39. *Booted Master*, 3, 42, 46, 75–77 and 163.

40. Wilson, *Boot-licking Slave*, 149.

41. Parker, *Bodies, Pleasures and Passions*, 52–3.

42. "A Susceptible Bachelor," *Englishwoman's Domestic Magazine*, October 1, 1870, 253.

43. "Nimrod," *Englishwoman's Domestic Magazine*, October 1, 1870, 254.

44. Stoller, *Sex and Gender*, 219.

45. Case history recorded by H. Hug-Hellmuth, quoted in Stekel, *Sexual Aberrations*, i, 295.

46. *Leg Show*, September 1994, 105.

47. Becker, *Denial of Death*, 237.

48. Becker, *Denial of Death*, 237.

49. Cited in Becker, *Denial of Death*, 236.

50. Becker, *Denial of Death*, 235–6.

51. Stekel, *Sexual Aberrations*, i, 227.

52. Stekel, *Sexual Aberrations*, ii, 51.

53. Meyers, *Scott Fitzgerald*, 12–14.

54. Becker, *Denial of Death*, 235.

55. Becker, *Denial of Death*, 236.

56. Glover, "Sublimation," 146–7.

57. Glover, "Note on Idealisation," 293–4.

58. Krafft-Ebing, *Psychopathia Sexualis*, 261–2.

59. Krafft-Ebing, *Psychopathia Sexualis*, 262–4.

60. For example that of Nizer, *Life in Court*, 199–204.

61. See for example Gebhard, "Fetishism and Sadomasochism," 159.

62. Quoted in Rossi, *Sex Life*, 183.

63. Dian Hanson "Just My Opinion: Perfect Strangers," *Leg Show*, September 1994, 4–5.

64. Gebhard, "Fetishism and Sadomasochism," 160.

65. Magnuson, "Hell on Heels," 128, 130 and 131.

66. Faith Bearden, "Cruel Shoes," *Bizarre*, 4 (1994), 46–9.

67. "Boots Are Made for Walking," *Bizarre*, 4 (1994), 54.

68. Stoller, *Pain and Passion*, 84–5.

69. "Vive La Difference," *Wall Street Journal*, October 15, 1984, 35.

70. Magnuson, "Hell on Heels," 130.

71. Ferragamo, *Shoemaker of Dreams*, 208 and 69.

72. A selection of catalogs from Frederick's of Hollywood and Victoria's Secret were examined, especially at the Kinsey Institute.

73. *High Heels*, February 1962, 2.

74. Magnuson, "Hell on Heels," 130.

75. Holly Brubach, "Shoe Crazy," *Atlantic*, May 1986, 87.

76. Frances Rogers Little, "Sitting Pretty," *Allure*, June 1994, 34–149.

Chapter 13. Sex and Sin

1. Thanks to Sue Constable, Alison Matthews David, Giorgio Riello, Peter McNeil, Oriole Cullen, Mosaic Williams, and the innumerable people who volunteered their personal experiences with red shoes.

2. Andersen, "Red Shoes."

3. The word "sexuality" was not used in its modern sense until 1889 and is here applied retrospectively when discussing the 1845 work.

4. Lévi-Strauss, "Two Faces."

5. Gerber, *Cochineal*, 5.

6. Andersen, "Red Shoes," paragraph 10.

7. Bredsdorff, *Hans Christian Andersen*, 275.

8. Bredsdorff, *Hans Christian Andersen*, 26.

9. Bredsdorff, *Hans Christian Andersen*, 304.

10. Wullschlager, *Hans Christian Andersen*, 259.

11. Wullschlager, *Hans Christian Andersen*, 8.

12. Handersen, "Red Shoes," trans. E. C. Haugaard, 236.

13. "The Snow Queen," website, third story, paragraph 6.

14. Hansen, "Andersen."

15. Handersen, "Red Shoes," trans. E. C. Haugaard, 232.

16. Haahr, "Red Shoes," 418.

17. Reaves, "Slip," 261.

18. Wullschlager, *Hans Christian Andersen*, 9.

19. Bredsdorff, *Hans Christian Andersen*, 154.

20. Hersholt, *Red Shoes*, paragraph 1.

21. Hersholt, *Red Shoes*, paragraph 6.

22. Proust, *Guermantes Way*.

23. The Alhambra, *The Red Shoes*. Programme, the British Library, Playbills 342.

24. Mackie, "Red Shoes."

25. Templeton, "OM Index," *Observer Magazine*, March 7, 2004, 12.

26. Freed of London, personal communication, August 10, 2004.

27. Marilyn Monroe Collection, website, paragraph 9.

28. D. Nahat, quoted in Chiapella, "Red Shoe Diary," website.

29. Mississippi John Hurt, "Richland's Woman Blues," c. 1920s, website, lines 6 and 9.

30. Gillian Welch, Alison Krauss, Emmylou Harris, "Didn't Leave Nobody But The Baby," in *O Brother, Where Art Thou?*, Mercury Records Inc., 170 069-2(11), 2000.

31. Tom Waits, "Red Shoes by the Drugstore," in *Blue Valentine*, Elektra, CD 7559-60533-2, 1978.

32. Estes, *Women Who Run With The Wolves*.

33. Kavaler-Adler, *Creative Mystique*.

34. Franz, *The Interpretation*; Bettelheim, *Uses of Enchantment*.

35. V. L. Heraty, "The Red Shoes Club," *Ta Da! International*, website.

Chapter 14. Beyond the Rainbow

1. Wilde, "House Beautiful," 179.

2. Dyer, *Matter of Images*, 1.

3. Shoes define class and occupational status. Rolley notes that few photographic representations of suffragettes show women in disarray, except for a photograph of a northern mill girl wearing clogs, who is without a hat. Punch satirized suffragettes as plain and old-fashioned, wearing "galoshes," and also with huge feet in elastic-sided boots. Rolley, "Fashion," 53 and 62.

4. Radford, "Dangerous Liaisons."

5. Hebdige, *Subcultures*; Hall and Jefferson (eds), *Resistance Through Rituals*; McRobbie, "Shut up and Dance," ch. 9; Polhemus, *Street Style*; Cole, *"Don We Now Our Gay Apparel."*

6. Simon Frith quoted by McLaughlin, "Rock Fashion," 270.

7. Wilson, "Deviant Dress"; Rolley, "Love, Desire"; and Lewis, "Looking Good," 92–109.

8. Lewis, "Looking Good," 94.

9. Cole, "Corsair Slacks"; Cole, "Invisible Men"; Cole, "Macho Man," Cole, *Don We Now Our Gay Apparel.*"

10. Schaffer, "Fashioning Aestheticism."

11. Sinfield, *Wilde Century*, 3; *Omaha Weekly Herald*, March 24, 1882, in Mikhail (ed.), *Oscar Wilde*, i, 58.

12. *The Daily Examiner* (San Francisco) March 27, 1882, in Mikhail (ed.), *Oscar Wilde*, i, 60.

13. Wilde, "House Beautiful," 178.

14. *The Portrait of Dorian Gray*, in Hyde, *Annotated Oscar Wilde*, 152.

15. Prison dress: see Cohen, 207. Former style: see de Bremont in Mikhail (ed.), *Oscar Wilde*, vol. I, 133.

16. Chauncey, *Gay New York*, 52.

17. Greenidge, *Degenerate Oxford?*, 107.

18. Weeks and Porter, *Between the Acts*, 79.

19. Weeks and Porter, *Between the Acts*, 79.

20. Hicks, *David Hicks*, 41.

21. Brighton Ourstory Project, *Daring Hearts*, 50.

22. The Roger Collection, Sotheby's London, January 1998.

23. Cohen, "Frock Consciousness," 159.

24. Sarah Bradford, "The Roger Family," in Sotheby's London, January 1988, 18.

25. We note here that our chapter is Anglo-American and does not cover major gay centers such as Berlin and Paris, which would produce different readings of queer dress codes.

26. Cole, *Don We Now Our Gay Apparel.*"

27. Martin, "The Gay Factor in Fashion."

28. Fischer, *Gay Semiotics*, 2.

29. Fischer, *Gay Semiotics*, 2.

30. Butler, *Gender Trouble*.

31. Sanders (ed.), *Stud*.

32. Dyer, *Culture of Queers*.

33. Dollimore, *Sexual Dissidence*.

34. Whitlock, " 'Everything is Out of Place.' "

35. Cohen, "Frock Consciousness."

36. Rolley, "Cutting a Dash."

37. Glendinning, *Vita*, 255.

38. Edwin Smith, *Vita Sackville-West's*

Boots, 1962, reproduced in McDowell, *Shoes. Fashion and Fantasy*, 129.

39. William Nicholson, *Miss Jekyll's Gardening Boots*, 1920. Oil/panel, Tate Gallery, London. We thank Alexandra Palmer for kindly alerting us to this image.

40. Tate Britain website, "Art of the Garden."

41. Lapovsky and Davis, *Boots of Leather, Slippers of Gold*.

42. Lapovsky and Davis, *Boots of Leather, Slippers of Gold*, 155.

43. Lapovsky and Davis, *Boots of Leather, Slippers of Gold*, 180.

44. Quoted in Lapovsky and Davis, *Boots of Leather, Slippers of Gold*, 156.

45. Brighton Ourstory Project, *Daring Hearts*, 52.

46. Brighton Ourstory Project, *Daring Hearts*, 51.

47. Wilson, Elizabeth, *Adorned in Dreams*, 240.

48. See Cooper, *The Sexual Perspective*, 262.

49. Halperin, *Saint Foucault*, 65.

50. Halperin, *Saint Foucault*.

51. *Sex and the City*, Season 2, Episode 18.

Chapter 15. Made in Italy

1. This text has been translated from Italian by Giorgio Riello and Peter McNeil.

2. Meldini, "Economia della Ricostruzione," iii, 127–8.

3. Chesne Dauphiné Griffo, "G. B. Giorgini," 68 and 71; *Lo Stato della Moda*.

4. See Malossi (ed.), *Sala Bianca*.

5. Corbellini and Saviolo, *Scommessa del Made in Italy*.

6. Ricci, "Artigianato della Moda," 229–55.

7. Porter, *Competitive Advantage of Nations*, 440.

8. Ferragamo, *Shoemaker of Dreams*.

9. Devlin, *Vogue*, 18.

10. *Materials and Creativity*.

11. Ricci (ed.), *Ideas, Models, Inventions*.

12. Ferragamo, *Shoemaker of Dreams*, 204.

13. "La Calzatura Italiana" and "Calzature."

14. Di Somma, "Salvatore Ferragamo," 60–3.

Chapter 16. Style through Design

1. Bondi and Mariacher, *Calzatura*, 11.

2. For a wider analysis see Fontana (ed.), *100 Anni*.

3. See Wilcox, *Mode in Footwear*; Barthes, *Fashion System*; McDowell, *Shoes. Form and Fantasy*; Probert, *Shoes in Vogue*; Girotti, *Calzatura, Storia e Costume*; Durian-Ress, *Schue*. See also Davanzo Poli (ed.), *Arts and Crafts of Fashion*, published in English, Chinese and Russian for exhibitions in Beijing and St. Petersburg.

4. Frigni and Tousijn, *Industria della Calzatura*; Varaldo, *Sistema delle Imprese*; Gabisso, *Struttura e Competitività*. For recent developments see Corbellino and Saviolo, *Scommessa del Made in Italy*.

5. For a wider analysis, see Fontana (ed.), *100 Anni*.

6. Bondi and Mariacher, *Calzatura della Riviera del Brenta*, 20.

7. Maldonado, *Disegno Industriale*, 48.

8. Morlacchi, "Progettazione," 12.

9. Morlacchi, "Progettazione," 18.

10. Bondi and Mariacher, *Calzatura*, 26.

11. Bondi and Mariacher, *Calzatura*, 26.

12. Morlacchi, "Progettazione," 13.

13. *School for Footwear*.

14. Morlacchi, "Progettazione," 14–15.

15. *Nuove Figure Professionali*, 55–61; *Indagine sulla Domanda*.

16. Morlacchi, "Progettazione," 15.

17. Morlacchi, "Progettazione," 15.

18. Morlacchi, "Progettazione," 18.

19. Becattini, *Distretti Industriali*; Becattini, *Distretto Industriale allo Sviluppo Locale*; Godman and Bamford (eds), *Small Firms*.

20. Fontana (ed.), *100 Anni*, 217–337; Roverato, *Dell'Industria Calzaturiera*.

21. Morlacchi, "Progettazione," 20.

22. Morlacchi, "Progettazione," 19.

23. Morlacchi, "Progettazione," 20.

24. Gottardi, *Anatomia*; Fontana (ed.), *100 Anni*; Anselmi (ed.), *Industria Calzaturiera Marchigiana*.

25. Bonaccorsi, "Disintegrazione Verticale."

26. Belussi, "Distretto Industriale"; Belussi (ed.), *Tacchi a Spillo*; Belassi and Gottardi (eds), *Evolutionary Patterns*.

27. Morlacchi, "Progettazione," 21.

28. Morlacchi, "Progettazione," 21.

29. Fontana, " 'Oggetti d'Arte Chiamati Scarpe,' " 331–36.

30. Becattini, *Distretto Industriale*, 183–86.

31. Bondi and Mariacher, *Calzatura della Riviera del Brenta*, 226; Fontana (ed.), *100 Anni*, xvii–xxii; Belassi (ed.), *Tacchi a Spillo*; Pampagnin, *Riviera degli Scarpari*; Roverato, *Dell'Industria Calzaturiera*.

32. Fontana (ed.), *100 Anni*, 37–100.

33. Fontana (ed.), *100 Anni*, 244–69 and 399–411.

34. Fontana (ed.), *100 Anni*, 245–55; *School for Footwear*.

35. See the series *Maestri Calzaturieri della Riviera del Brenta*. See also: *Calzature d'Autore*; Fontana (ed.), *100 Anni*, 419–30.

36. Fontana (ed.), *100 Anni*, 219–398; Belussi (ed.), *Tacchi a Spillo*.

37. Gottardi, *Anatomia*; Gottardi (ed.), *Trasferimento*; Gabisso, *Struttura*; G. L. Fontana (ed.), *100 Anni*, 365–96; Belussi (ed.), *Tacchi a Spillo*.

38. *Nuove Figure Professionali*, 37.

39. *Nuove Figure Professionali*, 56.

Chapter 17. Sole Representation

1. Dalí, *Secret Life*, 122. Dalí is most likely to be referring to an oil painting he produced in 1941, entitled *Original Sin*, which features a woman's foot and leg (probably that of his wife, Gala) encircled with a snake-shaped anklet, and about to plunge into one of two empty men's shoes.

2. Varnedoe and Gopnik, *High and Low*, 409.

3. Varnedoe and Gopnik, *High and Low*, 19.

4. Varnedoe and Gopnik, *High and Low*, 19.

5. Heidegger, "Origin," 413, 424.

6. Heidegger, "Origin," 423.

7. Heidegger, "Origin," 424.

8. Schapiro, "Still Life," 428. Both these essays were further critiqued by the French philosopher Jacques Derrida in an essay written in 1978, entitled "Restitution of the Truth."

9. On shoes in oil painting see also Bossan et al., *Représentation*. Note particularly the painting by François Bonvin, *Les souliers d'un réserviste*, 1876.

10. Donald, *Age of Caricature*, 54.

11. Donald, *Age of Caricature*, 50.

12. Varnedoe and Gopnik, *High and Low*, 410.

13. Varnedoe and Gopnik, *High and Low*, 410.

14. Varnedoe and Gopnik, *High and Low*, 410–11.

15. Varnedoe and Gopnik, *High and Low*, 411.

16. Varnedoe and Gopnik, *High and Low*, 411.

17. Burckhardt and Curiger, *Meret Oppenheim*, 49.

18. See Riviere, "Womanliness," 43.

19. Freud, "Three Essays," 155. Citing the phallic symbolism of the foot, in a footnote, Freud writes, "The shoe or slipper is a ... symbol of the *female* genitals."

20. Rossi, *Sex Life*, 160.

21. Turner, "Sodom," 45–6.

22. Steele, *Fetish*, 4.

23. See Anderson, *Imagined Communities*.

24. Michalski, *New Objectivity*, 30.

25. Marx, *Capital*, 46.

26. Bataille, "Esprit Moderne," 489. Quoted in Ades, "Surrealism," 68.

27. Ades, *Dalí*, 154.

28. Tzara, "Concerning a Certain Automatism."

29. Blum, *Shocking!*, 127.

30. Blum, *Shocking!*, 136.

31. Freud, "Uncanny," xvii, 240.

32. Gablik, *Magritte*, 124.

33. Marx, *Capital*, 46.

Chapter 18. Limousines for the Feet

1. Buchanan, "Rhetoric, Humanism, and Design," 26.

2. For examples of cultural studies literature citing the iconic status of trainers, see both Dyson, "Be Like Mike?," 70; and Busch, *Design For Sport*. Outlining the iconic status of sports shoes and the evolution of the industry as an exemplary "soft goods" or marketing-driven industry is journalist Tom Vanderbilt's *Sneaker Book*.

3. Vanderbilt, *Sneaker Book*, 2–8.

4. More than simply an icon of marketing power, the sports shoe has been interpreted as a key indicator of cultural, sociological and economic change. Vanderbilt, *Sneaker Book*, 3.

5. TV advertisement for Adidas shoes sold at The Athlete's Foot, August 2005, Channel 7 (Australian Television).

6. Vanderbilt, *Sneaker Book*, 2–9.

7. The Converse All Star was also known as the Chuck Taylor signature brand from 1923.

8. The process of vulcanization, refined through the bicycle (and later car) tire manufacturing process and patented by Charles Goodyear, is still used in traditional sneaker models such as Keds (1916), Converse All Stars (1917), Vans (1966), P. F. Flyer and Spalding tennis shoes. See Vanderbilt, *Sneaker Book*, 9, 33.

9. Garcia, *Where'd You Get Those?*, 57.

10. Garcia, *Where'd You Get Those?*, 57.

11. Vanderbilt, *Sneaker Book*, 4 and 18. Vanderbilt cites a 1950s study of a sneaker maker called Hood Rubber, which found that its manufacturing costs accounted for nearly half of its product costs. This is compared with a figure representing Nike's early 1990s performance, where manufacturing costs represented no more than twenty percent of purchase price. Vanderbilt, *Sneaker Book*, 4.

12. Vanderbilt, *Sneaker Book*, 18.

13. Katz, *Just Do It*, 7.

14. Cited in Vanderbilt, *Sneaker Book*, 85.

15. Cited in "The Running shoe – Symbol of Our Time." ABC Radio National's *The Sport Factor*, produced by Maria Tickle, December 27, 2002, 3 (transcript).

16. Cited in "The Running Shoe."

17. Vanderbilt, *Sneaker Book*, 25. Cites the president of Airwalk (a US sneaker company) as saying "We're a marketing company that happens to sell shoes."

18. Vanderbilt, *Sneaker Book*, 6.

19. Vanderbilt, *Sneaker Book*, 50.

20. Vanderbilt, *Sneaker Book*, 50–1.

21. Vanderbilt, *Sneaker Book*, 52.

22. Langehough makes the same point but as "transforming artifact" (instead of transporting symbol) in "Symbol, Status and Shoes," 25. See also Dyson, "Be Like Mike?" on the trainer as a transforming symbol.

23. See <www.5th-dimension.info/> for further information on Junya Watanabe's collaborations with Nike.

24. See comments made by Australian podiatrist Simon Bartold about the change of direction for the sports shoe industry in "Running Shoe," 4–5 (transcript).

Chapter 19. Conclusion. The Male Cinderella

1. The authors would like to thank Emanuele Lepri, Suzanne McLean, Elizabeth Semmelhack and Rebecca Shawcross for their intellectual support and criticism.

2. Cited in McNeil, "Norman Hartnell," 204.

3. Derrick and Muir, *Unseen Vogue*, 150.

4. See, in particular, Lehmann, *Tigersprung*.

5. Milam, "Playful Constructions."

6. Specter, "High-Heel Heaven," 108.

7. Ferragamo, *Shoemaker of Dreams*, 82.

8. Ferragamo, *Shoemaker of Dreams*, 66.

9. Ferragamo, *Shoemaker of Dreams*, 56.

10. Collins, "Fashion's Footman," 126.

11. Ferragamo, *Shoemaker of Dreams*, 16.

12. Ferragamo, *Shoemaker of Dreams*, 167–8.

13. Semmelhack, *Icons of Elegance*.

14. Bossan, *Art of the Shoe*; Semmelhack, *Icons of Elegance*, 8–9.

15. Ferragamo, *Shoemaker of Dreams*, 62.

16. *Absolutely Fabulous*, BBC Production.

17. Specter, "High-Heel Heaven," 106.

18. Ferragamo, *Shoemaker of Dreams*, 92.

19. Lipovetsky, *Empire of Fashion*.

20. Floch, *L'Indémodable* Total Look, 30.

21. Ferragamo, *Shoemaker of Dreams*, 32.

22. Ferragamo, *Shoemaker of Dreams*, 222–23.

23. Ferragamo, *Shoemaker of Dreams*, 214.

GLOSSARY

A. E. Marty, "La Pantoufle de Vair. Danseur Louis XIV," *Gazette du Bon Ton* 4 (February 1913), plate 1. Pochoir print. Collection of Peter McNeil.

This glossary has been compiled by the editors with the help of all the contributors. It also relies on the still limited scholarship on footwear and shoemaking terminology. It is based on the *Oxford English Dictionary* and supplemented by John Henry Thornton, and June M. Swann, *A Glossary of Shoe Terms* (Northampton Central Museum, 1986); Raphael Arthur Salaman, *Dictionary of Leather-Working Tools, c. 1700–1950* (London, 1986); June M. Swann, "Towards a Standard Shoe Glossary," in D. E. Friendship-Taylor, June M. Swann, and S. Thomas (eds), *Recent Research in Archaeological Footwear* (London, Association of Archaeological Illustrators and Surveyors, 1987), pp. 47–9; Francis Grew and Margrethe de Neergaard, *Shoes and Pattens. Medieval Finds from Excavations in London* (London, Her Majesty's Stationery Office, 1988), pp. 123–5; Marie-Josèphe Bossan, *The Art of the Shoe* (Romans, Park International, 2004) and Giorgio Riello, *A Foot in the Past: Consumers, Producers and Footwear in the Long Eighteenth Century* (Oxford, Oxford University Press, 2006), pp. 248–50.

Balmoral boot
A type of boot with front lacing, popular in Victorian times

Bata
General term for footwear in Nigeria

Bata epogi
Yoruba sandals made from hard barks

Bata golu
Yoruba golden slippers and shoes

Bata ileke
Yoruba bead-embroidered slippers

Bata onide
Yoruba brass sandals

Bata panseke
Yoruba sandals made of flat pods

Blücher boot
A strong half-boot named in honor of General Gebhard von Blücher (1742–1819)

Borzacchini
A boot-like shoe worn in medieval Italy

Boudoir slipper (or toilet slipper, or dressing slipper)
An easy-fitting slipper, often elaborately trimmed, worn indoors with a dressing gown or informal morning dress. The rough modern equivalent is the bedroom slipper

Branding
The identity created for a product through design, advertising, endorsements, and the graphic language of logos, signage and packaging

Brocade
A fabric (often silk) woven with a pattern of raised figures. Commonly used in eighteenth-century women's shoes

Brogue
Contemporary use of the word refers to a man's Oxford shoe with perforated and pinked leather decoration

Bronze leather
Kid or calf leather finished with cochineal to create a purplish-brown color of semi-iridescent quality

Buckle
Generally a metallic accessory to fasten a shoe

Buskin
In mid-nineteenth-century America, a leather shoe with a tied fastening. A buskin might tie high on the instep, but did not cover the ankle

Butterfly dream (hutie meng)
Chinese low-heeled satin booties with embroidered flowers and appliquéd butterflies – whose satin wings would flutter with each step taken by the wearer

Bu xie
At times called "Mao shoes." Because of their affordability and simplicity, they quickly became the shoe-wear of choice of many Chinese revolutionaries. Some have suggested that the shoes have survived because they predate the revolution, and are thus seen as symbols of Chinese culture

Calcagnini (calcagnetti)
Venetian denomination of the chopine

Calf
Leather of a calf (a young bovine animal) and part of the leg. It also indicates a stupid person

Calze solate
Literally "soled stockings," pair of stockings or hose with hard leather soles

Cambrione
A shank supporting the arch of the foot, traditionally made of strong leather. In the 1930s it was produced in metal by Salvatore Ferragamo

Camp
A cultural sensibility historically associated with, but not confined to, homosexual men. Involves irony, wit, excess and other coded communicative conventions

Caoutchouc
India rubber or mum elastic produced by the resinous juice of trees

Carriage boot
(a) An overshoe, often velvet trimmed with fur, worn over ordinary shoes or evening slippers for warmth; (b) a boot too dressy for walking but suitable for riding in a carriage to pay formal calls

Chopines
Platform shoes up to twenty inches tall, worn in Europe between the fourteenth and seventeenth centuries. *See also* "Pianelle"

Clicker
The workman who cuts out the component parts of the upper

Clog
A wooden-soled overshoe or sandal worn to protect the feet from mud and dirt; or a shoe with a thick wooden sole. Can also be a wooden-soled shoe (used in the north of England) or a shoe entirely made of wood (normally European continental). *See also* "Sabot"

Cobbler
Commonly a repairer of shoes, the cobbler can be also used as a term to identify poor shoemakers. In medieval and early modern Europe, the cobbler

is often paired with a birdcage and bird, symbols of the shoemaker's dedication to his occupation and the hard life of the "Gentle Craft"

Collabs
An abbreviation of "collaboration," referring to the partnerships between both high- and low-profile designers with sneaker or trainer companies in order to develop a specific shoe or customize an existing model

Congress
American term used from about 1847 for a boot or shoe having a triangular gusset of elasticized fabric ("goring") let into each side

Cordwainer
A shoemaker and member of the guild. The word derives from the cordovan (or cordwain) leather that members of the guild were allowed to use for the production of shoes

Cosciali
A light boot or a heavy stocking reaching the thigh and falling back

Currying
The process of coloring and dressing of leather after it has been tanned

Customization (or customs)
Refers to the altering of new-release or old-school models of sneakers – for example, cutting the tongues or ankle of the shoe, adding graphics or painting the outside surface of the upper – in order to make them one's own or even improve the design for function or comfort

Feminism
Activism, ideas, theoretical and creative activity devoted to the project of a desired equality of the sexes and to the reappraisal of gender relations throughout history

Footbinding
The binding of the foot in order to prevent its normal growth. This was a particularly widespread practice in pre-twentieth-century China

Footwear
A late nineteenth-century American term. It started to be used in the United Kingdom only in the 1920s

Foxing
American term for the leather parts forming or covering the toe (vamp) or

back part (quarter) of a wool serge gaiter-boot

Gait
Stance and style of gesture and movement while walking

Gaiter
A covering of fabric or leather for the ankle

Gaiter-boot
A side-lacing or elastic-sided boot generally made of wool serge, with leather foxing inserted at the toe and back part

Galosh (or golosh)
Originally used to indicate a wooden shoe or sandal fastened to the foot with thongs, or a wooden shoe with a leather upper. It was later use to designate an overshoe (sometimes made of rubber) worn to protect the ordinary shoe

Geta
A thonged wooden clog used in Japan

Grrl Culture
A complex term, embodying both popular culture and counterculture concepts, and reactions to feminism. Some have defined it as third-wave feminism

Half-boot
A boot cut high enough to cover the ankle, but not extending to the knee. "Half-boot" was the standard term for women's boots in the first half of the nineteenth century

Hide
The raw or dressed skin of a large animal that is mainly tanned into leather

Hussar boot
A type of boot named after the cavalry regiment

Kothornoi
In ancient Greece, high, soft boots, without laces. In the classical period they had thin soles, and were worn mainly by women, or by male actors playing female parts. It was probably only from the second century BC that *kothornoi* with platform soles were worn by actors playing any role

Kutsu
A shoe used in Japan, which encases the foot

Instep
The arched middle portion of the human foot, especially its upper surface

Jack boot (or jackboot)
A large top boot protecting the leg, worn by cavalry soldiers in the seventeenth and eighteenth centuries

Jockey boot
A top boot, named in the bootmaking trade, as reported by Mayhew in his *Morning Chronicle* letters

Lagolago
A kind of slipper used by some Ijebu monarchs in Nigeria in the late eighteenth and early nineteenth centuries

Last
The form or mold (generally made of wood) over which a shoe is constructed, and which gives the shoe its shape

Leather
Skin or hide prepared for use by a tanning process. *See also* "Bronze leather"

Mid-sole cushioning
The mid-sole, between the upper and the sole of the shoe, has seen various technologies inserted into it to assist cushioning of the foot. Nike Air – or pockets of pressurized gas – is one of these technologies.

Mule
(a) Venetian denomination of the chopine; (b) light indoor shoe without the back quarter, leaving the heel exposed

Nalin
Stilted wooden sandal with a toe strap, worn by women throughout the Ottoman empire

Nymphides
Special shoes worn by brides in ancient Greece

Pantofole
Italian for "slippers," also used in the early modern period in place of "*pianelle*"

Patako (or saka, or sakoto)
A platform clog sandal of about six inches in height, used in Nigeria

Patten (or pattin)
In the eighteenth century it was a type of overshoe, normally made of leather or with iron parts

Pianelle
Also known as *zibre* or *zibroni* (in Lombardy), *solee* (in Ferrara), *pantofole*, *calagnini* or mule (in Venice and

Tuscany), and more generically as *cioppine* or *chiapinetti*. Medieval and early modern Italian chopines, with leather or fabric uppers and cork or wooden soles, and could be as high as twenty inches

Platform shoe
Made of a high contiguous sole that is flat at the bottom with no indication of a heel. High heels, on the other hand, may feature thick platform soles but the heel must be distinguished from the sole (see, in particular, Elizabeth Semmelhack's chapter in this volume)

Poulaine
Long, pointy-toed footwear fashionable throughout Europe in the fourteenth and fifteenth centuries. Poulaines were also called "Crakows" after the Polish city, thought to be the place where they first became fashionable

Prunella
Type of wool serge commonly used for shoes in the early nineteenth century

Pump
A light shoe with a close fit and no fastening. In the eighteenth century, the word identified a low-heeled shoe

Quarter
One of the two parts of the upper between the heel and the vamp

Queer
Reappropriation, in the 1980s in the context of the cultural politics of AIDS of a formerly derogatory term referring to same-sex sexual activity or sociality. Often now denotes broadly non-hetero-normative attitudes and behaviors including, but not confined to, same-sex attraction

Queer shoe
Used in this volume to denote both the shoes worn by lesbians and homosexual men, often within subcultural codes. It is also used to denote ways of reading cultures of shoe-wearing in a non-normative manner – i.e. "queerly"

Sabot
Wooden shoe (normally made with a single piece of wood) used in France, especially in the countryside

Saka (or sakoto)
See "Patako"

Sandal
A type of footwear with an open top, frequently consisting of a sole fastened by straps or thongs

Satin
A silk fabric with a glossy surface

Serge
A firm, twilled wool designed for use in shoe uppers in the eighteenth and nineteenth centuries

Setta
A Japanese thonged sandal, woven from bamboo bark, with a leather sole

Skin
The pelt of a small animal

Slipper
A light shoe used mostly indoors (see also "Boudoir slipper")

Sneakerization of the economy
Refers to an economy that has encouraged the multiplication of niche markets for once inexpensive and fast-changing goods – such as accessories, sunglasses and sports shoes

Soft good
Refers to rapid-turnover products that represent the ascendancy of marketing concerns over production, for growing company profits

Stiletto
A lightweight, thin metal heel. The success of the stiletto was due to the technological advances of war. Prior to the Second World War, wood was the most frequently used material for high heels. By the 1950s, the search for a strong material led some shoe designers to make use of metal technology to develop the steel heel. Lightweight, thin, and able to sustain great pressure, the new steel stilettos allowed heel heights to soar (see, in particular, Elizabeth Semmelhack's chapter)

Straw nests
Chinese boots made from tightly woven stems and leaves of corn

Superfly
Superfly was a 1972 blaxploitation film, which starred Ron O'Neal as a cocaine dealer trying to leave the business. The term "fly" was and continues to be US slang meaning "attractive"

Suvarate
A kind of chopine common in central Italy, characterized by thick cork soles

Tabi
A split-toed cotton, silk or leather sock from Japan

Takalumi budede
Open shoe used by the Hausa in Nigeria

Takalumi bundin shirwa
Expensive embroidered sandals used by the chiefs and rich people in Nigeria

Tanning
The process of the conversion of skins or hides into leather through infusion in bark solutions

Tongue
Insert used to cover an opening at the vamp throat

Tappini
A type of clog used by prostitutes in medieval Sicily

Turned shoe
A low-cut shoe with such a light, flexible, single sole that it can be attached to the upper much the way clothing is made – by sewing the pieces together inside out and then "turning" the shoe right-side out to hide the seam allowance

Upper
The part of a shoe or boot above the sole and welt

Vamp
The part of a boot or shoe covering the front of the foot from the instep to the toe

Vulcanization
A technique for hardening rubber by heating and chemically combining it with sulphur. The process also makes the rubber stronger and more elastic

Waraji
Japanese woven straw sandal

Wellington boot
A high boot covering the knee in front and cut away behind; or a shorter boot worn under the trousers named in honor of the Duke of Wellington

Welt
The upper surface of the sole edge, where it protrudes beyond the upper

Welted shoe
A shoe with a sole having two layers (insole and outsole) connected to the upper by means of two seams and a welt

Zoccoleri
Venetian shoemakers who specialized in the making of the chopines

Zoccoli
Italian for "clogs." In Venice it was an alternative word for "chopines"

Zōri
Japanese woven thonged sandal

"ADJUSTABLE HIGH-HEELED SHOES - FROM 0 DEGREES TO 38 DEGREES." DESIGNED BY WEI-CHIEH WILLIAM TU.

CONTRIBUTORS

TUNDE MAURICE AKINWUMI is Associate Professor at the University of Agriculture, Department of Home Science and Management in Abeokuta, Nigeria, where he teaches history of costume. He received his BA and MA degrees in Art at Ahmadu Bello University Zaria and completed a Ph.D. in Art History at the University of Ibadan, Nigeria in 1990. He has worked for many years on the art historical and sociocultural aspects of African textiles and clothing.
EMAIL: tundemakinwumi @yahoo.com

SUE BLUNDELL is an Associate Lecturer in Classical Studies with the Open University, UK, and also teaches at the Architectural Association in London. Her published writing has been mainly on the subject of gender, and includes *Women in Ancient Greece* (1995) and *The Sacred and the Feminine in Ancient Greece*, co-edited with Margaret Williamson (1998). Greek women have led her to Greek dress, and hence to Greek shoes.
EMAIL: sblundell@aaschool.ac.uk

CHRISTOPHER BREWARD is Deputy Head of Research at the Victoria and Albert Museum, and Visiting Professor in Historical and Cultural Studies at London College of Fashion, The University of the Arts, London. Author of *The Culture of Fashion* (1995), *The Hidden Consumer* (1999), *Fashion* (2003) and *Fashioning London* (2004), he is currently working on a history of London's West End in the postwar period with colleagues at Royal Holloway and London College of Fashion, as part of the ESRC/AHRC-funded Cultures of Consumption program.
EMAIL: c.breward@vam.ac.uk

MARTHA CHAIKLIN received her Ph.D. from the University of Leiden and is currently an Assistant Professor at the University of Pittsburgh. She is the author of *Cultural Commerce and Dutch Commercial Culture – The Influence of European Material Culture on Japan, 1700–1850* (2003), as well as of a number of book chapters and articles. Despite repeated attempts at rehab, she had been unable to kick her shoe habit.

HILARY DAVIDSON is an independent scholar and designer who engages with interdisciplinary practice-based historic clothing research. Projects have included work with museums, films, theater and public workshops. She studied bespoke shoemaking in Sydney in the late 1990s, moved to England in 2001 and completed a Masters in the History of Textiles and Dress at Winchester School of Art, University of Southampton in 2004. The subject of her MA thesis, red shoes, is an enduring research interest. She owns eleven pairs, and counting.
EMAIL: ammazhon@mbox.com.au

GIOVANNI LUIGI FONTANA is Professor of Economic History at the University of Padova, Italy. He is the author of several books and articles on industrial, entrepreneurial and institutional economic history, including *100 Anni di Industria Calzaturiera nella Riviera del Brenta* (1998). He is President of the Italian Association for Industrial Heritage, Member of the Board of the International Committee for the Conservation of Industrial Heritage and Director of the MA program in Preservation, Management and Improvement of Industrial Heritage at the University of Padova.
EMAIL: giovanniluigi.fontana@unipd.it

ALISON GILL is a Lecturer in Design Studies and wrote her Ph.D. entitled "Wearing Clothes" on the intersections between fashion, critical theory and contemporary embodiment. She has written on contemporary graphic design and fashion with a dual interest in branding strategies and representations of the clothed body, including the athletic body, for the journals *Fashion Theory* and *Form/Work* and for other independent publications. These interests have emerged from her teaching of cultural theory and design history to graphic designers, illustrators, photographers and animators in the School of Communication Arts, University of Western Sydney.
EMAIL: a.gill@uws.edu.au

SALLY GRAY is a Sydney curator, writer and artist. She recently completed her PhD at the College of Fine Arts, University of New South Wales, on the queer artist David McDiarmid, who worked in Sydney and New York from the mid-1970s to the mid-1990s. Her research interests include fashion and the city, and cultural intersections between art and fashion.
EMAIL: salgray@ozemail.com.au

CLARE LOMAS is a Lecturer in Cultural Studies at the London College of Fashion, University of the Arts, London. Her areas of interests include oral history and methodological approaches for the fashion historian. Her recent research work focuses on the relationship between fashion and gay male identities in London from the 1950s to the 1970s.
EMAIL: c.lomas@fashion.arts.ac.uk

ALISON MATTHEWS DAVID is Assistant Professor in the Department of Fashion Design and Communication, Ryerson University, Toronto. Her research interests lie in the areas of nineteenth- and early twentieth-century fashion, particularly in military and textile technologies, tailoring, the history and social impact of the garment industry and the material culture of dress. Her current projects include a book for Berg entitled *Fashion Victims: Death by Clothing*, on

the dangers of fashionable dress. Writing this has inspired her to study the literal and figurative perils of high heels.
EMAIL: amdavid@ryerson.ca

PETER McNEIL holds the Chair of Design History, Faculty of Design, Architecture and Building, University of Technology, Sydney. He has published more than forty articles in journals such as *Fashion Theory*, *Journal of Design History* and *Art History*. His research interests include the relationship between dress fashion and other domains of art, architecture and design. Recent commissions include catalog essays for the exhibitions *Women of Influence* (2005) and *Everlasting: The Flower in Fashion and Textiles* (2005). His shoes occupy three rooms.
EMAIL: peter.mcneil@uts.edu.au

MARIA GIUSEPPINA MUZZARELLI teaches Medieval History at the University of Bologna, and History of Dress and Fashion at the University of Bologna at Rimini, where she researches the history of ideas. Among her recent works are: *Gli Inganni delle Apparenze. Disciplina di Vesti e Ornamenti alla Fine del Medioevo* (1996); *Guardaroba Medievale. Vesti e Società dal XIII al XVI Secolo* (1999); *Il Denaro e la Salvezza. L'Invenzione del Monte di Pietà* (2001), *Donne e Cibo. Una Relazione nella Storia* (with F. Tarozzi) (2003), and *Pescatori di Uomini. Predicatori e Piazze alla Fine del Medioevo* (2005); and she has edited *La Legislazione Suntuaria. Secoli XIII–XVI. Emilia-Romagna* (2002).
EMAIL: maria.muzzarelli@unibo.it

JULIA PINE worked for eight years at the Bata Shoe Museum in Toronto, Canada, in the capacity of Assistant Curator, and later Acting Curator. She is author of the book *Ontario's Amazing Museums* (1994), and writes and lectures on a variety of subjects. Currently completing her Doctorate in Culture Mediations, with a specialism in Visual Culture, at Carleton University, Ottawa, Canada, her focus is on cultural theory as it relates to twentieth-century art, fashion and popular culture.
EMAIL: pine_julia@yahoo.ca

NANCY REXFORD is author of *Women's Shoes in America, 1795–1930* (2000), which won the Costume Society of America's Millia Davenport Award for best costume book of the year 2000. Under grants from the National Endowment for the Humanities, she traveled around the United States studying not just footwear, but all types of women's clothing. As a consultant, she has dated and identified thousands of women's garments that survive in American museums and historical societies. She lives in Danvers, Massachusetts, where, alone against the tidal wave of sneakers, she carries on the venerable American tradition of wearing thin-soled slippers on the street.
EMAIL: nancy.rexford@verizon.net

STEFANIA RICCI has curated several exhibitions on Salvatore Ferragamo in Italy, England, United States and Japan, and since 1995 she has been Director of the Ferragamo Museum in Florence. She is the author of several books and articles on the history of fashion and dress. In 2006, she curated an exhibition in Mexico City on the life and work of Salvatore Ferragamo, and another in Florence on the history of color in shoes. She is a consultant for several museums, including the Museo Internazionale della Calzatura in Vigevano and she teaches the history of footwear at the Polimoda in Florence.
EMAIL: stefania.ricci@ferragamo.com

GIORGIO RIELLO is Research Officer in Global History at the London School of Economics and is soon to take the position of Lecturer in History at the University of Exeter. He has widely published on shoes and shoemaking, fashion and product innovation in the eighteenth and nineteenth centuries. He is the author of *A Foot in the Past: Consumers, Producers and Footwear in the Long Eighteenth Century* (2006) and is currently writing a book entitled *A Global History of Cotton Textiles, 1200–1850*.
EMAIL: g.riello@yahoo.com

ELIZABETH SEMMELHACK has been the Curator of the Bata Shoe Museum since 2000. During her tenure, she has curated numerous exhibitions, including *Heights of Fashion: A History of the Elevated Foot*; *The Perfect Pair: Wedding Shoe Stories*; *Beads, Buckles and Bows: 400 years of Embellished Footwear*, and *Icons of Elegance: The Most Influential Shoe Designers of the 20th Century*. She holds a BA from Bennington College, an MA in Art History from Tufts University, and was a Doctoral Fellow in Art History at Washington University.
EMAIL: Elizabeth.Semmelhack@batashoemuseum.ca

VALERIE STEELE (Ph.D., Yale University) is Director and Chief Curator of the museum at the Fashion Institute of Technology. She is the author of numerous books, including *Fetish: Fashion, Sex and Power* (1996); *Paris Fashion* (1999); and *The Corset: A Cultural History* (2001). She is also the founder and editor of *Fashion Theory: The Journal of Dress, Body & Culture* (www.fashiontheory.com). Often quoted in the media, she was herself the subject of a profile in *Forbes* (1992): "Fashion Professor," and in *The New York Times* (1999): "High-Heeled Historian." Steele has appeared on television programs including *The Oprah Winfrey Show* and *Undressed: The Story of Fashion*. After she appeared on the PBS special, *The Way We Wear*, she was described in *The Washington Post* as one of "fashion's brainiest women." She received an Iris Award for distinguished contributions to the decorative arts in 2002, and in 2003 she received the Artistry of Fashion Award at the American Images Awards ceremony.
EMAIL: Valerie_Steele@fitnyc.edu

ANDREA VIANELLO is an Assistant Professor of History at Saint Joseph's College of Maine. His research interests cover the diplomatic relations between European states in the eighteenth century, the history of poverty and assistance in early modern Europe, and the social history of work and fashion. He is the author of *L'Arte dei Caleghari e Zavateri di Venezia tra XVII e XVIII Secolo* (1993). His most recent work on this topic is a history of shoes and shoemaking in Italy from the Middle Ages to the present, published in the special volume on fashion in the *Annali* series of the *Storia d'Italia Einaudi* (2003).
EMAIL: avianello@sjcme.edu

PAOLA ZAMPERINI is a graduate of the University of Venice and was awarded a Doctorate in Chinese literature and gender studies at the University of California. She is currently Assistant Professor of Chinese Literature and Culture in the Asian Languages and Civilizations Department at Amherst College. She has been researching fashion in traditional and contemporary Chinese culture for the past decade, and has edited the special issue of *Positions*, entitled *Fabrications*, devoted to fashion dynamics in East Asia. Her latest book, *Lost Bodies. Representing Prostitution in Late Qing Fiction*, is forthcoming from Brill University Press.
EMAIL: pzamperini@amherst.edu

BIBLIOGRAPHY

ADAMS, J., *Remarks on the Country Extending from Cape Palmas to the River Congo*, London, Whittaker, 1823.

ADAMU, Mahdi, *The Hausa Factor in West African History*, Zaria, Nigeria, Ahmadu Bello University Press, 1978.

ADEDIRAN, A. A., "The 19th Century Wars and Yoruba Royalty," in Adeagbo Akinjogbin (ed.), *War and Peace in Yorubaland, 1793–1893*, Ibadan, Heineman, 1998.

ADÉOYÈ, C. L., *Asa Ati Ise Yoruba – The Custom and Practice of the Yoruba*, Oxford, Oxford University Press, 1979.

ADEPEGBA, Cornelius Oyeleke, *Yoruba Metal Sculpture*, Ibadan, Ibadan University Press, 1991.

ADES, Dawn, *Dalí*, London, Thames and Hudson, 1982.

ADES, Dawn, "Surrealism: Fetishism's Job," in Anthony Shelton (ed.), *Fetishism: Visualising Power and Desire*, London, Lund Humphries Publishers, 1995, pp. 67–87.

AKINJOGBIN, Isaac Adeagbo, *Milestones and Concepts in Yoruba History and Culture: A Key to Understanding Yoruba History*, Ibadan, Olu-Akin Publishers, 2002.

AKINWUMI, Tunde M., "Persistence and Change in Yoruba Costume: A Case Study of Oyo, c. 1850–1981," MA Thesis, Ahmadu Bello University, Zaria, 1981.

AKINWUMI, Tunde M., "The Commemorative Phenomenon of Textile Use Among the Yoruba: A Survey of Significance and Form," Ph.D. Thesis, University of Ibadan, 1990.

AKINYELE, Isaac Babalola, *Iwe itan Ibadan ati die ninu awon ilu agbegbe rè bi Iwo, Oshogbo, ati Ikirun*, Ibandan, Board Publications, 1911.

AKITA Hiroki, *Geta – kami no hakimono*, Tokyo, Hosei daigaku shuppankyoku, 2002.

ALBERTANI, Germana, "Lo Statuto di Bolzano del 1437," *I Dossier di Storiae*, 1–4 (2003).

Almanach des Modes, Paris, Rosa, 1814.

AMELUNG, W., "Rito di Alcune Sculture Antiche e di un Rito del Culto delle Divinità Sotterranee," *Dissertazioni della Pontifica Accademia Romana di Archeologia*, 9 (1907), pp. 115–135.

ANDERSEN, Hans Christian, "The Red Shoes," in *The Complete Andersen*, trans. Jean Hersholt, New York, The Limited Editions Club, 1949.

ANDERSEN, Hans Christian, "The Red Shoes," in *A Treasury of Hans Christian Andersen*, trans. Eric Christian Haugaard, New York, Barnes and Noble Books, 1993, pp. 231–236.

ANDERSEN, Hans Christian, "The Red Shoes," in Shari Benstock and Suzanne Ferriss (eds), *Footnotes: On Shoes*, New Brunswick, NJ and London, Rutgers University Press, 2001, pp. 305–310.

ANDERSON, Benedict, *Imagined Communities*, London and New York, Verso, 1983.

ANDERSON, Mark M., *Kafka's Clothes: Ornament and Aestheticism in the Hapsburg Fin de Siècle*, Oxford, Clarendon Press, 1992.

ANDERSON, Ruth Matilda, "The Chopine and Related Shoes," *Quadernos de la Alhambra*, 5 (1969), pp. 33–41.

ANDRY DE BOIS-REGARD, Nicolas, *Orthopædia, or, The Art of Correcting and Preventing Deformities in Children …*, London, Millar, 1743.

ANNAN, Mrs. A. M. F., "The Cheap Dress: A Passage in Mrs. Allanby's Experience," *Godey's Lady's Book*, 31 (1845), pp. 86–91.

ANSELMI, Sergio (ed.), *L'Industria Calzaturiera Marchigiana. Dalla Manifattura alla Fabbrica*, Ostra Vetere, Unione Industriali del Fermano, 1989.

Appeal from the Buckle Trade of London and Westminster to the Royal Conductor of Fashion, London, 1792.

ARDILL, Susan and Sue O'Sullivan, "Butch/Femme Obsessions," *Feminist Review*, 34 – Spring (1990), pp. 79–85.

ARNDT, William B., *Gender Disorders and the Paraphilias*, Madison, International Universities Press, 1991.

ASHELFORD, Jane, *The Art of Dress: Clothes And Society, 1500–1914*, London, The National Trust, 1996.

ASTON, W. G., *Shinto (Way of God)*, New York, Longman, Green and Co., 1905.

ATANDA, Joseph Adebowale, *The New Oyo Empire: Indirect Rule and Change in Western Nigeria, 1894–1934*, London, Longman, 1973.

AYANDELE, Emmanuel Ayankanmi, *The Ijebu of Yorubaland, 1850–1950: Politics, Economy, and Society*, Ibadan, Heineman, 1992.

BALZAC, Honoré de, "Théorie de la Démarche," in *La Collection des Chefs-d'Oeuvre Méconnus*, Paris, Boissard, [1833] 1922.

BARNES, Ruth and Joanne B. Eicher, "Introduction," in Ruth Barnes and Joanne B. Eicher (eds), *Dress and Gender: Making and Meaning in Cultural Contexts*, Oxford, Berg, 1993, pp. 1–7.

BARNI, Gianluigi and Gina Fasoli, *L'Italia nell'Alto Medioevo. Società e Costume*, Turin, Unione Tipografica Torinese, 1971.

BARTHES, Roland, *Fashion System*, New York, Hill & Wang, 1983.

BARTLETT, Cheryl S., *Stripper Shoes*, New York, 1st Book Library, 2004.

BASCOM, William R., "The Early Historical Evidence of Yoruba Urbanism," in Ukandi Godwin Damachi and Hans Dieter Seibel (eds), *Social Change and Economic Development in Nigeria*, New York, Praeger, 1973, pp. 11–39.

BATAILLE, Georges, "L'Esprit Moderne et le Jeu des Transpositions," *Documents*, 8 (1920).

BAUDENS, L., *On Military and Camp Hospitals and the Health of the Troops in the Field*, New York, Ballière Brothers, 1862.

BAUDOUIN, Benoît, and Giulio Negrone, *Balduinus De Calceo Antiquo, et Jul. Nigronus De caliga Veterum / Accesserunt ex Q. Sept. Fl. Tertulliani, Cl. Salmasi, & Alb. Rvbeni Scriptis Plurima Ejusdem Argumenti*, Amsterdam, Sumptibus Andreae Frisi, 1667.

BAYNES, Ken and Kate Baynes (eds), *The Shoe Show: British Shoes Since 1790*, London, Crafts Council, 1979.

BEARDEN, Faith, "Cruel Shoes," *Bizarre*, 4 (1994), pp. 46–49.

BECATTINI, Giacomo, *Distretti Industriali e Made in Italy. Le Basi Socioculturali del Nostro Sviluppo Economico*, Turin, Bollati Boringhieri, 1998.

BECATTINI, Giacomo, *Dal Distretto Industriale allo Sviluppo Locale*, Turin, Bollati Boringhieri, 2000.

BECKER, Ernest, *The Denial of Death*, New York, Free Press, 1973.

BEDARIDA François and Anthony Sutcliffe, "The Streets in the Structure and Life of the City. Reflections on Nineteenth-Century London and Paris," *Journal of Urban History*, 6 – 3 (1980), pp. 379–396.

BELFANTI, Carlo Marco and Giovanni Luigi Fontana, "Rinascimento e Made in Italy," in Marcello Fantoni (ed.), *Il Rinascimento Italiano e l'Europa: Vol. 1. Storia e Storiografia*, general editors Giovanni Luigi Fontana and Luca Molà, Vicenza, Fondazione Cassamarca and Angelo Colla Editore, 2005, pp. 617–636.

BELLOTTI, Edoardo (ed.), *Interrogatorio Volgare Compendioso et Copioso. Documenti sulla Confessione nel Secolo*

XV dal Ms. Aldini 24 della Biblioteca Universitaria di Pavia, Pavia, Guardamagna Editore, 1994.

BELUSSI, Fiorenza, "Il Distretto Industriale della Riviera del Brenta: Tipologia delle Imprese e Tendenze Evolutive," *Oltre il Ponte*, 9 – 43/44 (1993), pp. 118–134.

BELUSSI, Fiorenza (ed.), *Tacchi a Spillo. Il Distretto Calzaturiero della Riviera del Brenta come Forma Organizzata di Capitale Sociale*, Padua, Cleup, 2000.

BELUSSI, Fiorenza and Giorgio Gottardi (eds), *Evolutionary Patterns of Local Industrial Systems*, Aldershot, Ashgate, 2000.

BENSTOCK, Shari and Suzanne Ferriss (eds), *Footnotes: On Shoes*, New Brunswick, NJ and London, Rutgers University Press, 2001.

BERGMAN, David (ed.), *Camp Grounds: Style and Homosexuality*, Amherst, MA, University of Massachusetts Press, 1993.

BETTELHEIM, Bruno, *The Uses of Enchantment: The Meaning and Importance of Fairy Tales*, London, Penguin, 1976.

BILGER, Burkham, "Sole Survivor. One Man's Quest to Find the Best Shoes Ever Made," *The New Yorker*, February 14–21, 2005, pp. 152–167.

BILLS, Mark, "William Powell Frith's 'The Crossing Sweeper': an Archetypal Image of Mid-Nineteenth-Century London," *Burlington Magazine*, 146 (2004), pp. 300–307.

BISHOP, J. Leander, *A History of American Manufactures from 1608–1860*, New York, Johnson Reprint Corporation, [1868] 1968.

BLACKMAN, Inge and Perry Kathryn, "Skirting the Issue: Lesbian Fashion for the 1990s," *Feminist Review*, 34 – Spring (1990), pp. 67–78.

BLEWETT, Mary H., *We Will Rise in Our Might: Workingwomen's Voices from Nineteenth-Century New England*, Ithaca, NY, Cornell University Press, 1991.

BLUM, Dilys E., *Shocking! The Art and Fashion of Elsa Schiaparelli*, New Haven and London, Yale University Press, 2004.

BLY, Robert, *Iron John: A Book About Men*, Reading, MA, Addison-Wesley, 1990.

BONACCORSI, Andrea, "La Disintegrazione Verticale del Sistema," in Riccardo Varaldo (ed.), *Il Sistema delle Imprese Calzaturiere*, Turin, Giappichelli, 1988, pp. 189–236.

BONDI, Federico and Giovanni Mariacher, *La Calzatura della Riviera del Brenta. Storia & Design*, Venice, Edizioni del Cavallino, 1979.

BORSAY, Peter, "The Rise of the Promenade: the Social and Cultural Use of Space in the English Provincial Town, c. 1660–1800," *British Journal of Eighteenth-Century Studies*, 9–1 (1986), pp. 125–140.

BOSSAN, Marie-Josèphe, et al., *La Représentation de la Chaussure dans la Peinture*, Musée International de la Chaussure de Romans France, 2003.

BOSSAN, Marie-Josèphe, *The Art of the Shoe*, Romans, Parkstone International, 2004.

BOUCHER, François, *A History of Costume in the West*, London, Thames and Hudson, 1987.

BOURKE, Joanna, *Dismembering the Male: Men's Bodies, Britain and the Great War*, London, Reaktion Books, 1996.

BOXER, Charles R. (ed.), *A True Description of the Mighty Kingdoms of Japan & Siam by François Caron & Joost Schouten*, Amsterdam, N. Israel, 1971.

BREDSDORFF, Elias, *Hans Christian Andersen: The Story of his Life and Work 1805–75*, London, Phaidon Press Limited, 1975.

BRELICH, A., "Les Monosandales," *La nouvelle Clio*, 7–9 (1955–7), pp. 469–489.

BREWARD, Christopher, *The Hidden Consumer: Masculinities, Fashion and City Life 1860–1914*, Manchester, Manchester University Press, 1999.

BREWARD, Christopher, *Fashioning London: Clothing and the Modern Metropolis*, Oxford and New York, Berg, 2004.

BREWER, Daniel, "Lights in Space," *Eighteenth-Century Studies*, 37–2 (2004), pp. 171–186.

BREWER, John, *The Common People and Politics, 1750–1790s*, Cambridge, Chadwyck-Healey, 1985.

BREWER, John, *The Pleasures of the Imagination: English Culture in the Eighteenth Century*, London, Harper Collins, 1997.

BRIGHTON OURSTORY PROJECT, *Daring Hearts: Lesbian and Gay Lives of 50s and 60s Brighton*, Brighton, Queenspark Books, 1992.

BROOKE, Iris, *Footwear. A Short History of European and American Shoes*, London, Pitman Publishing, 1972.

BROWN, John, *Sixty Years' Gleanings from Life's Harvest: A Genuine Autobiography*, Cambridge, J. Palmer, 1858.

BRUBACH, Holly, "Shoe Crazy," *Atlantic*, May 1986, p. 87.

BRYANT, A. A., "Greek Shoes in the Classical Period," *Harvard Studies in Classical Philology*, 10 (1899), pp. 57–102.

BUCHANAN, Richard, "Rhetoric, Humanism, and Design," in Richard Buchanan and Victor Margolin (eds), *Discovering Design*: *Explorations in Design Studies*, Chicago and London, University of Chicago Press, 1995, pp. 23–66.

BURAKU kaiho kenkyūsho (ed.), *Buraku mondai jiten*, Osaka, Kaihō-shuppan, 1986, "Zōri," pp. 507–8.

BURGELIN, Oliver, "Abbigliamento," in *Enciclopedia Einaudi*, Turin, Einaudi, 1977, vol. I, pp. 79–104.

BURGIN, Victor, Janes Donald and Cora Kaplan, *Formations of Fantasy*, New York and London, Methuen, 1986.

BURKE, Peter, *The Fortunes of the Courtier. The European Reception of Castiglione's Cortegiano*, Cambridge, Polity Press, 1985.

BURKERT, Walter, *Lore and Science in Ancient Pythagoreanism*, trans. Edwin L. Minar Jr., Cambridge, MA, Harvard University Press, 1972.

BURTON, Sir Richard Francis, *Abeokuta and the Cameroons Mountains: An Exploration*, London, Tinsley Brothers, 1863.

BUSCH, Akiko (ed.), *Design For Sport*, London, Thames & Hudson, 1998.

BUTAZZI, Grazietta, "Un Paio di Pianelle Cinquecentesche delle Civiche Raccolte di Arte Applicata di Milano," in Dora Liscia Bemporad (ed.), *Il Costume nell'Età del Rinascimento*, Florence: EDIFIR, 1988, pp. 337–345.

BUTLER, Judith, *Gender Trouble: Feminism and the Subversion of Identity*, New York and London, Routledge, 1990.

CALIMANDREI POLIDORI, Enrico, *Le Vesti delle Fiorentine nel Quattrocento*, Rome, Multigrafica Editrice, 1973.

"La Calzatura Italiana Vista da Ferragamo e Cellofania," *Documento Moda* 2 (Summer 1942).

"Calzature," *Documento Moda* 3 (1943).

Calzature d'Autore. Rossìmoda. 50 anni per le Grandi Firme, Fiesso d'Artico, Villa Foscarini Rossi, 1997.

CAMPBELL, R., *The London Tradesman: Being a Compendious View of All the Trades, Professions, Arts, both Liberal and Mechanic, Now Practised in the Cities of London and Westminster…* London, printed by T. Gardner, 1747.

CAMPER, Petrus, *Abhandlung über die beste Form der Schuhe … Aus dem Französischen*, Berlin, 1783.

CAROSO, Fabrizio, *Nobiltà di Dame. Libro Altra Volta Chiamato Il Ballarino*, Venice, Il Muschio, 1605.

CASOLA, Pietro, *Viaggio a Gerusalemme di Pietro Casola*, edited by Anna Paoletti, Turin, Edizioni dell'Orso, 2001.

CASTIGLIONE, Baldesar, *Il libro del Cortegiano*, edited by Walter Barberis, Turin, Einaudi, 1998.

CECCHELLI, Carlo, *Vita di Roma nel Medio Evo. Le Arti Minori e il Costume*, Rome, Fratelli Palombi Editori, 1951–52.

CHAPMAN, Stanley D., "The Innovating

Entrepreneurs in the British Ready-Made Clothing Industry" *Textile History*, 24–1 (1993), pp. 5–25.

CHAUNCEY, George, *Gay New York: The Making of the Gay Male World 1890–1940*, London, Flamingo, 1994.

CHESNE DAUPHINÉ GRIFFO, G., "G. B. Giorgini: la Nascita di una Moda Italiana," in *La Moda Italiana. Le origini dell'Alta Moda e la Maglieria*, Milan, Electa, 1987, pp. 66–71.

CHOJNACKI, Stanley, "The Power of Love: Wives and Husbands," in Stanley Chojnacki, *Women and Men in Renaissance Venice: Twelve Essays on Patrician Society*, Baltimore and London, John Hopkins University Press, 2000, pp. 153–168.

CHRISMAN, Kimberly, "*L'Émigration à la Mode*. Clothing Worn and Produced by the French Émigré Community in England from the Revolution to the Restoration," MA Thesis, The Courtauld Institute of Art, 1997.

CLAIRIAN, L. J., *Recherches et Considérations Médicales sur les Vêtemens des Hommes, Particulièrement sur les Culottes. Augmenté de Notes Critiques, Historiques, et Ornée de Gravures.* Paris, A. Aubry, an XI [1803].

CLARKE, William H., *Travels and Explorations in Yorubaland, 1854–1858*, edited by J. A. Atanda, Ibadan, Nigeria, Ibadan University Press, 1972.

CLAYSON, Hollis, *Painted Love: Prostitution and French Art of the Impressionist Era*, New Haven and London, Yale University Press, 1991.

CLEMENTS, Paul, *Marc Isambard Brunel*, London, Longmans, 1970.

CLETO, Fabio, *Camp: Queer Aesthetics and the Performing Subject*, Ann Arbor, MI, University of Michigan Press, 1999.

COALDRAKE, William H., *The Way of the Carpenter*, New York, Weatherhill, 1990.

COECKE VAN AELST, Pieter, *The Turks in MDXXXIII; A Series of Drawings Made in That Year at Constantinople by Peter Coeck of Aelst*, London and Edinburgh, printed for W. S. M., [1533] 1873.

COHEN, Lisa, " 'Frock Consciousness.' Virginia Woolf, the Open Secret, and the Language of Fashion," *Fashion Theory*, 3–2 (1999), pp. 149–174.

COLE, Shaun, "Corsair Slacks and Bondi Bathers. Vince Man's Shop and the Beginnings of Carnaby Street Fashion," *Things*, 6 – Summer (1997), pp. 26–39.

COLE, Shaun, "Invisible Men: Gay Men's Dress in Britain, 1950–1970," in Amy de la Haye and Elizabeth Wilson (eds) *Defining Dress: Dress as Object, Meaning and Identity*, Manchester, Manchester University Press, 1999, pp. 143–154.

COLE, Shaun, "Macho Man: Clones and the Development of a Masculine Stereotype," *Fashion Theory*, 4–2 (2000), pp. 125–140.

COLE, Shaun, *"Don We Now Our Gay Apparel": Gay Men's Dress in the Twentieth Century*. Oxford and New York, Berg, 2000.

COLLINS, Amy, Fine, "Fashion's Footman," *Vanity Fair*, May 1995, p. 126.

COOPER, Emmanuel, *The Sexual Perspective: Homosexuality and Art in the Late Years of the West*, London, Routledge, 2nd edn., 1994.

CORBELLINI, Erica and Stefania Saviolo, *La Scommessa del Made in Italy e il Futuro della Moda Italiana*, Milan, Etas, 2004.

CORFIELD, Penelope J., "Walking the City Streets: the Urban Odyssey in Eighteenth-Century England," *Journal of Urban History*, 6–4 (1990), pp. 132–174.

COSENTINO, Francesca, *Osteoporosi e Invalidità Motorie nelle Arti Figurative*, Rome, Arti Grafiche Editoriali, 1999.

COWARD, David, "The Sublimation of a Fetishist: Restif de la Bretonne (1734–1806)," *Eighteenth Century Life*, 9–1 (1985), pp. 98–108.

COX, Caroline, *Stiletto*, New York, Harper Design International, 2004.

CRAIK, Jennifer, *Uniforms Exposed: From Conformity to Transgression*, Oxford and New York, Berg, 2005.

Crispin Anecdotes: Comprising Interesting Notices of Shoemakers, Who Have Been Distinguished for Genius, Enterprise and Eccentricity…, Sheffield, John Blackwell, 1827.

CROWDER, Michael, *The Story of Nigeria*, London, Faber and Faber, 1962.

CROWSTON, Clare Haru, *Fabricating Women. The Seamstresses of Old Regime France, 1675–1791*, Durham, NC, Duke University Press, 2001.

CUNNINGTON, Cecil Willet, *English Women's Clothing in the Nineteenth Century*, New York, Dover Publications, [1937] 1990.

DA CAPESTRANO, Giovanni, *Degli Ornamenti Specie delle Donne*, edited by Aniceto Chiappini, Siena, Edizioni Cantagalli, 1956.

DALÍ, Salvador, *The Secret Life of Salvador Dalí*, London, Vision Press, 1949.

Dalla Parte della Scarpa: Le Calzature e Vigevano dal 1400 al 1940, Vigevano, Diacronia, 1992.

DAVANZO POLI, Doretta (ed.), *The Arts and Crafts of Fashion in Venice from the 13th Century to the 18th Century*, Italian Trade Commission – Consorzio Maestri Calzaturieri del Brenta, 2005.

DAVIS, Robert C., "The Geography of Gender in the Renaissance," in Judith C. Brown and Robert C. Davis (eds), *Gender and Society in Renaissance Italy*, London and New York, Longman, 1998, pp. 19–38.

DE BECKER, Joseph Ernest, *Nightless City or History of the Yoshiwara Yūkwaku*, Rutland Vermont and Tokyo, Charles E. Tuttle, 5th edn., 1971.

DE CARACCIOLI, Louis-Antoine [attrib.], *La Critique des Dames et des Messieurs à Leur Toilette*, Inscribed "1770."

DE NEGRI, Eve, *Nigerian Body Adornment*, Lagos, Nigeria Magazine, 1976.

DE VEER, Elizabeth and Ann O'Hear, "Gerhard Rohlfs in Yorubaland," *History in Africa*, 21 (1994), pp. 251–268.

DEONNA, W., "Monokrepides," *Revue de l'Histoire des Religions*, 89 (1935), pp. 50–72.

DERRIDA, Jacques, "Restitutions of the Truth in Pointing ['Pointure']," in Donald Preziosi (ed.), *The Art of Art History: A Critical Anthology*, Oxford and New York, Oxford University Press, [1978] 1998, pp. 432–449.

DERRICK, Robin and Robin Muir, *Unseen Vogue. The Secret History of Fashion Photography*, London, Little Brown, 2002.

DES-ESSARTZ, [Jean-Charles], *Traité de l'Education Corporelle des Enfants en Bas Âge, ou Reflexions-Pratiques sur les Moyens de Procurer une Meilleure Constitution aux Citoyens*, Paris, Jean-Thomas Hérissant, 1760.

[DESHAIS-GENDRON, Louis-Florent], *Lettre à Monsieur xxx sur Plusieurs Maladies des Yeux, Causées par l'Usage du Rouge et du Blanc*, Paris, 1760.

DEVLIN, James Dacres, *The Boot and Shoe Trade of France as it Affects the Interests of the British Manufacturer in the Same Business*, London, A. Eccles, 1838.

DEVLIN, James Dacres, *The Shoemaker (Part 1)*, London, C. Knight, 1839.

DEVLIN, James Dacres, *The Shoemaker. The Guide to Trade (Part 2)*, London, C. Knight, 1841.

DEVLIN, James Dacres, *Critica Crispiana; or the Boots and Shoes British and Foreign of the Great Exhibition*, London, 1852.

DEVLIN, James Dacres, *Contract Reform: Its Necessary Shewn in Respect to the Shoemaker, Soldier, Sailor*, London, E. Stanford, 1856.

DEVLIN, Polly, *Vogue 1920–1980. Moda, Immagine e Costume*, Milan, Mondadori, 1980.

DI SOMMA, Giuseppe, "Salvatore Ferragamo: The Object of Design," in Stefania Ricci (ed.), *Ideas, Models, Inventions*, Livorno, Sillabe, 2004.

DIDEROT, Denis, and d'Alembert, Jean

Le Rond, *Encyclopédie; ou Dictionnaire Raisonné des Sciences, des Arts et des Métiers…*, Paris, 1751–65; Stuttgart, Friedrich Frommann Verlag, 1967 [facsimile of 1751–80 edition].

DOEFF, Hendrik, *Recollections of Japan*, trans. Annick M. Doeff, Victoria, BC, Trafford Press, 2003.

DOLLIMORE, Jonathan, *Sexual Dissidence: Augustine to Wilde, Freud to Foucault*, Oxford, Clarendon Press, 1996.

DONALD, Diana, *The Age of Caricature: Satirical Prints in the Age of George III*, New Haven, Yale University Press, 1996.

DONOGHUE, John D., *Pariah Persistence in Changing Japan – A Case Study*, Washington, DC, University Press of America, 1978.

DOWIE, James, *The Foot and Its Covering: Comprising a Full Translation of Dr. Camper's Work on "The Best Form of Shoe,"* London, Hardwicke, 1861.

DOYLE, Jennifer, Jonathan Flatley and Jose Esteban Munoz (eds), *Pop Out: Queer Warhol*. Durham, NC and London, Duke University Press, 1996.

DREWAL, Henry John and John Mason, "Beads, Body and Soul: Art and Light in the Yoruba Universe," *African Arts*, 31–1 (1998), pp. 1–27.

DUFFY, Michael, *The Englishman and the Foreigner*, Cambridge, Chadwyck-Healey, 1986.

DUBERMAN, Martin (ed.), *Queer Representations: Reading Lives, Reading Cultures*, New York and London, New York University Press, 1997.

DURIAN-RESS, S., *Schue*, Munich, Hirmer Vergal, 1992.

DYER, Richard, *The Matter of Images: Essays on Representations*, New York and London, Routledge, 1993.

DYER, Richard, *The Culture of Queers*, New York and London, Routledge, 2002.

DYSON, M. E., "Be Like Mike?: Michael Jordan and the Pedagogy of Desire," *Cultural Studies*, 7–1 (1995), pp. 64–72.

ECHERUO, Michael J. C., *Victorian Lagos: Aspects of Nineteenth-Century Lagos Life*, London, Macmillan, 1977.

EDMUNDS, L., "Thucydides on Monosandalism," *Greek, Roman and Byzantine Studies,* Monograph 10 (1984), pp. 71–75.

EIXIMENIS, Francesc, *Estetica Medievale dell'Eros, della Mensa e della Città*, edited by Gabriella Zanoletti, Milan, Jaka Books, 1985.

ELDERKIN, G. W., "The Hero on a Sandal," *Hesperia*, 10–4 (1941), pp. 381–387.

ELLIS, Havelock, *Studies in the Psychology of Sex*, New York, Random House, 1936.

ENTWISTLE, Joanne, *The Fashioned Body: Fashion, Dress, and Modern Social Theory*, Cambridge, Polity Press, 2000.

ESTES, Clarissa Pinkola, *Women Who Run With The Wolves: Contacting the Power of the Wild Woman*, London, Rider, 1993.

EVELYN, John, *The Diary of John Evelyn*, edited by E. S. de Beer, London, Oxford University Press, 1959.

FAGE, J. D., "Some Remarks on Beads and Trade in Lower Guinea in the Sixteenth and Seventeenth Centuries," *Journal of African History,* 3–2 (1962), pp. 343–347.

FAGG, William, *Yoruba Beadwork: Art of Nigeria*, New York, Pace Editions, 1980.

FEHER, Michel et al. (eds), *Fragments for a History of the Human Body*, New York, Zone, 1989.

FERRAGAMO, Salvatore, *Shoemaker of Dreams: The Autobiography of Salvatore Ferragamo*, London, Harrap, 1957.

FINE, Ben and Ellen Leopold, "Consumerism and the Industrial Revolution," *Social History*, 15–2 (1990), pp. 151–179.

FIORENTINI CAPITANI, Aurora and Stefania Ricci, "Considerazioni sull'Abbigliamento del Quattrocento in Toscana," in Aurora Fiorentini Capitani, Vittorio Erlindo and Stefania Ricci (eds), *Il Costume al Tempo di Pico e Lorenzo il Magnifico*, Milan, Edizioni Charta, 1994, pp. 51–75.

FIORENTINI CAPITANI, Aurora and Stefania Ricci, "Le Carte Vincenti della Moda Italiana," in Giannino Malossi (ed.), *La Sala Bianca: La Nascita della Moda Italiana*, Milan, Electa, 1992, pp. 91–130.

FISCHER, Hal, *Gay Semiotics: A Photographic Study of Visual Coding Among Homosexual Men,* San Francisco, NFS Press, 1977.

FLINT, Timothy, "Travellers in America," *The Knickerbocker, or New York Monthly Magazine,* 2 (1833), pp. 283–302.

FLOCH, Jean-Marie, *L'Indémodable* Total Look *de Chanel*, Paris, Presses Universitaires de France, 1995.

FLÜGEL, John Carl, *The Psychology of Clothes*, London, Hogarth Press, 1930.

FONTANA, Giovanni Luigi (ed.), *100 Anni di Industria Calzaturiera nella Riviera del Brenta*, Stra, ACRiB, 1998.

FONTANA, Giovanni Luigi, " 'Oggetti d'Arte Chiamati Scarpe': René Fernando Cavilla (interview)," in Giovanni Luigi Fontana (ed.), *100 Anni di Industria Calzaturiera nella Riviera del Brenta,* Stra, ACRiB, 1998, pp. 331–336.

FOSTER, Hal, *Compulsive Beauty*, Cambridge, MA and London, MIT Press, 2000.

FOUCAULT, Michel, *The History of Sexuality*, Harmondsworth, Penguin, 1992.

FRANCOU, B. (père), and Francou, J.-F. (fils), *L'Art du Bottier*, 1833.

FRANZ, Marie-Louise von, *The Interpretation of Fairy Tales*, Boston, Shambala Press, [1970] rev. ed. 1996.

FREUD, Sigmund, "Three Essays on the Theory of Sexuality," in James Strachey (ed.), *The Standard Edition of the Complete Psychological Works of Sigmund Freud*, London, Hogarth Press, [1905] 1953, vol. 7, pp. 125–245.

FREUD, Sigmund, "The Uncanny," in James Strachey (ed.), *The Standard Edition of the Complete Psychological Works of Sigmund Freud*, London, Hogarth Press, [1919] 1953, vol. 17, pp. 219–256.

FRICK, Carole Collier, *Dressing Renaissance Florence. Families, Fortunes and Fine Clothing*, Baltimore and London, Johns Hopkins University Press, 2002.

FRIGENI, R. and W. Tousijn, *L'Industria della Calzatura in Italia,* Bologna, Il Mulino, 1976.

FROLIC, Andrea N., "Wear it with Pride: The Fashions of Toronto's Pride Parade and Canadian Queer Identities," in *A Queer Country: Gay and Lesbian Studies in the Canadian Context*, Vancouver, Arsenal Pulp Press, 2001, pp. 257–284.

FUSS, Diane (ed.), *Inside/Out – Lesbian Theories and Gay Theories*, New York and London, Routledge, 1991.

GAIBISSO, Anna Maria, *Struttura e Competitività del Settore Calzaturiero in Italia,* Milan, Ceris and FrancoAngeli, 1992.

GABLIK, Suzi, *Magritte,* London, Thames and Hudson, 1972.

GALL, Gunter, *Deutsches Ledermuseum Katalog Heft,* 6 (1980).

GARBER, Marjorie, *Vested Interests. Cross-Dressing and Cultural Anxiety*, London, Routledge, 1992.

GARCIA, Bobbito, *Where'd You Get Those?: New York City's Sneaker Culture 1960–1987*, Sydney, Powerhouse Cultural Entertainment Books, 2003.

GARSAULT, François Alexandre de, *Art du Cordonnier*, Paris, [Académie Royale des Sciences], 1767.

GARZONI, Tomaso, *La Piazza Universale di Tutte le Professioni del Mondo*, edited by Paolo Cherchi and Beatrice Collina, Turin, Einaudi, 1996.

GAY, John, *Trivia; or, the Art of Walking the Streets of London,* London, printed for Bernard Lintott, 1716.

GAZDA, Elaine K. (ed.), *The Villa of the Mysteries in Pompeii. Ancient Ritual, Modern Muse*, Ann Arbor, The Kelsey Museum of Archaeology and The

University of Michigan Museum of Art, 2000.

GEBHARD, Paul H., "Fetishism and Sadomasochism," in Martin Weibberg (ed.), *Sex Research: Studies for the Kinsey Institute*, New York, Oxford University Press, 1976.

GERBER, Frederick H., *Cochineal and the Insect Dyes*, Ormond Beach, Florida, Frederick H. Gerber, 1978.

GHINATO, Alberto, "Apostolato Religioso e Sociale di San Giacomo della Marca in Terni," *Archivum Franciscanum Historicum*, 49 (1956), pp. 106–142 and 352–390.

GLENDINNING, Victoria, *Vita. The Life of V. Sackville-West*, Penguin, Harmondsworth, 1984.

GIROTTI, Eugenia, *La Calzatura, Storia e Costume*, Milan, BE-MA Editrice, 1989.

GLOVER, Edvard, "A Note on Idealisation," in *On the Early Development of Mind*, London, Image, [1938] 1956, pp. 293–294.

GLOVER, Edvard, "Sublimation, Substitution and Social Anxiety," in *On the Early Development of Mind*, London, Image, [1931] 1956, pp. 146–7.

GODMAN, Edward and Julia Bamford (eds), *Small Firms and Industrial Districts in Italy*, London, Routledge, 1989.

GOLDSMITH, Oliver (attrib.), *The History of Little Goody Two-Shoes; Otherwise Called Miss Margery Two-Shoes*, London, J. Newbery, 1766.

GOTTARDI, Giorgio, *Anatomia di un Sistema Industriale Locale*, Venice, Marsilio, 1979.

GOTTARDI, Giorgio (ed.), *Trasferimento di Tecnologie in un Settore Maturo*, Padua, Cleup, 1991.

GOWING, Laura, "The Freedom of the Street: Women and Social Space, 1560–1640," in Paul Griffiths and Mark S. R. Jenner (eds), *Londinopolis: Essays in the Cultural and Social History of Early Modern London*, Manchester, Manchester University Press, 2000, pp. 130–151.

GREENIDGE, Terence, *Degenerate Oxford? A Critical Study of Modern University Life*, London, Chapman & Hall, 1930.

GREIG, T. Watson, *Ladies' Dress Shoes of the Nineteenth Century*, Edinburgh, D. Douglas, 1900.

GREIG, T. Watson, *Ladies' Old-fashioned Shoes, with Supplement to Old-fashioned Shoes*, Edinburgh, D. Douglas, 1889.

GREW, Francis and Magrethe De Neergard, *Shoes and Pattens. Medieval Finds from Excavations in London*, London, Her Majesty's Stationery Office, 1988.

GRIFFIS, William Elliot, *The Mikado's Empire: Japan, its History and Culture*, New York and London, Harper Publishers, 1903.

GRIFFITH, Captain Wyn, *Up to Mametz*, London, Faber & Faber, 1931.

GRIMES, William, "The Chanel Platform," *New York Times*, May 17, 1992.

HAAHR, Joan Gluckauf, "The Red Shoes," in Jack Zipes (ed.), *The Oxford Companion to Fairy Tales*, Oxford, Oxford University Press, 2000.

HACKING, Ian, *The Taming of Chance*, Cambridge, Cambridge University Press, 1990.

HALL, Edwin, *The Arnolfini Betrothal. Medieval Marriage and Enigma of Van Eyck's Double Portrait*, Berkeley and London, University of California Press, 1994.

HALL, Joseph Sparkes, *History and Manufacture of Boots and Shoes… Being one of the Lectures Delivered at the Society of Arts*, London, 1853.

HALL, Joseph Sparkes, *The Book of the Feet: A History of Boots and Shoes. With Illustrations of the Fashions of the Egyptians, Hebrews, Persians, Greeks and Romans, and the Prevailing Style throughout Europe during the Middle Ages down to the Present Period*, London, Simpkin, Marshall & Co., 1846.

HALL, Stuart and Tony Jefferson (eds), *Resistance Through Rituals: Youth Subcultures in Post War Britain*, London, Hutchinson, 1975.

HALPERIN, David M., *Saint Foucault: Towards a Gay Hagiography*, New York, Oxford University Press, 1995.

HALPERIN, David M., *How to Do the History of Homosexuality*, Chicago and London, University of Chicago Press, 2002.

HANSEN, Albert, "H. C. Andersen. Beweis seiner Homosexualität," *Jahrbuch für sexuelle Zwischenstufen* (1901).

HANSON, Dian, "Just My Opinion: Perfect Strangers," *Leg Show*, September 1994, pp. 4–5.

HARVEY, John, *Men in Black*, London, Reaktion Books, 1995.

HAZARD, Blanche, *The Organization of the Boot and Shoe Industry in Massachusetts before 1875*, Cambridge, MA, Harvard University Press, 1921.

HEBDIGE, Dick, *Subcultures and the Meaning of Style*, London, Methuen, 1979.

HEIDEGGER, Martin, "The Origin of the Work of Art," in Donald Preziosi (ed.), *The Art of Art History: A Critical Anthology*, Oxford and New York, Oxford University Press, [1935] 1998, pp. 413–426.

HERDT, Gilbert (ed.), *Third Sex Third Gender. Beyond Sexual Dimorphism in Culture and History*. New York, Zone Books, 1994.

HESKETH-PRITCHARD, Major H., *Sniping in France*, London, Hutchinson, c. 1920.

HICKS, Ashley, *David Hicks: Designer*, London, Scriptum Editions, 2003.

HIROSHIMA-SHI REKISHI KAGAKU KYŌIKU IINKAI (ed.), *Geta-zukuri*, Hiroshima, Hiroshima-shi kyōiku iinkai, 1991.

HORLOCK, Thomas, *A Few Words to Journeymen Shoemakers about Gutta Percha… Illustrated with Wood Engravings*, London, W. Strange, 1851.

HUGHES, Bernard G. and Therle Hughes, *Georgian Buckles*, London, Greater London Council, 1971.

HURLOCK, Elizabeth B., "Sumptuary Law," in Mary Ellen Roach and Joanne Bubolz Eicher (eds), *Dress, Adornment and the Social Order*, New York, John Wiley, 1965, pp. 295–301.

HYDE, H. Montgomery (ed.), *The Annotated Oscar Wilde. Poems, Fiction, Plays, Lectures, Essays, and Letters*, New York, Clarkson N. Potter, 1982.

IHARA SAIKAKU, *This Scheming World*, trans. Masanori Takatsuka and David C. Stubbs, Rutland, Vermont & Tokyo, Charles E. Tuttle, 1965.

IKKU JIPPENSHA, *Hizakurige or Shank's Mare*, trans. Thomas Satchell, Rutland, Vermont & Tokyo, Charles E. Tuttle, 1965.

Indagine sulla Domanda e l'Offerta di Innovazione nel Settore Calzaturiero, Istituto per la Promozione Industriale, n.d., 2005.

Intorno alla Acconciatura del Capo e Calzatura delle Donne Veneziane, Secolo XV e XVI. Per Nozze Allegri-Berchet, Venice, Stabilimento Tipografico di Giovanni Cecchini, 1884.

INUI HIROMI, *Edo no shokunin*, Yoshikawa kobunkan, Tokyo, 1996.

ISICHEI, Elizabeth, *A History of Nigeria*, Longman, Lagos, 1983.

JAGOSE, Annamarie, *Queer Theory*, Melbourne, Melbourne University Press, 1998.

Jinrin kinmo zui, Tokyo, Heibonsha, [1690] 1990.

JOHNSON, Kim K. P. and Shannon J. Lennon, "Introduction: Appearance and Social Power," in Kim K. P. Johnson and Shannon J. Lennon (eds), *Appearance and Power*, Oxford and New York, Berg, 1999, pp. 1–10.

JOHNSON, Samuel, *The History of the Yorubas: From the Earliest Times to the Beginning of the British Protectorate*, Lagos, C. M. S. (Nigeria) Bookshops, 1921.

JONES, Ellen Carol, "Empty Shoes," in Shari Benstock and Suzanne Ferriss (eds), *Footnotes: On Shoes*, New Brunswick, NJ and London, Rutgers University Press, 2001, pp. 197–232.

JONES, Jennifer, "*Coquettes* and *Grisettes*: Women Buying and Selling in Ancient Regime Paris," in Victoria De Grazia and Ellen Furlough (eds), *The Sex of Things: Gender and Consumption in Historical Perspective*, Berkeley and London, University of California Press, 1996, pp. 25–53.

KALILU, R. O. R., "Leather Work in Oyo: Access to Material as a Factor in the Origin of an African Craft," *African Notes*, 15–1/2 (1991), pp. 105–112.

KALLAND ARNE, *Fishing Villages in Tokugawa Japan*, Honolulu, University of Hawaii Press, 1995.

"The Kano Chronicle," in Herbert Richmond Palmer (ed.), *Sudanese Memoirs: Being Mainly Translations of a Number of Arabic Manuscripts Relating to the Central and Western Sudan*, Lagos: Printed by the Government Printer, 1928, pp. 92–132.

KATZ, Donald, *Just Do It: The Nike Spirit in the Corporate World*, Holbrook, MA, Adams Media Corporation, 1994.

KAVALER-ADLER, Susan, *The Creative Mystique: From Red Shoes Frenzy to Love and Creativity*, New York, Routledge, 1997.

KERN, Stephen, *Anatomy and Destiny: A Cultural History of the Human Body*, Indianapolis, Bobbs Merrill, 1975.

KERR, Paul, Georgina Pye, Teresa Cherfas, Mick Gold and Margaret Mulvihill, *The Crimean War*, London, Boxtree, 1997.

KILMER, Martin F., *Greek Erotica on Attic Red-Figure Vases*, London, Duckworth, 1993.

KIPLING, Rudyard, *The Complete Verse*, London, Kyle Cathie, 2002.

KITAGAWA MORISADA, *Morisada mankō*, edited by Asakura Masahiko and Kashiwagawa Shūichi, Tokyo, Tokyodo shuppan, [c. 1840] 1992.

Kodansha. Enciclopedia del Giappone, Tokyo, Japan Society and Kodansha International, 1983.

KOIZUMI KAZUKO, *Dōgu to kurashi no edo jidai*, Tokyo, Yoshikawa kobunkan, 1999.

KOTCH, J., "The Pussy Posse," *Time Out: Special Issue, Lover Girls: From Lipstick Lesbians to Diesel Dykes*, June 21–28, 1995, London, Time Out Magazine Limited, 1995, pp. 28–31.

KUCHTA, David, *The Three-Piece Suit and Modern Masculinity: England 1550–1850*, Berkeley and London, University of California Press, 2002.

KYBALOVA, Ludmila, Olga Herbenova and Milena Lamarova, *Enciclopedia Illustrata della Moda*, Italian edition by G. Malossi, Milan, Bruno Mondadori, 2002.

LABI, Kwame Amoah, *Asante Kings of the Twentieth Century*, Legon, Institute of African Studies, 2000.

LADELE, T. A. A., O. Mustapha, I. A. Aworinde, O. Oyerinde and O. Oladapo, *Akojopo Iwadii Ijinle Asa Yoruba (Collection of Research Findings on Yoruba Customs)*, Ibadan, Macmillan Publishers, 1986.

LAMBERT, Andrew and Stephen Badsey, *The War Correspondents: The Crimean War*, Dover, Alan Sutton, 1994.

LANDER, Richard, *Records of Captain Clapperton's Last Expedition to Africa*, London, Colburn and Bentley, 1830.

LANDER, Richard Lemon and John Lander, *Niger Journal of Richard and John Lander*, edited by Robin H. Hallett, London, Routledge and Kegan Paul, 1965.

LANGEHOUGH, Steven, "Symbol, Status and Shoes: The Graphics of the World at Our Feet," in Akiko Busch (ed.), *Design For Sport*, New York, Cooper-Hewitt National Design Museum, Smithsonian Institution, 1998.

LAPOVSKY KENNEDY, Elizabeth and Madeline D. Davis, *Boots of Leather, Slippers of Gold: A History of a Lesbian Community*, Middlesex, Penguin Books, 1993.

LAUGHRAN, Michelle, " 'Infecting Souls and Sickening Bodies': Prostitution and the Question of the 'Mal Francese' in Sixteenth-Century Venice," unpublished paper, 2005.

LE CORBUSIER, *The Decorative Art of Today*, trans. James Dunnett, London, Architectural Press, 1987.

LEDGER, Florence E., *Put your Foot Down. A Treatise on the History of Shoes*, Melksham, Venton, 1985.

LEHMANN, Ulrich, *Tigersprung: Fashion in Modernity*, Cambridge, MA, MIT Press, 2000.

LEMIRE, Beverly, *Dress, Culture and Commerce: The English Clothing Trade before the Factory, 1660–1800*, Basingstoke, Macmilan, 1997.

LEVI PISETZKY, Rosita, *Storia del Costume in Italia*, Milan, Istituto Editoriale Italiano Fondazione G. Treccani, 1964–69.

LEVI PISETZKY, Rosita, *Il Costume e la Moda nella Società Italiana*, Turin, Einaudi, 1978.

LÉVI-STRAUSS, Claude, "The Two Faces of Red," in *Colors*, Tokyo, MOMA Kyoto/Mori Art Museum, 2004.

LEWIN, Ellen and William L. Leap, *Out in Theory: The Emergence of Lesbian and Gay Anthropology*, Urbana and Chicago, University of Chicago Press, 2002.

LEWIS, Reina. "Looking Good: The Lesbian Gaze and Fashion Imagery," *Feminist Review*, 55–1 (1997), pp. 92–109.

Liber Grossus Antiquus Comunis Regii (Liber Pax Constantiae), edited by Saverio Gatta, Florence, Deputazione di Storia Patria, 1962.

LIMOJON DE SAINT DISDIER, Alexandre Toussaint de, *La Ville et la Republique de Venice*, Paris, G. De Luyne, 1680.

LIPOVETSKY, Gilles, *The Empire of Fashion: Dressing the Modern Democracy*, trans. Catherine Porter, Princeton, Princeton University Press, 1994.

LIPPS, Ophelia, "Thanks for the Mammaries: The Rise and Fall of My Boobs," in Marcelle Karp and Debbie Stoller (eds), *The Bust Guide to the New Girl Order*, New York, Penguin Group, 1999.

LLOYD, Peter C., "Osifakorede of Ijebu," *Odu*, 8 (1960), pp. 59–64.

LLOYD, Peter C., "Osifekunde of Ijebu," in Philip D. Curtin (ed.), *Africa Remembered: Narratives by West Africans from the Era of the Slave Trade*, Madison, WI, University of Wisconsin Press, 1967, pp. 217–288.

Lo Stato della Moda, Rapporto Periodico del Censis, Florence, Edifir, 1989.

LONGFORD, Elizabeth, *Wellington: Pillar of State*, London, Weidenfeld & Nicholson, 1972.

LOOS, Adlofl, *Spoken into the Void: Collected Essays 1897–1900*, introd. Aldo Rossi, Cambridge, MA, MIT Press, 1982.

LUCHET, Auguste, *L'Art Industriel à l'Exposition Universelle de 1867*, Paris, Librairie Internationale, 1868.

LUDWIG, Gustav and Pompeo G. Molmenti, *Vittore Carpaccio. La Vita e le Opere*, Milan, Tip. Umberto Allegretti, 1906.

LYMAN MUNSON, E., *The Soldier's Foot and the Military Shoe*, Fort Leavenworth, KS, US Army War Department, 1912.

LYON, Todd, "Big Feet; or, How Cinderella's Glass Slipper Got Smashed under the Heel of a Size Ten Doc Marten," in Shari Benstock and Suzanne Ferriss (eds), *Footnotes: On Shoes*, New Brunswick, NJ and London, Rutgers University Press, 2001, pp. 291–298.

MACKIE, Erin, "Red Shoes and Bloody Stumps," in Shari Benstock, and Suzanne Ferriss (eds), *Footnotes: On Shoes*, New Brunswick, NJ and London, Rutgers University Press, 2001, pp. 233–250.

Maestri Calzaturieri della Riviera del Brenta, Stra, 1992.

MAGNUSON, Ann, "Hell on Heels," *Allure*, September 1994.

MALABARBA, Ivana, *Ai Piedi di una Donna*, Milan, Idealibri, 1991.

MALDONADO, Tomas, *Disegno Industriale: Un Riesame*, Milan, Feltrinelli, 1976.

MALOSSI, Giannino (ed.), *La Sala Bianca: la Nascita della Moda Italiana*, Milan, Electa, 1992.

Manuale di Calceologia per la Scuola Modellisti Calzaturieri della Riviera del Brenta, Fiesso d'Artico, Consorzio Centro Veneto Calzaturiero, 1991.

MARIACHER, Giovanni, "L'Arte dei Calzolai a Venezia dal XIII al XVIII secolo," in *I Mestieri della Moda a Venezia dal XIII al XVIII Secolo. Catalogo della Mostra tenutasi a Venezia al Museo Correr giugno-settembre 1988*, Venice, Edizioni del Cavallino, 1988, pp. 31–37.

MARRIOT, John, "The Spatiality of the Poor in Eighteenth-Century London," in Tim Hitchcock and Heather Shore (eds), *The Streets of London. From the Great Fire to the Great Stink*, London, Rivers Oram Press, 2003, pp. 119–34.

MARTIN, Richard, "The Gay Factor in Fashion," *Esquire Gentlemen*, 1993.

MARX, Karl, *Capital*, London, 1867.

Materials and Creativity, Florence, Salvatore Ferragamo Museum, 1997.

MATTHEWS DAVID, Alison, "Cutting a Figure: Tailoring, Technology and Social Identity in Nineteenth-Century Paris," Unpublished Ph.D. Thesis, Stanford University, 2002.

MATTHEWS DAVID, Alison, "Decorated Men: Fashioning the French Soldier, 1852–1914," *Fashion Theory*, 7–1 (2003), pp. 3–38.

MATTSON, Heidi, *Ivy League Stripper*, New York, Arcade Publishing, 1995.

MAY, Daniel J., "Journey in the Yoruba and Nupe Countries in 1858," *Journal of the Royal Geographical Society*, 30 (1860), pp. 212–233.

MAYNARD, Margaret, *Fashioned from Penury: Dress as Cultural Practice in Colonial Australia*, Cambridge, Cambridge University Press, 1994.

MCCLAIN, James L., "Space, Power, Wealth and Status in Seventeenth-Century Osaka," in James L. McClain and Wakita Osamu (eds), *Osaka – The Merchant's Capital of Early Modern Japan*, Ithaca, NY and London, Cornell University Press, 1999, pp. 44–79.

MCDOWELL, Colin, *Shoes. Fashion and Fantasy*, New York, Rizzoli, 1989.

MCDOWELL, Colin, *Manolo Blahnik*, New York, HarperCollins, 2000.

MCLAUGHLIN, Noel, "Rock Fashion and Performativity," in Stella Bruzzi

and Pamela Church Gibson (eds), *Fashion Cultures: Theories, Explorations and Analysis*, London and New York, Routledge, 2000, pp. 264–285.

MCNEIL, Peter, "Norman Hartnell (1901–1979)," in Robert Aldrich and Garry Wotherspoon (eds), *Who's Who in Gay and Lesbian History. From Antiquity to World War II. Vol. 1*, London and New York, Routledge, 2001, p. 204.

MCNEIL, Peter and Giorgio Riello, "The Art and Science of Walking: Mobility, Gender and Footwear in the Long Eighteenth Century," *Fashion Theory*, 9–2 (2005), pp. 175–204.

MCNEIL, Peter, "Fashion Victims: Class, Gender and Sexuality and the Macaroni, c. 1765–80," Ph.D. Thesis, University of Sydney, 1999.

MCNEIL, Peter, "Macaroni Masculinities," *Fashion Theory*, 4–4 (2000), pp. 373–404.

MCROBBIE, Angela, "Shut up and Dance: Youth Culture and Changing Modes of Femininity," in Angela McRobbie (ed.), *Post Modernism and Popular Culture*, London and New York, Routledge, 1994.

MEIJLAN, G. F., *Japan*, Amsterdam, W. Westerman & Zoon, 1830.

MELDINI, P., "L'Economia della Ricostruzione," in Omar Calabrese et al. (eds), *Italia Moderna. Immagini e Storia di una Identità Nazionale. Guerra, Dopoguerra, Ricostruzione, Decollo*, Milan, Electa, 1983–1985, vol. III.

MERCIER, Louis-Sébastien, *Tableau de Paris*, Amsterdam, 1783.

MERCIER, Louis-Sébastien, *Le Nouveau de Paris*, Paris, 1790.

MERCIER, Louis-Sébastien, *New Picture of Paris*, London, 1800.

MERRICK, Jeffrey, "Commissioner Foucault, Inspecteur Noël, and the "Pederasts" of Paris, 1780–3," *Journal of Social History*, 32–2 (1998), pp. 287–307.

MEYERS, Jeffrey, *Scott Fitzgerald*, New York, Harper Collins, 1994.

MICHALSKI, Sergiusz, *New Objectivity: Painting in Germany in the 1920s*, Köln, Taschen, 1990.

MIKHAIL, Edward Halim, *Oscar Wilde. Interviews and Recollections*, London, Macmillan, 1979.

MILAM, Jennifer, "Playful Constructions and Fragonard's Swinging Scenes," *Eighteenth-Century Studies*, 33–4 (2000), 543–559.

MILLSON, Alvan W., "The Yoruba Country, West Africa," *Proceedings of the Royal Geographical Society*, 13–10 (1891), pp. 577–587.

MOERS, E., *The Dandy: Brummel to Beerbohm*, London, Secker & Warburg, 1960.

MOLMENTI, Pompeo G., *Storia di Venezia nella Vita Privata*, Trieste, LINT, 1973.

MORLACCHI, Antonello, "Introduzione," in Antonello Morlacchi, Giuseppe Bellotti (eds), *L'Impresa Calzaturiera. Progettazione, Tecnica e Organizzazione: Vol. I. La Progettazione*, Trescore, Editrice San Marco, 1998.

MORITZ, Carl Philip, *Journeys of a German in England: a Walking Tour of England in 1782*, trans. Reginald Nettel, London, Cape, [1782] 1965.

MORROW, Katherine Dohan, *Greek Footwear and the Dating of Sculpture*, Wisconsin and London, University of Wisconsin Press, 1985.

MORYSON, Fynes, *An Itinerary*, [London] Glasgow, James Maclehose and Sons, [1617] 1905.

MOUNFIELD, Peter R., "Early Technological Innovation in the British Footwear Industry," *Industrial Archaeological Review*, 2 (1977–78), pp. 129–142.

MR. X, "The Cult of the High Heel," *Photo Bits*, March 25, 1910.

MUNSON, Edward, *The Theory and Practice of Military Hygiene*, London, Ballière, Tindall & Cox, 1901.

MUZZARELLI, Maria Giuseppina and Antonella Campanini (eds), *Disciplinare il Lusso. La Legislazione Suntuaria in Italia e in Europa tra Medioevo ed Età Moderna*, Rome, Carocci Editore, 2003.

MUZZARELLI, Maria Giuseppina, "Le Leggi Suntuarie," in Carlo Marco Belfanti and Fabio Giusberti (eds), *Storia d'Italia. Annali 19. La Moda*, Turin, Einaudi, 2003, pp. 185–220.

MUZZARELLI, Maria Giuseppina (ed.), *La Legislazione Suntuaria. Secoli XIII–XVI. Emilia-Romagna*, Rome, Pubblicazioni degli Archivi di Stato, 2002.

MUZZARELLI, Maria Giuseppina, *Gli Inganni delle Apparenze. Disciplina di Vesti e Ornamenti alla Fine del Medioevo*, Turin, Scriptorium, 1996.

MUZZARELLI, Maria Giuseppina, *Guardaroba Medievale. Vesti e Società dal XIII al XVI Secolo*, Bologna, Il Mulino, 1999.

MYERLY, Scott, *British Military Spectacle*, Cambridge, MA, Cambridge University Press, 1996.

"Nanaju ichi ban shokunin utaawase," in *Edokagaku koten sosho*, Tokyo, Kyowa shuppan, 1977.

NARDI, Peter (ed.), *Gay Masculinities*, London, Sage Publications, 2000.

NEWTON, Helmut, *Helmut Newton*, introd. Karl Lagerfeld, New York, Pantheon Books, 1987.

NISHIYAMA MATSUNOSUKE, et al., *Edo gaku jiten*, Tokyo, Kobundo, 1984.

NITSCHKE, Günter, *From Shinto to Ando-Studies in Architectural Anthropology in Japan*, London, Academic Editions, 1993.

NIZER, Louis, *My Life in Court*, Garden City, NY, Doubleday, 1961.

Nouvelle Encyclopédie des Arts et Métiers. Art de la Chaussure, Paris, no publisher, 1824.

Nuove Figure Professionali, Novi Formatori e Modelli Formativi nel Settore Calzaturiero Veneto, Stra, Politecnico Calzaturiero, 2004, pp. 55–61.

OAKLEY, John H. and Rebecca H. Sinos, *The Wedding in Ancient Athens*, Wisconsin and London, University of Wisconsin Press, 1993.

ODUYOYE, Modupe, *The Planting of Christianity in Yorubaland, 1842–1888*, Ibadan, Daystar 1963.

OGBORN, Miles and Charles W. J. Withers, "Introduction: Georgian Geographies?" in Miles Ogborn and Charles W. J. Withers (eds), *Georgian Geographies: Essays on Space, Place and Landscape in the Eighteenth Century*, Manchester and New York, Manchester University Press, 2004, pp. 1–23.

OGBORN, Miles, "Georgian Geographies?," *Journal of Historical Geography*, 24 – 2 (1998), pp. 218–223.

OGBORN, Miles, *Spaces of Modernity. London's Geographies, 1680–1780*, New York and London, Guilford Press, 1998.

OGDEN, Daniel, "Controlling Women's Dress: Gynaikonomoi," in L. Llewellyn-Jones (ed.), *Women's Dress in the Ancient Greek World*, London and Swansea, Duckworth and the Classical Press of Wales, 2002, pp. 203–225.

OGUNBA, O., "Crowns and Okute at Idowa," *Nigeria Magazine*, 83 (1964).

ORME, Nicholas, *Medieval Children*, New Haven and London, Yale University Press, 2001.

ORSI LANDINI, Roberta and Bruna Niccoli, *Moda a Firenze 1540–1580. Lo Stile di Eleonora di Toledo e la sua Influenza*, Florence, Pagliai Polistampa and Fondazione Arte della Seta Lisio, 2005.

OTTAVIANI, Nico and Grazia Maria (eds), *La Legislazione Suntuaria. Secoli XIII–XVI. Umbria*, Rome, Pubblicazioni degli Archivi di Stato. Fonti XLIII, 2005.

PAMPAGNIN, Vittorio, *La Riviera degli Scarpari. Storie di Uomini di Scarpe e di Lotte nella Riviera del Brenta e Dintorni*, Venice, Centro Studi Ettore Luccini, 2000.

PARKER, Richard G., *Bodies, Pleasures and Passions: Sexual Culture in Contemporary Brazil*, Boston, Beacon Press, 1991.

PARKINS, Wendy, "Introduction," in Wendy Parkins (ed.), *Fashioning the Body Politic*, Oxford and New York, Berg, 2002, pp. 1–18.

PEISS, Kathy, *Hope in a Jar: The Making of America's Beauty Culture*, New York, Henry Holt, 1999.

PERKINS GILMAN, Charlotte, *The Dress of Women. A Critical Introduction to the Symbolism and Sociology of Clothing*, Westport, CT, Greenwood Press, 2002.

PERRAULT, Charles, "Cinderella, or the Little Glass Slipper," in Shari Benstock and Suzanne Ferriss (eds), *Footnotes: On Shoes*, New Brunswick, NJ and London, Rutgers University Press, 2001, pp. 299–304.

PERROT, Philippe, *Fashioning the Bourgeoisie: A History of Clothing in the Nineteenth Century*, trans. Richard Bienvenu, Princeton, Princeton University Press, 1994.

PERTEGATO, F., "Tecniche di Lavorazione delle Calzature Rinascimentali," in Dora Liscia Bemporad (ed.), *Il Costume nell'Età del Rinascimento*, Florence, Edifir, 1988, pp. 347–354.

PETSCHE, Jerome E., *The Steamboat Bertrand: History, Excavation, and Architecture*, Washington, DC, National Park Service, US Department of the Interior, 1974.

PIPONNIER, Françoise and Perrine Mane, *Se Vêtir au Moyen Âge*, Paris, Adam Biro, 1995.

POLHEMUS, Ted, *Street Style: From Sidewalk to Catwalk*, London, Thames and Hudson, 1994.

POLIDORI CALAMANDREI, Egidia, *Le Vesti delle Donne Fiorentine nel Quattrocento*, Rome, Multigrafica, [1924] 1973.

POLIGNANO, Flavia, "Maliarde e Cortigiane: Titoli per una Damnatio. Le Dame di Vittore Carpaccio," *Venezia Cinquecento*, 2 (1992), pp. 5–23.

POND, James, *The Foot and its Covering*, London, Leather Trades Publisher, 1896.

PORTER, Michael, *The Competitive Advantage of Nations*, New York, Macmillian Press, 1990.

PRICE, John, "A History of the Outcaste: Untouchability in Japan," in George De Vos and Hiroshi Wagatsuma (eds), *Japan's Invisible Race – Caste in Culture and Personality*, Berkeley and Los Angeles, University of California Press, 1966.

PROBERT, Christina, *Shoes in Vogue since 1910*, London, Thames and Hudson, 1981.

PROUST, Marcel, *The Guermantes Way II*, London, Vintage, [1922] 1996.

RABINBACH, Anson, *The Human Motor: Energy, Fatigue, and the Origins of Modernity*, Berkeley, University of California Press, 1992.

RADFORD, Robert, "Dangerous Liaisons: Art Fashion and Individualism," *Fashion Theory*, 2–2 (1998), pp. 151–164.

RATOUIS, André, *Histoire de la Cordonnerie Précédé de l'Histoire de la Chaussure Depuis les Temps Plus Reculés Jusqu'en 1830*, Paris, 1886.

RATOUIS, André, *Théorie et Pratique de la Fabrication et du Commerce des Chaussures en 1865*, Paris, Meaux, 1866.

RAUSER, Amelia, "Hair, Authenticity, and the Self-Made Macaroni," *Eighteenth-Century Studies*, 38–1 (2004), pp. 101–117.

REAVES, Gerri, "The Slip in the Ballet Slipper: Illusion and the Naked Foot," in Shari Benstock and Suzanne Ferriss (eds), *Footnotes: On Shoes*, New Brunswick, NJ and London, Rutgers University Press, 2001, pp. 251–271.

REDFERN, William Beales, *Royal and Historic Gloves and Shoes*, London, Methuen, 1904.

REES, John F., *The Art and Mystery of a Cordwainer, or, an Essay on the Principles and Practice of Boot and Shoe-making*, London, Gale, Curtis and Fenner, 1813.

RENDELL, Jane, *The Pursuit of Pleasure: Gender, Space and Architecture in Regency London*, London, The Athlone Press, 2002.

RÉTIF DE LA BRETONNE, Nicolas Anne Edme, *Les Nuits de Paris, ou le Spectateur-nocturne*. Paris, Club du Libraire, [1787] 1960.

REXFORD, Nancy, "The Speaking Shoe," *Essex Institute Historical Collections*, 127 (1991), pp. 161–184.

REXFORD, Nancy, *Women's Shoes in America, 1795–1930*, Kent, OH, Kent State University Press, 2000.

RIBEIRO, Aileen, *Dress in Eighteenth-Century Europe, 1715–1789*, London, Batsford, 1984.

RIBEIRO, Aileen, "Fashion in the Eighteenth Century: Some Anglo-French Comparisons," *Textile History*, 22–2 (1991), pp. 329–345.

RIBEIRO, Aileen, "On Englishness in Dress," in Christopher Breward, Becky Conekin and Caroline Cox (eds), *The Englishness of English Dress*, Oxford and New York, Berg, 2002, pp. 15–27.

RICCI, Stefania, "L'Artigianato della Moda," in Gloria Fossi (ed.), *La Grande Storia dell'Artigianato. Il Novecento*, Florence, Giunti, 2003, pp. 229–255.

RICCI, Stefania (ed.), *Ideas, Models, Inventions*, Livorno, Sillabe, 2004.

RICCO, John Paul, *The Logic of the Lure*, Chicago and London, University of Chicago Press, 2002.

RICHARDSON, W. H., Jr., *The Boot and Shoe Manufacturer's Assistant and Guide, Containing a Brief History of the Trade, History of India-Rubber and Gutta-Percha and Their Application to the Manufacture of Boots and Shoes, etc.*, Boston, Higgins, Bradley & Dayton, 1858.

RICHTER, Giselle Marie Augusta, *Korai. Archaic Greek Maidens: A Study of the Development of the Kore Type in Greek Sculpture*, London and New York, Phaidon, 1968.

RIELLO, Giorgio, "*La Chaussure à la Mode*: Product Innovation and Marketing Strategies in Parisian and London Boot and Shoemaking in the Early Nineteenth Century," *Textile History*, 34–2 (2003), pp. 107–133.

RIELLO, Giorgio, *A Foot in the Past: Producers, Consumers and Footwear in the Long Eighteenth Century*, Oxford, Oxford University Press, 2006.

RIVIERE, Joan, "Womanliness as

Masquerade," in Victor Burgin (ed.), *Formations of Fantasy*, London, Methuen, [1929] 1986, pp. 35–44.

ROBERTSON, Pamela, *Guilty Pleasures: Feminist Camp from Mae West to Madonna*, Durham, NC and London, Duke University Press, 1996.

ROCHE, Daniel, *The People of Paris. An Essay in Popular Culture in the 18th Century*, trans. Marie Evans, Leamington Spa, Berg, 1987.

ROCHE, Daniel, *The Culture of Clothing. Dress and Fashion in the "Ancien Régime,"* trans. Jean Birell, Cambridge, Cambridge University Press, 1994.

RODRIGUES, João, *João Rodriques's Account of Sixteenth-Century Japan*, trans. Michael Cooper, London, Hakluyt Society, 2001.

ROGERS LITTLE, Frances, "Sitting Pretty," *Allure*, 1994, pp. 134–149.

ROLLEY, K., "Cutting a Dash: The Dress of Radclyffe Hall and Una Troubridge," *Feminist Review*, 35 – Summer (1990), pp. 54–62.

ROLLEY, K., "Love, Desire and the Pursuit of the Whole," in Juliet Ash and Elizabeth Wilson (eds), *Chic Thrills: A Fashion Reader*, London, Pandora Press, 1992, pp. 30–39.

ROLT, John, *On Moral Command*, London, Clowes and Sons, 2nd edn., 1842.

ROMANO, Dennis, "The Gondola as a Marker of Station in Venetian Society," *Renaissance Studies*, 8 (1994), pp. 359–374.

ROSS, Andrew, *No Respect: Intellectuals and Popular Culture*, New York and London, Routledge, 1989.

ROSSI, William, *The Sex of the Foot and Shoes*, London, Routledge and Kegan Paul, 1977.

ROUSSEAU, Jean-Jacques, *Emile*, trans. Barbara Foxley, London, J. M. Dent, [1762] 1993.

ROVERATO, Giorgio, *Dell'industria Calzaturiera in Riviera del Brenta ed Altri Saggi*, Padua, Il Telaio, 2004.

RUBBER GROWERS' ASSOCIATION, *Rubber and Footwear*, London,

Rubber Growers' Association, 1926.

RUGGIERO, Guido, *Binding Passions: Tales of Magic, Marriage and Power at the End of the Renaissance*, New York, Oxford University Press, 1993.

RUNTING, Ernest G. V., *First Aid for Foot Troubles, with Special Reference to Battalion Chiropody*, London, The Scientific Press, 1918.

RUSKIN, John, *St. Mark's Rest. The History of Venice Written for the Few Travellers Who Still Care for Her Monuments*, Leipzig, Tauchnitz, 1910.

RUSSELL, William, *Russell's Despatches from the Crimea, 1854–1856*, edited by Nicolas Bentley, London, Andre Deutsch, 1966.

SADLER, A. L., *A Short History of Japanese Architecture*, Rutland, Vermont and Tokyo, Charles E. Tuttle, 1941.

SÄFLUND, Marie-Louise, *The East Pediment of the Temple of Zeus at Olympia. A Reconstruction and Interpretation of its Composition*, Göteborg, Paul Åström Förlag, 1970.

SAGUTO, D. A., "The Wooden Shoe Peg and Pegged Construction in Footwear – Their Historical Origins," *Chronicle of Early American Industry*, 37 (1984), pp. 5–10.

SAND, George, *The Story of My Life*, trans. Dan Hofstadter, New York, Harper & Row, 1979.

SANDERS, Joel (ed.), *Stud: Architectures of Masculinity*, New York, Princeton Architectural Press, 1996.

SASAKU YUZURI and George De Vos, "A Traditional Urban Outcaste Community," in George De Vos and Hiroshi Wagatsuma (eds), *Japan's Invisible Race – Caste in Culture and Personality*, Berkeley and Los Angeles, University of California Press, 1966.

SCHAFFER, Talia, "Fashioning Aestheticism by Aestheticizing Fashion: Wilde, Beerbohm, and the Male Aesthetes' Sartorial Codes," *Victorian Literature and Culture*, 28–1 (2000), pp. 39–54.

SCHAPIRO, Meyer, "The Still Life as a Personal Object – A Note on

Heidegger and Van Gogh," in Donald Preziosi (ed.), *The Art of Art History: A Critical Anthology*, Oxford and New York, Oxford University Press, [1968] 1998, pp. 428–431.

SCHMIECHEN, James, *Sweated Industries and Sweated Labour: The London Clothing Trades 1860–1914*, London, Croom Helm, 1984.

School for Footwear Model Makers and Technicians, Stra, Centro Veneto Calzaturiero, n.d.

SCHULER, Carol M., "The Courtesan in Art: Historical Fact or Modern Fantasy?," *Women's Studies*, 19–1 (1991), pp. 209–222.

SCOTT, Joan, *Gender and the Politics of History*, Berkeley, University of California Press, 1988.

SEDGWICK, Eve Kosovsky, *The Epistemology of the Closet*, Berkeley, University of California Press, 1990.

SEI SHŌNAGON, *The Pillow Book of Sei Shōnagon*, trans. Ivan Morris, New York, Columbia University Press, 1991.

Seifūzoku, Tokyo, Yuzankaku, 1993.

SEIGLE, Cecilia Segawa, *Yoshiwara: The Glittering World of The Japanese Courtesan*, Honolulu, University of Hawaii Press, 1993.

SEIKI KIYOSEI, *The Art of Japanese Joinery*, trans. Yuriko Yokuko and Rebecca M. Davis, New York and Tokyo, Weatherhill, 1977.

SELVATICO, Pietro and Vincenzo Lazzari, *Guida Artistica e Storica di Venezia e delle Isole Circonvicine*, Venice and Milan, P. Ripamonti Carpano, 1852.

SEMMELHACK, Elizabeth, *Icons of Elegance: The Most Influential Shoe Designers of the 20th Century*, Toronto, Bata Shoe Museum, 2005.

SENSFELDER, M., *Histoire de la Cordonnerie*, Paris, 1856.

SEWELL, Captain C. W., MC, *A Resume on Weak and Tired Feet with Prescriptive Directions for Improving Function, Shape and Structure*, London, C. W. Daniel, 1924.

SHAW, T., "A Note on Trade and the Tsoede Bronzes," *West African Journal of Archaeology*, 3 (1973), pp. 233–238.

SHAWCROSS, Rebecca, "High Heels," in *Encyclopaedia of Clothing and Fashion*, edited by Valerie Steele, Detroit: Thomson Gale, 2005.

SHIODA TETSUO, *Hakimono*, Tokyo, Hosei daigaku shuppankyoku, 1973.

Shoe and Leather Lexicon: An Illustrated Glossary of Trade and Technical Terms Relating to Shoes, also Leather and Other Shoe Materials, and Allied Commodities, with Especial Reference to the Production, Distribution and Retail Merchandising of the Finished Article, Boston, Boot and Shoe Recorder Publishing Co., 3rd rev. edn., 1916.

SIGOURNEY, Mrs. L. H. et al., *The Young Lady's Offering: or, Gems of Prose and Poetry*, Boston, Phillips, Sampson & Co., 1851.

SILVERMAN, Kaja, "Fragments of a Fashionable Discourse," in Tania Modleski (ed.), *Studies in Entertainment: Critical Approaches to Mass Culture*, Bloomington, Indiana University Press, 1986.

SINFIELD, Alan, *The Wilde Century. Effeminacy, Oscar Wilde and the Queer Moment*, London and New York, Cassell, 1994.

SMITH, Robert S., *Kingdoms of the Yoruba*, London, Methuen, 1969.

SMITH, Thomas C., "The Japanese Village in the Seventeenth Century," *Journal of Economic History*, 12–1 (1952), pp. 1–20.

SMOLLETT, Tobias George, *Travels Through France and Italy*, London, R. Baldwin, 1766.

SOKOLL, Thomas, *Essex Pauper Letters 1731–1837*, London, The British Academy and Oxford University Press, 2001.

SOKOSKY, M., *Coup-d'Oeil sur les Imperfections de la Chaussure, et les Incommodité qui en Proviennent, Suivi de l'Examen d'un Procédé...*, Paris, Didot, 1811.

Soldier's Companion, London, c. 1800.

SOLNIT, Rebecca, *Wanderlust: A History of Walking*, New York, Viking, 2000.

SPARKE, Penny, *As Long as it's Pink: The Sexual Politics of Taste*, London, Pandora, 1995.

SPECTER, Michael, "High-Heel Heaven," *The New Yorker*, March 20, 2000.

SQUICCIARINO, Nicola, *Il Vestito Parla. Considerazioni Psicologiche sull' Abbigliamento*, Rome, Armando, 1986.

STEELE, Valerie, "*Femme Fatale*: Fashion and Visual Culture in Fin-de-siècle Paris," *Fashion Theory*, 8–3 (2004), pp. 315–328.

STEELE, Valerie, *Paris Fashion. A Cultural History.* New York and Oxford, Oxford University Press, 1988.

STEELE, Valerie, *Fetish: Fashion, Sex and Power*, New York, Oxford University Press, 1996.

STEELE, Valerie, *Shoes: A Lexicon of Style*, New York, Rizzoli, 1999.

STEKEL, Wilhelm, *Sexual Aberrations: The Phenomenon of Fetishism in Relation to Sex*, trans. Samuel Parker, New York, Liveright, 1930.

STOBART, Jon, "Shopping Streets as Social Space: Leisure, Consumerism and Improvement in an Eighteenth-Century Country Town," *Urban History*, 25–1 (1998), pp. 3–21.

STOBART, Jon, "Culture Versus Commerce: Societies and Spaces for Elites in Eighteenth-Century Liverpool," *Journal of Historical Geography*, 28–4 (2002), pp. 471–485.

STOLLER, Debbie, "Untitled," in Marcelle Karp and Debbie Stoller (eds), *The Bust Guide to the New Grrl Order*, New York, Penguin Group, 1999.

STOLLER, Robert, *Pain and Passion: A Psychoanalyst Explores the World of S&M*, New York, Plenum, 1991.

STOLLER, Robert, *Sex and Gender: On the Development of Masculinity and Femininity*, New York, Science House, 1968.

STOTT, Rebecca, *The Fabrication of the Late Victorian* Femme Fatale, London, Macmillan Press, 1992.

STRAUB, Kristina, *Sexual Suspects. Eighteenth-Century Players and Sexual Ideology*, Princeton, Princeton University Press, 1992.

SUMMERVILLE, Christopher, *March of Death: Sir John Moore's Retreat to Corunna, 1808–9*, London, Greenhill, 2003.

SWANN, June, *Shoes*, London, B. T. Batsford, 1982.

SWANN, June, *Shoemaking*, Princes Risborough, Shire Publications, 1986.

SWANN, June, *History of Footwear in Norway, Sweden and Finland: Prehistory to 1950*, Stockholm, Kungl Vittrhets Historie och Antikvitets, 2001.

SWAYSLAND, Edward, *Boot and Shoe Design and Manufacture*, Northampton, Tebbutt, 1905.

TAKEKOSHI Yosaburo, *The Economic Aspects of the Civilization of Japan*, London, George Allen & Unwin, 1930.

TEMPLETON, Tom, "The OM Index," *Observer Magazine*, March 7, 2004, p. 12.

TERAJIMA RYŌAN, *Wankan sansai zue*, Tokyo, Heibonsha, [1713] 1985–1991.

TERTULLIAN, *De Cultu Feminarum*, edited by Sandra Isetta, Florence, Nardini, 1986.

The Art of Preserving the Feet; or, Practical Instructions for the Prevention and Cure of Corns, Bunnions, Callosities, Chilblains, &c., London, Henry Colburn, 1818.

The Baboon A-la-Mode. A Satyr [sic] Against the French, by a Gentleman, London, S. Malthus, 1704.

The English Satirical Print 1600–1832, Cambridge, Chadwyck-Healey, 1986.

The French Dancing-Master and the English Soldier: or, the Difference betwixt Fidling and Fighting, Displayed in a Dialogue Betwixt an Englishman and a Frenchman, London, 1666.

The Life of the Right Honorable Charles James Fox, Late Principal Secretary of State for Foreign Affairs…, London, Albion Press, 1807.

The Town and Country Magazine, vol. IV, May 1772.

THOMPSON, Edward P. and Eileen Yeo (eds), *The Unknown Mayhew.*

Selections from the Morning Chronicle 1849–50, London, Merlin Press Reprints, [1852] 1971.

THOMPSON, Robert Farris, "The Sign of the Divine King: Yoruba Bead-Embroidered Crowns with Veil and Bird Decorations," in Douglas Fraser and Herbert M. Cole (eds), *African Art and Leadership*, Madison, University of Wisconsin Press, 1972, pp. 227–260.

THORNTON, John Henry, "Brunel the Bootmaker," *Journal of the British Boot and Shoe Institution*, 20–8 (1969), pp. 170–174.

THUNBERG, Carl Peter, *Travels in Europe, Africa and Asia*, London, Richardson, Cornhill and Egerton, 1810?

TICKLE, Marie (producer), "The Running Shoe – Symbol of Our Time," *The Sports Factor*, ABC Radio National, December 27, 2002 (transcript).

TIMMONS, Traci Elizabeth, "Habiti Antichi et Moderni di Tutto il Mondo and the 'Myth of Venice,' " *Athanor*, 15 (1997), pp. 28–33.

TODD, Ellen Wiley, *The "New Woman" Revised: Painting and Gender Politics on Fourteenth Street*, Berkeley, University of California Press, 1993.

TORRES, Gerry, "The Marikina Shoe Museum," Unpublished Paper, 2004.

TOSI BRANDI, Elisa, *Abbigliamento e Società a Rimini nel XV Secolo*, Rimini, Panozzo 2000.

TRASKO, Mary, *Heavenly Soles: Extraordinary Twentieth Century Shoes*, New York, Abbeville Press, 1989.

TROLLOPE, Frances, *Domestic Manners of the Americans*, edited by Donald Smalley, New York, Alfred A. Knopf, [1832] 1949.

TROY, Nancy J., *Modernism and the Decorative Arts in France: Art Nouveau to Le Corbusier*, New Haven, Yale University Press, 1991.

TURNER, Grady T., "Sodom on the Hudson," in *NYCSEX: How New York City Transformed Sex in America*, London, Scala, 2002.

TURNER, Mark. W., *Backward Glances: Cruising the Queer Streets of New York and London*, London, Reaktion Books, 2003.

TZARA, Tristan, "Concerning a Certain Automatism of Taste," in Pontus Hulten (ed.), *The Surrealists Look at Art*, Venice, CA, Lapis Press, [1933] 1990, pp. 201–213.

URBANI De Gheltoff, G. M., *Di una Singolare Calzatura già Usata dalle Donne Veneziane*, Venice, Tip. M. Fontana, 1882.

USMAN, Yusufu Bala, "Some Aspects of the External Relations of Katsina before 1804," *Savanna*, 1–2 (1972), p. 175–197.

VANDERBILT, Tom, *The Sneaker Book: Anatomy of an Industry and an Icon*, New York, New Press, 1998.

VARALDO, Riccardo (ed.), *Il Sistema delle Imprese Calzaturiere*, Turin, Giappichelli, 1988.

VARNEDOE, Kirk and Adam Gopnik, *High and Low: Modern Art and Popular Culture*, New York, Harry N. Abrams, 1990.

VAUGHAN, Walter, *An Essay Philosophical and Medical Concerning Modern Clothing*, London, Robinsons, 1792.

VEBLEN, Thorstein, *The Theory of the Leisure Class*, New York, Modern Library, [1899] 2001.

VECELLIO, Cesare, *Degli Habiti Antichi et Moderni di Diverse Parti del Mondo*, Venice, Damian Zenaro, 1590.

VIANELLO, Andrea, *L'Arte dei Calegheri e Zavateri di Venezia tra XVII e XVIII Secolo*, Venice, Istituto Veneto di Scienze Lettere ed Arti, 1993.

VIANELLO, Andrea, "La Storia della Calzatura in Italia," in Carlo Marco Belfanti and Fabio Giusberti (eds), *Storia d'Italia, Annali 19: La Moda*, Turin, Einaudi, 2003, pp. 627–666.

VIDAL-NAQUET, Pierre, *The Black Hunter. Forms of Thought and Forms of Society in the Greek World*, trans. A. Szegedy-Maszak, Baltimore and London, John Hopkins University Press, 1986.

VIGARELLO, Georges, *Concepts of Cleanliness. Changing Attitudes in France since the Middle Ages*, trans. Jean Birrell, Cambridge, Cambridge University Press, 1988.

VON KRAFFT-EBING, Richard, *Pscyhopathia Sexualis with Especial Reference to the Antipathic Sexual Instinct: A Medico-Forensic Study*, trans. F. J Rebman, New York, Physicians and Surgeons Book Company, [1886] 1906 and 1934.

VON LA ROCHE, Sophie, *Sophie in London. Being the Diary of Sophie v. la Roche*, London, J. Cape, [1786] 1933.

WADE, Carslon, *Panty Raid and Other Stories of Transvestism and Female Impersonation*, New York, Selbee, 1963.

WALDREP, Shelton (ed.), *The Seventies: The Age of Glitter in Popular Culture*, New York and London, Routledge, 2000.

WARNER, Michael (ed.), *Fear of a Queer Planet*, Minneapolis and London, University of Minnesota Press, 1993.

WASS, Betty Marguerite, "Yoruba Dress: A Systematic Case Study of Five Generations of a Lagos Family," Ph.D. Thesis, Michigan State University, 1975.

WEBB-JOHNSON, Cecil, *The Soldiers' Feet and Footgear*, Calcutta, Thacker, Spink & Co., 1915.

WEEKS, J. and K. Porter (eds), *Between the Acts: Lives of Homosexual Men, 1885–1967*, London, Rivers Oram Press, 1998.

WELLESLEY, Lord Gerald and John Steegmann, *The Iconography of the First Duke of Wellington*, London, J. M. Dent & Sons, 1935.

WELLS, Herbert G., *This Misery of Boots* (reprinted with alterations from the *Independent Review*, December 1905), London, The Fabian Society, 1907.

WHITLOCK, Gillian, " 'Everything is Out of Place': Radclyffe Hall and the Lesbian Literary Tradition," *Feminist Studies*, 13–3 (1987), pp. 555–582.

Whole Art of Dress, Or, The Road to Elegance and Fashion [by a Cavalry Officer], London, Effingham Wilson, 1830.

WIGLEY, Mark, *White Walls, Designer Dresses: The Fashioning of Modern Architecture*, Cambridge, MA, MIT Press, 1995.

WILLETT, Frank, *Ife in the History of West African Sculpture*, London, Thames and Hudson, 1967.

WILCOX, Ruth Turner, *The Mode in Footwear*, New York, Scribners, 1948.

WILSON, Elizabeth, *Adorned in Dreams: Fashion & Modernity*, London, Virago, 1985.

WILSON, Elizabeth, "Deviant Dress," in *Feminist Review*, 35 – Summer (1990), pp. 67–74.

WILSON, Eunice, *A History of Shoe Fashions: A Study of Shoe Design in Relation to Costume for Shoe Designers…*, London, Pitman, 1969.

WILSON, George, *Boot-licking Slave*, n.p., n.d.

WHITFORD, J., *Trading Life in Western and Central Africa*, London, Cass, 1877.

WOLLSTONECRAFT, Mary, *A Vindication of the Rights of Women*, London, Penguin Books, [1792] 2004.

WRIGHT, Lee, "Objectifying Gender: The Stiletto Heel," in Judy Attfield and Pat Kirkham (eds), *A View from the Interior. Feminism, Women and Design*, London, The Women's Press, 1989, pp. 7–19.

WRIGHT, Thomas, *The Romance of the Shoe*, London, C. J. Farncombe & Son, 1922.

WULLSCHLAGER, Jackie, *Hans Christian Andersen: The Life of a Storyteller*, London, Penguin, 2000.

YAMAKAWA KIKUE, *Women of the Mito Domain – Recollections of Samurai Family Life*, trans. Kate Wildman Nakai, Tokyo, Tokyo University Press, 1992.

YAMAMOTO Tsunetomo, *Hagakure: The Book of the Samurai*, trans. William Scott Wilson, Tokyo, Kodansha International, 2002.

YANAGITA Kunio, *Meiji taisho shi –seiron hen*, Tokyo, Heibonsha, 1967.

YASUMI Ryōan, *Ryokōyōjinshū*, ed. Sakurai Masanobu, Tokyo, Yasaka shobo, [1810] 2001.

ZACHARIE, I., *Surgical and Practical Observations on the Diseases of the Human Foot*, London, Adams Brothers, [1844] 1876.

ZAKIM, Michael, "Sartorial Ideologies: From Homespun to Ready-Made," *American Historical Review*, 106–5 (2001), pp. 1553–1586.

ZAKIM, Michael, *Ready-Made Democracy. A History of Men's Dress in the American Republic, 1760–1860*, Chicago and London, University of Chicago Press, 2003.

Music

Kate Bush, *The Red Shoes*, EMI Records, CDEMD1047/8272772, 1993.

The Red Shoes, dir. Michael Powell, with Moira Shearer, Anton Warbrook and Robert Helpmann. J. Arthur Rank, 1948.

Run DMC, "My Adidas,", released on Raising Hell, Profile Records, 1986.

Tom Waits, "Red Shoes by The Drugstore," in *Blue Valentine*, Elektra, CD 7559-60533-2, 1978.

Gillian Welch, Alison Krauss, Emmylou Harris, "Didn't Leave Nobody But The Baby," in *O Brother, Where Art Thou?*, Mercury Records Inc., 170 069-2(11), 2000.

The Wizard of Oz, dir. Victor Fleming, with Judy Garland and Margaret Hamilton, Metro-Goldwyn-Meyer, 1939.

Video

Advertisement for Adidas shoes sold at The Athlete's Foot, August 2005, Channel 7 (Australian Television).

Websites

5th Dimension, www.5th-dimension. info/forum/ (new shoe releases and reviews, favorites and rare items)

J. Chiapella, "Red Shoe Diary," *Metro* (San Jose, CA), October 18–24, 2001.<www.metroactive.com/ papers/metro/10.18.01/arts-0142. html>

Concealed Garments Project, University of Southampton Textile Conservation Centre. <www. concealedgarments. org>

Heraty, Velva Lee, "The Red Shoes Club," *Ta Da! International*. <www.sixdegreesofsuccess.com/ redshoes/index.htm>

Mississippi John Hurt. Richland's Woman Blues, c.1920s. <blueslyrics. tripod.com/artistswithsongs/mississippi _ john _hurt_3.htm>

"The Snow Queen," Hersholt. <www.andersen.sdu.dk/vaerk/ hersholt/TheSnowQueen_e.html>

Marilyn Monroe Collection. <www. marilynmonroecollection.com/ Flash/Christies.htm>

Manuscripts and Archival Materials

Imperial War Museum Manuscript 02/43/1, Stevens, Private Richard E. P., "Diary and Letters."

John Piggott, Outfitter's Catalogue, London, 1907 [Copy at the Museum of London Ephemera Collection].

Moses, E., *Fashion's Favourite or The Mart of the Many*, London, 1847 [Copy at the Museum of London Ephemera Collection].

WOMAN'S SHOE BY DELMAN, 1930S. BATA SHOE MUSEUM, TORONTO, P96.150. REPRODUCED BY KIND PERMISSION OF BATA SHOE MUSEUM.

INDEX